"In a world stricken with fear and turmoil, Valarie Kaur shows us how to summon our deepest wisdom and show up to the labor with bravery—and revolutionary love. Stunning, timely, and timeless."

—Elizabeth Gilbert, author of *Eat Pray Love*

"Valarie Kaur is a prophetic voice of our generation. Her wisdom ignites and inspires me, lighting the way through the darkness. This book will do the same for you."

—America Ferrera, actress, activist, organizer

"A beautifully written exposé of activism, rebirth and 'revolutionary love' that is much needed for all readers in our current times."

—*Library Journal* (starred review)

"This is a book that will change your life. Valarie Kaur reframes and renews the tradition of nonviolent social change for our time. Drawing deeply on the gritty love of women of color in everything from childbirth to creating community amid violence, she reaches out to all who understand, with Auden, that 'we must love one another or die.' Tested and tempered by suffering, transcending with hope and joy, Kaur shows us how to love others, opponents, and ourselves in ways that will move us closer to the beloved community."

—Parker J. Palmer, author of *Let Your Life Speak, Healing the Heart of Democracy,* and *On the Brink of Everything*

"Valarie Kaur writes prose like poetry. Her stirring life journey and clarity in the call to action aligns and resonates with treasured voices for social change of their era, from Sojourner Truth to Dorothy Day and Martin Luther King, Jr., and places in our hands this gift for the urgent now we face in the challenges of our times."

—John Paul Lederach, author of *The Moral Imagination*

"Valarie Kaur is a revolutionary for justice who shows us how to labor for the world we dream of. In my darkest moments, I remember my Sikh sister's call to 'breathe and push!'"

—Rev. William J. Barber II, president of Repairers of the Breach and co-chair of the Poor People's Campaign: A National Call for Moral Revival

"Love-firebrand . . . Part personal history, part inspiring manifesto, her immensely readable book implores and inspires us toward love as 'sweet labor: bloody, fierce, imperfect, and life-giving.'"

—Rainn Wilson, actor

"Valarie Kaur's inspirational book, *See No Stranger*, is rooted in radical honesty, vulnerability, and fierce commitment to building a world in which we all belong. Her powerful memoir offers a moral compass for our time."

—Michelle Alexander, author of *The New Jim Crow*

"*See No Stranger* is achingly beautiful—dangerously beautiful. It weaves an intimate coming-of-age narrative with an activist story and a spiritual journey, all somehow perfectly framed in a research-backed manifesto for social change."

—Eboo Patel, founder of Interfaith Youth Core

"Kaur's expansive world view, unflinching approach to social justice, and abiding faith in wonder will make this a compelling read for all who perceive the inevitable intertwining of the personal and the political."

—*Booklist* (starred review)

"Valarie's work and this memoir reframe the tropes of the American immigrant story into a spiritual odyssey of discovery and confrontation. . . . A beautifully written story of hope amid the wreckage of our current political and racial division."

—Rev. Dr. Otis Moss, III, Trinity United Church of Christ

"Valarie Kaur, with brilliance and passion, offers us the most needed and pure medicine for our times: a call to awaken from 'us' and 'them,' and dedicate ourselves to all-inclusive, wise loving. The intimate, raw stories in *See No Stranger* will break and awaken your heart; the profound teachings and compelling vision will inspire you to serve and savor our precious world."

—Tara Brach, author of *Radical Acceptance* and *Radical Compassion*

"A soulful memoir mined in the stories of race, gender, Sikh wisdom, and love—where the personal and political merge and spirit and action emerge. Valarie Kaur is a visionary worker for justice and this book is her radiant offering."

—V (formerly Eve Ensler), playwright, activist, founder of V-Day

"This book and the woman who gave birth to it have so much to offer the struggle for peace and justice as we move into a most complex and crucial century. Open up your heart as you open these pages and let yourself be inspired and invigorated by the way Ms. Kaur breaks it down."

—Ani DiFranco

"Inspiration comes from the sheer humanity of Kaur's investigations, from the depth and breadth of her research and footwork, along with the generosity of her explanations. . . . The narrative is a weaving of stories with an infusion of Sikh culture and feminist theory, grounded in scholarship and extensive footwork. . . . These are edgy and emotionally laden encounters—both gripping and difficult to read. . . . The many stories and paths to reconciliation that this book offers are reasons alone to read it.

—*Ms.* magazine

"*See No Stranger* is immediate medicine for our troubled times. It will inspire your soul to repair the world by loving everything and everyone."

—Mark Nepo, author of *The Book of Soul* and *More Together Than Alone*

"Mohandas Gandhi and Martin Luther King, Jr., now have a bold new visionary to complement their understandings of truth force and beloved community."

—Rev. Scotty McLennan, author of *Finding Your Religion*

"*See No Stranger* is an invitation to love mightily, a guide book to put that love into action, and a love story that speaks to the universal connection that binds us as One."

—Seane Corn, author of *Revolution of the Soul* and co-founder of Off The Mat, Into The World

"Kaur is a constant source of light who the world needs now more than ever."

—W. Kamau Bell, comedian and Emmy Award–winning host of
United Shades of America

"As I finished the book, I realized that the biggest wonder isn't that I could hear Kaur over the trumpeting of the external elephants in the room. It's that I could hear Kaur over the terrible rumblings that are taking root within me: the relentless drumbeats of grief, anxiety, and despair. Even against that pulse, I was able to make out Kaur's fierce, bloody, imperfect, and life-giving call. *See No Stranger* was written for such a time as this."

—*Christian Century*

"Her wisdom reads like the prayer the world needs to be screaming and singing right now. Through Valarie's retelling of the years after 9/11 until the birth of her daughter, she speaks a new world into existence—it is the world we are craving and she imagines it until it is very nearly real."

—Rabbi Stephanie Kolin

"In the first chapter of Valarie Kaur's book, I felt I was reading the best definition and description of love I had ever come across. As the chapters unfolded, I felt I was seeing rage, grief, healing, and joy all in a fresh light. *See No Stranger* is deep, brilliant, sensitive, emotionally moving, and absolutely needed at this critical moment in our history. It is, simply put, among the best books I've ever read."

—Brian D. McLaren, author, speaker, activist

"*See No Stranger* is an invitation to rebirth. With the gentle care of a mindful doula, Valarie Kaur unfolds this riveting memoir of joy, heartbreak, rage, and wonder, welcoming us to engage her story as a way of fully seeing our own. This is undoubtedly one of the most transformative books I've ever read, challenging me to imagine a world where everyone belongs. A world filled with Revolutionary Love. A world that is possible, if we are courageous enough to breathe and then push."

—Rev. Traci Blackmon, United Church of Christ

"Inspires us to become who we believe we are."

—Lawrence Lessig, legal scholar and activist

"In a world ravaged by anger and hatred, Valarie Kaur offers a vision of 'Revolutionary Love,' not as platitude or panacea, but rather as a powerful weapon against intolerance and injustice. It may well be our only hope for peace and understanding in these troubled times."

—Reza Aslan, author of *Zealot: The Life and Times of Jesus of Nazareth*

"Valarie Kaur is the powerful, prophetic leader we need, and this book is a gift to all of us, and an invitation for us all to reflect, learn, grow, and fight."

—Sally Kohn, author of *The Opposite of Hate: A Field Guide to Repairing Our Humanity*

"Valarie Kaur has the ferocity of ten thousand tigers. She also has the ability to soften in the hardest of moments and the leadership ability to move this nation to a new place entirely. If you do not read anything else this year, read *See No Stranger*."

—Buffy Barfoot, host of the podcast *Things That Will Help*

"Valarie Kaur has written a book of remarkable courage and deep insight. Kaur maps singularly personal experiences of suffering and shared collective agonies of inequality as she seeks to understand the terrain of our humanity. She guides readers through painful journeys of violence while insisting healing is necessary and possible for ourselves and for our nation. This is a book for our shattered souls and our battered world. This is a book that takes seriously the power of both hate and love, while leading us insistently toward love."

—Melissa Harris-Perry, Maya Angelou Presidential Chair at Wake Forest University

"This is the book we've been waiting for—a beautifully written, personal, and urgent call for the revolutionary love our country and our world so desperately need."

—Rabbi Jill Jacobs, executive director of T'ruah: The Rabbinic Call for Human Rights

"A must read for all of us who struggle to create a society of inclusion and care beyond boundaries."

—Sister Simone Campbell, former executive director of NETWORK

"In this beautifully written book, Valarie Kaur takes us by the hand and brings us to a world where pain can be met by courage, prejudice can be met by insight, and the ravages brought about by profound disconnection can be met with the revolutionary power of love."

—Sharon Salzberg, author of *Lovingkindness* and *Real Change*

"A breathtaking narrative! Love and violence, personal and public, spirituality and activism are most beautifully textured in the life of an American Sikh woman."

—Nikky-Guninder Kaur Singh, Sikh scholar and professor of religion

"This book shook me to the core. . . . [It] is a smart, efficient, feminist and antiracist memoir that should be required reading. The author is a powerhouse and like AOC, Ruth Bader-Ginsberg, and Malala Yousafzai, Valarie Kaur is a great example of persistence, kindness, and strength."

—Kai Spellmeier

"Moving, inspiring, filled with the powerful medicine we need, *See No Stranger* is an act of bravery and love."

—Jack Kornfield, author of *A Path with Heart*

"This is the book we have been waiting for. It is a guide for anyone who believes that politics alone will not solve our current cultural and spiritual crisis. This book calls us up and calls us into the hard and necessary work to heal our wounds and reimagine the world."

—Van Jones, CEO of REFORM Alliance and CNN host

"Yes, love is dangerous business, and yet Valarie Kaur shows us that it's the only way out of the moral and spiritual crisis of our day. Love is sweet labor, and *See No Stranger* is the guidebook."

—Rabbi Sharon Brous, co-founder of IKAR

"Valarie Kaur is a remarkable human being, whose exhortation to 'Breathe and Push' electrified tens of millions in the wake of the devastating 2016 election. *See No Stranger* is a singularly powerful book. I cannot recommend it strongly enough."

—Jim Wallis, founder and ambassador of *Sojourners*

see
no
stranger

one world
new york

see
no
stranger

a memoir and manifesto
of revolutionary love

valarie kaur

2021 One World Trade Paperback Edition

Copyright © 2020 by Valarie Kaur

Published in the United States by One World, an imprint of Random House, a division of Penguin Random House LLC, New York.

ONE WORLD and colophon are registered trademarks of Penguin Random House LLC.

Originally published in hardcover in the United States by One World, an imprint of Random House, a division of Penguin Random House LLC, in 2020.

LIBRARY OF CONGRESS CATALOGING-IN-PUBLICATION DATA
Names: Kaur, Valarie, author.
Title: See no stranger / Valarie Kaur.
Description: First edition. | New York: One World, [2020] |
Identifiers: LCCN 2019055042 (print) | LCCN 2019055043 (ebook) |
ISBN 9780525509110 (trade paperback) | ISBN 9780525509103 (ebook)
Subjects: LCSH: Love—Political aspects. | Love—Social aspects. |
Social conflict—History—21st century.
Classification: LCC BF575.L8 K37 2020 (print) | LCC BF575.L8 (ebook) |
DDC 177/.7—dc23
LC record available at https://lccn.loc.gov/2019055042
LC ebook record available at https://lccn.loc.gov/2019055043

PRINTED IN THE UNITED STATES OF AMERICA ON ACID-FREE PAPER

oneworldlit.com
randomhousebooks.com

9 8 7 6 5 4 3 2

for Kavi and Ananda

and my mother, without whom . . .

There are no new ideas. There are only new ways of making them felt.
—*Audre Lorde*

contents.

THIS BOOK IS FOR ANYONE WHO FEELS BREATHLESS. MAYBE MOVING through this world, in your body, is enough to make you feel constriction in your chest. Maybe you're holding someone close to you who is struggling and suffering. Maybe you are reeling from the latest mass shooting, or the refugee crisis at the border, or the looming threat of climate change, or the blistering pace of a global pandemic. Maybe, like me, you are breathless from all of the above. I thought my breathlessness was a sign of my weakness, until a wise friend told me what I wish to tell you: *Your breathlessness is a sign of your bravery. It means you are awake to what's happening right now: The world is in transition.*

introduction.

I T WAS NEW YEAR'S EVE 2016. MY FRIEND REV. WILLIAM BARBER II HAD invited me to speak at the Metropolitan AME Church, a historic black church in Washington, D.C. Like millions of Americans, I was still in shock over the results of our presidential election. I looked out at that crowded church and saw grief and anticipation in people's eyes.

"The future is dark," I said. "But what if—what if this darkness is not the darkness of the tomb but the darkness of the womb? What if our America is not dead but a country that is waiting to be born? What if the story of America is one long labor? What if all of our grandfathers and grandmothers are standing behind us now, those who survived occupation and genocide, slavery and Jim Crow, detentions and political assault? What if they are whispering in our ear, 'You are brave'? What if this is our nation's greatest transition?"

The crowd erupted in cheers and shouts and cries of "Hallelujah!" Reverend Barber was on his feet, his great bear hands outstretched over me.

"What does the midwife tell us to do?" I cried over the roar.

"Breathe! And then? Push!"

In the weeks that followed, the address was viewed about forty million times around the world, and my words began to appear on protest signs. I received thousands of inquiries from people asking: *How do we breathe? How do we push? How do we keep laboring for justice when we feel hopeless?* I also became a target of online hate from the Far Right and got messages that I should be deported or killed, and my son, too. I was a civil rights activist and lawyer who had labored with brown and black communities since 9/11. I was also a Sikh American, a woman of color, for whom these struggles were deeply personal. Now I was also a new mother, and exhausted. I needed to answer these questions for myself, as much as for others.

And so, I stepped back from crisis response. I spent a year living outside the country in a remote part of the rain forest in Central America with my family. I was given a gift that is rare among women who are activists and mothers: a room of my own and time to think. My husband and my father pulled a writing desk up the mountain with ropes. My mother unpacked one hundred pounds of handwritten journals I had kept since the age of seven. In the mornings we hiked with our two-year-old son Kavi, and in the afternoons I worked at my desk alone as mist drifted through the green valley. The rain forest felt like a womb—warm, wet, safe, and generative. I read texts on ethics, social justice, and the science of human behavior, and I pored over the stories of my life—spiritual teachings of my Sikh roots, hard lessons of frontline activism, primal truths discovered in the labor of childbirth. I began to see patterns of wisdom. And I began writing this book.

❧

This book is for a world in transition. We have been witnessing the rise of Far-Right ethnic supremacist movements in the United States, across Europe, and around the globe—propping up demagogues, mainstreaming nativism, undermining democracy, politicizing the very notion of truth, and failing to safeguard the most vulnerable among us. The United States is also in the midst of an unprecedented demographic transition. Within twenty-five years, the number of people of color will exceed the number of white people for the first time since colonization, and we are at a crossroads: Will we descend into a kind of civil war—a power struggle with those who want to return America to a past where only a certain class of white people hold political, cultural, and economic dominion? Or will we begin to birth a nation that has never been—a multiracial, multifaith, multicultural democracy where we strive to protect the dignity of every person?

With the climate crisis, the stakes are existential. The same supremacist ideologies that justified colonialism—the conquest, rape, massacre, and enslavement of black and brown people around the globe—those same ideologies built industries that accumulate wealth by pillaging the earth, poisoning the waters, and darkening the skies. Global temperatures climb, seas rise, storms intensify, fires rage. Humanity itself is in transition. Are we on the brink of mass suffering and extinction—or will we marshal the vision, skill, and solidarity to deliver a sustainable future?

Is this the darkness of the tomb—or of the womb?

Some days are so deadly, I can taste the ash in my mouth. Other days, I see glimpses of the nation, the world, that is wanting to be born: a society awakened to the truth of our interdependence. I choose to labor for that world. Sound government is necessary *but not sufficient* to take us across the threshold. We need a shift in consciousness and culture. A revolution of the heart. A new way of being and seeing that leaves no one outside our circle of care. A love without limit. *Revolutionary* love.

Revolutionary love is the call of our times.

If you cringe when people say that love is the answer, I do, too. I am not talking about sentimentality or civility or thoughts and prayers. I am talking about love as labor, a conscious embodied practice. Social reformers and spiritual teachers through history led entire nonviolent movements anchored in the ethic of love. Time and again, people gave their bodies and breath for one another, not only in the face of fire hoses and firing squads but also in the quieter venues of their daily lives. Black feminists like bell hooks have long envisioned a world where the love ethic is a foundation for *all* arenas of our society. It's time to reclaim love as a force for justice.

Here is my offering:

Love is a form of sweet labor: fierce, bloody, imperfect, and life-giving—a choice we make over and over again. Love as labor can be taught, modeled, and practiced. This labor engages *all* our emotions. Joy is the gift of love. Grief is the price of love. Anger protects that which is loved. And when we think we have reached our limit, wonder is the act that returns us to love.

"Revolutionary love" is the choice to labor for *others,* for our *opponents,* and for *ourselves* in order to transform the world around us. It begins with wonder: *You are a part of me I do not yet know.* It is not a formal code or prescription but an orientation to life that is personal and political, sustained by joy. Loving only ourselves is escapism; loving only our opponents is self-loathing; loving only others is ineffective. All three practices together make love revolutionary, and revolutionary love can only be practiced in community.

This book tells the story of how I discovered ten practices of revolutionary love in a tumultuous journey of awakening. My story begins where many stories start—in a moment when we wonder how to breathe through the world we're in and how to push to transform it. Each chapter of the book unfolds my story chronologically and explores a practice of revolutionary love, drawing on research in history, ethics, religion, and science. Along the way, I use birthing labor as a universal metaphor, a way to tap into the bravery required to create new worlds. As you go on this journey with me, I invite you to take what is useful into your own life. May this work nourish the root of your deepest wisdom, so that the next time you feel breathless and need direction, you find a compass in your hands.*

* You can find "the revolutionary love compass" at the back of the book. Then, go deeper with the Revolutionary Love Learning Hub, where you can find educational guides, training courses, videos, and home practices to bring revolutionary love into your life and world. Visit the Learning Hub at valariekaur.com.

The story unfolds in three parts. **Part One: See No Stranger** is about learning how to love others. When we *wonder* about people, *grieve* with them, and choose to *fight* with and for them, we can build the kind of solidarity the world needs. **Part Two: Tend the Wound** is about learning how to love even our opponents. When we *rage* in safe containers to tend to our own wounds, and *listen* to understand theirs, we can gain the information we need to *reimagine* solutions. **Part Three: Breathe and Push** is about learning how to love ourselves, how to *breathe* amidst labor, *push* ourselves to go deeper, and summon our wisest selves in times of *transition*.

Revolutions happen not only in grand moments in public view but also in the spaces where people are coming together to inhabit a new way of being. We birth the beloved community by *becoming* the beloved community. I offer these ten practices of revolutionary love—told through my journey but infused with the wisdom of many others—to help us build beloved community where we are, even as we navigate the real and trying moments of our daily lives—the numbing grief of a global pandemic; the difficult conversations with children about difference and danger; the intimate work of apology, repair, and reconciliation. Imagine a critical mass of people across the nation and around the world who are making love a conscious practice—block by block, heart to heart. What institutions will we build, what stories will we tell, what world will we birth? I wrote the first draft of this book while pregnant and finished it hours before my daughter was born. Her name is Ananda, which means "joy." This book, written in the throes of all that struggle and hopeful anticipation, is about how to labor with joy.

see
no
stranger

part I.

see no stranger

loving others

Jo to prem khelan ka chaao
Sir dhar tali gali meri aao

If you want to play the game of love with me,
step forth with your head on your palm.
  —*Guru Nanak*

1.
wonder.

I
N THE BEGINNING, THERE WAS WONDER. OUT IN THE COUNTRY, FAR FROM city lights, the night air was clear enough to gaze into the long shimmering galaxy that stretched across the sky. I would stand in the field behind our house and talk to the stars like they were my friends, just like I talked to the cows over the fence or the horses across the road. Once, while playing in a stream, I saw a butterfly dancing over the water and put out my finger and asked it to come to me—and the butterfly came. It perched on my finger for a long time, long enough for me to peer closer at its wings and praise it before it flew away. Back then, there was no question: The earth under me, the stars above me, the animals around me, were all part of me. And wonder was my first orientation to them all, the thing that connected me to them: *You are a part of me I do not yet know.*

I grew up on forty acres in Clovis, California, where the land stretched on all sides of us like an open palm. We were surrounded by peach orchards, orange trees, eucalyptus groves, strawberry fields, and olive trees that my father's father had planted along our dirt road. My family had farmed this land for nearly a century. My little brother and I would run through the fields, play in muddy ditches, and drink at the water pump in front of the two-room wooden cabin my father was born in. In the summers, my mother and I would walk the orchards collecting fruit in our shirts, stepping over apricots that had fallen to the ground and spoiled because the fruit was that plentiful. In the winters, when the tule fog rolled into the valley, my father would pull me up onto our tractor and I would sit at his side like a princess as we disked the fields until the sky darkened over the Sierra Nevada mountains. We belonged to the land.

At night, my grandfather, my mother's father, would tuck me into bed. With his hand on my forehead, stroking my hair, he recited his favorite prayer, the *shabad* called *Tati Vao Na Lagi.* The hot winds cannot touch you. There was a tremor in Papa Ji's voice, just as there was a tremor in his hands, and the tremor rose and fell in an arc that rocked me to sleep as he hummed the *shabad.* Papa Ji was always humming— while surveying the tomatoes in his garden, arms clasped behind his back like the army captain he had once been; while sitting at the kitchen table, cutting ice cream into slices like a cake; while tying his turban in the mornings, slowly and carefully, as if each layer contained secret histories; he was always humming. The sacred music resounded within him, spilling out when he parted his lips.

"Do you dream?" I asked Papa Ji one night.

"Oh yes, my dear."

"What did you dream last night?"

"I was a young man on the beaches of Gaza, and I was running fast like I used to run. My superior officer, British, challenged me to a race, and I was winning," he said and laughed. Papa Ji was wondrous to me, as infinite and inexhaustible as the night sky. He had worlds of stories in him, ancient stories he would bequeath to me in slivers— stories of gurus and saints, warriors and poets, soldiers and farmers— and these stories formed a long shimmering history that spanned centuries from India to America and ended with me.

My favorite was our origin story: the story of Guru Nanak, the first teacher of the Sikh faith. Five centuries ago, the story goes, halfway around the world in a village in Punjab on the Indian subcontinent, there lived a young man named Nanak. He was deeply troubled by the violence around him, Hindus and Muslims in turmoil. One day, he disappeared on the bank of a river for three days. People thought he was dead, drowned. But Nanak emerged on the third day with a vision of Oneness: *Ik Onkar,* the Oneness of humanity and of the world. This vision threw him into a state of ecstatic wonder—

vismaad—and he began singing songs of devotion called *shabad*s, praising the divine within him and around him. In other words, he was in love. Love made him see with new eyes: Everyone around him was a part of him that he did not yet know.

"I see no stranger," said Guru Nanak, "I see no enemy." Guru Nanak taught that all of us could see the world in this way. There is a voice inside each of us called *haumai*, the I that names itself as separate from You. It resides in the bowl that holds our individual consciousness. But separateness is an illusion. When we quiet the chatter in our heads through music or meditation or recitation or song, the boundaries begin to disappear. The bowl breaks. For a moment, we taste the truth, sweet as nectar—we are part of one another. Joy rushes in. Long after the moment passes, we can choose to remember the truth of our interconnectedness, that we belong to one another. We can *choose* to "see no stranger." When Papa Ji was humming the *shabad*s day and night, he was not praying as much as practicing a constant communion with all things. It was his way of remembering the truth—rehearsing his wonder.

> *Wondrous are the forms, wondrous are the colors.*
> *Wondrous are the beings who wander around unclothed.*
> *Wondrous is the wind, wondrous is the water.*
> *Wondrous is the fire, which works wonders. . . .*
> *Beholding these wonders, I am wonderstruck.*
> *O Nanak, those who understand this are blessed.*
>
> (ASA DI VAR, SRI GURU GRANTH SAHIB, GURU NANAK, 463–464)

"Waheguru, Waheguru!" Papa Ji would say. It was our word for God, but he would say it throughout the day like it was a deep breath. *"Wahe"* is an expression of awe, and *"guru"* is the light that dispels darkness. So even God's name was an expression of wonder at the divine around us and within us.

"Look at the hose!" Papa Ji would exclaim, spraying water into the sunlight, making rainbows. *"Kamal hai!"* Isn't that amazing? My brother, Sanjeev, and I would rush through the rainbows, but Papa Ji was teaching us a lesson, to cultivate our *orientation* to wonder. When our father came home from irrigating the fields, we would sit close to him as he drew pictures of the solar system on a chalkboard and talked about the universe, his voice rising with excitement: "The sun's light takes exactly eight minutes and twenty seconds to reach us! The light of faraway stars reaches us long after they have died!" When it thundered, our mother would cry out in joy and pull us outside with her to dance in the rain, mouths open to catch raindrops, just like during the monsoons of her childhood. When I wrote little poems about the rain or stars or land, Papa Ji kept them all in a special red binder. On weekends, our cousins and aunties and uncles and grandparents, who all lived on the land with us, would come over to eat and dance together in the night, bhangra beats pounding through our bodies, fingers sticky from pakoras, sparks flying from the fire. On the farmland of California, under the stars, inside the music of my enormous family, the stories of my ancestors, and the sounds of my grandfather's prayers, I was at home in my body and at home in the world.

৩৩

Wonder is our birthright. It comes easily in childhood—the feeling of watching dust motes dancing in sunlight, or climbing a tree to touch the sky, or falling asleep thinking about where the universe ends. If we are safe and nurtured enough to develop our capacity to wonder, we start to wonder about the people in our lives, too—their thoughts and experiences, their pain and joy, their wants and needs. We begin to sense that they are to themselves as vast and complex as we are to ourselves, their inner world as infinite as our own. In other words, we are seeing them as our equal. We are gaining information about how to love them. Wonder is the wellspring for love.

It is easy to wonder about the internal life of the people closest to us. It is harder to wonder about people who seem like strangers or outsiders. But when we choose to wonder about people we don't know, when we imagine their lives and listen for their stories, we begin to expand the circle of those we see as part of *us*. We prepare ourselves to love beyond what evolution requires.

The call to love beyond our own flesh and blood is ancient. It echoes down to us on the lips of indigenous leaders, spiritual teachers, and social reformers through the centuries. Guru Nanak called us to see no stranger, Buddha to practice unending compassion, Abraham to open our tent to all, Jesus to love our neighbors, Muhammad to take in the orphan, Mirabai to love without limit. They all expanded the circle of who counts as *one of us,* and therefore who is worthy of our care and concern. These teachings were rooted in the linguistic, cultural, and spiritual contexts of their time, but they spoke of a common vision of our interconnectedness and interdependence. It is the ancient Sanskrit truth that we can look upon anyone or anything and say: *Tat tvam asi,* "I am that." It is the African philosophy: *Ubuntu,* "I am because you are." It is the Mayan precept: *In La'Kech,* "You are my other me."

What has been an ancient spiritual truth is now increasingly verified by science: We are all indivisibly part of one another. We share a common ancestry with everyone and everything alive on earth. The air we breathe contains atoms that have passed through the lungs of ancestors long dead. Our bodies are composed of the same elements created deep inside the furnaces of long-dead stars. We can look upon the face of anyone or anything around us and say—as a moral declaration and a spiritual, cosmological, and biological fact: *You are a part of me I do not yet know.*

But you don't have to be religious in order to open to wonder. You only have to reclaim a sliver of what you once knew as a child. If you remember how to wonder, then you already have what you need to learn how to love.

Wonder is where love begins, but the failure to wonder is the beginning of violence. Once people stop wondering about others, once they no longer see others as part of them, they disable their instinct for empathy. And once they lose empathy, they can do anything to them, or allow anything to be done to them. Entire institutions built to preserve the interests of one group of people over another *depend* on this failure of imagination. Violence comes in the form of policies by the state and sometimes bloodshed in the streets. More often, it comes in forms that are hard to see, unless we find a way to make them visible through our stories.

As a child, I learned how to wonder. I also quickly learned what appears in its absence.

☙❧

I was six years old, playing with a friend during recess. I was pretending to be a baby, walking on my knees holding the hand of my friend who was pretending to be my mommy. We were rounding the bases of a baseball diamond, which was our house, when a boy ran up to us, an older boy we did not know. He came to us urgently, like a messenger on a mission.

"Get up, you black dog!" he said. He was glaring at me.

"I'm sorry, that's not right. I'm playing a baby, not a dog," I wanted to say. But his mouth was tight and his eyes were cruel. He was not waiting for an answer; he was waiting for compliance. I still wanted to correct him: "But I'm brown, not black, so you should say 'brown dog.'" But this, too, didn't matter: He was white and I was brown, which made me black, and this disgusted him.

"Get up!" he yelled again.

And so I got up. I did not yet have the language to say no. The bell rang and the boy walked away satisfied.

My friend had stopped holding my hand. The game had ended, our connection broken by a slur that was cast with supreme confidence: *You are dark, which means I can tell you what to do.* I was not angry at the boy. His words were not personal. He was articulating something that I did not know until then. It was like gathering important information—*Oh, I had never seen myself through your eyes before.* But my face was burning, and I was ashamed.

Another day at recess, I was sitting in the bathroom stall at school when I heard the words "Let's break down the door!" I froze. A group of girls who were white started to beat my door down. *Thud. Thud. THUD.* The door swung open, and my body came into view—small, brown, skinny, hair in two long braids, sitting on the toilet, clutching my dress, underwear at knees, wide-eyed and terrified. They looked at me for a long time and walked away. Power was theirs to exercise, and the choice to abandon the mission was a sign of absolute power. My face was flushed as I rushed out of the bathroom, but I did not say a word. I was not angry at the girls. They had seen my naked-ness and smallness and brownness, and that made me ashamed.

Shame became part of childhood after that, stitched into my story in the form of a thousand small insults, stares, and slurs that made me feel strange to myself—as if I did not have the right to feel at home in my body. It almost worked. But each time I felt the burning under my skin, strong and stinging, making me lose my breath, Papa Ji's room was my sanctuary. I went to his bedside and buried my face in his choc-olate brown sweater. He would stroke my forehead and make me recite with him three times: *Tati Vao Na Lagi, Par Brahm Sarnai*—The hot winds cannot touch you, you are shielded by love. And I could breathe again. This *shabad* was my key to get back home, back into my body.

Love is dangerous business, Papa Ji explained. If you choose to see no stranger, then you must love people, even when they do not love you. You must wonder about them even when they refuse to wonder about you. You must even protect them when they are in harm's way.

Guru Nanak called for a revolution of the heart. He inspired people to practice equality, service, and social justice. His followers were called Sikhs, students of truth, and Sikhs became known as war-riors, sworn to defend all people in harm's way. Papa Ji told me stories of ancestors who rode into battle with sword in hand to defend vul-nerable communities of all kinds and gave their lives to challenge the oppression of empire: Guru Arjan was martyred in a cauldron of burning sand, Guru Tegh Bahadur beheaded, Baba Deep Singh went on fighting with his head in his hand.

In 1699, the tenth Sikh teacher, Guru Gobind Singh, formed the Sikh community into the Khalsa, which means "pure and free," a kind of beloved community. He gave the community new last names that signified a sense of sovereignty—"Singh" for men and boys, meaning "lion" or "warrior-prince"; "Kaur" for women and girls, meaning "warrior-princess" or "sovereign woman warrior." He adorned us with five articles of faith, the five "K's"—a steel bracelet called a *karra,* a comb called a *kangee,* an undergarment called a *kach,* a dagger called a *kirpan,* and long uncut hair called *kesh.* "Sikhs do not hide," Papa Ji would say. We couldn't. These articles were meant to make Sikhs visible, so that we could never hide in a crowd, or hide from the call to fight for justice. Men and some women wrapped their long hair in a turban—the most visible way for us to signal our commitment to love and serve others. At the time, the turban was only worn by royalty in India, but we all had the responsibility to serve, so the turban became our crown.

I liked to sit on the dresser and watch Papa Ji tie his turban. It was a process: He fastened one end of the cloth to a doorknob, held the other end across the room, stretched it tight, and shook it up and down, up and down, making the cloth ripple. He then tied his long hair into a bun, gathered the six yards of cloth into large folds, released it from the knob, and began wrapping the *pag,* the turban, until it was crisp and tight. The tremor in his hands made it slow work.

"What is higher than truth?" Papa Ji would ask me.

"Living the truth," I answered.

"Changa," he said. "Good."

"Truth is high, but higher still is truthful living," says Guru Nanak. *"Sachahu orai sabh ko upar sach aachaar."*

"Everyone in this country says, 'I love you, I love you, I love you!'" Papa Ji liked to say. "All talk! No action! That's not love." Love and labor were inseparable. Love called forth our deepest bravery, and Papa Ji was the bravest person I knew—he had pulled people out of danger many times, as a soldier in the British Indian Army during World War II, in the midst of the mass violence and forced migration

of the Partition of India in 1947, and during the 1984 pogroms against
Sikhs in India. Through it all, he wore his turban even when it marked
him for persecution—and he recited his prayer *Tati Vao Na Lagi*. The
shabad was his key to bravery, even when he was afraid, and so it became mine, too.

The Sikh ideal was the *sant-sipahi,* the warrior-sage. The warrior
fights. The sage loves. It was a path of revolutionary love. Papa Ji was
my warrior-sage: He went *into* the fires of this world with the eyes of
a sage and the heart of a warrior. He was teaching me how to reclaim
our warrior tradition for courageous nonviolent action, here and
now.

"Do not abandon your post," said Papa Ji whenever I came to him
in tears. I was a little girl in two long braids who liked writing poetry
and riding on tractors, but my grandfather saw me as a warrior. I always nodded yes.

So I did my best to hold my post in the world, and Clovis was my
entire world. California's Central Valley, midway between San Francisco and Los Angeles, was an enormous swath of farmland. People
from out of town did not seem to understand the culture of the valley
where land was wealth and water was life. So our farming towns were
insular, conservative, parochial, and predominantly Christian. We had
long histories of diverse communities of color—indigenous peoples
had lived on this land for thousands of years followed by farmers and
laborers who were Latinx, Asian, and South Asian. But the dominant
culture in my childhood was white. The most common questions
people asked me as a kid had daggers inside them—"Where are you
from?" was always followed by "Where are you *really* from?" I formed
the worst defenses: "I'm from India but I don't worship idols," or
"I'm Indian but not the Wa-Wa-Wa kind," mimicking a chief I saw in
cartoons. And when our friends came over for dinner, "Don't worry.
We don't serve monkey brains like in *Indiana Jones*." In other words,
we may *look* like savages but we are civilized savages—can we play?
My family had lived in the United States for a century but Sikh Americans still had no place in the nation's racial imagination, which meant

that I was illegible, unable to be read except by negation: not Native American, not Hindu, not monkey-brains eating. I had fallen for the great bribe of white supremacy: the promise of acceptance for people of color who put down other people of color.

Then my family started taking trips to India, where everyone was brown like us, a sea of turbans in the street like Papa Ji's. I realized how much my eyes had adjusted to whiteness. The characters in my books, the heroes in the cartoons, every one of my dolls—they were all white. White people were not strange to me because they were all around me, so I would even forget that I was brown until I was reminded by a question or slur. Here I could be part of everyone! Our family's house was in the old royal city of Patiala in Punjab. The house had a court-yard in the center, where the roof opened up to the sky. Star House. Night after night, we sat together in the courtyard on a *manjee* with cups of *cha* as Papa Ji played the *dholki,* the small drum that went *taka-taka-taka-taka*. My mother and aunties sang, and my brother and I danced with our cousins as my dad recorded on a gigantic video cam-era on his shoulder. The stars shone overhead, and it was as though the stars and the *dholki* and the singing and the beating of my heart were all in unison. *Vismaad*. Ecstatic wonder. I wanted to stay in this feeling forever. But it didn't last. Whenever we went out to the bazaars, I wore a *salwar kameez* and kept my voice low to hide my accent, but everyone still seemed to know that I was the girl from Amreeka just by how I walked. The stares bore into me, and I started to feel ashamed every time we stepped outside, though I did not know why I was ashamed. I felt strange in both worlds, stares in one, slurs in the other.

❧

Our minds are primed to see the world in terms of *us and them*. We can't help it. The moment we look upon another person's face, our minds discern in an instant whether or not they are one of *us*—part of our family or community or country—or one of *them*. This happens *before* conscious thought. Our bodies release hormones that prime us to trust and listen to those we see as part of *us* and to fear and resent *them*. It is easier to feel empathy and compassion for one of *us,* much harder for one of *them*. When one of *us* does something bad, we tend to attribute it to circumstance, but when one of *them* does the same, we attribute it to essence—*Oh, that's just how they are*. We think of *us* as complex and multidimensional; we tend to think of *them* as simple and one-dimensional. We are much more likely to intervene when we already see a victim of violence as part of *us*. We tend to stand by when people we see as *them* are harmed, whether by policies of the state or violence on the street. In other words, who we see as one of *us* determines who we let inside our circle of care and concern.

The most powerful force shaping who we see as *us and them* is the dominant stories in our social landscape. They are produced by ideologies and theologies that divide the world into good or bad, saved or unsaved, with us or against us. Stereotypes are the most reductive kind of story: They reduce others to single, crude images. In the United States, the stereotypes are persistent: black as criminal, brown as illegal, indigenous as savage, Muslims and Sikhs as terrorists, Jews as controlling, Hindus as primitive, Asians of all kinds as perpetually foreign, queer and trans people as sinful, disabled people as pitiable, and women and girls as property. Such stereotypes are in the air, on television and film, in the news, permeating our communities, and ordering our institutions. We breathe them in, whether or not we consciously endorse them. Even if we are part of a marginalized community, we internalize these stereotypes about others and ourselves. In brain-imaging studies, for example, nearly half of black people, queer people, and women exhibited unconscious fear and distrust in response to pictures of people who looked like them. In other words, we live in a culture that makes us strange to ourselves.

❧

In sixth grade, I discovered History Day, a national competition where students spend an entire year researching an event in history.

Most students at our school chose the American Revolution or the Civil War or a world war. I realized that I had stories no one else knew, so I started harvesting South Asian and Sikh histories. My brother, brilliant and wildly imaginative, became my accomplice. Each year, we produced papers, exhibits, videos, and performances that told our family's stories. We competed through high school, won national medals, and became the school's History Day champions. I discovered that the margin can be a space of strength—I could see what others could not see; I could tell stories no one had heard. This is how I came to manage my own strangeness: I learned how to tell stories that inspired wonder and invited people to see me through new eyes. It didn't always work right away.

One day in eighth grade, my best friend, Lisa, and I were working on our History Day projects in the library. I was researching the Partition of India, when Britain left India in 1947, created Pakistan, and Sikhs, Hindus, and Muslims became one another's enemies almost overnight. Lisa and I were passing notes to each other, giggling in our own bubble, when Lisa looked up suddenly and said, "Valarie, I can't wait until Judgment Day." There was beautiful anticipation in her eyes. "Just think, it will only be you and me and all the good people."

I realized that by "good people," Lisa was talking about Christians. But Lisa knew everything about my family and me. She had heard all my stories. She knew that I was Sikh. I was confused.

"Where will everyone else go," I asked, "everyone who isn't Christian?"

She looked at me startled. "Well, you know, down *there*." It was too unpleasant to say out loud.

That's when I realized that my best friend believed that I was going to hell. She just didn't know it yet. I had to be the one to break it to her.

"Lisa, you know I'm not Christian, right?"

She went pale.

"But I thought Sikhism was a sect of Christianity."

"Um, it's not," I said.

The bubble broke, the bell rang, and we left each other without another word. We didn't talk about it again until a few months later. We were sitting with our friends at lunch and talking about the Honors Bio lecture on evolution when somehow the conversation turned into an argument about what happens after we die. At some point, I realized what this group of my friends who were all Christian were trying to tell me.

"So *all* of you believe that I'm going to hell?" I asked.

They shifted in their seats and looked down at the cement. Only Lisa looked me in the eye, Lisa who loved me and pitied me and wanted to save me. There were tears in her eyes and mine, too.

Our friendship ended after that. We still exchanged many letters trying to persuade each other—she stressed that I needed to accept Christ to be saved, and I replied that I didn't need Jesus to be good—but our attempts always failed. As long as Lisa believed I was going to hell, she could not love me as before. Wonder is an admission that you don't know everything about another. Lisa had stopped wondering about me. She had decided that she knew my fate and had no more to learn.

On the drives to school, my brother and I would gaze out the window at Clovis, its country fields and churches passing by. The signs in front of the buildings—small storefronts and megachurches alike—read JESUS IS LORD. REPENT. Lisa did not invent her theology—she had inherited it. That theology hovered over the land like the breath of God, like the air we breathed. It showed up everywhere in this small town that was our entire world—on lawn signs and billboards, in the mouths of preachers on television and talk radio, at prayer circles around the flagpole at our public high school. Her theology defined our moral universe; I was the one disturbing it. Lisa had begged me to say the words to make the universe make sense again. How could her best friend, who she wanted to love, *not* be a Christian? To be a brown girl, to be Sikh, was to be a problem neither of us could solve.

I started taking philosophy classes at Fresno State during free periods and wrote essays on religious pluralism—the view that there can be many different paths that hold truth. I found new friends in high school, outliers like me, including Brynn Saito, a granddaughter of Japanese and Korean American farmers like my own grandparents. We talked about art and truth, wrote poems on napkins, crammed for APs, made mixed tapes, ditched class, searched for shooting stars. I was not alone. Still, some nights, the burning under the skin returned, strong and stinging and strange.

I had recurring dreams of Judgment Day: I was standing on a bank looking out at dark storm clouds forming over the sea. A golden spiral staircase appeared on the water. This was the way to heaven. Families hurried onto boats and paddled hard to reach the staircase. I got swept up in the rush and was so close that I could touch the golden rail. But I was alone. Where was my family? I let go and rushed back over the bank through the woods down into underground caverns where we had been hiding. I found them and told them to hurry. Everyone was ready with packs on their backs, my parents and brother and cousins, but Papa Ji was missing. I finally found him in a dark room and took his hand, but his tremor made us go slow. By the time we reached the bank, the staircase was gone. The storm clouds moved in, the sea tossed up, and I looked at my family one last time before the fire.

One summer day, I came home to find a woman sitting at our kitchen table. One of our neighbors had brought this woman from her church to our house in an effort to convert my family and me.

"Oh, Lord, they are so hungry for you!" cried out the woman with wide eyes when she saw me. She glided over to me, placed one hand on my heart, the other on my back, and pinned me down in a chair. She asked me to repeat after her.

"I accept Jesus Christ as my only Lord and Savior," she said.

"I can't say that," I said.

"One Way. One Truth. One Life!" she cried.

"But I think that there are many paths," I said.

"Oh, Lord, the Devil is speaking to her!" she cried out. "Every time you hear that voice putting doubt in your head, it is the Devil speaking to you!" She paused and hovered her hands in the air. "I can feel him! The Devil is inside you now, child. The Devil is *living* inside you."

She closed her eyes and cried: "Help me, Lord! Help me banish the Devil from her!" Everything grew quiet for a moment. Then there were sounds I had never heard before, syllables that clanged like metal. She was rocking me back and forth, crying out in words that were not words, casting the Devil from my heart with all her strength and might. When it was done, the woman was exhausted.

I rose to my feet. "Thank you," I said. I was not sure what else I was supposed to say after an exorcism.

I went outside and started to run. The suburbs were encroaching on the farmland all around us, so I ran east into the country, past chickens and cows and horses and barns. The tall dry grass was gold in the setting sun. My muscles pumped blood. I was not angry with the woman. It was not personal. She believed she was a messenger of the moral universe: I did not belong here. She had merely done her duty and tried to defeat the Devil that ensnared me. But the Devil's voice was my own voice, and so the exorcism was really just an attempt to cast me out of my own body, to make me a stranger to myself. She was still back at the house. Had she converted my little cousins? Was I standing on the bank alone?

I gazed out at the land and remembered what it was like before, when I was still a little girl riding on tractors, connected to the earth and ash and oak trees, the peaches and apricots spoiled and rotting on the ground, the tule fog in the valley, and the stars at night. It had been so long since I had experienced that boundless sense of wonder that had defined my childhood. I longed for it now. I had belonged to the land once. Why couldn't I get back to that feeling?

Much later I would learn the deeper history of this land. My alienation was minuscule compared to what had once happened here. Before my family arrived in California's Central Valley, this land was not farmland. It was home to the Yokut and Wintu peoples for thousands of years. Their society was among the most linguistically diverse in

North America. When this land became part of the United States, the first governor of California armed local militias and sanctioned the extermination of all indigenous peoples. Scalp bounties were posted, some for $5 a head. Men, women, and children were hunted like animals. The indigenous population of California fell from 150,000 to 30,000 in just twenty-seven years from 1846 to 1873, making the California genocide the most documented genocide in North America. By the time my family arrived in 1913, there were only 600 Yokut people left in the valley. There was no trace of their civilization on the forty acres where we planted our crops. We could not see it, but there was blood in our soil.

Learning this history has helped me understand my small struggle in those same fields that day. In the United States, white supremacy is intertwined with Christian supremacy, one an extension of the other. Any theology that teaches that God will torture the people in front of you in the afterlife creates the imaginative space for you to do so yourself on earth. The European colonizers who arrived on this soil assumed that dark bodies could not contain the inner life they experienced in themselves. Once they no longer saw the faces in front of them as equal, they could call people strangers on their own land, savage to the touch, ripe for conversion: They could concentrate them, enslave them, pillage them, consolidate their resources, and build an empire on their soil in the name of God and country. Generations of brown and black peoples and their white allies fought hard enough for freedom so that in my childhood, the colonizing forces that worked on my small brown female body were minimal in comparison. I was one of the lucky ones. The least that I could do was resist the exorcism: "Thank you but you will not make me strange to myself."

Sometimes I imagine: What if first contact in the Americas had been marked not by violence but by wonder? If the first Europeans who arrived here had looked into the faces of the indigenous people they met and thought not *savage* but *sister* and *brother,* it would have been difficult, perhaps impossible, to mount operations of enslavement, theft, rape, and domination. Such operations depend on the lie that some people are subhuman. If they saw them as equals instead, might they have sat down and negotiated a shared future? Imagine institutions on this soil built on the premise of equality rather than white supremacy. Imagine the forms of community that might have emerged, and how that would have evolved through generations. What would my childhood have been then? I reach the limits of my imagination. The dream evaporates. What does it take to reclaim wonder now after so much trauma and devastation?

Back then, I did not have this language, or history. I only felt the burning inside. As the sun set, I recited Papa Ji's prayer *Tati Vao Na Lagi* and breathed again—and returned home. The exorcist was gone and my family was there as before; no one had been converted. We were still together.

Papa Ji asked me to go with him to the gurdwara on Sunday. It was his seventy-eighth birthday and he wanted us to listen to the *shabad*s together. I had not gone to the gurdwara on Dakota Street in downtown Fresno in a long time; I was immersing myself in books, not music and community. I took off my shoes, covered my head, and followed Papa Ji inside the *diwan* hall, the prayer hall. We bowed our heads before the Guru Granth Sahib, the book that contained our canon of *shabad*s, the devotional poems composed by Nanak and other Sikh gurus as well as Hindu and Muslim poets and saints. In this book, the divine has hundreds of names. Sikhs gather together to sing, recite, and chant these poems in community. The gurdwara was filled with sacred music. We sat down and listened as the voices of the singers rose and dipped and soared with the *vaja* and tabla, the harmonium and the drum. Papa Ji's eyes were closed. The sound that was always resounding within him echoed all around us now. He was somewhere I could not reach, residing inside the music. I was so preoccupied with the thoughts in my head, I could not hear it.

I gazed at the Guru Granth Sahib at the front of the room, and the blue and silver canopy that hung over the book. Stitched into the canopy was the first utterance in our scriptures: ੴ—*Ik Onkar,* Oneness.

At the base of the book, there were flowers and *kirpans,* thick-edged swords and daggers that represented the courage of warriors centuries past who had fought and bled and died for us. The *kirpan* was the article of faith that signaled that we would always be prepared to fight for justice. I looked out at the *sangat* sitting and listening together, men with colorful turbans, women with bright *chunni*s over long braids, children on their laps. This long hair, these tall turbans, were meant to be seen, so that you could spot us in a crowd and know that we would feed you, shelter you, serve you, even fight for you. Because warriors do not hide.

But weren't we hiding this Sunday morning, Papa Ji and me? Weren't we hiding in our gurdwaras, these little islands of India, as preachers rose in pulpits at the churches that surrounded us to condemn us at this very moment? I imagined Lisa and my friends and teachers sitting in a church as their pastors taught them that we were primitive and pitiable and needed to be saved. If this theology hovered over the land like the breath of God, it was because these preachers were pumping it into the air.

That's it. I decided that I needed to go to the source. I needed to confront the priest in front of the congregation. I needed to fight for us. My muscles were taut, ready to lunge. I was learning how to fence at school—*Lunge! Touch!*—and my legs were strong. I had stopped shaving the hair off my body—if it was an article of faith to keep our hair long and uncut, then I would not cut any of it. I imagined becoming a woman warrior, black hair tied at the nape, legs unshaven, blood of my ancestors running through my veins.

Papa Ji's eyes were still closed when I got to my feet and ran out of the gurdwara onto the street, past children on bicycles who stared at me—a brown girl in a *salwar kameez* with clenched fists. I marched up to the church on the corner and knocked on the door. The church was locked. I marched another block, found another church, and banged on the door again. I heard organ music inside. The music stopped, the door opened, and a white woman with silver hair in a flower-printed dress looked at me. This was not the priest I was expecting. The church behind her was empty. That's when I learned that these Christians definitely finished their morning prayers before we did. I thought of something to say.

"Excuse me, do you think I could sit and listen?" I asked. My head was hot and dry.

A breath.

"Of course," she said and she let me in. She was the church organist practicing for a concert the following Sunday. I sat in the empty pews and saw the cross looming at the front of the church, the sign of my damnation. What was I doing here? I was locating the closest exit when she set her fingers down on the keys.

Sound burst from the organ like a thousand birds out of a tree. It lifted and swelled and echoed on the stained glass, making my chest ache. I closed my eyes and heard in the full-throated chorus of the organ the sound of the *vaja,* rising and trembling, like a gull on the wind. Maybe I was still sitting in the gurdwara and hadn't left at all, but I was soaring higher and higher now, back through the ages or up into the heavens, and here was Jesus in the woodwork, head bent over me, arms open, a smile that was sad and wide like the sea, and he was embracing me, and he became nothing, and I became nothing, and there were only the lines from his hands making an arc weaving across the shimmering blue and silver canopy of the sky. The lines spelled out *Ik Onkar.* ੴ.

The music ended and tears were pouring down my face. I tried to understand what just happened. This was my first experience of *vismaad* since childhood, that spontaneous moment of ecstatic wonder, the taste of Oneness sweet as nectar, the gift I had longed for . . . and it happened inside a Christian church.

"What do you feel?" The organist was looking at me.

I remembered my mission here. I wiped my tears and gathered myself up tall. I saw this woman as every Christian, every white person, who had hurt me, who had made me feel like a dog and condemned me to hellfire.

"I just can't believe that there could be a God who would send me to hell," I said. There was a pause as she looked at me. I was ready to fight.

"I can't either," she said. She saw my shock and explained. "I think that there are many paths. It just doesn't make sense otherwise. Of course, some people don't agree." Then she laughed. There was a sparkle in her eye. I started crying, she handed me tissues, and I threw my arms around her. Her name was Faye and she was the first Christian I had ever met who did not believe I was going to hell. I would go on to meet many more people like her and learn that there are many ways to be Christian, just as there are many ways to be Sikh. Our traditions are like treasure chests filled with scriptures, songs, and stories—some empower us to cast judgment and others shimmer with the call to love above all. There are no true or false interpretations. There are only those that destroy the world we want and those that create it. We get to decide which ones to hold in our hearts. Just as I chose to hold in my heart a vision of Sikh faith that Papa Ji gave me, so, too, Faye chose a vision of Christianity that saw me as beloved: *You are not a stranger to me,* Faye had said with her music and her embrace. *You are a part of me that I do not yet know. Sit down. Tell me who you are.* We stayed there in the empty church and talked for a long time. When I returned, Papa Ji was waiting for me at the gurdwara under a great tree with roots knotted deep into the earth. We went home together.

When Faye opened the church door and saw me standing there, it would have been easy to turn me away. Instead she let me in. Who is knocking on your door? Who have you not yet let in? If unconscious, *pre-conscious,* implicit bias infects us all, how do we reclaim wonder as our primary orientation to the world and one another?

Seeing no stranger is an act of will. In brain-imaging studies, when people are shown a picture of a person of a different race long enough for comprehension, it is possible for them to dampen their unconscious fear response. We can change how we see. We shouldn't confuse this with suppressing our biased thoughts. Saying to yourself *Don't be racist, don't be racist* doesn't work. It actually increases the frequency and power of the original biased thought! Instead you have to choose to think of the face in front of you as belonging to a person. In these studies, it was as simple as wondering what they like to eat for dinner. Only then does fear dissipate. Therefore, when we encounter each other throughout the day, it is not our primal reflex that we are responsible for—it is the succession of conscious thought.

I started a simple practice. As I move through my day and come across faces on the street or subway or on a screen, I say in my mind, *Sister. Brother. Sibling. Aunt. Uncle.* I start to wonder about each of them as a person. When I do this, I am retraining my mind to see more and more kinds of people as part of *us* rather than *them*. I practice this with animals and parts of the earth, too. I say in my mind: *You are a part of me I do not yet know.* I practice orienting to the world with wonder, preparing myself for the possibility of connection.

We all absorb stereotypes, but we can undo what has been done to us. In recent years, breakthroughs in neuroscience demonstrate the plasticity of the brain—that we can rewire neural circuits and create new neurons not just in childhood but throughout our lifetime. Experience can lead to structural changes in the brain in a matter of months, and these changes can occur even more rapidly in response to continuous repetition. In this manner, scientific discoveries dovetail with traditions of spiritual training: We become what we practice. It is possible to train our eyes to see others differently—*to see no stranger*.

Wondering about others helps us to wonder about ourselves. What stereotypes have we absorbed? Where do they come from? All of us assume that we are good people. When we set aside the labels "good" and "bad," we can begin to wonder about our effect on the world, which of our actions create the world we want, and which destroy it. We can begin to let go of the stories that no longer serve us. It took an instant for my best friend to see me through the lens of a theology that severed our connection. Stories that divide the world into *us and them* have the singular power to disconnect us. But stories that expand the collective *we* have the power to return us to one another.

My encounter with Faye brought me joy and returned me to wonder at a time when I could have shut down. I could not have known then where wonder would lead me—that I would go on to study religion in college and in graduate school; that one day I would be invited to preach in an Episcopal church under a cross and weep upon receiving the Eucharist from my friend Tracy, who is now a priest; that I would go on to work in interfaith spaces and organize with faith leaders like Brian McLaren and Parker Palmer, progressive Christian thinkers whose books eventually reached my friend Lisa. There was no way I could have known that one day I would receive a Facebook notification that would reopen the exchange of letters between Lisa and me. Fifteen years after I thought our friendship was over, Lisa would reach out with an apology. She would still be Christian and I would still be Sikh, but she would have long abandoned the particular theology that had tried to sever us from one another. She had gone on her own journey, encountered new ideas, knocked on doors that opened her to new wonders, and had eventually come back to our friendship. In the end, we learned that love was the way, the truth, and the life.

❧

How I wish that my story could end there! How I wish that a thousand Fayes were enough to repair the world, and to repair me! But shame inflicts deep damage. We all carry memories of wonder, but we carry memories of shame, too. That shame returns when we receive messages from the world, sometimes within our homes, that make us feel alienated and strange in our bodies. We are told that we are not smart enough, pretty enough, strong enough, straight enough, or good enough to belong. Some of us are also told that we are not white enough, not civilized enough, and therefore not *human* enough. By the time I left home for college, I still needed to learn how to wonder about *myself*, the parts of *me* that I did not yet know. Only when I could explore my own internal world without shame—the grief and rage I had suppressed—could I begin to love myself.

To be a person of color in America is to live on the precipice—any moment your world can erupt in violence. But this isn't a problem just for people of color—or Americans. We all live under the cloud of potential shaming and potential violence as long as we live in a society that enforces hierarchies of human value, where violence is often perpetuated by institutions of power. Individual acts of love are not enough. We need to be part of movements that help us wonder, grieve, and fight *together*.

Those who love us never leave us alone with our grief. At the moment they show us our wound, they reveal they have the medicine.

—*Alice Walker*

2.
grieve.

VIOLENCE IS A RUPTURE. VIOLENCE MAKES A HOLE—NOT JUST THE damage it inflicts on the body of a person but the pain it causes in the body of a people. The hole swallows up language, memory, and meaning and leaves us in a scarred and stripped landscape. Hannah Arendt calls this *the private realm,* the dark shadowy place that violence throws us into, shocked and speechless and alone in our loss. Human beings cannot remain in this silence and survive, and so we have to learn to say what is unsayable. We tell a story about violence to make sense of it, and the story returns us to the public realm where grieving is possible. The act of naming the violence and grieving loss *in community* is how the hole turns into a wound that can heal. But what happens when we don't have time and space to grieve because the violence is ongoing? As soon as we find our voice, we are thrown into the hole again. The only choice is to find a way to speak—and grieve—even when our wounds are still open and bleeding. This is how I speak to you now.

❦

Stanford University is nicknamed "the farm" but really it is more like a beautiful garden. When I arrived, the entrance was lined with palm trees that swayed in the wind, the hills shone gold in the distance, and ivy grew on Spanish-style architecture under a sky that was always blue. As soon as I set my bags down, I felt a surge of astonishment. I wasn't supposed to be here, but here I was. It was easy to spot the others who felt like me, first to go far from home for college. It would have been easy to feel lost or intimidated, but my advisers—Linda Hess, Tommy Woon, and Scotty McLennan—were dedicated to creating a strong sense of community for first-year students like me. My roommate, Mariah, was more like a sister, and our dorm was home. For the first time in my life, I felt seen by the surrounding world. And that meant that I felt free.

I was the only Sikh undergrad I knew who was not premed. The Sikh students I met came from families who had immigrated here in the 1960s, when the United States changed its policies to woo doctors and engineers from around the world, including South Asia. Many in this first generation of immigrants intended for their children to follow "safe" professional paths. I came from an old farming family. My parents were as astonished as I was that I made it out of the valley, and they made no further demands of me. So I studied what I wanted: philosophy, religion, and international relations. I dreamed of becoming a professor of religion, but I was also drawn to the "underside" of history—the voices of survivors and what they had to teach us. I got trained in oral history, how to collect, preserve, and interpret survivors' stories.

In my sophomore year, my friend Irene and I directed a multimedia project called "Living History: Voices Crossing Borders" and brought to campus the voices of survivors and descendants on multiple sides of violent conflict. As I watched Catholics and Protestants from Northern Ireland grieve together, I wondered if the same was possible for my grandparents' generation. I wrote a proposal for an honors thesis to start an archive of oral histories of Sikhs, Hindus, and Muslims who survived the massacres of the 1947 Partition of India. If I started now, maybe I could build on this work as a religious studies professor, I thought. I got a university grant to travel to Punjab to begin fieldwork in the fall of my junior year. I had it all planned out.

It was early September, and I was home. My father woke me up and pulled me to the television—a ball of fire burgeoning into a blue sky. We watched as a second plane exploded into the South Tower of the World Trade Center and people jumped from high stories, disappearing into the bottom of the screen. We did not see the impact. We only felt the weightlessness of the fall. That's what it was like for all of us who were watching helplessly from afar—we were not inside our bodies, we were inside screens, watching the Twin Towers collapse, over and over again, on an endless loop, until the face of the person responsible appeared on every screen, every channel, and in every newspaper: Osama bin Laden of the terrorist network al-Qaeda. His face: Brown skin. Black beard. Round turban.

Our nation's new enemy looked like my family.

The violence was instant. On city streets across the nation, Muslim, Sikh, Hindu, Arab, and South Asian Americans were beaten, chased, shot, and stabbed, and our homes and houses of worship were set ablaze, in thousands of acts of hate across the country in the wake of September 11, 2001. I didn't get news of the hate crimes on television. I got it online. This was before the advent of social media. All we had was email, but it was enough for people to post news on community LISTSERVs: *My brother's been shot! My sister's been stabbed! Our grandfather was beaten! Our gurdwara burned down!* The story of 9/11 divided into a split screen: On television, President Bush declared that we were a nation united in grief and resolve. Over email and on the phone, we heard that our families were under attack. The president repeated that we were not at war with Islam while initiating national security policies that targeted Muslim American communities. It was hard for me to feel anything at all. I was suspended in that sense of weightlessness that never went away, the fall before the impact.

On September 15, I was still at my parents' house when I got a phone call from a close friend in Phoenix. Balbir Uncle had been killed. Breathless details spilled out of the phone. He was standing in front of his gas station in Mesa, Arizona, about to plant crates of flowers, when a gunman reeled around the corner in a black pickup truck, tipped the barrel of a gun out the window, and shot him five times in the back. He bled to death where he fell, his turban knocked to the side. Balbir Singh Sodhi was a Sikh American, a family friend I called uncle, killed by a man who called himself a patriot. He was the first of nineteen people killed in hate crimes in the immediate aftermath of 9/11. Their murders barely made the evening news.

I went to my childhood bedroom and shut the door. My head was heavy and hot. My chest was tight, and it was hard to breathe. Thousands had been killed in the terrorist attacks on September 11. That morning, Chacha Jas, my father's brother who worked three blocks away from the Towers, dove under his desk as debris shattered his window. He stumbled down the stairs with a cloth to his mouth and made it out of Manhattan alive. He knew many who did not. I wanted to learn their stories, go to the vigils, and light candles for the families. I wanted to grieve. But we could not leave our homes for fear that someone would kill us. Balbir Uncle was dead and the nation was preparing for war.

I ran my fingers along the spines of the philosophy and religion and international relations texts I was reading in my courses. There must be a book that could help me now. I went past the academic textbooks, philosophical treatises, and sacred scriptures until my fingers stopped. I pulled down *Harry Potter and the Sorcerer's Stone*. Harry Potter. No one would have to know.

I had never read the series. I only knew that I didn't want to be in my body, or in this world at all. So I read, and kept reading, book after book. For days, while the country raged outside, I was in another world where the heroes were students who wielded their own magic, where spells pronounced correctly had the power to cast out darkness, and love made a shield. Harry was not the strongest. He was not the smartest. But he was brave, and bravery was a choice. "Sikhs do not hide," I could hear Papa Ji saying. There was no such thing as fearlessness. There was only the choice to hide or to go toward the thing you are most afraid of. I put the books down.

The university canceled my trip to Punjab. Too dangerous, they said. I was to return to campus immediately. I kept thinking about Balbir Uncle's body lying out on the asphalt of the gas station for hours, blocked off by police tape, unable to be touched. I thought back to my family's survival stories in India—the massacres of India's Partition in 1947, the Sikh pogroms of 1984—and how these acts of violence were cataclysmic for the Sikh community but barely mentioned in my history textbooks. Documentation determined which atrocities were remembered and which were forgotten, whose lives were deemed grievable and whose disposable, and whether the rest of the world intervened. I didn't know how to stop the hate violence, but I knew we needed to document it for any kind of intervention to happen. I had a Hi8 camera and a Honda Civic. And I had time. My cousin Sonny could come with me as cameraman. My heart beat fast. I wrote to my adviser Professor Linda Hess. She replied:

"You're in a position to enter this unique moment in history, the huge energy generated by these events, and catch the life of it. It's like entering the whirlwind."

I wrote a new proposal. The university approved. We were on the road within a week.

This is how it happened that in the immediate aftermath of 9/11, in the thick of mourning and the heat of nationalist fervor, my cousin and I drove across America for months, from city to city, coast to coast, sleeping on couches, following news of hate crimes as they popped up in our email inbox, taking trains and planes to get to crime scenes faster. Sonny managed the tapes and batteries. I prepared the interview questions. The journey was urgent and frenetic and disorienting. We caught the stories like shards of a mirror, each reflecting a fragment of the truth.

AT GROUND ZERO—

The rubble was still smoldering. We walked slowly past walls of ribbons and flowers and photos of missing people. We pressed up against the orange barricades to get a clear view. Smoke rose from smashed steel. We were quiet and reverent. Amrik Singh Chawla stared into the smoke with us. He was a New Yorker who had asked us to meet him here. He hadn't been back to this spot since 9/11. On that morning, he had been three blocks south of the World Trade Center. He remembered jumping out of a cab and seeing a huge tire on the street, embedded in the cement—it took him a few moments to understand that this was the tire of the first airplane that had crashed into the North Tower. He heard a roar and looked up to see a second plane flying low and fast overhead into the South Tower. Metal debris and paper and pieces of bodies fell around him. He ran. A woman crawled on her hands and knees toward him, bloodied, and he pulled her to safety beneath scaffolding. He turned south on Broadway, running with thousands of other people. Two men across the street pointed at him and yelled, "You terrorist, take off that fucking turban!" They ran toward him, cutting against the crowd. More joined them. "Hey, you fucking terrorist!" Amrik ran into a subway and onto a train as the doors closed. He had run for his life for the second time in fifteen minutes. As far as we know, Amrik was the first person attacked in hate in the aftermath of 9/11, within minutes of the South Tower explosion. He was chased before Osama bin Laden's face was ever broadcast on television.

IN MANHATTAN—

I was standing on the street with a Sikh doctor, holding an umbrella in the rain, listening to his story over the roar of the construction. Navinderdeep Nijher was one of the first doctors at Ground Zero. On the morning of the terrorist attacks, he drove across the Brooklyn Bridge to get into the city as thousands were running to get out. He and his team set up a triage center and temporary morgue in the lobby of the American Express Building and ran into the epicenter to search for survivors. In the clouds of ash and smoke, he made out the contours of a van turned upside down with a body inside, then more bodies and body parts strung along the West Side Highway. *There aren't going to be any survivors,* he thought. Then he saw one: a police officer on the ground, confused and dehydrated. Navinderdeep lifted him up and carried him back to the triage center. It had been eight hours since the attacks. The police officer was the first survivor found. Navinderdeep stayed at the triage center all night, treating firefighters. In the haze of floodlights, he saw bodies carried past him covered in gray ash—one man with half his head missing, another with his toes missing. Body parts arrived in bags. Nausea overcame him. He kept his head down and focused on saving the life in front of him. Three days later, he stumbled home to sleep for a few hours, got up, and went out for a walk. "There goes one of those terrorists!" someone shouted. More people pointed at his turban and yelled, "Hey, you terrorist, go back to your country!" He rushed back home. His roommate told him not to go anywhere alone. From then on, he went only from home to hospital, hospital to home, for weeks, even after *Newsweek* published an article that named him one of the heroes of 9/11. Here was a young doctor who had found the first survivor at Ground Zero, a native New Yorker with a thick accent to prove it, but as with thousands of Sikh and Muslim Americans, nothing could protect him from hate on the street. Navinderdeep did what he knew how to do—he kept his head down and focused on saving the life in front of him.

IN WASHINGTON, D.C.—
I recognized Sher Singh's face from television. On September 12, he was on a train bound for Boston when the train stopped in Providence and dozens of uniformed officers boarded his compartment, guns up. "Put your fucking hands up!" they said. They escorted Sher Singh off the train platform through angry crowds. Sher Singh was arrested because of an anonymous tip that reported that he *looked* suspicious. He was released within a few hours, but footage of his arrest—a brown man with a black beard and tall turban, led away in handcuffs—was broadcast on national news for days announcing that the United States had caught the first suspected terrorist. No correction was issued by any media outlet. The image of turbaned and bearded men as terrorists, a stereotype that had already been circulating in Hollywood films and the news media for decades, was now seared into the nation's collective imagination.

IN QUEENS——

There was a mattress on the floor of a bedroom, and an old man who looked like my grandfather lying on it, moaning in pain. I kneeled at his side. "Waheguru, Waheguru," he kept saying, God's name. On 9/11, Attar Singh had gone to the gurdwara to pray for the dead. He was walking home from the gurdwara that evening when a group of young men chased him, shot him with paintball guns, and beat him with baseball bats. "Where does it hurt?" I asked. *"Ethay. Ethay. Te ethay."* He pointed to spots on his arm, his back, his leg. Police caught his assailants, but Attar Singh dropped the charges, saying it was a time for forgiveness. He would be the first of many Sikh grandfathers with turbans and white beards to be beaten, shot, or killed to slurs like "terrorist" and "Osama." It's hard to think of another community where grandfathers are specifically targeted for hate. Attar Singh died a few months after I interviewed him.

IN SAN DIEGO——

We walked into an Indian video store owned by a Sikh woman entrepreneur. She showed us the scars on her head. On the morning of September 30, Swaran Bhullar was driving to work and stopped at a light on Cabot Street when two men on a black motorbike pulled up next to her and opened her door. "This is what you get for what you people have done to us," one said. "I'm going to slash your throat." Three cuts sliced open her scalp. She drove away, bleeding, but alive. As we spoke, there was a noise in the back of the store and she jumped. "I'm afraid for my children," she said. "We came for security, but what kind of security do we have here?" Her neighbor had brought her American flags after her son was yelled at on the road. "For protection," she had said. The flag was on the back of Swaran's car when she was attacked. She shrugged. "I guess it didn't work." She was one of many women who had to manage the direct trauma of hate after 9/11, even as they focused on protecting their families.

IN SACRAMENTO—

We sat in the prayer hall of the Sikh gurdwara and heard how, on the morning of September 12, a man had pulled his truck into the parking lot and blocked the entrance. "You people have no respect! Lower your flag!" he yelled, pointing to the religious flag in front. He came back the next day with a tractor, blocked the entrance, locked the gates with his chain and lock, jumped over a fence into a sacred pool of water called the *sarover,* and yelled that he wouldn't get out. "He was standing in the water with his shoes on," said Pargan Singh, the gurdwara chairman, who was more upset by the water than anything else. This gurdwara was one of the first of many houses of worship— mosques, temples, and gurdwaras—that would be vandalized or set on fire or graffitied in the months to come. When I came home to my own gurdwara in Fresno to find the words THIS IS NOT YOUR COUNTRY sprayed across the wall, my chest hurt. Sacred spaces are extensions of our own bodies, and when they are violated, our bodies hurt from the inside. I could not imagine then that in the years to come, mass shootings in houses of worship would come to be a repeated strategy for white supremacists seeking to inflict the most pain on communities they wanted to terrorize.

IN SAN JOSE—

I sat on the lawn and talked to an eight-year-old Muslim boy in his backyard. Sameer Akhter picked at the grass and cast his eyes down and told me what it was like at school. "Some people say I'm from Afghanistan and I'm bin Laden's son," he said. "What do you say?" I asked. "Nothing. I try to ignore it. . . . One time, this kid called me bin Laden's son, and all of their friends were putting their lunch pails on my face like this and they called me bin Laden's face. They smashed lunch pails on my face so I couldn't breathe." He said, "I'm not the bad guy, and I don't want to be the bad guy. I want to be a good guy and I don't want to go to jail." "What do you want to be when you grow up?" I asked. "I want to be a baseball player," he said. "Because I like baseball." Sameer was the first of many Muslim, Sikh, and other brown kids I interviewed who experienced cruelty in the schoolyard. Half of Muslim students—and nearly seven out of ten turbaned Sikh students—report being bullied in school. It was hard to meet these children knowing that they would not remember a time before 9/11, that hate would be part of their coming of age, that "terrorist" would become their "n-word."

IT WENT ON LIKE THIS FOR MONTHS—

The beatings, shootings, and stabbings were mostly reported as isolated incidents in the local news. But the FBI would report a 1,600 percent increase in anti-Muslim hate crimes in the year that followed 9/11—a number that reflects only a fraction of the violence that actually occurred because so many incidents were not reported or classified as hate crimes at all. When crimes were recorded, the government lumped them together as "anti-Muslim" even though the targets were as wide-ranging as Christian Arabs, South Asian Hindus, and Black Muslims. Even Native Americans were told to "go back to your country." The most consistent and immediate targets for hate were Sikh Americans—the only people in the United States who wear turbans not as optional cultural garb but as part of our faith, an extension of our bodies. There were half a million Sikhs in the United States. We most visibly resembled the nation's new enemy, and now the nation was at war. As Sonny and I crisscrossed the country, we passed American flags on buildings and patriotic music blasting from radios and red, white, and blue billboards. And then we would arrive at the site of violence.

At first, I tried to play the part of oral historian, sitting behind the camera holding a clipboard of carefully crafted questions. Sonny tried to play the part of cameraman focused on lighting and sound. But for all our displays of professionalism, we were still just two kids showing up at the front doors of people we called "Auntie" and "Uncle," because that's how we addressed our elders. They would call us *"Beta,"* my child, because that's how young people are addressed, and let us into their homes and serve us *cha* and tell us what happened. Since we would arrive soon after the violence had happened, sometimes when the blood was still fresh on the ground, invariably at some point we would reach the limits of language and they would begin to cry, and we would begin to cry with them. I didn't understand it then, but recording the stories was secondary to our real work—grieving together.

Grief is the price of love. Loving someone means that one day, there will be grieving. They will leave you, or you will leave them. The more you love, the more you grieve. Loving someone also means grieving *with* them. It means letting their pain and loss bleed into your own heart. When you see that pain coming, you may want to throw up the guardrails, sound the alarm, raise the flag, but you must keep the borders of your heart porous in order to love well. Grieving is an act of surrender.

Many of us are taught to avoid grief and to fear suffering and death. Our dead are wheeled out of sight, their bodies incinerated behind crematorium walls or buried beneath sterile marble tile. But grieving openly is an ancient practice. In our blood lie memories of ancestors who participated in grief rituals in all corners of the world: drums and fire, music and moaning, incense and incantations, bodies burned in moonlight, ashes poured into silver waters. We know how to grieve. We just have to remember it. The wisdom across faith traditions is that grieving is done in community.

Grief does not come in clean stages: It is more like the current of a river, sweeping us into new emotional terrain, twisting and turning unexpectedly. In one moment we need to cry and rage, in another we feel nothing at all, and in another we feel a sense of acceptance, until we find ourselves one day sobbing on the steering wheel of a car as a song plays on the radio. Grief has no end really. There is no fixing it, only bearing it. The journey is often painful, but suppressing grief is what causes the real damage—depression, loneliness, isolation, addiction, and violence. When we are brave enough to sit with our pain, it deepens our ability to sit with the pain of others. It shows us how to love them.

Some forms of grief are impossible to bear alone. In the wake of trauma, when it feels like we're thrown into a hole, we need to be able to tell the story of what happened in order to return to a sense of community. We must be able to say: *This was wrong and must not happen again.* Telling the story is the prerequisite to justice. But for the story to matter, someone we trust must be listening. It is not easy to listen. A story of violence is like "a living presence transmitted in real time, entering the body of those who are listening," says Elizabeth Rosner, the daughter of Holocaust survivors. "Something entirely *un*bearable that must, somehow, be borne, and then passed on." But it is worth it. Grieving together, bearing the unbearable, is an act of transformation: It brings survivors into the healing process, creates new relationships, and energizes the demand for justice. We come to know people when we grieve with them through stories and rituals. It is how we build real solidarity, the kind that shows us the world we want to live in—and our role in fighting for it.

❦

As we traveled from city to city, home to home, I was learning how to grieve with people and be present to their stories. I would get quiet in my head in order to watch and listen to what was unsaid as much as what was said—the silence, sweat, tears, murmurs, sighs, and exhales. I tried to notice the sensations in my body without letting my own pain become so acute that I couldn't attune myself to theirs. I tried to create long stretches of silence, so that they could rest or say more or cry more or find a new thought. I was learning how to witness emotions without getting overwhelmed by them. When I wanted to shut down, I tried again to wonder about the person in front of me and ask the next question.

The hardest part of every testimony was not hearing people describe the violence but watching them try to understand why it happened. It required them to see their own bodies through the eyes of others who saw them as foreign or suspect or terrorist. For many, this was not a new experience. They had witnessed surges of hate crimes in the past—Sikh, Muslim, Arab, and South Asian Americans were beaten in the wake of the Iran hostage crisis, the first Persian Gulf War, and even the Oklahoma City bombing, where the perpetrator was white. Stereotypes and stories that associated Islam with violence, brown skin with foreignness, and turbans and beards with terrorists had been around for decades. But this felt different. The scale and scope of violence after 9/11 changed people's daily lives and how they saw themselves in America. Social psychologists speak of terror management theory: Human beings under threat are conditioned to draw close to those we already see as part of our own group and to exclude and attack those we see as other. America already had to see Sikhs as "them" in order to exclude our community so powerfully and efficiently from "us."

The loss of our bodies was ancient and familiar. Many of our grandparents and great-grandparents had survived the 1947 Partition of India, the largest, swiftest, and most violent forced migration in history. Fourteen million were displaced, an estimated two million killed, and as many as one million women were raped. Some of our parents and grandparents had also survived the 1984 anti-Sikh pogroms in India, where eight thousand to seventeen thousand Sikhs were killed in the course of three days. I did not know a Punjabi Sikh family who did not have a story of terror in their bloodline. Sikh ancestors had been persecuted throughout South Asian history, since the time of our founding Gurus. Today we know that trauma is passed down from parents to children through generations, epigenetically. It is a revolutionary scientific discovery. Perhaps this is why the trauma after 9/11 felt so familiar. But Sikhs had also inherited a story of resilience—a warrior tradition with cultural and spiritual practices that were developed through the centuries. Perhaps this accounts for the fiery courage I saw in Sikh elders determined to live, work, and raise their children in America anyway. If the trauma of violence and oppression is inherited from our ancestors, might we also inherit their resilience and bravery?

❧❧

"How much longer do you want to do this, Didi?" Sonny asked me after three months.

"Until it's over," I said.

People stared at us wherever we went. They yelled at us to go back to our country, gave us the finger, ran up to our car window and cursed us at stoplights, nothing between us except the thin sheet of glass. It was always Sonny's turban that drew them. Each time, I could feel my face get hot and my heartbeat speed up. But I directed my energies to the job we were doing. "Get out the camera!" We were always too late to get it on tape, until it happened directly with no glass between us.

We were sitting down to lunch at Union Station in Washington, D.C., waiting for a train to take us to the next interview, when we heard someone say, "Go home." The man who said it glared at Sonny's black turban as he walked past us. We followed him with the camera and stopped him.

"Hey, you told me to 'go home,' right?" Sonny asked him.

"Yeah, basically," the man said. "I don't care where you're at, from, whatever. I was just wondering if you was a Christian."

He was nonchalant, even proud. He looked into the camera lens and said his name was Daniel.

"Who do you think I am?" Sonny asked.

"I don't care. I know you're Muslim," Daniel said.

"Why do you say I'm Muslim?" Sonny asked.

"Because you're wearing a turban," he said.

"How do you understand that only Muslim people wear turbans?" Sonny asked.

"Because American people don't wear turbans," he said.

"And all American people aren't Muslim?"

"The majority of American people aren't Muslim."

"I'm from Punjab, India," Sonny said.

"India," he repeated.

"India," Sonny said. "I'm Sikh."

"Sheek?"

"Sikh."

"Sheikh."

"Not a sheikh. A Sikh."

"What's that?"

"There's a lot of people who wear turbans," Sonny said. "If you have a message, why don't you go ahead and tell them."

"Well, accept Christ," Daniel said, looking into the camera. "Repent and be baptized. Be saved."

"I accept the same values as Christians do—" Sonny began.

"Accept Christ that he died on the cross for your sins," Daniel said.

"Sikhs believe in equality—" I started to say.

"Six?" Daniel's brother had found us and chimed in. He was hearing the word "Sikhs" as the number six. "6-6-6 is the number of the beast." He went on, saying our religion was a religion of the Devil. I said we had to go.

Hate violence after 9/11 came from the same forces that had attempted to convert me as a child. What I had escaped in my hometown was out here, too, plaguing the entire nation because it helped found the nation: the notion that the people who called themselves white and Christian had dominion over this land; we who were brown or black did not belong here unless we were willing to submit to them. In the best of times, we were to be saved. In the worst of times, we were to be slain. Daniel and his brother were unashamed and unequivocal: *American people don't wear turbans. You wear a turban. Therefore, you are not American.* By the logic of a syllogism, we did not belong here. We were a problem that could only be solved with the words "Go home," or could only be explained as the work of the Devil. White supremacy had always been twinned with Christian supremacy in America—slavery was justified as a Christian mission, indigenous people were forced to convert at the barrel of a gun, "Confucian" and "Hindoo" laborers were barred from citizenship. What was happening now had happened many times before, to many people before us. September 11 did not cause the violence. September 11 uncovered what was already there.

All this time, as we were struggling to understand and grieve the loss of our bodies, the nation barely noticed. Instead the nation was marshaling its energies for war, telling itself a story about its goodness and greatness and power to deliver justice to enemies of freedom. The fact of white supremacist hate contradicted this story, so the scope and extent of the violence, and our pain, never entered mainstream consciousness. America did not grieve with us. America did not find our lives worthy of grief or our stories believable. We were left to grieve in the dark, but with this consolation: We could still grieve with each other.

I thought of Balbir Uncle. I had not yet gone to see the Sodhi family after his murder. It would be the hardest place to go, the place where the pain was most personal. Sonny and I packed up our camera, flew back west, and drove through the desert cities to the outskirts of Phoenix.

IN MESA, ARIZONA—
The gas station at Eightieth and University looked like any other— a red, white, and blue Chevron sign on the corner, a convenience store called the Mesa Star set back from the pumps—with the exception of the piles of flowers and cards and candles on the spot where Balbir Uncle was killed. For me, this gas station was the Second Ground Zero, the ground zero for all the people killed *in response* to 9/11, not just those killed in hate crimes but also the hundreds of thousands of civilians and soldiers killed in the "war on terror" that followed 9/11. It was not a national site of mourning—there were no barricades or tourists here. But I would make my pilgrimage here many times to sit next to Balbir Uncle's memorial on the corner of the

property, in quiet and stillness while people pumped gas behind me. I sat on the concrete and said my grandfather's prayer: *Tati Vao Na Lagi*. The hot winds cannot touch you.

Rana Sodhi was Balbir Uncle's younger brother—calm, soft-spoken, and kind. We set up our camera in his living room. I knew the Sodhi family from the gurdwara I used to visit in Phoenix with close friends, but I had never visited their home before. The kids whirled around us, while Rana and his brother Harjit put on mics for the interview. The aunties were in the kitchen, bringing *cha* to a boil and frying pakoras to serve us. The Sodhis were one big joint family, cousins growing up like siblings, aunties and uncles like second parents, which meant constant commotion in the house. There was always some drama in the corner, always some sweet togetherness, always steel cups of *cha* in the kitchen. I grew up like that, too. But the Sodhis were tighter than most Punjabi families I knew—eleven siblings all together, six brothers in America, their spouses and kids living together, making a life together as small business owners. They opened one gas station, then another, then a restaurant, driving cabs in between, working seven days a week to build a future where their children could exceed them.

Balbir had been the eldest brother in America. He came here escaping the anti-Sikh pogroms and subsequent human rights abuses in India in the 1980s. He sent money home to his wife, who lived back in Punjab with his parents and daughters, and set up his sons to drive cabs in San Francisco. Then he came to Arizona and opened the Mesa Star gas station with his brothers. That was only one year ago, but the entire neighborhood already knew him. When customers said they didn't have enough money for gas, he would let them fill up anyway and go on their way. The kids called him "Mr. Bill." He handed them candy and filled their cups with soda and let them skateboard in the parking lot. Rana had warned him, "Someone will sue you for getting hurt on your property." But Balbir would just smile. "These children are God's children," he would say. "Let them enjoy it." His devotion often baffled his family. Whenever he drove past a church, Balbir always bowed his head. His son challenged him once: "Dad, why are you doing that? We're not Christian." Balbir would answer, "God is everywhere."

Of all the brothers, Balbir was the only one whose family stretched across two continents and three cities. His own children were grown so he spent most of his evenings and weekends with his brothers Rana and Harjit and their families. As soon as he walked through the door, pockets filled with candy, his nieces and nephews would tackle him. He always brought them treats, took them swimming, surprised them with pizza, chased them around the living room and tickled them. He was their favorite uncle.

Now Balbir Uncle was gone, and this was a house in mourning. The kids were quiet. Rana smiled when he handed me my *cha,* then his face grew still again.

"Tell us what happened," I said.

On the morning of 9/11, Rana got a call from Balbir, who told him to turn on the television. "Don't go to work today," Balbir said. "It's not safe."

"Then why are *you* working today?" Rana asked his big brother. Rana was running his own gas station in Phoenix. Balbir's was in Mesa, just outside the city.

"I'm in a safe area," Balbir said.

The next day, Balbir and Rana went out together to shop for inventory. People were yelling at them from cars: "Fuck you! Go back to your country!" Their phones were ringing. Other Sikh families were reaching out to them for help. Haunted by memories of the pogroms they had survived in India, the Sodhi brothers knew how nationalist fervor and racial slurs could break into violence. They rushed to do something before someone was killed. So Balbir, Rana, and Harjit went to the gurdwara to meet with GuruRoop Kaur Khalsa. She was a white woman who had converted to Sikhism and a community leader who knew the power of the news media. They created a strategic plan together. They would print cards that read "I'm a

Sikh." They would hold a press conference and community meeting at the gurdwara that Sunday.

"I really want to go to New York and help those people," Balbir told Rana. Rana shook his head. "You have to have skills for that! You have to be a doctor or an ambulance driver." Sometimes he couldn't decide whether his brother was saintly or just naïve.

The Sodhi brothers worked on Saturdays. That Saturday, September 15, Rana got a call from Balbir at around two P.M. "Bring me a couple of American flags," he said. "I want to put them on my store." Rana was already looking for them. The stores were out. Balbir had gone to Costco that morning to purchase crates of flowers to plant in front of his gas station. They were out of flags there, too. He noticed the jar on the checkout counter—THE SEPTEMBER 11TH RELIEF FUND. Maybe he couldn't go to New York but at least he could give something. Balbir emptied out his wallet and stuffed $75 in the jar. "I'll keep looking for a flag," Rana said. "See you tonight," Balbir said.

Forty-five minutes later, Rana's phone rang again. There had been a shooting at Balbir's gas station. *Robbery,* Rana thought. He closed up his store and rushed to the Mesa Star.

Balbir's body was lying facedown on the ground, near the sidewalk in front of the gas pumps, in a pool of blood, crates of flowers on the ground next to him. Rana cried out. Police officers had already strung up yellow police tape. They pushed Rana back. "This is a crime scene," they said. "You cannot touch the body."

Rana's brother Harjit held him and told him what happened. Balbir had been standing in front of his gas station speaking with a landscaper when he was shot in the back. It happened outside and nothing was stolen. *Hate crime,* they thought. Rana called GuruRoop: "Do something! Do something!" She steadied herself and got to work. Harjit called home and his kids answered. *"Chalday Vaday Papa!"* Your uncle is no more! His nieces and nephews began to wail. Then they locked the doors and turned on the alarm and waited.

A few local reporters arrived on the scene. An officer instructed the brothers not to tell the media it was a hate crime. But Harjit was the one brother who had no shyness in him. "Our brother was killed because of his turban and beard," he sobbed to a reporter.

"How do you feel about Americans?" the reporter asked.

Harjit was incensed. "Why don't you think *I'm* American? I'm American also. We may have different dress but my children are in this country, my business is in this country. Why are you asking me this question?"

The killer's name was Frank Roque. He was a Boeing aircraft mechanic at a local repair facility. That morning, he had boasted at a sports bar that he was "going to go out and shoot some towelheads. . . . We should kill their children, too." After killing Balbir, he drove to a Mobil gas station ten miles away and shot at a Lebanese American clerk from his truck. He missed. He then drove to his former house, bought by an Afghan American family, and fired multiple rounds outside. After the shooting rampage, he went to a local bar and announced, "They're investigating the murder of a turban-head down the street." He was proud. When he was arrested, he yelled, "I'm a patriot! Arrest me and let those terrorists go wild!"

Later that same day, Waqar Hasan, a Pakistani father of four daughters, was killed in his grocery store in Dallas, Texas. Mark Stroman, the man who killed him, then went to a gas station and killed Vasudev Patel, a father of two from India. A few days later, Stroman shot Rais Bhuiyan, a Bangladeshi immigrant, who survived. Rana and Harjit had heard of the killings, too. "It has to stop," they said.

Rana's and Harjit's voices faded off at this point in the story. We sat there together, pakoras now cold on the table, letting the silence grow. After a few minutes, Rana left the room and returned with a book. "This is Balbir's diary," he said. "Read what he wrote on the last page, his last entry before he died." He handed it to me. It said in Punjabi: "Waheguru, I am ready for whatever job or duty you assign me."

"He came to the world for this purpose," Rana said. "To give us the opportunity to tell people, the whole world, who Sikhs are."

A few days after his brother was killed, Rana was stopped at a streetlight in Phoenix when a man in the car next to him held up a knife and glared. Rana called his wife, who implored him to come home, but he stayed at work. That night, his son begged him, "Papa, don't go to work with your turban." Rana tried to tell him not to be afraid. Sikhs don't hide, he said. A few weeks later, Rana's nephew Daman came home from school devastated. A kid had yelled, "Go back to Afghanistan," and tried to beat him with a stick. The danger did not end with Balbir's murder; it had only begun. Rana would spend the years to come trying to tell his brother's story everywhere he could, in school auditoriums, at vigils, with reporters—not just for Balbir but for his children, too. Even as he told his story, he wanted to hear from others—including Frank Roque. He had always wanted to ask the killer why. Neither of us thought that would ever be possible.

Before we left Arizona, I stopped at the gas station one more time. Balbir's eldest son, Sukhwinder, was there. He had returned to Mesa to take his father's place and run the Mesa Star. He had worn a hat before but had started keeping his hair long in a turban. "My dad died for this," he told me. "I don't want to cut it anymore." He wept and collected himself, but I still heard the grief beneath every word.

Sukhwinder had talked to his father two hours before he was killed. "You should come and take over the gas station," Balbir had said to his son. "I'll drive a cab for a couple months, save up some more money, and go back to India to be with Mom." The distance was getting too hard for them. It was going to be their twenty-fifth wedding anniversary in November—time to be reunited. After his murder, Joginder Kaur had come to Arizona for her husband's funeral and then returned to India. Sukhwinder wept once more, crossed his arms, and looked out at the orange sunset. "The thing I miss the most is that my children won't ever get to meet him," he said. I looked at the horizon with him. There was one more interview I knew I had to do. I used the last of my research grant to book a flight to India.

IN INDIA—

We drove through the noise and heat and haze of New Delhi into the wide countryside of Punjab. The fog hung low on the land. It reminded me of the Clovis of my childhood. My family had come with me, my mother and father helping the driver decipher directions scribbled on a piece of paper, my brother, Sanjeev, prepping the camera. We passed fields and farms until we found a long dirt road that led us to a village and, in this village, a house. She was there—Joginder Kaur, Balbir Sodhi's widow, a silhouette in the doorway, dressed in white, the color of mourning. Balbir's elderly parents rushed to the car to embrace us with the same warmth I felt from his family in Arizona. They ushered us inside and served us *cha* and biscuits. Joginder Auntie was quiet. My mother and I sat down next to her on the *manjee* to interview her. There were dark circles under her eyes. She began to tear up at the mention of her husband's name.

"Everyone tries to console me," she said in Punjabi, "but I do not have one moment of peace. Everything is empty to me." She wiped away tears with a cloth. "He was ready to come see me. He had a ticket to come here in November. But God did not give us even two months to meet each other. We were separated, and we remain separated. I miss him so much that I wish I could talk to him in my dreams but there's nothing." She began to cry again. She was the incarnation of grief.

I looked down at my list of questions and felt dumb. I put the list down and wrapped my arms around her. My mother wrapped her arms around me, and we all wept together. That was the only thing we could offer, as if to say: *You are grieving, but you do not grieve alone.* All this time, I had kept my body behind the camera, as if I was separate from the story. But I was always part of my community; the pain in their body was in mine. In our shared tears, I remembered something I had forgotten: Separateness is an illusion. *The bowl breaks.* We are part of one another. I became aware of a sensation inside me, an ache that exceeded language. After so many months on the road, listening to so many stories, grieving with so many people, I turned my attention to the place in me where the pain made a hole. *This is what it feels like to live with an open wound,* I thought. *She must feel it, too.*

"I have just one question," I said. "What would you like to tell the people of America?"

I was ready for bitterness. She stopped crying and looked at me.

"Jo pyar ohana ne mainu dikhaia, mai kade nahi bhula sakdi," she said. I can never forget the love they showed me.

Love?

"I went there," she said. "I can never forget their love. They did as much as they could for me. They gave me so much love." She was describing her husband's memorial. "I had no friends or community there. But everyone gathered together. Hindu, Muslim, Christian. Everyone was crying. Sikhs weren't the only ones who were crying. Everyone was crying."

She wanted me to thank America for loving her.

Now I was racking my brain and trying to remember what was hard to see in the thick fog of grief. They were never alone in it, the Sodhi family. After the shooting, hundreds of neighbors spontaneously showed up at the gas station and left cards and flowers and candles burning through the night. There was still a trace of them when I arrived months later. Thousands had attended Balbir Uncle's memorial, the one that Joginder Auntie came for. *Why?* I wondered. Why did so many people grieve with us in Mesa and Phoenix when in the wake of other hate crimes around the country, we were left alone with our pain? I remembered GuruRoop Kaur Khalsa.

After Rana Sodhi called GuruRoop from the gas station on the day of the killing, she began to work around the clock. The first prong of her strategy was media outreach. GuruRoop teamed up with Jaswant Singh Sachdev, a Sikh doctor, advocate, and beloved elder in the community. Together they organized a press conference the day after the shooting. They briefed reporters, so that by that evening, local news was able to convey the basics of the Sikh faith and Balbir Sodhi's story—that he had come to America to escape religious persecution in India, that he was kind and generous to his neighbors and their children, that he would now never meet his own grandchildren, that his widow's heart was broken. Then GuruRoop and Dr. Sachdev contacted the local interfaith network of churches, synagogues, and mosques and asked the faith leaders and congregations to show up in person to pray with them—to grieve with them. And they did. Just one week after the murder, three thousand people came to Balbir Uncle's memorial for prayers and tears and resolutions against hate, and this outpouring of love was enough to change Joginder Auntie's experience of the loss. She bore the pain, but she did not bear it alone. She shared it with people she had never met before. "They didn't even know me," she kept saying. "But they cried with me."

America as a whole did not grieve with us after 9/11, but it happened in pockets throughout the country where our stories were told and people showed up. In person. On the ground. At the memorials. To grieve with us.

Most of the people who came to Balbir Uncle's memorial had never heard of Sikhs before, or known anything about our faith or history or struggles. But hearing his story in the local news and from their pastors and rabbis helped them see him not as a foreigner or a suspect but a neighbor, even a brother. The story was enough to turn Balbir Uncle—a brown, bearded, and turbaned man from a different faith—from "one of them" into "one of us." His story sparked their wonder and drew them close to our pain. They may not have had a clear view of the broader policies and historical forces that led to Balbir Uncle's murder, but grieving with us was the first step to understanding us. For Joginder Auntie, their act of love was a balm. Nothing could bring back her husband, but communal grieving made it possible to breathe. It quieted any impulse to let the pain create another reason to divide the world into "us and them." She learned to live with her wound.

I could not help asking myself: Would people have shown up if Balbir Uncle had been less virtuous? Did people of color have to be perfect in order for our lives to be grievable? I marveled at the labor it took to prove our humanity—it seemed like we had to be superhuman in order to be seen as human. But looking back at history, even that has not been enough.

How many have had to grieve *alone* in the wake of mass violence in the United States? I thought of the indigenous peoples of North America who, after enduring campaigns of coordinated slaughter, were sent to boarding schools to have their cultures and native tongues ripped out of them. The miracle is that they survived and continue to live in a nation that cannot see them, let alone grieve with them, because national recognition, truth, and reconciliation would mean admitting that there is blood on our hands. I thought of the black people who are told that the systems of slavery and Jim Crow are sins of the past and have no bearing on the disparities in health and income and education and safety of black people today, that the mass incarceration of black bodies is their fault and that the police who kill their sons and daughters are worthy of exoneration. America does not know how to grieve black lives, because doing so would mean accepting that there was never complete abolition: Slavery transmuted into segregation, which morphed into discriminatory laws, and now into policies that appear neutral on their face but still disparately violate people of color. I thought of my own community—how generations of Asian, South Asian, Muslim, and Arab Americans as well as Latinx people are still seen as perpetual foreigners and therefore easily criminalized. They have been incarcerated in camps, banned, detained, deported, parents separated from their children, repeatedly, in the last century, in the name of an illusory "security," without apology.

New horrors keep arising from old impulses. The past keeps bleeding into the present. No civilization in the world is exempt. But what is particular to America is that many who suffered enormous loss and destruction have had to do so alone, had to marshal language to tell the story, only to find that there was no one to hear it because their suffering contradicts the story that the nation keeps telling itself—the story of American exceptionalism. *America is a beacon of light, the singular enforcer of truth.* Our story of exceptionalism doesn't allow us to confront our past with open eyes. A nation that cannot see its own past cannot see the suffering it has caused, suffering that persists into the present. A nation that cannot see our suffering cannot grieve with us. A nation that cannot grieve with us cannot know us, and therefore cannot love us.

What does it look like for a nation to grieve together? I am not talking about the routine rituals of grief—singing the national anthem, lowering the flag, firing rifles into the air, or the stilted offerings of "thoughts and prayers." I am talking about sitting with pain together, modeling how to do that in public view, reflecting quietly on our deepest values, and mourning the dead, all of the dead. It requires acknowledging the ways historically oppressed people continue to suffer—and the ways people with good intentions continue to benefit from that suffering. It requires witnessing the pain of trauma without trying to control or colonize or minimize it—then listening, and continuing to listen. Soothing words are not enough, not when trauma has traversed centuries. But if we are present to pain—if we sit together in the rooms of the heart, curtains drawn, and grieve together—we can begin to ask: How do we fight for one another?

There have always been people who did what the nation as a whole did not. They crossed the line and took the hand of someone who did not look like them and wept with them, as if to say: *You are grieving, but you do not grieve alone.* There is nothing romantic about suffering. But when others are present to suffering, that presence begins to tend our wounds. When we allow ourselves to be changed by the experience of another's pain, we build bonds with people we once called strangers. Sharing in one another's grief can also lead to sharing in one another's joy.

America's greatest social movements—for civil rights, immigrants' rights, women's rights, union organizing, queer and trans rights, farmworkers' rights, indigenous sovereignty, and black lives—were rooted in the solidarity that came from shared grieving. First people grieved together. Then they organized together. Often, they sang and celebrated together. "We sang our grief to clean the air of turbulent spirits," writes poet Joy Harjo. This is not the dominant narrative of American history, but, if you look closely, you can see many stories of solidarity. In response to great violence or injustice, there are people who rush to bury the dead, cut down the lynching noose, or attend the memorials to say: *Not in my name*. When people who have no obvious reason to love each other come together to grieve, they can give birth to new relationships, even revolutions.

❧

You may say: *It's too much—all this grief, all this violence and injustice, it's too hard*. You are right: The mind can comprehend one death, but it cannot comprehend thousands, especially when one's own community, nation, or ancestors played some part in causing the death. Mother Teresa once said, "If I look at the mass, I will never act. If I look at the one, I will." And so, begin with one. Can you choose one person to practice wondering about? Can you listen to the story they have to tell? If your fists tighten, or your heart beats fast, or if shame rises to your face, it's okay. Breathe through it. Trust that you can. The heart is a muscle: The more you use it, the stronger it becomes. Then the next time a black boy in your city is killed by a police officer, or a turbaned Sikh father is beaten, or a Jewish person is stabbed, or a trans woman is murdered, or an indigenous woman goes missing, or a Muslim child is attacked, show up. Show up at the public vigils and memorials to grieve, in person. You don't need to know people in order to grieve with them. *You grieve with them in order to know them*.

If you are like me, sometimes you are just too tired. Too tired to cry. Too tired to feel. When that moment comes, I ask you not to judge the emotions in your body. Let them come and go. There is something called "empathy fatigue" that happens when we get overloaded by other people's pain. The good news is that you don't need to feel empathy all the time. *Love is not a rush of feeling: Love is sweet labor*.

What matters is the work your hands do. So, breathe and rest and, when you are ready, see if you can wonder about the world just a little, just enough to show up to the labor one more day. Let wonder surprise you.

❧

I left Joginder Auntie's side that day in India deeply grateful. If the love she received at Balbir Uncle's memorial made it possible for her to go on, then *her* love made it possible for *me* to go on. I returned home and slept for days. But, under the fatigue, I felt different in my body. The journey into the whirlwind, listening to all those stories, had expanded my sense of self. It was as if all those stories lived inside me now. I could access them as if they were memories or dreams. I felt their pain but also their wisdom. They were lessons in resilience, the human capacity to overcome unimaginable loss and go on.

I asked myself: If a story in the local news could mobilize thousands of people to show up at Balbir Uncle's memorial, then what might happen if we told our stories to the nation? I returned to college determined to do my part to turn the footage we had collected into a documentary film. The film would be a time capsule of the aftermath of 9/11, a kind of oral history, so that people in the future could understand what happened. But, like so many of us who jumped into this crisis to try to protect our communities, I would learn the hard way that we were not witnessing the end of a backlash, but the beginning of something worse. We would be in perpetual motion for decades to come: Crisis response would come to define our careers, and ultimately our lives. Grieving would not be enough. We would have to learn how to fight.

FIFTEEN YEARS LATER, NEW YORK CITY—
I found myself at Ground Zero again. A woman rushed up to me from the other side of the orange barricades, pinned a ribbon on me, told the police officers I was with her, and led me into the memorial where

families gathered around a stage. It was the fifteen-year anniversary of 9/11. Kerri Kelly and I had met each other only a few months earlier at an organizing meeting. Her stepfather, Lt. Joseph Gerard Leavey, was a firefighter who was one of the first responders killed that day. Kerri was also a seasoned activist. When she learned that my family friend had been killed in the hate that followed 9/11, she asked me to spend this difficult day with her. So I showed up.

There was rubble the last time I was here. Now I gazed at clean marble and inverted water fountains and green trees that rustled in the cool breeze. We listened to the reading of the names of the dead and waited for Joe's name. It was solemn and peaceful. Kerri squeezed my hand and gestured to the right. Donald Trump stood a few feet away from us, flanked by men in black suits.

"I'm so angry that he's here," said Kerri. We were two months away from the 2016 presidential election, and this man was the GOP candidate. There was no way he was going to win. Still his presence was unbearable: He represented to her all of the cruelty that had been unleashed in Joe's name. She began to lead me away from the crowd.

"Shouldn't we wait here for the L's?" I asked. They were on the D's.

"Every name is Joe's name," she said. She led me into the 9/11 Memorial Museum. She apologized for some of its Islamophobic undertones and took me down corridors into a small dark room. A map of the Twin Towers flickered on a screen. We sat down and watched. Names appeared on the map on the screen, followed by a recording of a person's voice. Joe Leavey's name appeared on the map, identified as a firefighter who was on the fortieth floor of the South Tower. A recording of his voice had been recovered in the rubble. It was made at 9:57 A.M., two minutes before the South Tower fell. We heard his last words before he died. He told his unit: "I'll be right up." Then crackle and silence.

My chest cracked open. I began to sob. Kerri looked at me tenderly and put her arms around me and we cried together. My grief for Joe was fresh, hers practiced, so that when she stopped crying, I just kept going. I was grieving Joe, but because every name was Joe's name, I was grieving all of the people who died in the attacks. I realized that, after fifteen years, I had never been given the chance to grieve 9/11. Not even a day. Not even an hour. This was the case for so many of us who jumped into crisis-response mode to protect our own families and communities from hate. We were robbed of the space to breathe, let alone the right to grieve with our country. Now the tears came, fifteen years later, and it was a relief. Kerri had given me the gift of time and space to grieve with her.

How can we presume to grieve people we never knew, people who don't look like us or share the same history with us? Here is the answer: Grieve with those who loved them. Grieve with the living. That is the revolutionary act.

When we were done, Kerri took me outside and ran her fingers over Joe's name etched into the stone. An American flag lay next to it, dappled with water droplets from the fountain.

"So much killing in Joe's name," Kerri said. She was sad and weary. I realized that Kerri had been robbed, too.

I thought back to how it started. Before Americans even had time to process our shock and count our dead after 9/11, our energies had been redirected for war. On the very night of the attacks, President Bush declared a "war against terrorism" and divided the world into *us and them:* "You are either with us or against us." Grieving is a process that takes time and stillness and presence. It is impossible to grieve and prepare to kill at the same time. So, despite all the performances of national mourning, we as a nation had little time and space to be present to our pain and all that it had to teach us. Unresolved grief inside a person is tragic; unresolved grief inside a nation is catastrophic: It releases enormous aggression. In the name of the dead—in Joe's name—the U.S. war on terror that began in Afghanistan would come to span at least two decades, three presidencies, and seventy-six countries; cost more than $5.6 trillion; and kill more than one million people. One million. And every year on the 9/11 anniversary at

Ground Zero, Joe's name is read and broadcast to the nation to justify it. Meanwhile, the same aggression that powers a perpetual war abroad has created new norms for the hate and criminalization of Muslims and immigrants at home. It fueled the resurgence of a white nationalist movement that would, in time, overtake the highest offices of the nation.

It did not have to be this way.

History is littered with the wreckage of mass violence on the scale of 9/11. But 9/11 was the first attack that occurred as a global televised experience, unfolding in real time for all the world to see. No tragedy has been so roundly condemned. In those first days after the attacks, the world as a whole poured its goodwill into us, despite any grievances with the United States. What if we hadn't squandered that goodwill? What would have happened if we had used that outpouring of love as a balm for the wound? I remembered Harry Potter and the choice of bravery. It takes bravery to grieve well. We could have grieved with all of our fellow Americans, not just the ones who looked like us, but also the ones who looked like the people we feared. We could have grieved with people around the world and drawn connections between their suffering and ours. The mass killing of three thousand people and the trauma of a world that watched could have sustained a kind of public grieving that expanded our sense of who counts as "us" beyond what anyone had previously experienced. It could have made us safer. Today we might have remembered 9/11 as the tragedy that initiated an era of global cooperation rather than global war.

Standing there together arm in arm, in our stillness and our sadness, Kerri and I mourned what might have been. We decided that if the nation could not model shared grieving, then we would. We had learned that grieving is an act of revolutionary love: Grieving together, we ease each other's suffering and come to know each other. Only when we know each other can we understand *how* to stand up and fight for each other—and the world we want. And so, four days after I joined Kerri at Ground Zero to mourn Joe, she joined me in Arizona to mourn Balbir Uncle with me on the anniversary of his murder. One act of revolutionary love inspires another. What happened after that changed the story for me and the Sodhi family forever. I just wish we would not have had to wait fifteen years, and lose so much more.

Power without love is reckless and abusive, and love without power is sentimental and anemic. Power at its best is love implementing the demands of justice, and justice at its best is power correcting everything that stands against love.

—*Dr. Martin Luther King, Jr.*

3.
fight.

THE FIGHT IMPULSE IS ANCIENT AND FUNDAMENTAL. IT IS BIOLOGICAL.
Sometimes we fight to protect who or what we love from those who would destroy it. Other times we fight *with* the ones we love to protect them or ourselves. We must summon the wisdom to discern between threats that are real rather than imagined, and respond in ways that give life rather than deal death. The question therefore is not whether or not we will fight in our lives but *how* we choose to fight. I learned how to fight from my ancestors. My mother's father, Papa Ji, connected me to my Sikh warrior tradition. But it was my other grandfather who taught me what it meant to fight in America.

My family's story in the United States begins with Kehar Singh, my father's father. We called him Baba Ji. Born in British India in 1892, he was one of a few thousand young men who left Punjab at the turn of the century seeking freedom from economic and political tyranny. At nineteen, he took a train from Punjab to Calcutta, a steamship to Hong Kong, then Manila, and on September 22, 1913, his ship docked at the port in San Francisco and Baba Ji was escorted to an immigration station on Angel Island. He presented a passport issued by the British Empire, but the immigration officials threw him behind bars, along with every other turbaned Sikh who had arrived on the *Nippon Maru*. This was a time when zealous white nativists warned of a "Tide of Turbans" and a "Hindoo Invasion." The U.S. Immigration Commission even called South Asian immigrants, the majority of whom were Sikh, "the least desirable race of immigrants thus far admitted to the United States." On the East Coast, Ellis Island was a symbol of welcome for European immigrants. But on the West Coast, officials were marshaling the power of the state to expel as many Asian immigrants as possible. Baba Ji was slated for deportation on the grounds that he was likely to become a "public charge," dependent on the government for subsistence, because there was too much prejudice against his class of people for him to earn a living. The state cited racism to justify its racism. He was interrogated and imprisoned in a cell in squalid conditions for four months. Deportation was all but assured—until the records show the sudden appearance of a lawyer, a white immigration attorney named Henry Marshall, who filed a writ of habeas corpus. My grandfather was released from detention on Christmas Eve 1913.

Baba Ji made his way down into the Central Valley as a laborer, working in fields during the day, sleeping in barns at night, twisting his body into farm crates to keep safe from snakes. He was a simple farmer, but he went on to help found the first Sikh gurdwara in America in Stockton, California, serve as a secretary in the revolutionary Gadar Party to free India from the British Empire, and support heroes like Bhagat Singh Thind, a Sikh soldier who challenged racist laws that denied Indian immigrants U.S. citizenship before the Supreme Court. For decades, Asians were barred from owning land, becoming citizens, or returning to the United States if they ever left. But my grandfather and his generation fought alongside Japanese, Chinese, Filipino, and other immigrant groups, until they eventually secured equal rights under the law. The 1946 Luce-Celler Act allowed South Asians to become U.S. citizens; the 1965 Immigration Act prohibited discrimination on the basis of race in the government's decision to admit immigrants, a landmark victory inspired by the civil rights movement.

Now, one hundred years after Baba Ji made America home, I thought that all of our hardest battles were behind us. I was wrong.

❧❧

On the morning of August 5, 2002, Rana Sodhi was getting ready for work when the phone rang.

"Your brother's been shot."

Rana was confused. Balbir was already gone—almost a year now.

"Sukhpal," said his cousin on the line. "Your brother Sukhpal."

It's happening again, Rana thought. *Waheguru, Waheguru.*

A few months earlier, Sukhpal had called him, upset. His friend, another turbaned Sikh cabdriver, had been attacked. "He was stopped at a red light, pulled from the cab, and beaten. Not robbed, just beaten," Sukhpal kept saying. Rana was worried about his brother. He told his wife, "Maybe it's time to bring Sukhpal to Phoenix to live with all of us. We can open a small business together."

The details were sparse. Sukhpal had been driving his cab in San Francisco at night. A bullet hit him in the neck. The car crashed into a pole, and he was killed. That's it. Nothing was stolen. Nothing was found. Just his dead body in the car.

Rana was numb. It took him two weeks to call his parents to deliver the news. After Balbir was killed, his parents had wanted all of their sons to return to them in India. But Rana had told them, "No, this is a good country. We've received a lot of support from our neighbors." Balbir's death had meaning. He was the first person killed in a hate crime after 9/11. He died so that we could tell the world who Sikhs are and prevent more killing, he explained. Balbir was a martyr. Now he didn't have an answer for his parents, or for himself. Whose life was Balbir's murder meant to save if not his own brother's?

Sukhpal Sodhi's death would not be counted as a hate crime. No person was caught, no motive identified, no greater meaning ever emerged. Even though news of Sukhpal's killing sent shock through Sikh households across America, it would not catalyze a public response. No crowd would show up to grieve with the family or the new widow this time.

I drove through the desert to Phoenix, past the now-familiar red rocks and cactuses, to Rana's house. I sat in the living room with the Sodhi family and cried with them—again. I had no answers for them, just sorrow. The kids had now lost two uncles. "I didn't cry as much this time," said eleven-year-old Daman. "I guess it's because I knew that crying is not going to do anything—I already tried it."

I returned to campus, devastated. It was my senior year of college. I had been poring over one hundred hours of interview transcripts to write an honors thesis about the scope of the "post-9/11 backlash." But now it was a year later, and each day was bringing news of more assaults, vandalism, beatings, arsons, and murders. I could not understand why. Once I even had a chance to ask a Supreme Court justice at a lecture about the rise in hate against our communities. He said that it was a "blip" in history and made a popping gesture with his fingers. In fact, everyone seemed to talk about hate crimes after 9/11 as if they were "crimes of passion"—"acceptable" rage expressed in unacceptable ways. A temporary madness. But in crimes of passion, the blood cools down. America's blood did not cool. Hate crimes peaked in the wake of 9/11 but then remained high. Outright violence was the tip of the iceberg—what remained invisible were the racial slurs and stares, the subtle acts of bigotry that were coming to shape the daily life of anyone who was brown or wore a hijab or a turban. And it was taking a toll on my boyfriend.

Ram Singh was a Sikh medical student I met at a conference in Los Angeles, where he was in residency. He was tall and handsome and liked to make me laugh. He would make the long drive up to Stanford just to spend a day with me, showing up at my dorm with a box of cookies. In the beginning, our relationship was sweet and simple, embedded in shared culture. We studied Punjabi together, danced all night at bhangra parties, and spent holiday breaks at each other's houses. His home in New Jersey became my second home. His parents treated me as their daughter-in-law, and I liked to spend long hours talking with them, sitting on the edge of their bed with a cup of *cha*. I loved his parents. We had it all planned out: Ram would become a surgeon, I would become an academic, and we would make each other happy. But after 9/11, I noticed that the slurs on the street made his fists clench—"Hey, Osama!" "Hey, you terrorist." Ram took a summer trip to Europe and returned with stories of how he was called a dog and thrown out of nightclubs. There was no escaping it.

"Why should I treat people in the hospital who are just going to spit on me on the street?" he asked me.

I reached for his hand. I wanted to make him feel safe. But he pulled his hand away and tried to laugh.

"I'm fine," he kept saying. I could grieve with people around the country but I did not know how to grieve with the man I was going to marry. I focused my energies on reading and writing in the library, analyzing the root causes of hate, as if my honors thesis was somehow going to save him, and us.

As the months went by, Ram stopped smiling as much. He lost his temper more. He lost his temper with me. His grievances were small at first—he would criticize my appearance when we went out. "Your jeans are too loose," he said when I didn't wear a belt. "Why can't you be more girly?" he said when I didn't paint my nails. "Keep your voice down, people are looking at us," he said when I got excited about something. He could hear me pee in the bathroom. "Can't you make it silent like other girls?" That one was tough—I had to practice a lot of different angles.

One day, Ram put our relationship on "pause."

"I need time alone," he said. "But no one can know. You can't tell your parents or Papa Ji. I don't want anything to ruin our future."

I pictured a tape recorder with a big Pause button. We had been together for nearly three years. We would have our wedding back in New Jersey after he was done with school. His Nani had picked out the palkee for our wedding.

"Do we still count our anniversaries on pause?" I asked.

Ram paused and un-paused our relationship from then on. He had somehow managed to tether me to him like a yo-yo—close enough to pull me in when he wanted me, far enough away that he could tell other women he was single and "find himself." I covered for him and told my family that nothing was wrong.

One night, we were talking about the future we were trying very hard not to ruin. I told him I wanted to have children, and I also wanted to travel and make films and write books and make a difference in the wider world. Ram grew quiet. "If you want to be a man," he said, "get a sex change." I could feel the burning under my skin. This time, I gathered my things and left his apartment, but he still somehow managed to be the one slamming the door. He didn't have to tell me that we were back on pause.

I needed a break from thinking about my thesis and the news and my paused long-term relationship, so when I saw flyers advertising tryouts for a production of *The Vagina Monologues* on a campus billboard, I auditioned without knowing anything about it. I discovered it was a work by playwright Eve Ensler, who had interviewed hundreds of women about what their vaginas would say if they could speak. The script was shocking and hilarious and sad and inappropriate in polite company. I devoured it.

We had rehearsals every week that started with the group of actors sitting in a circle and checking in. I was in awe of these other women who had such self-assured relationships with their bodies. I realized that I had come to see my body only through Ram's eyes, and it was ugly and inadequate. I wanted to change that. Our premiere was on Valentine's Day, my birthday. That morning, I realized that I had never actually *seen* my vagina before. I wrote in my journal: "February 14th—Valarie turns twenty-two, Valarie performs in the Vagina Monologues, Valarie looks at her vagina." I put the journal down, rolled out my purple yoga mat, and held out a tiny makeup mirror. When I finally positioned myself correctly after much difficulty, I caught my first glimpse. "Oh god," I said. I was repulsed. But I kept looking and said "Oh god" again because there were layers and layers, as if each layer contained secret histories, and I started humming. "This is part of me, part of me, part of *me,*" I said, in wonder. *A part of me that I do not yet know.*

That night, my friends came to the play, and so did my family, and so did Ram. I had been assigned the monologue "Crooked Braid," a new addition to that year's script. It was based on interviews with indigenous women from the Oglala Lakota Nation on the Pine Ridge Reservation in South Dakota. My monologue was about a woman whose husband battered her. She braided his long black hair for him, all crooked. He walked in the street all macho and proud, but his braid was so crooked, she couldn't help but smile. One day he came home drunk after sleeping with another woman. She snuck in and snipped his braid clean off. She ran. Returned to him years later when his hair had grown out. Watched her son grow up to be a batterer like his father. The monologue ended with all our voices on the stage:

> They took our land.
> They took our ways.
> They took our men.
> We want them back.

My friends Mariah, Shannon, Jess, Mo, and Irene all rushed up to me after the show. Irene handed me a bouquet of red roses, a letter tied to each stem: *V for Vagina, A for Activist* . . . My parents hugged me, proud. We had birthday cake, and I was on top of the world. Then Ram and I were alone. I had invited him to the show because I thought that seeing me up on that stage, beautiful and saying something important, would make him fall in love with me again.

"If you were my daughter, I would slap you," he said. He was talking fast, moving his hands, incensed. A man doesn't deserve his hair cut ever, no matter what.

"But . . . but he battered her," I said.

"The girl I fell in love with three years ago wouldn't have been part of this," he said.

Ram didn't just want to put our relationship on pause—he wanted to pause me. During our time apart, I was finding my voice (and my vagina), and this scared him. But I didn't fight for myself. I cried myself to sleep and apologized the next morning. I couldn't see then what is obvious now. "Crooked Braid" was a kind of distorted mirror of my own relationship. He never hit me, just hurt me with words that came from his own sense of shame and discomfort in his body, his inability to negotiate being brown and Sikh and male in America. But I could not see my own bruises, only his. So I stayed with him. I stayed because I did not want to lose him to a world that was trying to kill him. I stayed because I wanted to do everything I could to protect our future and our families. I stayed because I thought I had no other choice. How many women who bear the displaced aggression of wounded men make the same calculation?

They took our men.
We want them back.

With my relationship back on pause and the play over, I started paying attention to the news again. In the spring of 2003, our country was preparing for an invasion and occupation of Iraq. Top members of the Bush administration were using the pretense of 9/11 to execute a long-standing agenda for regime change in Iraq that would profit U.S. corporations and secure military and economic control of a region that had long eluded them. A year and a half after 9/11, any evidence justifying the invasion was weak at best and fabricated at worst. But the nation was hungry for a fight, and this desire blotted out the rest of our senses. It allowed our government to shift our focus from Afghanistan to Iraq, successfully exchanging one Muslim target for another. The public was fed the administration's rationale, and Congress did not object to the war save for a few lone voices.

It was around this time that I heard Dr. King speak. I sat in the pews of Memorial Church on Stanford's campus. Scotty McLennan, dean of religious life, had organized this event, but he was not the one speaking. A lone black man stood in the pulpit. He stepped up to the mic and suddenly his voice boomed against the stained glass and shook my chest, and Dr. King came alive. This man was an actor performing selections of King's 1967 speech "Beyond Vietnam," but it felt like King himself was speaking to us here and now from the other side of the grave—the radical King who declared that our real enemies were not individuals but unjust systems, the three evils of "poverty, racism, and militarism." It was time to end the wars that recruit poor people and people of color, because "sending men home from dark and bloodied battlefields physically handicapped and psychologically deranged cannot be reconciled with wisdom, justice, and love." It was time to create new systems of justice and equality, and birth a new America. But to do so, we needed a kind of nonviolent revolution that shifted collective consciousness, "a radical revolution of values." For King, inspired by Gandhi before him, nonviolent direct action was not just a moral imperative but a *strategic* necessity.

When I returned to my dorm room that night, my skin tingled and my throat ached as if all my words were stuck there. I called my best friend from back home. Brynn answered from her dorm room at Berkeley. She had seen the scholar-activist Edward Said speak that same night, and both of us felt a deep desire to respond.

"What do we do? What do we do?" we asked each other. We needed to do something.

"I'm not smart enough," I said. "I'm not good enough. I don't know enough. But it's like there's something deep in me that's aching to get out."

"Oh my god, we're pregnant!" Brynn said, and we laughed. "We are going to birth all that's inside us. It's going to be painful, but we just have to trust that it will come. And we'll look back and remember the night we were confused and uncertain."

Brynn and I had always seen the best in each other. A few years earlier, when we were back home, we sat in the car in the parking lot of our high school, looking at the orchards, took each other's hands, and vowed to think of our lives as a great quest. She would become an acclaimed poet; I would become an activist. But back then, we were two Asian American girls, longing to shake off the dust of the farmlands of the Central Valley, determined to help each other be brave. Just like our grandparents.

When they were our age, Brynn's grandparents Alma and Mitsuo were forced from their homes in California's Central Valley and sent to a concentration camp in the deserts of Arizona. They were among 120,000 Japanese Americans, two-thirds of them American citizens, including children and infants, imprisoned during World War II. They felt anguished and alone, indefinitely detained in some of the harshest desert landscapes in North America. Many of their farms and homes were pillaged. Risking his own safety, my grandfather Kehar Singh traveled to those camps to see his Japanese American neighbors, bringing food and company and witness. He looked after some of their farms so that they would have a life to return to when they were freed. He brought home a petrified rock from the desert on one of these visits. I held the rock in my hands now and felt its weight. I could not help but wonder whether the white lawyer who freed Baba Ji from detention at Angel Island had shown him his first act of solidarity on U.S. soil. Dr. King had articulated for us the *need* to fight racism and poverty and war together; perhaps our ancestors pointed us to *how*. "Ancestral solidarity," Brynn called it. They showed up for each other—the white lawyer who fought for the Sikh farmer, the Sikh farmer who fought for his Japanese American neighbors, and their descendants now. They fought injustice *together*. Brynn and I decided that that was how we would fight, too.

∽✦∾

Any act to change the world around us begins *within* us. It starts with a sense of agency, a sense that we have the power to effect change. The Latin root of the word "power" means "to be able." When we feel helpless in the face of injustice, it is easy to give in to the idea that this is just the way things are, because it's the way things have always been. Then someone comes along and sparks our imagination, a prophetic voice from the past, or a friend on the phone. We begin to see that the norms and institutions that order this world are not inevitable but constructed—and therefore can be changed. The Brazilian educator Paulo Freire calls this internal shift "critical consciousness," the moment we tap into our own power to change the world around us. It feels like waking up. That night, I could not feel my own power, but

I could see Brynn's, and she could see mine. We woke each other up. We didn't know what to do next, but we didn't have to know. We just had to hold on consciously to our conviction, and be ready to act when the world said *Now*.

❧

A few days later, I saw flyers on campus about a national student strike. College students across the country were going to hold a coordinated walkout on March 5 to protest the government's plans to invade Iraq. I slept in that morning and almost didn't go. Then I remembered Brynn and our vow and got ready, cursing under my breath, and rushed to the main quad on campus. Sunlight slanted through palm trees and rippled over hundreds of students sitting on the ground. Professors with microphones delivered teach-ins on preemptive war and histories of resistance and liberation theology. I sat down and listened for a long time. Someone who knew about my honors thesis about hate crimes asked me to speak. The next thing I knew I was standing under a tree, holding a mic, a hundred students looking up at me. My legs were shaking, and my heart was beating in my ears.

"Hi," I said. "Um, well, I can only tell you what I know." I took a deep breath and began to describe Balbir Uncle's murder after 9/11 and then the survivors of hate I had met, and story after story spilled forth from me. My voice began to quicken and rise and I wasn't on that sun-drenched quad anymore; I was inside the stories I was telling. I described what I was seeing, and the audience saw what I was seeing, and, for one long moment, the boundaries dissolved: There was no separation between the feeling in the audience and the feeling in me and the feeling in the people whose stories I was telling. *Vismaad*. The bowl was breaking. I heard someone quietly weeping. The audience was with me, on the journey with me, but I didn't know where I was taking them. I didn't know what conclusion we were going to reach together, until I got to the end of all the stories and the conclusion was waiting there for me: "If this war happens," I said, "hate against Muslims and Sikhs will go on, here at home. I think there won't be an end to the violence."

There was silence. Then applause. I felt relief in my throat, but my mind was racing as I tried to understand how I had reached that conclusion. A student rushed up to me and introduced herself as Rachael, a senior in my class. "That story you told about the turbaned man who was arrested on the train? The first suspect after 9/11?" "Yes?" I said. "I was there," she said. Her voice cracked. We sat down and she told me her story.

Rachael Neumann had been visiting friends in Boston during the 9/11 attacks. Overcome with shock, she knew she needed to get home to her family in New York and booked a train ticket for the next day, September 12. She noticed two turbaned men walking around at South Station and her body seized up. She was scared. She caught herself. *Rachael, why are you profiling them?* She had Sikh classmates at school. She knew who Sikhs were. But she still heard herself say, *Why don't they just take off their turbans, for their own protection?* Other people at the train station were staring at them, too. "Everyone was thinking 'turban equals terrorist,'" Rachael said. "Because that's all we saw over and over again. Flash the turban and flash the Towers and that's what sticks." When Rachael boarded Amtrak No. 173 and found her seat, the two turbaned men were seated in front of her. *Out of all the seats on the train,* she thought. She shook it off and settled in.

The train stopped in Providence. "Ladies and gentlemen, please remain seated," said the conductor. "We're having a problem with the track." No one bought it. The chatter began. People began to introduce themselves—they were firefighters, doctors, and nurses from Boston all heading into New York for the relief effort.

Rachael looked out the window and noticed swarms of people moving fast—the first wave of them in plain clothes, then a second wave in windbreakers with bold letters on their backs. The train compartments in front of her and behind her were being evacuated, but

Rachael's car was left alone. *What are they not telling us?* she asked. She started to panic. Then, out the window, she saw thirty to fifty officers. SWAT gear. Bulletproof vests. Dogs.

The doors of the train car flew open. Four officers rushed in with automatic guns pointed in Rachael's direction. "Put your fucking hands up! Put your fucking hands up!" Rachael ducked. *Holy shit, I'm dead,* she thought. *If they shoot, it will go right through this seat and into me.* The two turbaned men were standing with their hands up. One dropped his cell phone. "What the fuck was in your hand? Give us that phone!" They frisked the men and turned them around and frisked them again, then handcuffed them and led them off the train.

"Did those men have anything else?" an officer yelled. Rachael remembered another cell phone. She jumped up and pointed to it. "That's their phone! That's theirs!" she cried. Maybe it was a bomb. "Get it off! Get it all off!"

The officers left and everyone started crying. Rachael started crying. The man next to her was crying. Outside the window, suddenly there were news cameras and bright lights and hundreds of spectators. One of the turbaned men was being pushed through the crowd. An officer taunted, "How's Osama bin Laden?" Someone yelled, "You killed my brother!" People were shouting, "Kill him!"

This was the real thing, thought Rachael. She made it home to her family and didn't watch the news for a week. She baked bread, sat quietly, and grieved with her parents. She didn't try to find out what had happened on the train that day. She didn't want to know that the men were terrorists, and she didn't want to know that they weren't. "I knew they were innocent deep in my heart," she told me. "I just didn't want that to be verified. Until I heard you speak."

I told Rachael that Sher Singh was a twenty-eight-year-old software engineer, a soft-spoken and gentle man. He had been arrested on an anonymous tip that he and his friend *looked* suspicious. Sher Singh was carrying a *kirpan,* a small ceremonial dagger, a Sikh article of faith, and so he was the one handcuffed and interrogated for five hours before his release. Rachael sighed. "I wish I could apologize to him," she said. "I wish I could apologize for making him not a person in my head for a year and a half. I wish I could tell him that I was sorry."

About a year later, I was able to deliver Rachael's message to Sher in person when I visited him in D.C.

"I forgive her," he said softly. "And I wish her the best in life."

Rachael's story gave me the answer I had been searching for.

Why didn't America's blood cool? Our leadership kept the nation in a heightened state of terror. The image of the brown turbaned "Muslim terrorist" seared into Americans on 9/11 was reinforced over and over again by a government that arrested, detained, deported, registered, and surveilled Muslims, Arabs, South Asians, and immigrants. Sher Singh was just the first of thousands of innocent people to endure this treatment. After his release, federal officials rounded up, detained, and interrogated more than twelve hundred Muslim and Arab men in the course of two months. Like Sher Singh, none was found to have any connection to terrorism. Next the administration rolled out a series of immigration policies that targeted Muslim and Arab men who were noncitizens. Under the Alien Absconder Initiative, at least one thousand were arrested, two-thirds of them deported. None was convicted of terrorism. Then, under the National Security Entry-Exit Registration System (NSEERS), nearly eighty-four thousand men from twenty-four Muslim-majority countries had to specially register their presence in the United States. They were fingerprinted, photographed, and interrogated. Around three thousand were detained and nearly fourteen thousand deported. Again, none was convicted of terrorism. Meanwhile, the administration began sweeping domestic surveillance of Muslims and immigrants, authorized by the USA PATRIOT Act that had been hastily passed by Congress only forty-five days after 9/11. Once again, no one surveilled under the PATRIOT Act has been convicted of terrorism. Over and over again, the government cast a wide net, curtailing civil liberties and terrorizing entire communities in the name of national security, but it did not make the nation any safer. This is what happens when the state profiles people based on their race, religion, or national origin instead of focusing on behavior. It doesn't work. It also creates a vicious cycle: Profiling by the government signals to the public whom they should fear, and in turn the public's fear pressures the government to profile.

In a twist of fate, Rachael would come to hear Sher's story and apologize, but there would be no public apology or reconciliation for the thousands of people targeted by the state. Instead, government profiling continued to signal to the public that people who were brown or turbaned or Muslim should be treated as automatically suspect and potentially terrorist. This is why hate crimes remained high and never again fell back to the levels they were at before 9/11. State violence fueled public hatred, which led to more violence. This was a new instance of an old pattern: State violence has been tethered to hate violence throughout U.S. history for indigenous people, black people, queer people, and immigrant groups in every generation. The government incarcerated Brynn's grandparents after Pearl Harbor in response to virulent hatred for Japanese Americans, an act that in turn motivated more pillage, propaganda, and violence. As long as the United States carried out a war on terror that bombed Muslim-majority countries abroad and profiled Muslims and immigrants at home, hate violence against our communities would continue.

Already the Bush administration had repurposed the military base at Guantánamo Bay, Cuba, to incarcerate prisoners in the war on terror and had authorized their indefinite detention. The administration argued that these detainees were not on U.S. soil and therefore outside the reach of the U.S. Constitution. Our federal courts were already positioned to try people for terrorism. International law was already set up to manage prisoners of war. But the administration insisted on creating a new legal regime that was more like a legal black hole. It treated detainees as if they were beyond the reach of existing human rights law. And it worked. By the spring of 2003, the public had largely accepted the images of Muslim men in cages detained without trial or charge at Guantánamo—just as it had accepted the profiling and surveillance of Muslim Americans at home. When a nation collectively condones the stripping of civil and human rights of a group, it has delineated who is acceptable to hate.

This was wrong. It was unjust. But what was I to do? As the war drums grew louder in the spring of 2003, I could feel a sense of alarm rise inside me, not for what might happen to me if I acted but what might happen to me if I did nothing.

I resolved that if we were serious about fighting hate in America, we had to challenge the institutions whose actions perpetuated hate. Specifically, we had to fight the policies of the Bush administration— the policies that launched the wars based on lies and stripped the rights of whole groups of people. Not everyone agreed. Ram did not agree. He thought we needed to keep our heads down. Let it pass. It was a problem of "mistaken identity." Sikhs bore the brunt of hate violence, often because we were confused with Muslims. To keep ourselves safe, we needed to distance ourselves from Muslims. We needed to show our patriotism through flag pins and photo ops with the president. Some even displayed bumper stickers that said WE ARE SIKH NOT MUSLIM. This reminded me of the I AM CHINESE, NOT JAPANESE buttons during World War II.

Brynn's words echoed in my ears: "ancestral solidarity." People of color survived oppression throughout our history through acts of solidarity. Shallow solidarity was based on the logic of exchange— *You show up for me, and I will show up for you*. But deep solidarity was rooted in recognition—*I show up for you, because I see you as part of me*. Your liberation is bound up in my own. We needed to show up for communities who were subject to state violence, *and* for the people in the countries our government was about to bomb, *and* for the soldiers about to be sent into battlefields that did not need to exist. All this meant that we needed to try to stop the war, I reasoned. Ram thought that protesting in the streets was the last thing we needed to do. Good thing he still had me on pause.

A few days after the national student strike, I showed up at an organizing meeting on campus with some of my closest friends—

Shannon, Jess, and Irene. We sat in a circle in Stanford's White Plaza, an outdoor gathering space where generations of students before us had held protests and rallies. I knew why I had to fight but I had no idea how. "We've been protesting this war, but our voices keep falling on deaf ears," said Shahid Buttar, a third-year law student and Muslim American who spoke with precision and passion. "So we are turning to nonviolent direct action, in the tradition of King." Direct Action to Stop the War was an organization created by San Francisco Bay Area activists whose blockading and disruptive tactics had been honed through twenty years of urban direct-action organizing. They were inspired by King, who taught, like Gandhi before him, that it was right to break just laws in order to stop unjust state action. Now they were organizing on college campuses. "A sign-up sheet is going around for arrestable and non-arrestable roles," said Shahid. Arrestables were those who were willing to risk arrest in an act of civil disobedience. Non-arrestables were legal observers, media liaisons, police liaisons, medics, and those who offered ground support. I signed my name under "non-arrestable." My friends and I teamed up with Shahid to form an affinity group. I didn't quite know what that meant, but I could hear my heart beating in my ears. Our training began the next day. We were trained as legal observers with the National Lawyers Guild and learned how to document protests to protect against police brutality. We were taught how to engage the media and negotiate with the police and keep people calm during an arrest. We began showing up to support antiwar rallies and direct actions in protests around the San Francisco Bay Area. We marched with protesters in the streets, ran with breakaway marches down Market Street, photographed people in white body bags who dropped to the asphalt in "die-ins," and witnessed dozens of arrests. Night after night we met in my dorm room, pored over blueprints for the next action, prepared communication with law enforcement and news media, and reviewed our training. I was swept up by the momentum, relieved to be in motion, inside another whirlwind. My friends and I gave ourselves a name—the Pocket. If we were ever far apart, we had to remember only that we belonged to each other, that we were always part of a pocket held together by a kind of invisible magic, shielded by love.

Then, amid a groundswell of global protest, the ultimatum arrived. In a televised address, President Bush gave Saddam Hussein forty-eight hours to leave Iraq or the United States would begin military action "at a time of our choosing." The antiwar movement had failed to stop the war. As the deadline approached, I went to the common room in my dorm and waited in front of the television set. The whole day felt quiet. The air was still, the trees were silent. As if the earth had exhaled and forgotten to take another breath.

The deadline struck: five P.M. Pacific Time on March 19. But President Bush did not deliver an address from the Oval Office. The first image was a live feed from Baghdad at night. Bright flashes. Three thousand bombs. The news anchor seemed genuinely surprised when the correspondent on the ground reported that the Iraqis he talked to were upset that they were being invaded. A few minutes later, President Bush appeared on the screen: "My fellow citizens, at this hour, American and coalition forces are in the early stages of military operations to disarm Iraq, to free its people, and to defend the world from grave danger." "Operation Iraqi Freedom" had begun with "a broad and concerted campaign" of "shock and awe." The first of an estimated seven thousand civilians were killed in the bombing that night.

My friends came over, and we held each other for a long time, without words. Then we gathered our bags and drove into the city. Our affinity group had agreed to be part of a large coordinated effort planned by Direct Action to Stop the War to shut down business as usual in San Francisco as soon as the war began. We spent the night at a house close to the morning's action. We practiced chants and reviewed the game plan. I couldn't sleep. There was a knot in the center of my chest. I had shifted my name to the "arrestable" category, because I wanted to offer everything I had to this moment, to give my all to the fight. *I am probably going to be arrested tomorrow,* I thought. *Oh my god, I've never done anything like this before. What will my parents say?* I looked at my friends in their sleeping bags—Shannon, who planned to go to medical school *and* law school, because she knew marginalized people, including the black community, her community, needed formidable advocates; Jess, who wanted to become an immigration attorney after spending time in Central America and learning about the humanitarian crises propelling so many people to seek refuge in the United States. They were brilliant and young and earnest and powerful. We were strong together. I felt the breath in my body and slept.

❧

Dawn broke over the city. We made our way down the hill, quietly beating our drums, singing to ourselves, "Ain't gonna let nobody turn me around," and marched up to the intersection of Third and Folsom, a busy intersection just south of downtown. One hundred Stanford students and professors were already there in their own affinity groups. Everyone had trained for this moment; everyone knew the plan and had a role. Shannon, Jess, and I took each other's hands, made two long lines along the intersection, and blocked the street. Traffic ground to a halt. The sound of horns grew deafening. Students went from car to car passing out our mission statement along with pastries; others stood by as medics with first-aid kits; others were legal observers ready with notepads and cameras; and we "arrestables" kept our lines strong. The megaphone passed from hand to hand as different students assumed the role of chant leader. When it got to me, my palms were sweaty. I started with an easy chant, my voice shaking: "Say no to war! *No to war!* Say yes to peace! *Yes to peace!* Say we want peace! *We want peace!*" The crowd roared back and I could feel their voices inside me and began to pace up and down the lines, chanting louder. Crowds of people gathered on the street corner to watch us and join us and chant with us. News cameras arrived.

Then the police arrived, a marching army of helmets and batons. Officers went down the line of students blocking the street and asked each of them if they were willing to be arrested. They nodded and sat down in unison. I suddenly found myself alone with the megaphone in the center of the intersection—the now-seated students facing me, their arms locked together making a thin human wall, the police positioned behind them like tall statues, and behind them, a growing crowd. The cameras were pointed at us. An officer approached and asked me to sit down, too. Everyone was watching and waiting. There was no passing the megaphone now. I was stuck with it. I panicked. *What am I going to say? What am I going to say?* I returned to what I'd learned in those interviews across the country with grieving Sikh families—*What needs to be heard?* Shannon and Jess tried to smile across the way. I had a piece of paper in my pocket. It was the mission statement we had written about why we were here. I looked at the police with their hard batons, took a breath, and lifted the megaphone.

"This is a nonviolent direct action," I said. "We are standing up to an administration that has taken our country to war. The police are doing their job today and they are letting us do ours." The officers slowly lifted their visors and rested their batons and I could see their faces now.

I looked at the drivers stuck in their cars. "We acknowledge that blocking this intersection today affects the people of San Francisco indiscriminately. This is meant to reflect and call attention to the indiscriminate nature of the attack on Iraq. Civilians are being killed this very moment in our name, for our sake, and we cannot remain silent. Thank you for bearing witness to our protest. We did not vote on this war, and our representatives failed to stop it. Our last resort is nonviolent direct action." Everyone began to chant: "This is what democracy looks like!"

"The United States is the world's superpower." I was gaining steam now. "But there is a second superpower growing in the land around the globe and that is the people. The people have the power." Everyone began to chant: "There ain't no power like the power of the people 'cause the power of the people don't stop!"

At this point, the police officers had peeled off a few protesters at the ends of the human wall to let a line of traffic pass through. Those protesters joined me in the intersection. I recognized a Stanford professor and asked him to speak, and he delivered a short lecture on the history of Iraq and the reasons this war did not have a legal basis. Then he handed the megaphone back to me and we held a moment of silence for the dead and began to sing again. The next few hours proceeded this way: singing, chanting, listening to lectures, observing silence, reading our mission statement in unison as more media cameras showed up and the crowds swelled to hundreds, the applause grew louder, and the police looked on, and some even smiled. This was something powerful—part teach-in, part demonstration, part concert of resistance—and I wasn't afraid of the megaphone anymore. I was calm and present and there was nowhere else I wanted to be on this day in history but here. When the police arrested me and carried me to the van, the crowd cheered, and I heard my name. It was Professor Linda Hess, my adviser, the woman who had sent me into the whirlwind after 9/11 a year and a half before, standing in the crowd and cheering me on. The students on the street broke into the Toyi-Toyi, the South African dance of resistance. I felt the rush of history behind me, the fighters who had gone before us on this soil and around the world, and it made me feel invincible.

In the police van, it was suddenly quiet. The cheers outside were muffled. "I'm sorry," someone said. The woman handcuffed next to me was my mother's age and she was looking at me sadly. "In 1982, I was arrested for protesting nuclear weapons in front of the Lawrence Livermore Lab," she said. "Amber was just a baby then." Her daughter Amber was sitting next to her, also handcuffed, leaning her head on her mother's shoulder. "I'm sorry that you're having to do this now," her mother said to both of us. "I'm so sorry my generation failed you. And I'm so proud of you." She had tears in her eyes.

When the van arrived at the pier, we were issued traffic citations and immediately released. My cell phone rang. "Daddy?" I asked. My father was a deeply sincere and kind man who believed in the best in people, including our leaders. We had spent many nights at home arguing about this war over the dinner table. Now I was straining to hear his voice over the noise in the street. "I still believe in this war," he said. "I still trust the president. But today you put your body and life on the line for what *you* believe, and—I'm so proud of you."

I took a breath and my phone rang again. This time, it was my teammate Shahid. Protests were heating up and they needed legal observers in the Financial District. "Got it," I said. Shannon, Jess, and I rushed back downtown. Thousands of people flooded Market Street. Shouting and chanting, marching and moving, but instead of the clear and crisp organization of the morning, there was chaos and confusion. Police officers were pushing in on the crowd, helmets down, shields up. I knew this formation—they were sweeping the street, trapping hundreds together in order to initiate a mass arrest. People shouted back in anger. Tensions mounted. Batons were out. People were going to get hurt. I had a megaphone.

"This is a nonviolent action," I began. "This is not about the people versus the police. This is about the administration waging war." My voice fell flat against the building. I tried again. "The police are trying to do their job. We are doing our job. Let's show them how we wage peace." Still no response. Some rolled their eyes at us. Linda Hess had taught me some civil rights songs back in her office. "My generation has a whole treasure chest of songs to give you, my dear," Linda had said. So I started singing. I had a terrible singing voice, but I started singing, and Jess and Shannon sang with me.

"We shall overcome. We shall overcome. . . ." The three of us stood between the police and protesters, turned our back to the police, faced the crowd with the megaphone, and kept singing. I don't know why I was not scared. It was as if the megaphone and the song were our shield. "Deep in my heart, I do believe, that we shall overcome some day." The crowd started to join us, and it felt as though the song slowed down time, and everyone had a chance to breathe. There was a black woman wailing loudly, angry and desperate, and officers were closing in on her, batons out. Shannon, Jess, and I moved to her and continued singing, and the woman got quiet and began humming with us. The officers were backing away. The space between the police and the crowd grew, and soon there was enough space for the people to resume the march again. We had broken up the arrest. The three of us became roaming peacemakers after that. We moved up and down Market Street and found the corners where the police were about to push in or beat protesters. We put our bodies between them, reminded everyone why we were there, and sang the old songs. Over and over again, it worked.

Years later, I would look back on this day in San Francisco and realize how lucky I was not to have been hurt. I would study police departments' excessive use of force on people of color and join protests in the wake of police killings of young black people in places like Ferguson and Baltimore. I would learn about histories of systemic racism and police brutality from the Movement for Black Lives and track the names of the dead whose killers were never indicted, a never-ending list that included Tamir Rice, Eric Garner, and Sandra Bland. I watched as America's police departments became increasingly militarized, armed with surplus military equipment and weapons from the war on terror. Police officers rolled down city streets in assault vehicles, decked in full battle uniforms and assault rifles, and I was no longer able to see their faces. When we can no longer see the faces of the people sworn to protect us, public safety is an illusion. I did not know all this that day in San Francisco. I thought appealing to the conscience of individual officers would be enough to prevent the unnecessary use of force. This was before I knew better. This was before I got injured.

When Shannon, Jess, and I returned to campus that day, we were still on top of the world. We had experienced the power and promise of nonviolent civil disobedience. Newspapers reported that twenty-two hundred antiwar demonstrators were arrested in San Francisco in the first few days of the war. Millions had protested across the country and around the globe. What needed to happen next? We needed to keep building momentum to bring the war to an end. I thought of those drivers stuck in traffic. "From now on, we should no longer target intersections and places that indiscriminately hurt people," I wrote to the team. "Instead, we should stage sharply directed actions at institutions that are most directly linked with the war. There are more effective and efficient ways to fight." Everyone felt the same way. So our season of organizing began: teach-ins and marches and direct action protests against military contractors and the president himself when he visited the Bay Area to crow under a "Mission Accomplished" banner. Thousands of people marched with us. We were riding the wave of momentum. It almost felt like we could stop the war.

I could wield the megaphone. I could do a press interview on the fly. I could face down the police. But I couldn't face my boyfriend.

Ram found me on campus on the day of Holi, the South Asian festival of color that celebrates the triumph of good over evil. We were standing in Wilbur Field. Students were laughing and running and shrieking and throwing powdered dyes into the air as colors were flying all around us. The colors were inspired by the love story of Krishna and Radha in Hindu mythology. The legend goes, Krishna loved Radha deeply but was so self-conscious of his dark blue skin that he shied away until one day, he playfully painted the face of his beloved the same color as his own, making her like him.

"How could you do this to me?" Ram was saying. He wasn't throwing colors, he was throwing words. "People have been seeing you on the news, getting arrested. They're asking me what's going on, and I don't know what to tell them. It's so embarrassing. How could you be so stupid? How could you hurt me like this?"

He was yelling, this time not behind closed doors but out in the open, on campus, in front of everyone. I began to cry. "Let's go," he said. He drove me home. I let slip that my parents knew that we were on pause. He got quiet. "You betrayed me," he said. He had made me promise not to tell my family. "You've hurt me more than anyone else in my entire life. Maybe one day I can forgive you. But I'll never forget."

Then he kissed me. I was relieved. I was still going to be his wife. I was surprised by his kiss and by my relief. "I already gave my heart to Ram," I wrote in my journal. "I don't know how to get it back, or if I can. That's it! I gave my heart to him long ago and now no matter what he does or how many reasons he gives me to leave, I can't." I had not yet learned that abuse cannot be the price of love.

The months went on, and our relationship went on.

The wars went on, too. Soldiers began to come home in coffins from the wars in Afghanistan and Iraq. The administration had assured the country that the wars would be short, the casualties minimal—another lie. Even as we watched Iraq descend into chaos, we could not have imagined that nearly two decades later, the wars would continue. Today, a new generation of American soldiers enlist to fight in wars on terror that began before they were born.

The months went on, and so did the policies that targeted Muslim and immigrant communities. A multimillion-dollar industry emerged to produce anti-Muslim propaganda, think tanks, and trainings for politicians who vilified Muslims. The Bush administration's post-9/11 policies set a precedent for even more brutal state practices, paving the way for the Muslim bans and family separation policies of the Trump era. Our government's response to 9/11 initiated a contraction of civil and human rights so powerful that it continues twenty years later with a new generation barely aware that it could be otherwise.

The hate violence went on, too. Balbir and Sukhpal Sodhi's names are now written on a long list of the dead. Today Americans are seven times more likely to be killed by a white right-wing extremist than a terrorist who kills in the name of Islam. And Muslim and Sikh Americans specifically are five times more likely to be targets of hate than we were before 9/11. At this moment, a brother, an uncle, or a child somewhere in America is hearing the word "Terrorist!" A new generation of our young people have no memory of what it was like before 9/11, before the threat of hate was braided into our daily lives.

Back in 2003, I did not know all that was to come. But I knew enough by the time of my college graduation to believe that we had fought—and failed. We didn't stop the war. We didn't stop the policies. We didn't stop the hate. All that energy and momentum and power of thousands of people in the streets, all that history rushing at our backs as we offered up our bodies and our voices, all that bravery and conviction—what good was it? What good was our fight?

As graduation day neared, I felt defeated. Laura Donohue, a political science professor who had watched me through college, called me into her office. "I never say this to my students," she said. "But I say this to you: You have to go to law school."

No, no, I was going to be an academic. First a master's and then a PhD in religious studies. These were the credentials I wanted.

"Look, you have an activist heart, and you're going to keep ending up out *there*," she said. "You are a woman. You are a woman of color. This war is going to have repercussions for years to come. You're going to need to make people listen to you. If you want to be heard, if you want to be protected, no matter what else you do, you have to get your law degree."

She was talking about degrees as if they were swords and shields for the battle. She did not know it but she was returning me to language I knew well. She was returning me home.

Sikhs are a warrior people. In the halls of our gurdwaras, there are portraits of our Ten Gurus, our ten teachers. The first is Guru Nanak, founder of the faith, his eyes soft and palm lifted with the inscription *Ik Onkar*, Oneness. The tenth is Guru Gobind Singh, arrows at his back and falcon on his shoulder. He is the one who led Sikhs into battle against an oppressive empire and called us to become *sant-sipahi*, warrior-sages. When you love someone, you fight to protect them when they are in harm's way. If you "see no stranger" and choose to love all people, then you must fight for *anyone* who is suffering from the harm of injustice. This was the path of the warrior-sage: The warrior fights, the sage loves. *Revolutionary love*.

I had drifted from these stories. I assumed that being part of the antiwar movement meant that I had to be ashamed of this martial history. I saw all violence as reactive, confrontational, and destructive, no matter its justification. Nonviolence was thoughtful, disciplined, and creative. I knew which side I wanted to be on, so I had thrown war metaphors out of my vocabulary and downplayed my heritage. But this denied me the ability to draw upon the strength and wisdom of my own ancestors. The fight impulse is ancient and fundamental. These ancestors fought with swords and shields, bows and arrows, because they had no choice. They did not have a sophisticated matrix of legal and political avenues to defend civil and human rights, nor international law to mediate conflicts between nations. We have these avenues today. We no longer need literal weapons like our ancestors. But we could still learn from how they marshaled the fighting impulse on the battlefield. My professor saw me out there holding nothing but a megaphone. *You are a woman and a woman of color,* she had said. *If you want to fight, you need armor.*

❧

I thought again of the paintings on the walls of our gurdwaras. The Sikh gurus professed equality between women and men and people of all genders, which was revolutionary in their time. Our scriptures, stories, and songs all teach gender equality, unequivocally. Yet almost all of the women on the gurdwara walls are portrayed first and foremost as mothers, sisters, and wives. Bibi Nanaki, the first Sikh disciple, is presented as Nanak's sister; Mata Khivi, who established *langar,* the communal meal served in all gurdwaras, is presented as the second guru's wife. There was no woman on the wall who stood in her own right. Except one. Here she was, her sword catching the light—Mai Bhago, the first Sikh woman warrior, whose story my grandfather had told me as a child. She was strong and beautiful and fierce.

In the year 1705, the legend goes, during a great battle against an empire, forty soldiers abandoned their post and returned to their village. This village woman Mai Bhago turned to them and said, "You will not abandon the fight. You will return to the fire. And I will lead you." She donned a turban, mounted a horse, and, with a sword in her hand and fire in her eyes, she led them where no one else would. She became the one she was waiting for.

"Do not abandon your post," Papa Ji had told me in childhood.

I always wanted to be the warrior in the story. But I was the deserter, too. I was the one who wanted to give up, but inside me was a woman warrior who kept taking my hand and leading me back into the fire anyway, again and again. Why did she keep leading me back? In the story, the forty deserters who followed Mai Bhago back into the field all died in that battle. They fought for a future they did not live to see. They did not know that they would be remembered or that their fight would make a difference. They did not know that our people would go on to live in every part of the world and recite their names in every *Ardas,* the prayer at the end of every Sikh service. Today we call the forty warriors the *Chali Mukte,* the Forty Liberated Ones, not because they were liberated in death but because they were liberated in life. For the warrior-sage, the fight is not just a means to an end. The fight is a way of being in the world, an ongoing labor of love. The woman warrior in me kept leading me back into the field, because it was the only way to keep loving the world, and myself, *here and now*. That would have to be enough.

"One more thing," said Professor Donohue before I left her office. "You need a man who sees you up on that stage and is proud of you. Not someone who will diminish you."

How did she know? I walked out of the office stunned. But I still could not figure it out. If I left Ram, which would I be—the warrior or the deserter?

I called Ram's father to tell him that I would not be coming home for the holidays this year, the first time in four years. I said that it was because my family had plans, but really it was a way to give myself time to think.

"*Beta,* I see what's happening," he said. "I know that you're not happy."

How did *everyone* know?

"Listen," he said. "It is very important that you do what I say."

"*Haan Ji,* Uncle Ji." I promised to do what he said. In any generation before ours, Ram and I would have been married by now. The words "girlfriend" and "boyfriend" did not exist in traditional Punjabi families, so his family had treated me as a fiancée for the past four years. I started preparing the response of a good daughter-in-law: I will give it another chance. I will work harder. Marriages require sacrifice. I will sacrifice, like all the women in my family before me.

"Move on," he said.

"Uncle Ji?" I did not hear him right.

"Move on," he said again. "Be free. You have great things to accomplish in this world. You can't have anyone holding you back, even if it's my own son."

No, no, no.

"Just promise me one thing," he said. He was choking up now. "I am losing you as my daughter-in-law," he said. "But I cannot lose you as a daughter. Call me now and then. Tell me how you are."

I was crying now, and he was crying, too.

"Yes," I said. "I promise."

Ram did not know how to let me go, and I did not know how to leave him. But his father fought for my life and my future when I could not. Ram and I had to learn how to love ourselves before we could learn to love another. I wrote him a letter ending the relationship and freed us both.

❧

Dr. King named three evils—racism, poverty, and militarism. But he left out a fourth—sexism. The assumption that women and girls are less than equal and therefore deserve less dignity and freedom is perhaps the most ancient, pervasive, and insidious evil of them all. But sexism is not a single issue. "There is no such thing as a single-issue struggle because we do not live single-issue lives," said black feminist Audre Lorde. "Intersectionality," a term coined by scholar Kimberlé Crenshaw, is a concept that black women have used since Sojourner Truth's "Ain't I a Woman" speech in 1851. It describes how women fight on multiple fronts: Women of color must fight racism in addition to sexism; if they are poor and rural women, they must also fight poverty; if they are queer women, homophobia; if they are trans women, transphobia; if they are disabled women, stigma and barriers to access; if they are undocumented women, the threat of detention, deportation, and family separation. Since multiple inequalities determine our power and privilege and lived experience in society, these inequalities must be fought *together*, by all of us. Otherwise we fail our movements and ourselves.

Sikh women in America must fight on at least three different fronts: hate and racism out in the world, ignorance and invisibility even within progressive spaces, and sexism within our own community. Sikh advocates were starting to gain traction on women's issues like domestic violence, sexual assault, and gender discrimination— until 9/11 happened. Then many of us put our issues on the back burner. It was more urgent to protect our brothers, fathers, husbands, and sons. But the threat of hate violence never ended. It took many of us years to start organizing for women and girls again. It is *still* hard for me to speak publicly about sexism in my community when we live in a nation that continues to see turbaned men as violent patriarchs. But any time I do, I find new chances to build solidarity, with women from different communities, with other Sikh women, and with men who are allies. We are stronger together. Now I look for the spaces where women are confronting issues like racism, sexism, classism, militarism, homophobia, and transphobia in the same breath. We cannot fight on multiple fronts alone and last. We need allies in our lives, and in our movements, who wonder, grieve, and fight with us and for us. Perhaps a better word is "accomplices," a term invoked by indigenous leaders. We need accomplices who will conspire with us to break rules in order to break chains, as Ram's father did for me.

What does it mean to be a warrior-sage for a new time? Who will you fight for? What will you risk? It begins with honoring the fight impulse in you. Think about what breaks your heart. Notice what it feels like to have your fists clench, your jaw close, your pulse quicken. Notice what it feels like to want to fight back. Honor that in yourself. You are alive and have something worth fighting for. Now comes the second moment: How will you channel that into something that delivers life instead of death? Breathe. Think. Then choose your sword and shield. You don't have to know the answers. You just have to be ready for the moment when the world says: *Now*.

I believe that we can *all* be warrior-sages. Like Papa Ji, I choose to interpret the Sikh warrior tradition in the most expansive, compassionate, nonviolent, and life-enhancing way I can. Not everyone interprets our tradition this way. Every great wisdom tradition in the world—Judaism, Christianity, Islam, Hinduism, and Buddhism—has been used to justify cruelty and violence, or to inspire a revolutionary kind of love. I choose love. I know that military metaphors don't work for some people. Too much actual bloodshed. For those who are drawn to it, I think the warrior-sage concept can be useful as a means of tapping into our bravery. Nonviolence is often seen as passive and soft. But warrior metaphors show nonviolent action for what it is—fierce, strategic, demanding, and disciplined. Nonviolent movements around the globe have ushered in more durable democracies that are less likely to regress into civil war. There are some situations where force is necessary to defend oneself and resist state violence. But force should be a last resort. "Only when all other methods fail is it proper to hold the sword in hand," says Guru Gobind Singh. For the cost of violence is high. To break another's bones, to take their life, is to forgo wonder: *It is to cut off a part of ourselves that we do not yet know*. I choose nonviolence because it is moral *and* strategic.

So, I invite you to step into this rich part of my tradition with four questions. First, what is your sword, your *kirpan*? What can you use to fight on behalf of others—your pen, your voice, your art, your pocketbook, your presence? Begin where you are, your home or campus or community, on the front lines or behind the scenes. Second, what is your shield, your *dhal*? What can you use to protect yourself and others when the fight is dangerous—your camera, legal counsel, a group of allies, public witness? Your safety matters. Third, what is your instrument, your *dilruba*? In Sikh legend, our ancestors designed the *dilruba,* a string instrument small enough for soldiers to carry on their backs into the battlefield, so that they could lift their spirits in music, song, and poetry in the mornings before they faced the fire. I have a painting of the woman warrior Mai Bhago with a sword and shield in her hands, and a *dilruba* on her back. So, I started learning how to play the actual instrument! I still can only play a scale, but the music helps me breathe. The sound of the strings reverberates inside me and centers my mind. Your *dilruba* can be what centers you—singing, dancing, drumming, walking, yoga, *kirtan,* prayer, meditation. Finally, who is your sacred community, your *sangat*? You just need three kinds of people. Someone like Brynn who sees the best in you. Someone like Shannon or Jess who is willing to fight by your side. And someone like Ram's father who can fight *for* you when you need help. Bring them together and you've created a pocket of revolutionary love.

part II.

tend the wound

loving opponents

My fear of anger taught me nothing. Your fear of that anger will teach you nothing, also.

—*Audre Lorde*

4.
rage.

I ALWAYS THOUGHT THAT THE OPPOSITE OF LOVE WAS RAGE, THE EXTREME, irrational, uncontrollable expression of anger, the force that drove people to hurt others with their words or weapons. Rage was to be tamed and wrestled down like a wild animal within us. We were only as evolved or spiritual or good as our ability to subdue it. Only when our rage was subdued could we unlock our human potential to love others, even our opponents. I don't know when I learned this, but it ran so deep that it must have been at the onset of memory. It must have been inherited. To find rage, I had to look at my mother.

My first memory of my mother is her crying. I knew even as a small child that my mother was beautiful—dark brown eyes, raven hair, radiant smile. The world turned to look at her wherever we went, but only *I* saw her cry, behind closed doors, in the bedroom, where the *surma* under her eyes ran down her face in black lines and stained the sheets. I would bring her tissues, and she would take my hand in hers. The membrane between our hearts was porous, and so my mother's sadness became my own. I did not know that my mother's rage had nowhere to go except into her tears. I glimpsed her rage only in flashes, when milk spilled on the table, or when one of the children wet the bed.

My mother grew up in India in the old royal city of Patiala in Punjab, where she studied literature and planned to be a teacher. When she was eighteen years old, her family heard about a young man visiting from America looking to get married. He and his mother were visiting different homes, talking with the fathers of households while the daughters silently served them tea, as was custom. My mother agreed to meet this man only if the cups of *cha* were already on the table—she would not be a doll on display. Papa Ji, my mother's father, met the young man at the door, shook his hand, and liked him instantly. The two families talked in the house with the rooftop that opened to the sky. My mother eyed my father quietly, the bachelor with sideburns and bell-bottoms. When they were left alone for a few minutes, my mother said to him in perfect English, "Don't you feel bad coming to this country and seeing all these girls and breaking their hearts just to take your pick of a bride?" My father opened his mouth and closed it again. He was in love. She thought he was handsome. Two weeks later they were married. My mother boarded her first-ever flight and together they traveled from India to the family farm in California.

My father was born and raised on that farm and grew up picking peaches and plums, milking the cow, and laboring alongside his father, who had arrived at the turn of the century to make a home in the California heartland. By now his father, Baba Ji, was old and frail. He spent each day sitting in the rocking chair under the red pipe-cleaner tree. Grandmother was the matriarch of the household, managing the daily work of the farm and the family's small collective fortunes. My mother was the first daughter-in-law in the family. Grandmother treated my mother as a servant in their home. Grandmother expected her to cook and clean for her and her three sons, pick peaches in the fields when called upon, and bear children. My mother had no rest and no say. My father, an honest and good man and a loyal son, had not yet learned how to be a husband. When my mother confided in him at night, she would find him sitting at the kitchen table in the morning, seeking his mother's counsel. My mother tried to write to her family, but Grandmother read all the letters she sent to India, and all the letters that came back. Baba Ji of the rocking chair was her only friend—until I was born.

My mother was twenty years old, lonely, homesick, and on the verge of a nervous breakdown when she gave birth to me on Valen-

tine's Day. Upon news of my birth, relatives sent my family not con-
gratulations but condolences, because I was not a boy. This could have
been the thing that broke my mother, the ancestral shame of bearing
a girl. But Grandmother, defiant and proud, admonished these relatives, brought me home to the farm, held me high, and called me her
diamond, the first grandchild in the house. She showed me the love
she did not know how to show my mother. This is how I grew up as
my mother's witness, confidante, and advocate. I learned how to trans-
late her sadness, which was my own sadness, to my father and the rest
of the family and win small victories, like visits to India to see my
mother's family.

On those childhood trips to India, I sat on *manjee*s with my mother
and my aunts and all the aunties who were our neighbors and drank
cha, sweet and milky. No one could hear us up here on the rooftop
cota, sitting under the colorful clothes that hung on lines and waved in
the breeze. Here in the company of these Punjabi women, my mother
could finally confide the fullness of her pain, and all the aunties would
nod and shake their heads and click their tongues, *"Tut-tut-tut."*
Then it would be someone else's turn. One woman was sent back to
her parents' house for not being able to conceive a child. Another was
denied food after she bore a third daughter in a row. Another couldn't
get married because she was "too dark." Another's husband beat her
when he drank, in places where no one could see the bruises. Each
story stirred anger within me. My mother wasn't alone. She belonged
to a congregation of women who bore pain with silence. The aunties
doled out advice. *Stay strong. Paath karro.* Pray. "Why don't you just
leave?" I blurted out in my American English. They all turned to look
at me, the seven-year-old with two long braids, yellow plastic bar-
rettes, and a jean jacket, perched on the edge of the *manjee.* "I mean,
why don't we tell someone who can help?" I was hushed. There was
nowhere to go, no mechanism to break the silence, and so no place for
my kind of indignation. It was our responsibility as women to keep
families together, they explained. Any solutions had to be pursued
within the confines of the home. The aunties turned to my mother

and said, "At least your American husband is trying to love you." In my mother's case, the aunties were right. In time, my father learned how to love my mother. He would no longer see himself as her guardian, looking to Grandmother for cues. He would learn to stand beside her as her companion. Together they moved out of Grandmother's house and built their own house on our land next door. On their own, they were free to nurture a shared passion for adventure. On camping trips to the Sierra Nevadas, my father would make my mother *cha* in the morning, and my mother would fry the fish he had caught, and they would hike to secret waterfalls and sneak in kisses just to gross us out. Their fights were like storms that would roll in, and soon pass, for their greatest shared passion was my brother and me. My mother was determined to give me the life that she had been denied, dismissing me from chores so that I could write stories. At night, my father sang to me "When You Wish Upon a Star" and told me that I was strong and smart. I was the first girl in my ancestral line whose parents told her that she could become anything she wanted.

I knew I was lucky, so I worked hard to be a good girl. In my journals, I drew portraits of my body with my feet trapped in the muck of sins—rage, envy, desire—and my arms reaching up toward the sky, toward goodness and purity. The upper half of me was the real me; the lower half was the shameful me that I needed to transcend. I had absorbed the gender norms I saw in movies, books, and billboards: Men and boys were to measure their worth by displays of their aggression and machismo, women and girls by their politeness and absence of anger—in the fairy tales, in the workplace, and in bed. I think this is why for as long as I can remember, my response to getting hurt as a girl was always paralysis followed by shame, never anger. I bypassed rage, or subdued it as soon as it arose. That's what it meant to be a good girl—to have the compassion of a savior, forgiveness on the sleeve. After all, rage was the opposite of love.

This was a lie.

The opposite of love is not rage. The opposite of love is indifference. Love engages all our emotions: *Joy is the gift of love. Grief is the price of love. Anger is the force that protects that which is loved.* We cannot access the depth of loving ourselves or others without our rage. I finally found this force inside myself—and inside my mother—in the course of my own love story.

❧

We met at a museum.

It was the opening night of the Spinning Wheel Film Festival, featuring films by and about the Sikh community, held at the Royal Ontario Museum in Toronto in October 2003. I had just graduated from college. My senior honors thesis about hate crimes after 9/11 won a university award, but I still hadn't found the support to turn my footage into a film, so I accepted an invitation to screen some of my footage as a work in progress at this festival. My parents and I walked into the museum, dazzled by a sea of turbans and *chunni*s. Never before had we seen so many people dedicated to supporting Sikh and South Asian artists in the diaspora to tell our own stories in film, television, media, and the arts. It would be the first of many festivals to come. After the speeches, samosas, and bhangra, a car arrived to take the filmmakers back to the hotel. Everyone piled in, the door slammed, and the car sped off, leaving my parents and me alone on the street in the cold—along with a young filmmaker.

"Hi, I'm Sharat," he said and put out his hand. His smile was wide. We split a cab and talked the whole way. Sharat Raju was fresh out of the American Film Institute and had been invited to screen his award-winning thesis film. He was earnest, self-effacing, and wondrously at ease. He made my parents laugh; I thought he was handsome.

The next day, we all went to see Sharat's film. *American Made* told the story of a Sikh family whose car breaks down on the way to the Grand Canyon. Stranded on the side of the road, the son tells his turbaned father that people won't stop to help them because he looks like a terrorist. I was undone. Sharat had made the fictional version of what I had documented on the road. The film would go on to win dozens of international awards and air on PBS for years, the first fictional portrait of a Sikh family after 9/11 on television. It was tender and funny, heartbreaking and so . . . professional. On the last day of the festival, I handed him my honors thesis and missed my flight because we talked so long. I thought it was the last time I would see him, but he called me when he landed in L.A. "I read your thesis on the plane, and what you have here is gold," he said. "I don't want to just say good luck; I want to help you make this film." A professional film. I mailed him my box of tapes.

We talked every day after that, hatching plans to turn the footage into a documentary film that would become *Divided We Fall: Americans in the Aftermath*. My parents noticed that the only time I smiled during the day was when Sharat called. I was still nursing a broken heart after breaking up with Ram and my would-be family. Any time I woke without crying was a rare day. But Sharat waltzed into the frame with his wide smile, unbridled laughter, and endless stories, and, before long, whenever the phone rang, my heart leapt into my throat.

We fell in love at another museum—the Art Institute of Chicago.

Chicago was Sharat's city, and he had adored this museum since he was a child, so we took the day off from our film shoot to go there. We danced through the museum together like two electrons whirling around each other, never touching. "Here are the Chagall Windows where they kiss in *Ferris Bueller's Day Off*," he said. I turned to gaze into the luminous blue panels, marveling at the musical instruments and books and people falling up toward the sky until it felt like the ground was falling from beneath my feet, and I had to sit down. *Vismaad*. I thought of a poem in a book my mother once gave me. It captured what it felt like to be wonderstruck. My throat was hot. I began to recite.

> *Last night the moon came dropping its clothes in the street.*
> *I took it as a sign to start singing,*
> *falling up into the bowl of sky.*

The bowl breaks. Everywhere is falling everywhere.
Nothing left to do.
Here's the new rule: break the wineglass
and fall toward the Glassblower's breath.

"Rumi," I said. Sharat grinned. If my skin had been lighter, he would have seen me blush.

He took me upstairs to the sculpture gallery to see the Rodin statues. Ah, here was the hero among the Burghers of Calais! He was the one who surrendered himself to save his city, willing to die so that his people would live. His life would be spared, but he did not know it yet. His face was mournful and brave. Stanford had a cast of these Burghers in the main quad. All through college, I would visit them at night and find new ways to experience them. I looked at Sharat and grew bold.

"Now what you need to do is keep your eyes on his face," I said. I took Sharat's hand, warm in mine, and began circling around the statue. "You are standing still. It's the Burgher who's moving. See, he's spinning, becoming alive, moving in the world." The Burgher spun around and around, faster and faster. We were drunk and dizzy.

Then we walked into a small gallery and looked up at a portrait of a man tipping a pitcher of water to his lips. My body was flushed with heat from the spinning, and I could feel Sharat near me, and I started to smile. We had been "professional" all this time, but now I was sweeping him into my inner world, and he was letting me, willingly, joyfully. He asked why I was smiling at the sad painting of the man drinking from the pitcher. I could not think of a reason. The jig was up. I pulled him to the corner of the room.

"How is your heart?" I asked.

"Um, okay," he said. He thought I was asking about a heart condition in his family.

"No, I mean, is your heart saying anything right now?" I tried again. He began to break into a smile. I couldn't look at him. I looked at his sweater.

"I'm crazy about you," I said and closed my eyes. An eternity passed.

"I'm crazy about you, too," he said. There was a sweet wetness on my lips. *Oh, he's kissing me,* I realized. *I should kiss back.* It had been so long. *How does this go?* I pressed closer and he held me closer and there was nothing but his arms and the kiss and the world spinning around us and shining a spotlight where we stood. *Vismaad.* We tumbled out of the museum and leaned our backs against one of the big iconic lions on the front steps and kissed again, feeling the sunlight on our faces to make sure that it was real, that it wasn't some museum trick, that the magic held in the world outside.

"What if you grow tired of me?" he asked as we tumbled into a cab.

"I won't," I said.

"But what if you do?"

I lifted my head from his chest and looked into his eyes and ran my fingers through his curly mop of hair. I wasn't interested in being his bride-to-be. I had suffered too long for a future that never came. I had clung to the "perfect" husband, and it had nearly killed me.

"The future does not exist," I declared and noticed the way his lips curled up at the ends in an always-smile like faces of the Buddha. I put my head back down on his chest. "We shall swing from Moment with a capital M to Moment with a capital M."

We spent the summer together in L.A., dancing through more museums, watching sunsets over the Pacific, lying in the sand at Venice Beach. When the world darkened, Venus appeared in the summer sky, hanging over the crescent moon like a bindi. He kissed my fingertips at night. I wanted to go slow, so we made a castle of kissing. In the morning, in the shower, I remembered how Ram had hated my feet. And the hair on my fingers. It was still hard for me to see my body through anyone's eyes but his. But that was starting to change. Sharat and I would lie on top of the covers, without clothes, in daylight. He was teaching me not to be ashamed.

One night, I spread the blanket on the floor of the bedroom. Safe and free, soft and warm, I drew his body to mine. We had been consciously waiting to have sex. I wanted him now, in the Moment with a capital M. "I'm ready," I said. We must have kissed for hours. I drew him closer. Then—stabbing pain. Like a knife. A knife into vagina. I pulled away. I took a breath and drew him to me again. Razor blade against pink muscle. I was confused and hot with shame. He kissed my eyelids, then my lips. "It's okay," he said. "It's okay." He held me through the night. I knew that sex could hurt, but I was pretty sure that this was not how it was supposed to feel.

I went to the doctor for my first Pap smear and asked her to go slow please. The speculum came out, hard and cold, then I felt the stabbing pain again, and my muscles made a wall. "Relax," she kept saying. Then she got frustrated. She didn't have *this* much time for a routine exam. I ran out of the office in tears. It was not a doctor's job to make a patient feel more ashamed than she already was. I tried to figure out what was wrong on my own. I searched online and discovered the term "vaginismus," one of many underdiagnosed and underresourced women's health conditions. Vaginismus is the involuntary tightening of the pelvic floor muscles when the vaginal canal is touched. The source of the touch doesn't matter—a Q-tip, a cotton ball, a fingertip. The muscle spasms happen automatically, the nerve endings send stinging pain through the pelvic floor, no matter how hard the mind tries to stop it, and penetration becomes difficult or, in severe cases, impossible. I had a severe case. It is estimated that one in five women have this condition, and many suffer for years without support or information. How in the world did this happen? I scrolled down to read the list of causes. One possible cause for vaginismus was "sexual assault early in life."

Oh.

I had never called it that.

It had happened a long time ago. In a large extended family, first cousins are more like siblings, and second and third cousins are like first cousins. We all played and fought together and made rafts out of blankets on the floor of the living room where we fell asleep like puppies. One night, when I was a teenager, I woke up to a hand moving up my thigh. I froze.

Hair on goose bumps. Wires crossed. Skin crawling. There was burning beneath the skin, and the burning was blue. Rain pattered on the skylight overhead, a thousand drops in the night, but no drop reached me. No drop touched the body twisted in the sheets. The body was frozen like a fish in the net, and the body was mine.

I was paralyzed as if not breathing or moving an inch would protect me. But freezing just made it easier for the molestation to happen. I willed my body to move, to flee. *Come on, get up. Come on!* I turned to my side, got to my feet, and rushed out of the house. I had just gotten my driver's license. I drove to a friend's house, legs clenched under me, and threw rocks at her window. She let me in, made a bed for me, gave me hot chocolate with a peppermint stick, and held me as I cried and cried. I could still feel his hardness on my back like a slug, but I did not tell her. I would not tell anyone. The next day, I mustered the courage to call the boy who hurt me. I couldn't remember how we were related, but we still called each other brother and sister. "You did something wrong," I began to say. He sobbed and said that he would kill himself if he ever hurt me. "It's okay," I said. "It's okay." I consoled him, then buried it. After all, there was no penetration. I decided that I had the compassion of a savior, and I was not going to be the one to set off any new war.

In the months and years that followed, my pelvic floor tightened under me, my thighs became hard wooden things, and I never noticed. I never gave language to what happened, so I did not notice how it was changing my physiology. I had no reason to think anything was wrong. I never wore tampons. I never had a gynecological exam. In college, Ram and I decided not to have intercourse until our wedding night, which never came. I had looked at my vagina, yes, but had never gone *inside*. How many girls are never given a road map to their own bodies, or vocabulary for their body's desires? In a culture where female pleasure was never discussed and therefore did not seem to exist, I discovered that the safest place for orgasms was my dreams.

Fast-forward—Now I was an adult and here was this beautiful man in real life who wanted to love me and touch me, all of me, but my body made a brick wall and I could not persuade it to do otherwise. If only I had told someone what had happened earlier.

Hold on, I *had* told someone. Early in our relationship in college, I had told Ram that a relative had touched me inappropriately when I was young. What was it that he said? "Did you reciprocate?" Those were his first words. He was asking me if I enjoyed it. I felt sick to my stomach and shook my head no. We never talked about it after that. Now it made sense: If you do not know how to respect women, then you cannot believe them. Respect comes from the root word *"respicere,"* to look at. Ram could not look at me—he could not see my body's desires, let alone my body's pain, so how could he believe me? But instead of responding with outrage, I just let my shame deepen.

That mistake would no longer be repeated. I went to my mother and told her. She held me and choked back tears and told me I was not alone. She grew up in a time when penetration was expected on the first night of arranged marriages, and stories of sexual violence, incest, and domestic violence were hushed as soon as spoken. As a little girl in India, my mother did not know any woman whose body had not been violated in some way. But these women followed the unwritten rule in the sky: Silence is survival. The Sikh faith professes radical equality between women and men and all genders, but Punjabi culture was still steeped in patriarchy. She had hoped that it would be different for our generation, here in America. But patriarchy and gender oppression are not local anomalies. There is no nation, no community, and no corner of the earth where women and girls are as safe as men. One in three women are sexually assaulted in their lifetimes. No culture is immune. The solution is not silence. The solution is more solidarity.

Sharat and I worked hard to solve the problem together. We tried plastic dilators and pelvic floor muscle exercises—and lots of wine. No luck. Every time I started to apologize, he stopped me. "I'm just happy to be here," he said, and kissed me again. He was in no rush. He was going to stay here with me, on top of the sheets, in the sunlight, unashamed and content.

Our beautiful summer came to an end. I was starting graduate school in the fall—Harvard Divinity School for a master's degree in religion and ethics. Maybe law school one day. The day before my departure, Sharat took me to our favorite spot on Venice Beach by the rocks. We stood on the brink of the vast shimmering sea and held each other tight, the wind whipping my hair all around us.

"I know we are going from Moment to Moment," I said, "but won't it be hard living on opposite sides of the country?"

"I love you," he said. "A whole continent doesn't matter."

I had a week before the school year began, so I made a stop in New York City to see my beloved friend Brynn. She was starting a master's program in religious studies at New York University while I was doing the same at Harvard. "Look at us, on the quest!" we marveled, echoing our vow in high school. We walked through the city, arm in arm, talking about the state of the world. At this point, the war in Iraq had gone on more than a year, and Republicans were trying to rally support for the war on terror and for President Bush's reelection. They were about to host the 2004 Republican National Convention in New York City, and the city had turned into a cauldron of protest. On Sunday, Brynn and I joined thousands of people in a march organized by United for Peace and Justice, one of the largest protests in U.S. history, and felt the rush of solidarity. Then I got a call from Shahid, my fellow organizer from Stanford, who was helping protesters plan direct action in the streets all week. "They're going to need legal observers," he said. I had a few extra days in the city, so he gave me instructions on where to show up to film the protest—to protect against any police misconduct.

This is how it happened that on Tuesday, August 31, 2004, I showed up alone on a street corner in the Financial District of New York City, video camera in hand, wearing a green badge that read LEGAL OBSERVER—NATIONAL LAWYERS GUILD. It was early morning; the air was crisp and still. Suddenly a handful of protesters rushed into the cobblestone street, strung red and yellow yarn to stop traffic, and handed out flyers to halted cars. The buildings were too tall, the sunlight too dim, and the streets too narrow to make out what happened next. "Get down! Get down!" someone shouted. Now I could see: Men in oversize jerseys were running into the street and clobbering the protesters to the ground. One young man was pinned to the ground by an officer, blood on his face. More were now pinned against a wall, blood on their knees. Then a mass of uniformed police officers flooded the street. It happened so fast, I didn't know where to focus my camera.

"NYPD. You're under arrest," someone said. I looked up from my camera to see a Latinx woman in civilian clothes and suddenly felt my arms yanked behind my back by someone else. My camera fell from my hands and shattered on the ground.

"I'm a legal observer! I'm not part of this action! You did not give me a warning!" I heard myself repeat.

I felt something like razor blades digging into my wrists—I was thrown against the wall and realized I had been handcuffed in plastic cuffs with sharp edges. *Fine,* I thought. *They will take us to a facility, hand us a traffic citation, and release us.* But by the time they herded us into a cramped van, I was already beginning to lose sensation in my hands. The van stopped. The doors swung open, and I squinted in the light that reflected off the silver water of the Hudson.

The officers escorted us into an empty warehouse—a makeshift detention center on Pier 57. I looked at the big empty cages lined with barbed wire and diesel gas spilled on the floor. The warehouse would soon detain thousands of protesters and bystanders arrested in police sweeps and mass arrests that week and be dubbed "Guantánamo on the Hudson." An officer in a crisp white shirt and black-rimmed glasses seemed to be giving orders. They called him Lieutenant. One of the protesters began to repeat calmly, "I cannot feel my left hand." The officers looked down at clipboards. The man got louder until the lieutenant ordered his handcuffs replaced. He turned to the women arrestees and yelled: "Do any of you need your cuffs replaced?"

"It would be nice if you could . . ." began the woman next to me, a journalist who like me had been swept up in the arrest.

"I'm not going to do it because you're *uncomfortable!*" he shouted.

At this point, I had lost all feeling in my right hand.

"Please, sir," I began. "My cuffs are on tight. Could you please—"

The lieutenant circled behind me, grabbed my wrists and hands, and then—with one clean force—twisted them hard. Knife sliced hand off wrist. I thought my hand had fallen off. Pain shot up into the base of my skull like a gun shoved under skin. "See she's fine!" he said. The last thing I saw was the back of that crisp white shirt receding from me. And then the world went black. My mouth was open but no sound came out, and in my mind all I heard was Papa Ji's whispering tremor: *Ik Onkar.*

Go on.

Ik Onkar. Satnam. Karta Purakh. Nirbhau. Nirvair. Akaal Murat. Ajuni. Saibhang. Gurprasad. Jap.

The words on the torture wheel, the words in the boiling cauldron, the words on the lips of the women who wailed on their knees, soaked with blood. All the paintings of my childhood, the ones on the walls of the gurdwara, taught me that *this* is what you recite under torture: the *mul mantar,* the root verse. The sound forms the vessel, and the vessel carries the body across the ocean of pain. Life is the ocean.

Aad Sach. Jugaad Sach. Hai Bhi Sach. Nanak Hosi Bhi Sach.

Panic. Movement. A snap and the cuffs were off. I brought my right hand to the front of me and opened my eyes. My hand was still there, trembling, purple gashes across the veins. I could not feel the gashes, or my hand. There was arguing. The lieutenant was yelling at the Latinx officer who arrested me, because she did not empty my pockets. "That is incorrect procedure, Officer Diaz!" he yelled. He was in a rage. She was startled, flustered. I looked at his badge. CAMPO. I wanted to say something to Lieutenant Campo, but before I could, he said, "Take her away."

I was transferred to headquarters, booked, photographed, fingerprinted, and herded down hallways chained to other detainees. Male officers stared at my body, smirking. Some whistled circus tunes. I tried to look straight ahead. I hardened my gaze, and my body was stiff. I still couldn't feel my hand. My requests for medical treatment and legal counsel were denied, but I managed a phone call to my friend Shahid. Nearly eighteen hundred people had been arrested in mass sweeps. Lawyers were working hard to get us out. They believed that the delay in completing desk appearance tickets, the simple transaction we needed to get released, was part of a deliberate attempt to discourage protesters from returning to the street. It appeared that the city was holding protesters long enough to keep the streets empty during President Bush's acceptance speech at the Republican National Convention. Some fifty detainees were beginning a hunger strike. I was taken to a cell. There was an open toilet in the corner, and a stench filled the air. Lying on the floor, nursing my dead hand on my chest, deep blue gashes in my wrists, I stared up at the fluorescent lights and thought: *I am a citizen. I speak English. I am educated. What happens to people without my privilege?* The thought overwhelmed me.

I had always thought that my privilege—citizenship, education, literacy—formed a sort of membrane of protection between me and state violence. But in entering a fight against the state and its foot soldiers, on behalf of brown people, as a brown woman, those privileges thinned to nothingness. The officers who hurt and harassed me operated as arms of the state, and the state was marshaling all its power to suppress dissent. Now the state had my body, which meant that it also had the power to silence my voice and break my skin and justify it. My professor was right—I needed a sword and shield. I also needed something more. In that moment, curled up on the floor of the cell, I knew that I would need to access something deeper and more fiery in me if I was going to face this kind of Goliath. I just didn't know what it was or how to find it.

After many hours, my name was called. I rose to my feet and they took me down the labyrinth of hallways, handed me a ticket, and deposited me outside the building. The security guard in charge of lifting the front gate stood there, smirking. I waited under a yellow spotlight as he threw his eyes up and down my body, one last time, one last harassment, as if my small brown body was theirs, had always been theirs.

An eternity passed. The gate lifted. My friend Shahid along with a team of medics rushed to receive me. "I'm so sorry," he said. He was telling me that I had been detained sixteen hours but that it was over now, that I was safe. I nodded blankly. He put me in a cab to Brynn's place in the East Village. It was two in the morning when I stumbled into her apartment. Brynn had gone out to get soup when she heard I had been released. So, I stood at the kitchen sink and ran my hands under hot water for a long time. When Brynn walked through the door, she took one look at me, rushed to my side, and cried. I finally cried, too.

"We're on the quest," Brynn said as she wrapped a blanket around my shoulders.

"We're on the quest," I said, and started laughing, sobbing and laughing. We had promised each other that we would show up in the world and fight and make each other brave—*ancestral solidarity*—but now we were learning firsthand what our ancestors had known, that the fight is dangerous, the fight is deadly. When the sun rose, Brynn took me to the emergency room at New York University. A doctor treated the gashes in my right wrist and set my arm in a splint. Out on the street, a police car went by and the sound of the siren sent me into a panic. When Brynn took me to a café to eat, I saw a police officer ordering food and wanted to run. *No, no, no.* I could not live in this world with an enemy that terrified me. All police officers could not be my enemy. I was determined to heal; I just didn't know how.

First attempt to love my opponent: Understanding.

A few days later, I left the cocoon of Brynn's apartment, took a train to Boston, and started my master's program at Harvard Divinity

School. I started taking classes on violence, ethics, religion, and evil
with Professors Hille Haker, Michael Jackson, and Diana Eck. I pored
over Kant and Heidegger and Arendt, seeking to understand human
cruelty, to understand the lieutenant who had hurt me. My right arm
was still in a splint. I turned the pages with my left hand. I was captivated by Hannah Arendt's concept of the banality of evil. She covered
the war crimes trial of Adolf Eichmann, a man who displayed no guilt
for his actions in the Holocaust and simply repeated that he was trying
to do his job. Arendt found him to be not a fanatic or sociopath but an
exceedingly ordinary person who could have made a different moral
choice but chose instead to follow orders. I thought I was beginning
to understand Lieutenant Campo. He was following orders, too. He
must have rationalized his actions as moral because they aligned with
the norms of the system in which he operated, an institution to which
he had pledged his allegiance. But the more I read and thought I understood, the more I felt the pain in my wrist shooting into my arm,
shoulder, and neck. My injury wasn't healing; it was getting worse. I
typed an email with one finger and sent it to Brynn and Sharat, then
turned over in bed and gazed at the tree out my window.

Pain
penetrates me
drop
by
drop.
    —*Sappho*

this is how it feels, my wrist, neck. in bed all day.

I saw another doctor who assured me that my injury would heal in
time. He recommended acupuncture to manage the pain. I found an
acupuncturist and noticed that my name was inside her name; I took
it as a sign. Valerie Courville wielded her needles masterfully and
found the points in my body that needed relief. She would become

one of my lifelong friends and healers. "You have to treat your own body with the same compassion as you treat others'," she told me, cradling my head in her hands on the treatment table. I resisted. My injuries fell far short of what other people suffered. The police officer hurt my arm but did not break it; my molestation did not rise to the level of rape. As long as I compared my suffering with others', I could not access compassion for myself, only more shame.

Second attempt: Compassion.

One night, I attended a loving-kindness workshop on campus inspired by Buddhist meditation practices. The meditation was meant to cultivate the qualities of compassion—warm feelings for yourself, for others, and for your opponents. I closed my eyes as the facilitator led us with her soothing voice.

"Bring to your mind's eye a picture of your own face. Now say to yourself, 'May I be happy. May I be healthy. May I be safe. May I be at peace.'"

I saw myself and my eyes welled up with tears. Still I made my first concerted effort to send myself this tender wish. This was progress.

"Now picture someone you love and send them the same wish."

I pictured Sharat and smiled.

"Now picture someone who is neutral and send them the same blessing."

I pictured the homeless man asleep on the bench in Harvard Square on my way here and dutifully sent him my affection.

"Now picture someone you consider an enemy."

Lieutenant Campo—his white face, his black-rimmed glasses, gun at his side.

"Say to this person, 'May you be happy.'"

Panic.

"May you be healthy."

Panic rising like fire in a cage.

"May you be safe."

Can't breathe.

"May you be at peace."

I ran out of the room and found a water fountain and drank and drank and took a breath. I could not access compassion for the officer, as much as I tried. What was wrong with me? Why couldn't I love my enemy? I had absorbed the lie that love requires us to rush to tend to our opponents' wounds before we tend to our own.

Third attempt: Empathy.

I saw a campus flyer of a hooded prisoner standing on a box, arms extended, with live wires on fingertips. Harvard students were putting on a play about Abu Ghraib. It was the first theater production to examine the prisoner abuse and torture at the hands of U.S. soldiers during the Iraq war. Abu Ghraib was a watershed moment—a scandal we thought would expose the widespread abuse occurring in military detention centers and hasten an end to the war. The play was meant to keep attention on the scandal and humanize both the detainees and the soldiers in the story. I auditioned for a part. Maybe doing this play would help me practice empathy for the officer who hurt me—to sense his experience and perspective on the world.

I was assigned the role of Huda—a character based on the real story of an Iraqi woman named Huda Alazawi, who in December 2003 was arrested by U.S. soldiers after she inquired about her missing brother. The officers kept her overnight, and in the morning they threw something cold at her feet. Her brother's dead body. Huda was detained for months. Like most detainees at Abu Ghraib, she had done nothing wrong except show up in the wrong place at the wrong time. I went to sleep with Huda's lines and woke up with Huda's lines, and her story lived in me: the white man in the uniform, the brown woman in handcuffs, the institution that contained them, the body that was violated.

During one of our rehearsals, our student writer-director Currun Singh introduced a new scene to the play—a nightmare-fantasy sequence where the soldiers abuse the prisoners to dark seductive music. The theater goes dark, the lights flicker, and Huda is one of the prisoners tortured by a soldier who is writing words on her body. We started to rehearse. I assumed a helpless position.

"Stop," said Currun. "Switch roles. Huda, you write on Darby."

Okay, I am no longer the tortured. I am the torturer. Got it. Sergeant Joseph Darby was the soldier who would become the whistle-blower at Abu Ghraib. He was always different from the others. Huda was different from the other prisoners, too: professional, educated, equipped with language for outrage. The role reversal was symbolic. My right hand still wasn't working, so I took the marker in my left hand. The music began and I began to pretend-write on my captor's body.

"No!" Currun shouted to me over the music. "Touch him. Push him. Stalk him. Jump him. Then write on him again." Okay, I started to circle him and write.

"No, you are not writing real words!" Currun shouted louder. "What are you writing? Write real words. Write FEAR. Write PRISON." *Got it. Fear. Prison.*

Then he said, "Write AYAD." My mind conjured the face of Huda's brother who was dead. I thought of my own brother. My fists clenched, and the music rose, and I wrote their names while circling, stalking, jumping, and attacking this man who was responsible, spinning around him, faster and faster, the music louder and louder, and then—I hit him. I socked him in the arm. Hard. I stopped.

"Oh my god, I'm sorry," I said. "I'm so sorry."

"It's okay," said the actor. But I could not go on with the scene. Huda, who was the abused one, suddenly had power and she punched Darby. I mean, *I* punched him. I was not directed to do this. My muscles were sore and my throat ached. I went outside into the cold night and found myself in the midst of glowing tents, jugglers, kettle corn, music and dancing, an arts festival in Harvard Square, but I could not feel any of it.

"She has a lot of rage, I'm realizing," I wrote Sharat. "Maybe I do, too. And it's frightening and revealing to see how that rage comes out once she/I have gained some power over someone else." I thought of Arendt's analysis that we each have the potential to be the prisoner and the guard, to bear the violence and commit the violence. Now I had seen a flash of rage inside me—a monster in me like the monster in them—but this did not make me feel any better. It made me ashamed, of them and of myself.

The play ran in a black-box theater on Harvard's campus in the spring of 2005. Even before opening night, it made national news. It was attacked by the Right for its attempt to cultivate empathy for the Iraqi prisoners, and by the Left for its attempt to cultivate empathy for the U.S. soldiers at Abu Ghraib. It was criticized for what made it brilliant. On the final night of the show, in the final minutes of the play, in the middle of my last line, I broke down onstage. I put my face in my hands and wept for a full minute. I was plunged into the emotions of all the players in this story. But the torrent of empathy did not heal my arm. A year after my arrest, the pain was now chronic. Sometimes at night, I imagined an ax coming down on the top of my right shoulder. One clean cut. "You can have my arm, it's yours." I did not know with whom I was bargaining but I was serious.

❧

Throughout divinity school, Sharat would come to stay with me in Cambridge, and I would go to stay with him in L.A. We worked on our documentary film together, and, when we weren't in the editing room, he was distracting me from pain. My parents, brother, and cousins saw how much he made me laugh. So we were all excited and nervous when his parents came to visit us in Clovis for the first time over the winter holiday. His father talked medicine and literature in fascinating mini-lectures. His mother listened with large eyes. My mother laughed and laughed. My father responded eagerly, some new story sparkling in his mouth. It was going so well.

We were on a driving tour of town when my brother, Sanjeev, called me in the car. "Don't come home," he said. "It's not safe. Roshan knows that our parents are meeting. He says he's going to kill Sharat. I don't know what he's going to do."

Roshan Singh was the relative who had molested me when we were kids. It was his assault on my body that Sharat and I were trying hard to solve. Now Roshan was treating my body like a vessel of honor to be protected from further violation. When he found out that Sharat and I were dating, he said that I was betraying our community and our faith and bringing disgrace to our family because Sharat wasn't Sikh. Now he was issuing death threats.

"Something wrong?" asked Sharat's dad.

"No, nothing," I said. I made up an excuse for us to drive to the foothills. Sharat took my hand. Sanjeev found Roshan and managed to talk him down, so that we could all return to the house that night.

"People who want to kill others because they are not righteous enough actually want to kill something inside themselves," Sanjeev said when he came to my room to console me. "There must be something inside Roshan that he absolutely hates. I'm here for you, Val."

We hugged each other. It was going to be okay. After all, I thought, time healed all wounds.

Fourth attempt: Forgiveness.

Six months later, my phone rang.

"I want to talk." It was Roshan. He must have been ready to make amends. It had been half a year since the death threats. I felt ready to forgive him. I thought forgiveness meant forgetting about the past. I had done it before and could do it again. So I didn't tell anyone where I was going when I left the house and drove to the park, where Roshan had asked me to meet him. The park was empty. The trees rustled softly. There was a brook in the distance. Roshan was standing at the water's edge, looking into the current. When I got closer, I saw that his eyes were red from crying.

"Have I been a good brother?" he asked me. It seemed important to answer precisely.

"No," I said slowly. "Not to me."

Roshan reached down for a black umbrella lying on the bench and picked up something long and hard he had hidden beneath it—a rifle.

"Are you going to kill me?" I cried out.

The gun was spinning in the sunlight, round and round, pointing at him, at me, at him, at me. *No, this was not how it was going to end*.

"You have no control over me anymore," I heard myself say. Then I turned my back and walked away. I did not run; I walked. I do not know how I had the power to do this. Roshan called my name, but I kept walking. It dawned on me that I had just told a man with a loaded gun that he had no control over me and turned my back on him. The rifle could fire at any moment. Would anyone hear it? Would anyone find me? The brook kept babbling and I kept walking. I reached the car, and my hands trembled on the steering wheel. It was hard to make them work, but I drove away. I fumbled with the phone and dialed Sharat's number. He was in our editing room in Los Angeles.

"We have to make sure he hasn't shot himself," Sharat said. "Circle back around, at a distance." Roshan was still standing there where I left him, staring into the water.

"Don't go home," Sharat said. "It's not safe."

We called my parents. My father tracked Roshan down as he was speeding away to the foothills and talked the gun out of his hands. Then my father sat down with me, my mother, and Papa Ji. I told them the truth, all of it—the molestation and the death threats and now this.

"Why didn't you tell me?" my father asked me.

"I didn't want Roshan to get hurt," I said. I had wanted to forgive him. Now I wanted to call the police.

"Don't call the police," said Papa Ji. My beautiful grandfather, my pillar of wisdom, was telling me to keep this in the family. *Stay strong*. *Paath karro*.

"No." It was my mother who said it. She stood up between Papa Ji and me with a rage in her eyes that I had never seen before. "For too long have women in this family silenced abuse," she said. "It ends here," she said. "It ends with my daughter."

My mother handed me the phone. My father nodded and put his hand on my shoulder. I held the phone in my hand. Would the officers see Roshan as a terrorist? Would they hurt him? I thought of all the women who cannot call the police on their husbands, brothers, and sons—black women, Latinx women, Muslim women, Asian women, indigenous women, trans women, any woman with good reason to think that the police will see their men as animals instead of people and abuse them, detain them, deport them, or pull the trigger too soon. What is "national security" for women whose families are not secure in this country, whose bodies are not secure in their own homes? What is "national security" for women whose race or religion or status makes it dangerous to trust the officers sworn to protect us? I thought of the lieutenant who hurt me. How could I trust anyone who wore his uniform? Did I have any other choice? I dialed 911. When the officers came, I sat them down in the living room and begged them not to hurt him. The officers listened earnestly. They took Roshan quietly in the middle of the night and held him for twenty-four hours, long enough for me to make a plan.

"You have shamed us," Papa Ji said to me. This was now my fault. I had violated the unwritten rule to keep my silence. I had sparked the flame to set off the war. My mother, father, and brother defended me, but it wasn't enough. I kept imagining Roshan crossing the field with the gun, coming for me. My mother found me in our backyard on my knees in the grass, crying.

"Go," she said. "You're not safe here. Go to Sharat. Build your life. I will handle them."

She set me free. My mother. I left. I left home and never went back, not to the home it was. Home was the California farmland and fields and my family, my cousins and aunts and uncles and grand-parents, tangled up in each other's lives. It was more like a little village in Punjab. Now I was cast out of that world because I had broken my silence. Sharat took me to his apartment in Los Angeles and wrapped his arms around me and didn't let me go through the panic attacks.

"I have no home," I said into his chest.

"That's not true," he said. "Home is right here."

I was beginning to learn that home is the space within us and between us where we feel safe—and brave. It is not a physical space as much as it is a field of being.

I finished divinity school six months later and got accepted to law school—finally my chance to acquire that sword and shield. But my right arm now hung like a dead limb by my side, unable to lift a pen or turn a doorknob. My body had become a map of injuries from physical assault and sexual assault—thigh to vagina, wrist to neck. So I deferred law school for a year, then another, and lived with Sharat in Venice Beach. For two years, Sharat cooked our meals, washed my hair, drove me to appointments, and held me when I woke from nightmares. Sometimes the monster in my dreams was the relative, other times the lieutenant; every time, the monster won.

Final attempt: The first step to loving our opponents is rage.

"Close your eyes," said Tommy Woon. He was one of my advisers from college, a dean of multicultural education and a trailblazer in healing historical trauma. He operated on the premise that healing begins in the body, and the brain follows. Trauma alienates us from our bodies, he explained. When we face a threat, our bodies release a flood of stress hormones so that we can protect ourselves. We can fight, flee, or freeze. If we can't do any of those fully, then our internal alarms never turn off. Memories of the trauma keep flooding our thoughts; panic keeps gripping us; the past keeps bleeding into the present. In extreme cases, we cope by numbing and dissociating— abandoning our bodies so that it is difficult to feel sensation. Tommy believed that I had a "disrupted fight impulse." I did not need to relive my trauma through talk therapy. I needed to access my fiercest emotions and reclaim my agency—in my mind *and* body. One way to do this was to experience an alternative narrative.

"Take yourself back to the detention center on the Hudson on the day of your arrest," he said. "You ask the lieutenant to loosen your cuffs. He is about to circle behind you, but he stops. You are transforming into something big and powerful before his eyes. You are becoming a—"

I spotted my childhood stuffed tiger, Raja, on my bed.

"Tiger," I said.

"Okay, picture yourself as a tiger," he said. "What do you want to do?"

"Roar," I said.

"Sense all the impulses to roar," he said.

I towered over the lieutenant with vicious fangs and roared in his face so hard that his black-rimmed glasses fell off.

"Okay, he's running. What are you going to do?" said Tommy.

"Chase him," I said. I imagined chasing him down the length of the detention center, out the door, into the streets of New York City. My fists clenched and my legs were about to spring and Tommy had me move my fists and legs to release the motion inside them.

"You've caught him," said Tommy. "Now what do you want to do?"

"Destroy him," I said.

No, no, no. I did not say that. I could not do that.

"Go ahead," said Tommy, softly. "It's okay."

I showed my fangs and started to rip the lieutenant's clothes into shreds.

"Good," Tommy said. "This is good."

This is good, I repeated. *How could this be good?* I kept tearing into the lieutenant until I got to his flesh.

"Don't override your impulses," he said.

I tore into the lieutenant's flesh until there was nothing left but blood and bone and muscle on the cobblestone street.

"Notice what this feels like in your body," said Tommy. I was breathing hard and felt embarrassed, but I also felt energy rising in me and wanted to leap up.

"Celebrate," said Tommy. I stood and stretched my arms to the sky and felt big and relieved and satisfied.

"Now think of the lieutenant again," said Tommy.

I pictured myself as the tiger sniffing the bloodied clothes on the ground and noticed that the lieutenant wasn't there. Instead there stood a frail man, a naked and anxious man, a white man who did not know what else to do with his anxiety but rage at the women of color in proximity to him. He was the product of a system that sanctioned routine violence as the outlet for rage, whether at a detention center in New York City or at a prison in Abu Ghraib.

"Now go back to the park where you met Roshan," Tommy said. "He picks up the gun. You tell him he has no power over you. Now *show* him."

I became the tiger again. I chased Roshan the length of the park, caught him by the brook, and consumed him, blood dripping from my teeth into the water. When it was done, Roshan wasn't there. There stood a boy, a fragile brown boy who had watched his alcoholic father beat a mother who would not leave him, a boy who was taught that women were vessels of honor to be revered and defended and if necessary dominated, a young man who came of age in post-9/11 America where he couldn't walk down the street without hearing "Osama!" Roshan had come to believe that the Sikh community's very survival in America depended on who his sisters married. He did not know what to do with his insecurity other than to hurt me.

When I tore up these men with my fangs, I was not destroying them. I was destroying my projections of them. My mind had turned them into monsters—bad guys with infinite power over me. But there is no such thing as monsters in this world. There are only human beings who are wounded. These men had hurt me out of their own suffering. It was common, it was banal. When we cannot see that evil is driven by a person's wounds, not their innate nature, we become terrified of each other. But the moment we see their wounds, they no longer have absolute power over us. I could not see the wound in them until I tended to the wound inside me. And that required me to access my rage.

❧

Neurobiologists call oxytocin the love hormone: The more oxytocin in the body, the more care and nurturing mammals show for their babies. Oxytocin decreases aggression in a mother's body overall with one exception—in defense of her young. When babies are threatened, oxytocin actually increases aggression. For mothers, rage is part of love: It is the biological force that protects that which is loved.

When I learned this, I thought of my mother and the ferocity in her eyes when she had fought for me. I did not know that she had that kind of rage roaring inside her. She couldn't access it for herself. But she could access it for me. Now I was learning how to access it for *myself*.

My rage showed me that I was worth protecting, that the gashes in my wrist and the burning in my thighs did not have to end my life in order to merit outrage, that racism and sexism were not abstract oppressions but flesh-and-blood violations that lived in the body, and that the body *had* to find a way to unleash all of its mighty ferocity to protect itself in order to know itself to be alive. The tiger had always been with me, inside me; I just had to find a way to release it and ride it. And where did it deliver me? To a place where my assailants no longer had psychological power over me, because I had reclaimed the sovereignty of my body.

I thought of all of us who have been trained to suppress our rage—women, especially women of color. Rage is a healthy, normal, and necessary response to trauma. It is a rightful response to the social traumas of patriarchy, white supremacy, misogyny, homophobia, transphobia, and poverty. But we live in a culture that punishes us when we show our teeth—we are called hysterical when we raise our voice; we are less likely to be believed when we tell our story with fury; and, if we are anything other than deferential with an officer, we might get hurt or shot, and even then, our deference might not make a difference. Black and brown people have been schooled in the suppression of our emotions as a matter of survival. "We learned when we were very little that black people could die from feeling rage and expressing it to the wrong white folks," says bell hooks. "We learned to choke down our rage." We now have the data to prove what community healers know well: Repressing anger comes at a cost to our health. It results in high rates of autoimmune diseases. It amplifies our perception of physical pain.

The opposite of repression is also dangerous. Too many men have been socialized to unleash rage without apology. For men, rage is often a secondary emotion that masks sadness or shame. Violence is the socially conditioned default for male rage, and the proliferation of guns has made male aggression deadlier than ever: Mass shooters are typically men, and the majority of these men have physically abused the women in their lives. We might think that the solution is teaching our boys not to show aggression. But suppressed anger always finds a way to explode. For women and girls, it is more likely to explode internally as self-hatred or stress or illness. For men and boys, it is more likely to erupt as violence against others.

The solution is not to suppress our rage or let it explode, but to process our rage in *safe containers*—emotional spaces safe enough to express our body's impulses without shame and without harming ourselves or others. I could not access my rage until Tommy gently beckoned me to release it into the container he fashioned for me. He became my accomplice. Safe containers take many forms: shaking, weeping, venting, writing, art, music, dance, drama, meditation, trauma therapies, rituals, and ceremonies of all kinds. Only when we give rage an external expression outside our bodies can we be in relationship with it. We can then ask: What information does my rage carry? What is it telling me? How do I want to harness this energy?

❧❧

I called Deonnie, my friend and roommate all through divinity school. We had studied devotional traditions in India together with Professor Anne Monius at Harvard. "What if we took that backpacking trip to see the places we studied?" I asked. The shooting pain in my arm was subsiding, thanks to my sessions with Tommy. My body was now strong enough to carry a pack, and I had saved up enough money for a trip. We seized the moment. That summer, for two months, we traveled from south to north India and witnessed the fluidity of spiritual devotion: Sikhs meditating in Hindu temples in Punjab, Buddhists bowing in Sikh gurdwaras in the high mountains of Leh, Hindus making offerings before portraits of Mother Mary in the cities of Delhi and Bangalore. Academics in other parts of the world had divided religions into separate "isms," but, in India, faith traditions flowed into and out of one another like rivers.

In Kolkata, Deonnie took me to the Kalighat Temple and introduced me to the subject of her academic study—the Hindu goddess Kali. We walked through the temple barefoot, our feet stained red from crushed flowers and the blood of goats. Kalighat is one of the only major temples in India where animal sacrifices are performed daily. In Hindu practice, you give the deity what they desire. Krishna, the god who dances with his flute, is offered milk-based sweets. In this temple, Kali, the mother of life, is offered blood. The goat meat is then distributed to the homeless, sold to devotees, or donated to Mother Teresa's Home for the Dying next door. I began to watch the goat sacrifices, one clean cut of the head after another. The bleating filled my ears and the drums beat in my chest and the smell of blood filled the air. It smelled like menstrual blood. The crowd pressed my body into the *garba griha*—the "house of the womb" or innermost sacred shrine—until I was thrust in front of her: a black stone, draped in sari cloths of all colors, three large eyes that penetrated me. I saw Kali, and she saw me. A priest pressed a red dot on my forehead with such mighty force that I almost fell back. As the bells rang out I stumbled outside and sat on the cool stone for a long time.

I thought about Kali's origin story in the Hindu tradition. According to one famous story, all the gods were in battle against a great demon, Mahisha, who could not be defeated, so they poured their energies together to create the goddess Durga. When Durga went to battle with the demon, her ferocious energy concentrated in her forehead and out sprang Kali. She was the fiercest form of the goddess, clad in a tiger skin, wearing a garland of skulls, mouth agape, tongue rolling out as she drank the blood of life. Kali in her many forms was most beloved as the Divine Mother, to be revered and feared and loved, because she protected us. The rage of Kali made me wonder: Can we see our own rage as animal *and* divine?

Divine rage is fierce, disciplined, and visionary. It is the fearsome wrath of Ekajati, or Blue Tara, when she fought demons in Tibetan Buddhist legends. Or the fury of Jesus when he overturned the tables of the money changers in the temple in Christian scripture. The aim of divine rage is not vengeance but to reorder the world. It is precise and purposeful, like the focused fury projected into the world from the forehead of the goddess. It points us to the humanity of even those who we are fighting. Kali is clad in a tiger skin: It is only *through* accessing her ferocity that divine rage can take form in the world. Perhaps our task as human beings is to find safe containers for our raw reactionary rage—and then choose to harness that energy in a way that creates a new world for *all* of us.

❧❧

Now I see instances of divine rage everywhere. I see it in the activists who storm the stage at political rallies, disrupt confirmation hearings, and confront senators in elevators. I see it in the indigenous rituals that appear in the wake of atrocities, like the fierce Maori Haka dance that erupted across New Zealand spontaneously in the wake of the white supremacist mass shootings in the mosques of Christchurch:

Students beat their chests, grimaced, and cried out, not with "thoughts and prayers," but with the kind of rage that demands action. I see it in people who stand up to tell the truth at school board meetings, in workplaces, on social media, and at their kitchen tables. There are many ways to confront one's opponents without anger. But in the case of ongoing social injustices, expressing outrage is often the only way to be heard.

Divine rage can make people uncomfortable: It can feel disruptive, frightening, and unpredictable. There are those who wish to police such rage in the name of civility. But civility is too often used to silence pain that requires people to change their lives. Rather than taming public expressions of moral outrage, perhaps it is up to the rest of us to train our ears to "hearing beyond what we are able to hear," in the words of theorist Judith Butler, so that we can discern the truth of the pain of injustice and confront our own complicity and responsibility. Just as we need accomplices to hold protected spaces where the most traumatized among us tend to our grief, so, too, do we need accomplices to stand by us when we express our rage, *and* help others to understand it.

"Anger is loaded with information and energy," says Audre Lorde. "Every woman has a well-stocked arsenal of anger potentially useful against those oppressions, personal and institutional, which brought that anger into being. Focused with precision it can become a powerful source of energy serving progress and change." Lorde asks us to tend to the rage within us as a symphony, "to listen to its rhythms, to learn within it, to move beyond the manner of presentation to the substance, to tap that anger as an important source of empowerment." It is a rhythm: Step away to *rage,* return to *listen,* and *reimagine* the solutions together. It becomes a kind of dance—to release raw rage in a safe container, in order to send divine rage into the world, like focused fury. The way of the warrior-sage is not only loving-kindness but loving-revolution, or revolutionary love.

❧❧

When I returned from India, I brought home a painting of Kali and placed it on our mantel in Venice and meditated on her. I had started learning Kathak, a classical Indian dance, where the dancer tells stories with her feet and hands and eyes, embodying the full spectrum of human moods and emotions. Every day, I tied my *ghungroo* around my ankles, stood before the picture of Kali, and pounded my feet into the ground until the sound of the bells echoed in the room and within my body, and the fire rose in me, and then I did the chakars, spinning around and around. Our tiny apartment was my safe container. Sometimes, I took my bells to Venice Beach to dance in front of the sea, my hands making the shape of wind, waves, and dolphins I imagined in the water.

Once, after the dancing was done, I watched the sun dip into the Pacific and gazed at the vast horizon. A man sitting with a guitar looked over at me, chewing on a piece of straw, and said, "You had to run to the edge of the world, didn't you?" I smiled. Then I saw a flashing fin. Maybe it was the man's whimsical recognition or the heat of the Kathak dance, but I found myself sprinting toward the ocean. The water was cold, but still I leapt into it, calling after the dolphins, knee-deep in frothy waves. Suddenly they came: two dolphins, cutting through the water, a single eye peering into mine, a flash, then gone. I laughed and cried out and stretched my arms to the dome of sky and felt the bowl breaking. *Vismaad*.

Sharat looked up from a book to find me in our doorway, shoeless, dripping wet.

"I'm home," I said, grinning.

"At last," he said.

On the other side of rage awaits the ability to wonder again at the spinning world.

How do we hold people accountable for wrongdoing and yet at the same time remain in touch with their humanity enough to believe in their capacity to be transformed?

—*bell hooks*

5.

listen.

THERE COMES A POINT, IN THE AFTERMATH OF CRUELTY OR INJURY, when I start to wonder about my opponent: *Why did they do that? Say that? Believe that? Vote that way? What is at stake for them? What is driving their behavior?* And I want to find out. Sometimes it's not safe for me to do this. I need to tend my own wound and keep processing my rage, grief, and trauma. But when it is safe, I think about how to listen to their story.

One might say: *Why should anyone try to listen to the white nationalist marching in the street, or the demagogue locking children in cages, or a former abuser? For too long, marginalized people have been asked to feel for their oppressors at the expense of their own dignity. Enough. We have a right to withhold our empathy.*

No one should be asked to *feel* empathy or compassion for their oppressors. I have learned that we do not need to *feel* anything for our opponents at all in order to practice love. Love is labor that returns us to wonder—it is seeing another person's humanity, even if they deny our own. We just have to choose to wonder about them.

Why is it that such labor always falls on the ones who have been the most oppressed? They have already ground our bones and profited from our sweat and tears and suffering. How much more is expected of us? We don't owe our oppressors anything.

I do not owe my opponents my affection, warmth, or regard. But I do owe *myself* a chance to live in this world without the burden of hate. "I shall permit no man, no matter what his color might be, to narrow and degrade my soul by making me hate him," said Booker T.

Washington. It reminds me of a line from Toni Morrison's novel *Love:* "Hate does that. Burns off everything but itself, so whatever your grievance is, your face looks just like your enemy's." I refuse to let anyone belittle my soul, or diminish my own expansive sense of self. The more I listen, the less I hate. The less I hate, the more I am free to choose actions that are controlled not by animosity but by wisdom. Laboring to love my opponents is how I love myself. This is not the stuff of saintliness. This is our birthright.

Listening is also a strategic choice: The more I listen, the more I understand. I am persuaded that there is no such thing as monsters in this world, only human beings who are wounded. I start to gain critical information about how we can respond to their greed, insecurity, anxiety, or blindness in ways that hold them accountable *and* fight the institutions that empower them. Listening enables us to fight in smarter ways for justice—not only to remove bad actors from power but to change the cultures that radicalize them. Listening is how we succeed.

The question therefore is not *whether* or not to listen to our opponents. The questions are: *When* is it *my* role to listen? When am I emotionally and physically safe? When can I take on the labor of listening when others are not safe to do so? We can all be one another's accomplices. At any given time, there are some opponents I cannot wonder about—I need others to do that labor for me as I tend to the wounds they inflict. But there are some opponents I find I am in a position to listen to. In these moments, it is time to turn to the practice of *how*.

It begins with the art of listening to stories.

❧

By the fall of 2006, the war in Iraq was at a fever pitch, and the list of hate crime victims was growing. Sharat and I were still working to turn the footage I had collected after 9/11 into a film about hate crimes called *Divided We Fall*. We didn't get the grants we applied for.

We couldn't find wealthy donors willing to take a chance on us. We had no money. But every time I buried my head in my hands, Sharat repeated a truth another independent filmmaker had passed on to him: "If you run after your project, people will chase you." So we ran after our project despite everything. Our friends began to volunteer as researchers, editors, and production assistants, working for free, because they believed in the project and they believed in us. Sharat and I didn't want to let them down. So we broke the first rule of filmmaking and maxed out our personal credit cards. We crisscrossed the country again, this time with our film team, shooting on 16 millimeter film. Blogs had just become a thing. I began blogging stories from our interviews with scholars, advocates, and more survivors of hate, and little donations started to trickle in—first ten dollars, then twenty dollars, then fifty dollars. We raised enough money for postproduction, tapping into crowdsourcing before it became a term. The central focus of the film emerged: "Who counts as American?" The Sikhs and Muslims in our film made a declaration—we see *ourselves* as American—and challenged our audience—how do *you* see us?

We premiered the film on September 15, 2006—five years after Balbir Singh Sodhi's murder. Rana Sodhi invited us to premiere the film in Phoenix on Balbir Uncle's death anniversary. We showed up, nervous then amazed. Four hundred people came. The Sodhi family had worked with local Sikh and interfaith leaders to turn a carpenters' union building into a movie theater. They rolled out a red carpet in a parking lot and kicked off the night with Punjabi food, hot *cha,* and *kirtan,* the poetry of Sikh scriptures set to song. Five years after 9/11, our community was still in crisis-response mode, but now we were no longer relying solely on others to tell our stories. We were telling our own stories *and* creating our own alternative spaces in which to share them.

With the family's blessings, we made the rounds of film festivals and won a few awards. Educators who had been following our blog began to invite us to screen the film on campuses, hungry for ways to talk about the escalation of hate in America since 9/11. Suddenly we were catapulted into a film tour to colleges and universities across the country. Sharat and I went from city to city, screening the film in classrooms and auditoriums, sometimes to audiences of a few dozen, other times a thousand. Our film was often required viewing for students, so the young people we engaged were diverse in political beliefs and backgrounds, a cross section of our generation. We were on the road for two years and reached about three hundred campuses and communities.

Each night the film played, I stood in the back of the theater and watched the audience—their sighs, laughter, gasps, tears, and silence. Their listening was an embodied experience. They were giving their senses to the screen. That was the singular power of cinema, the great empathy machine, to transfer our stories into their bodies in one seamless dream. The lights lifted. It was done. Our stories belonged to them now.

Sharat and I took the stage as students and community members lined up at the mics. One after another, people confessed how they had seen Sikhs as foreigners or suspects or terrorists. Until they heard our stories.

"Whenever I saw turbaned men at the airport or on the street, I was afraid. I didn't realize that until now."

"I had no idea that these hate crimes happened."

"I didn't know anything about Sikhs."

"I'm so sorry."

The film was forcing people to confront the conscious and unconscious ways that they were seeing other faces, *our* faces. Each night turned into a sort of town hall experience—intimate, raw, emotional, and demanding.

In Connecticut, a Japanese American woman said: "My grandparents were interned in the camps during World War II. No one raised their voice for them then. I will raise my voice for you now."

In New York City, a gay man stood and said: "I realize now that I must fight for the rights of Sikhs to wear their turbans, just as I fight for the rights of queer people to come out of the closet. We have to fight *for* one another."

In Chicago, a black man pointed to his dreadlocks and said: "My braids are *my* turban."

In story after story, people of color, queer people, and white allies were making connections that I had not made, linking their struggles to mine. They admitted that they had seen Sikhs as strangers or outright opponents. Now they were vowing to stand with us, to fight with us. We had made the film so that others would listen to *our* stories. What I did not expect was for the film to open spaces for me to listen to *their* stories. At the end of each night, people lined up to talk to me, often crying in my arms as I tried to find the right way to say "I see you." I began to understand that the pain that I had felt to be uniquely my own belonged to many. The Sikh story was bound up with the stories of all people still striving to be *seen* in America, our struggle situated in the larger struggle for civil and human rights. A larger "we" came into view: I could no longer be the activist who labored only for her own people. I had to listen to other communities' stories with the same wonder and humility with which they were listening to mine. I had to grieve with them, I had to fight for them, as they were doing for us.

✧

Deep listening is an act of surrender. We risk being changed by what we hear. When I really want to hear another person's story, I try to leave my preconceptions at the door and draw close to their telling. I am always partially listening to the thoughts in my own head when others are speaking, so I consciously quiet my thoughts and begin to listen with my senses. Empathy is cognitive *and* emotional—to inhabit another person's view of the world is to *feel* the world with them. But I also know that it's okay if I don't feel very much for them at all. I just need to feel safe enough to stay curious. The most critical part of listening is asking *what is at stake* for the other person. I try to understand what matters to them, not what I think matters. Sometimes I start to lose myself in their story. As soon as I notice feeling unmoored, I try to pull myself back into my body, like returning home. As Hannah Arendt says, "One trains one's imagination to go visiting." When the story is done, we must return to our skin, our own worldview, and notice how we have been changed by our visit. So I ask myself, *What is this story demanding of me? What will I do now that I know this?*

When I listen that deeply, it feels like a dance between two poles, between myself and another person, between what is at stake for them and what is at stake for me. I call this the circle of listening. The dance can take place in any length of time—ninety seconds or ninety minutes. I can be listening to a friend on the phone or a survivor's testimony or an opponent's story. The process is the same—I draw close to them, return, respond, and draw close to listen again, moving in a circle animated by wonder. Sometimes I feel empathy; that is, I feel *as* they are feeling. Other times—say, when a child in my care is wailing—I don't need to feel empathy in order to know how to respond. In fact, sometimes empathy gets in the way.

For decades, documentary filmmakers have told stories about immigrants and refugees and survivors of violence. Empathy was the goal. The idea was that if we just humanized people, it would motivate audiences to action. But witnessing suffering does not necessarily lead to meaningful action. The credits roll; we go home or swipe the screen. We think that something has been accomplished because we are emotionally spent, but nothing has changed. We can have all the empathy in the world for a group of people and still participate in the structures and systems that oppress them. We might believe we are listening, but we have journeyed only half of the circle. We have drawn close to the story and lost ourselves in another's experience, but we haven't returned to ourselves and asked: What does this demand of *me*? Is it the reckoning of my privilege? Is it an expansion of whose struggles connect with mine? What will I *do* differently now?

Our documentary film could have fallen into the empathy-as-destination trap. But when the lights went on, Sharat and I stood on the stage in the flesh, and our presence demanded a response. Often Sikhs and Muslims who lived in the community stood up in the audience and told their stories, too, voices cracking. Listening led to action. Students formed working groups, others penned essays for the school newspaper, some formed new friendships. Empathy gave rise to solidarity.

As we toured with the film, campuses began to ask us to stay longer so that I could give lectures and workshops on storytelling and social change. Every week I taught in a different part of the country, honing my skills. I thought I was becoming an expert in the art of listening across divides—until I had to try it at home.

❧

Papa Ji was sick. Parkinson's disease was starting to take a toll on my grandfather's body. All this time, Sharat and I were living out of suitcases, returning to our apartment in Venice as our base. I hadn't returned to my family's home in Clovis since the incident with Roshan. My family was still talking to him. Every time I thought of him, I felt rage, then returned to the image of him as a frail and wounded kid. It was not my responsibility to help him, to sit down and listen to him, but I would not get in the way of others who would. This was my loving act: to see my worst opponent as someone who deserved healing and let others tend to his wound. I let my brother, parents, and cousins love Roshan the best they could. Meanwhile, I was steering clear of Clovis—until my parents called me about Papa Ji's decline, and I rushed back to see him.

Papa Ji was wrapped in a soft blue blanket that looked like a cocoon, as if he was transforming into something new and beautiful beneath the layers. Only his head was visible. His eyes were watery and his mouth moved slowly to take in spoonfuls of dal and *chol*. I rushed to his side, took the spoon in my hand, and began to feed him.

"You may be happy now," Papa Ji said slowly, vocal cords strained. "But this happiness won't last when the community disowns you and you do not become the leader you were meant to be, and Sikhi is lost on your children."

I held the spoon in midair. He was talking about the fact that Sharat was from a Hindu family in South India—and not Sikh.

"Papa Ji, you taught me that Sikhi calls us to a path of love," I said slowly. "You taught me to believe in equality."

"Not all husbands are equal," he said. "Ram was no good, that's fine, but you are meant for a tall and handsome sardar. Maybe we find him in Punjab."

I reached for Papa Ji's hand, even as my body stiffened.

"Papa Ji, Sharat makes me a better Sikh," I said. I explained how we were traveling the country now with a film that was helping change how people saw our community, that Sharat was helping me heal from the pain in my body, that his love was making me brave. We wanted to get married with his blessing.

"I wish I die before I see your wedding day," he said. He never raised his voice. He just said it again. "I hope that God takes me away before I ever see you married. You are betraying the gurus and you will suffer for this."

I began to sob.

"You are not a Sikh."

I couldn't listen anymore. I ran out of the room.

The belief that had driven Roshan to hurt me also lived in Papa Ji. They both believed that marrying someone of a different religion or race or the same gender threatened a way of life that needed to be preserved. They both assumed that I was relinquishing my faith and betraying my people. But I was not abandoning my faith; I was deepening it. I did not know how to make him understand.

That night, we had a family meeting to discuss options for Papa Ji's medical care, all of us crammed into a bedroom where he could not hear us. It was hot and stuffy. Suddenly one of my uncles blocked the doorway and pointed his finger down at me.

"You're the one making Papa Ji sick," he said. "You're the one killing him."

My mother and father began to shout at my uncle. I squeezed through the opening in the doorway and ran into the suburbs that had replaced the farms and fields around our house. The tired tears tumbled out. Was my love for Sharat killing my grandfather?

In the morning, my mother and father helped me pack. It was not my job to stay and listen. They would do that work. I rejoined Sharat on the road and resumed the listening tour out in the world that I could not yet do in my own family.

☙❧

Back on the road with the film, we toured the South. One night in South Carolina, a white evangelical man stood up after the film and described how he felt under siege in America. "People think that you and I have nothing in common," he said to me. "But you and I are not that different. I, too, am seen as an outsider."

He was making a well-meaning gesture, connecting his status as a white evangelical man with mine as a brown Sikh woman, framing both of us as minorities. Far from challenging him, I rushed to embrace the comparison.

"Yes! We all have been seen as outsiders at some point in our lives," I reasoned. "Even a white straight evangelical Christian man has been depressed at some point, or picked on, or felt outside the mainstream. We all have ancestors who were persecuted at some point in history and we all carry these ancestral memories in us. We all share the desire to be seen the way we see ourselves."

There was nothing wrong with this insight of commonality. The problem is that I did not follow it up—I did not ask the man to say more about where his feeling of being a minority came from, and so I never found out whether it was our nation's increasing diversity and equality that threatened his position of supremacy and made him feel under siege. Nor did I suggest the ways in which this man and I were *not* similar, that his ancestors had likely possessed power over mine, allowed them to be stripped of citizenship, and profited from their labor, and that these histories shape the world we both live in today, affording him access and privilege that I did not enjoy by virtue of the body I occupied.

Instead I let it be a feel-good moment.

I had fallen for the trap in so many dialogues—the rush to be polite, to seek out sameness but not difference, to steer clear of discomfort and avoid hard truths. But the purpose of listening across lines of difference is not agreement or compromise. It is understanding. True understanding is not possible unless we risk changing our worldview. Otherwise we think we have built bridges to one another, but the bridges are rooted in sands that can shift with the tide. Solidarity is only possible if we are brave enough to reckon with the past and how the past shapes the present. In the United States, this means confronting the reality of white supremacy.

I did not talk about white supremacy onstage. I never even uttered the words out loud. I was afraid that it would make people shut down, that it would make them feel like I was calling them racist and attacking them personally rather than inviting them to look at the world and their social location with new eyes. Instead I referred to white supremacy as a fringe belief that only a subset of people held. But it was and is not a fringe belief. White supremacy is a system based on the notion that white Christians are superior and therefore deserve economic, political, and cultural dominion on this soil. This single powerful idea motivated the rape, pillage, conquest, concentration, incarceration, and slaughter of indigenous, black, and brown peoples throughout U.S. history. White supremacy forces an ordering of human value. And from that ordering comes every other form of inequality in the United States.

White supremacy as an *ideology* had been pushed to the margins of American culture. But white supremacy as a *system* of structural advantage that favors white people persists: It animates the institutions we operate in. It is why our nation's policies on immigration, criminal justice, and national security continue to criminalize communities of color, maintaining the climate in which hate crimes keep happening. We keep talking about hate crimes as radical acts driven by individual intention. But they are only the most visible evidence of this broader system at work.

Still I kept finding ways to talk about hate in America without naming white supremacy. I wanted to believe that the well-meaning Southern man was right—that no matter who we were or where we were from or what we had done, we had only to find common ground to heal our nation, that individual connections could transcend systems of injustice, that we could join hands and look to the future without having to reckon with the past. I wanted reconciliation without truth.

Around the same time that we were touring the country, a young presidential candidate was rising to prominence with a vision of unity. In Barack Obama, I heard my generation's longing to form a more perfect union that transcended the cruelties of our racial past. Obama joined all our disparate struggles together as parts of one great struggle for the American Dream, and he asked us to unite behind that dream. It was an impossible notion: A black presidency had never been and so could never be. And yet Obama's personhood alone ignited our imagination—a white mother, an African father, a childhood spent partly in Asia, an immigrant past, and life as a black man whose encounters with racism did not deter his faith in the nation's promise. Obama was like a prism that we could turn in our mind's eye until we saw ourselves. He would be not only the first black president but also the first who carried our diversity in his being and breath. He held up a sparkling vision of a nation that had never been, but could be.

After eight long years documenting hate and murder and memorials during President Bush's tenure, I ached for the America that Obama sang into being onstage. So even while we continued to tour with the film, Sharat and I leapt into Obama's 2008 presidential campaign. The campaign used a storytelling model to build solidarity, the same process we saw work on campuses. Organizing meetings began with people in a room taking time to tell the story of why they were there. People who met as strangers bonded instantly and became foot soldiers in one great army. We recruited our families and friends. Brynn, Irene, Jess, and the rest of the Pocket were there. Even my father, driven out of the Republican Party by rabid racism and warmongering that had become increasingly explicit, joined us and made calls to turn people out to the polls. The antiwar movement wasn't dead: It had reemerged more diverse, disciplined, inspired, and powerful than before in the form of a political campaign. This time, instead of planning protests, we were running phone banks and canvassing neighborhoods. Sharat and I helped organize precincts on the ground in Texas, California, and Pennsylvania. Our goal was razor-sharp: to get Barack elected.

On election night, November 8, 2008, Sharat and I gathered with others in a bar in Philadelphia where we had been organizing all week and watched the television screen in hopeful anticipation. The entire bar counted down to the closing of the polls state by state. We held our breath. 10—9—8. It felt like a countdown to a new era. 7—6—5. Heart racing. 4—3—2. Sharat drew me close. 1. Obama's picture appeared. We had done the impossible! Confetti flew! Party horns blasted! Sharat and I kissed and laughed and wept and hugged people we didn't know. Soon after, we huddled together at the foot of the Washington Monument on Inauguration Day to watch our man sworn in as president of the United States in the far distance, people of all colors on all sides of us, jubilation in the air, as if the birth of a new America was imminent.

Then—everyone went home.

After the election, Obama's team folded his organization—thirteen million strong—into the Democratic National Committee. He shifted from a transformative candidate inspiring the masses into a moderate politician struggling for consensus. I understood the impulses behind President Obama's approach. I shared them—the rush to find agreement, the aspiration to transcend our polarized past, the belief that finding common ground was more important than reckoning with a history of difference, domination, and subordination. But there is no reconciliation without truth. I wish Obama had chosen to look back and hold the previous administration accountable for war crimes. I wish he had prioritized policies to uplift historically oppressed peoples without apology. I wish he had initiated truth and reconciliation commissions for genocide and slavery and opened the discussion for reparations. But how much can we demand of one man whose opposition was already determined to destroy him? During the Obama era, our movement regrouped in pockets to occupy Wall Street and march with Dreamers and proclaim that Black Lives Matter. We saw glimpses of the nation we were birthing into being—but nothing on the scale of the broad-based intersectional movement that might have been had the thirteen million of us stayed connected, vigilant, and organized.

In the meantime, a subset of Republicans built a lean grassroots machine of their own, harnessing the fresh surge of racial resentment under Obama, calling for local "tea parties" to oppose the president at every turn, capturing local and state seats, and setting the stage for the zealous white nationalist movement that would deliver a Trump presidency. We never noticed the scope and intensity of racial hatred in these spaces until eight years later when an angry groundswell unfurled the banner in 2016 to MAKE AMERICA GREAT AGAIN. The Obama era did not transcend our racial past: It revived that past with a vengeance.

My friend Professor Melissa Harris-Perry once told me that after Obama's election, she held up a picture of President Lyndon Johnson and Dr. Martin Luther King, Jr., to her class.

"Which one is Obama?" she asked her students.

The students shouted, "King! King!"

"No," she said. "Obama is President Johnson. Obama is constrained by the office of the presidency. President Johnson could not deliver civil rights victories without Dr. King. The president needs a King. The president needs *Kings,* plural. We must be his Kings."

Imagine if we as a nation had treated Obama's election, not as the end of white supremacy, but as our first real opportunity to dismantle it. Imagine if, on the day after the inauguration, we had gathered in the same spaces where we had organized in order to discuss truth and reconciliation in America. We might have initiated it ourselves, block by block, practicing that hard, genuine listening together—listening in order to confront the past and create a new future. What if people like that well-meaning Southern man and me had the support to keep listening to each other, even when it got hard, until we could anchor our solidarity in real understanding? Imagine if we had each assumed our role as Kings—as voices in a dialogue that allowed for reckoning and reconciliation on national and local levels, the sort that could lead to real, binding unity. We might have been able to respond more swiftly to the militant right-wing white nationalism that resurged under a black presidency. Some of us might have been able to tend to the rage and grief of disaffected white people before they were whipped into racist nationalist fervor. In those eight years of opportunity, might *we* the people have begun to birth the America that Obama had lifted before our eyes?

Is it still possible now, after we have lost so much?

❧

One afternoon, I was sitting alone and writing at a table at a Mexican restaurant in El Porto, a neighborhood in greater Los Angeles.

"Those fucking sand niggers!"

I froze. The group of white men at the table next to me were hunched over beers but their voices boomed. They said the phrase again. I recoiled and wanted to leave. Then I glanced over at those men and remembered the practice for wonder that I had developed for myself and said in my mind *These men are your uncles* a few times until the word "uncle" replaced "bigot." Then I walked over.

"Excuse me," I said.

They turned to face me—five older white men, slightly drunk, amused to see a lone young brown woman addressing them. They were smirking, throwing their eyes up and down my body.

"What, did we say something racist?"

"I wasn't listening to your conversation," I said. "All I heard was the words 'sand nigger' a few times, and I had to say something." I took a breath. "You see, people in my community have been beaten and killed while hearing those words. I'm a Sikh and men in my community wear turbans as part of our faith. They've been called 'Osama' and 'terrorist' and 'sand nigger' on the street. Those words carry a lot of hate. I just needed you to know what it means to me."

"Oh, I'm sorry that I hurt your feelings," one of them said, mocking me. He was the one who had said the words. His name was Richard. "But you have to understand 9/11. You don't remember 9/11."

"I do," I said. "A man I knew, Balbir Singh Sodhi, was killed in a hate crime after 9/11. The man who killed him was sitting in a bar the day before he shot him—using words like yours. And no one said anything to him then. That's why I had to say something to you now. These are dangerous words. This is how violence happens."

The men got quiet.

"I'm not gonna shoot nobody," said Richard.

"But the guy sitting behind you who's hearing you talk like that might say, 'Yeah, he's right,' and grab his gun."

"Well, he's a moron, then," said Richard. "You know who's really causing all this violence, don't you? You can't tell me Muslims have a peaceful religion."

"They do," I said. "A fraction does not represent a whole. Think about your upbringing. Weren't you raised to treat people who were different from you with respect? Weren't you raised not to blame an entire group of people for the actions of a few?"

"Look, the Quran tells you to kill infidels," Richard argued. "It says for Muslims to go out and kill infidels. That's us!"

"The Quran also says that if you kill one person, it's as if you have killed all of humanity," I said. "Every religious scripture has passages that can be used to condone violence, or to promote love. Think of how the Bible has been used throughout history. Think of the Crusades. Or the KKK. They thought their religion justified violence, too. But that doesn't mean all Christians are evil."

"It's not just a few people," he said. "Have your people ever—*ever*—said anything to condemn all this terrorism?"

"Yes," I said, exasperated. "I just posted a video called 'Muslim Americans Speaking Out' on Facebook while sitting at that table. Sikhs and Muslims have been speaking out *every time* in the wake of every terrorist attack since 9/11. You just haven't listened to us."

The other men egged him to go watch the video on my laptop. Instead he said, "What's Sikh? I don't know anything about Sikh. What do you believe?"

"Sikhism is a major world religion, just like Christianity or Judaism or Islam or Hinduism," I recited. "We believe in One God, equality, and social justice. Many Sikhs wear articles of faith—like keeping our hair long and uncut—to show our commitment to serve others."

"That sounds pretty good," one of them said.

"That's why it's so sad that Sikhs who wear turbans are instead seen as terrorists or called 'sand nigger,'" I said.

I thought I was getting somewhere. I just kept going.

"You know, I was sitting at that table next to you and I could have thought, *You're all just a bunch of bigots*. I would have never come over here to talk to you. But instead I thought, *Those are my uncles sitting over there. You* are my uncles. I came to talk to you because I hoped that you would hear me. I hoped that you would see me as your niece. Or your little sister. I think that's why you're listening to me now."

Some of them were nodding. This felt like a breakthrough—calling myself a sister really seemed to create an opening.

"If you keep using words like 'sand nigger,' you put other people in boxes," I said. "You'll never be able to really see them or hear their stories or realize that they are your brothers and sisters, too."

They asked if I came to this restaurant often, and I said sometimes. They said they would see me around and got up to leave. This was *their* neighborhood joint—*their* territory, not mine. I shook their hands. I thanked them for listening. I thought that perhaps I had been heard and something had been achieved.

One of them stayed behind.

"Look, I'm not a bigot," he said. His name was Steve. He leaned close and looked at me earnestly. "I'm married to a Mexican woman. I listen to jazz and blues all the time. You have to understand that we've put up with an asshole for a president. We want our country back. We need to stop those Muslims from killing us. We need to build a wall to keep all those immigrants from flooding our country and taking our jobs. We need to . . ."

It was like listening to the most virulent right-wing talk radio, live, in person. My entire body seized up. My chest constricted. I focused on taking a deep breath.

"Okay," I said, searching for an entry point. "Do you understand that hate crimes against my community are skyrocketing because of these beliefs?"

"You know what we should do?" he said. "We should teach you all how to fight and send you back to your country."

"What? Where would I go back to?" I said, thrown. "My family has lived here for more than a hundred years. My grandfather came to California in 1913. With that way of thinking, my grandfather would never have been allowed in this country, and neither would yours."

"My ancestor signed the Declaration of Independence," he said. "My family owned slaves in Louisiana."

He wasn't proud when he said this, but he wasn't ashamed, either.

"Look, you're not a sand nigger," he went on. "He's not a sand nigger." He was pointing at the Latinx bartender. "But there are niggers out there. If you line up ten black people, eight of them are niggers and two of them are blacks."

"Wait, what?"

"You know what I'm talking about," he said. "They're lowlifes covered with tattoos who don't have jobs. We call them niggers. They're not human beings."

"Let me get this right," I said carefully. "You don't think that every person is a human being?"

"No, they're not," said Steve.

"I believe that every person is a human being," I said.

"I don't," he said.

"Um," I said. "That makes me sad."

Steve had to go. He shook my hand and left. I sat down for a long time without moving, so furious that I was still like a stone. I had walked over to their table feeling all bold. I thought I could say something that would reach them. But I ended up being the one shaken by what I heard. I needed to wash my hands, I thought. How could I have let him touch me?

❧

Deep listening is about drawing close to someone's story. It turns out it is extremely difficult to draw close to someone you find absolutely abhorrent. How do we listen to someone when their beliefs are disgusting? Or enraging? Or terrifying? How do we keep listening when the words are so offensive and dangerous that it seems that the only rightful response is hostility? An invisible wall forms between us and them, a chasm that seems impossible to cross. We don't even know why we should try to cross it. Those beliefs don't deserve our attention. In these moments, we can choose to remember that the goal of listening is not to feel empathy for our opponents, or validate their ideas, or even change their mind in the moment. Our goal is to understand them. Why would someone believe that not every person is a human being? In understanding the cultural forces that shape such a belief, and the institutions that embolden people to act on it, we can better focus on what we need to fight: not a few bad actors, but entire policies, platforms, and echo chambers that perpetuate supremacy. In order to create a safer world for all of us, we must not only defeat such opponents but invite them into transformation. That means finding a way to overcome our own emotional resistance and choose to ask questions about them. This takes work. Neuroscientists call it "cognitive load"—trying to understand the perspective and pain of people we are inclined to hate is a dramatic cognitive challenge. The load only lightens with practice.

When listening gets hard, I focus on taking the next breath. I pay attention to sensations in my body: heat, clenching, and constriction. I feel the ground beneath my feet. Am I safe? If so, I stay and slow my breath again, quiet my mind, and release the pressure that pushes me to defend my position. I try to wonder about this person's story and the possible wound in them. I think of an earnest question and try to stay curious long enough to be changed by what I hear. Maybe, just maybe, my opponent will begin to wonder about me in return, ask me questions, and listen to my story. Maybe their views will start to break apart and new horizons will open in the process. Maybe the memory of the exchange will play a critical role in their transformation in the future. Then again, maybe not. It doesn't matter as long as the primary goal of listening is to deepen my own understanding. Listening does not grant the other side legitimacy. It grants them humanity—and preserves our own.

❧

As I sat in the restaurant bar, the words "sand nigger" replayed in my mind. The word "nigger" was inside the phrase "sand nigger." The simple statement "Black Lives Matter" was not true *on its face* to people like Steve, for whom black people were not human beings. And just as there were niggers, there were sand niggers and dehumanizing slurs for every other marginalized group. I began to understand the centrality of antiblack racism in America. All this time, I believed we all had different struggles that intersected with each other—black people, brown people, queer people, and poor people. No one group was at the center. Since the genocide and colonization of indigenous peoples, antiblack racism has been the country's most enduring mechanism for creating hierarchies of human value—every other form followed from it. Antiblack racism ordered the nation's most durable white supremacist systems—from slavery to Jim Crow to mass incarceration—and perpetuated racism against other communities, including my own. I knew that our struggles as communities of color were interconnected, but I was beginning to understand that our movements needed to *center* black lives if we were to combat the hate of the men at this table.

I wondered what more I could have learned had I listened for longer to these men. I didn't listen as well as I could have, since I was mostly paying attention to form a counterargument and spending my energy trying to defend my position. So I wrote down their words and kept listening to their voices in my mind until I was able to quiet my reaction of disgust—and then it happened. I heard the suffering inside their hate: their sense of violation since 9/11, their anxiety about keeping their jobs, their terror as a nation where white people like them had economic and cultural control seemed to disappear, their relief upon the rise of political figures who validated their hate. These men inhabited a world filled not with people but with subhumans who threatened them. What a painful way to live. Their pain did not justify their hate. But once I could listen from inside their pain, I no longer saw white nationalists like them as simple, homogenous, or evil. I saw them as deeply human, deeply complex, and deeply wounded. That of course did not make them any less dangerous.

I had decided in the restaurant that it was safe enough for me to walk over to the men's table. In retrospect, I'm not sure that it was. Someone had to listen to them. Someone had to gather information in order to understand them. Someone had to tend to their wound. I'm just not sure it had to be me.

❧❧

Everyone has a role in the labor of birthing a new America. If you find yourself in harm's way right now, then it is *not* necessarily your role to listen to the people who are terrorizing you. Or to tend to any kind of wound in them. Your primary responsibility is to survive, find safety, and tend to the wounds they inflict on you—to build bonds with people who are willing to wonder about you, grieve with you, and fight with and for you. In finding ways to breathe, you are creating the kind of energy and joy that can sustain us all in the struggle. That is your act of revolutionary love.

But, by virtue of whatever privilege you have, if you find yourself safe enough to do the brave work of listening to your opponents, you have a vital role to play. My friend Sister Simone Campbell helps me understand some of the people I cannot talk to in person. As an attorney and progressive nun, she crisscrosses the country as part of "Nuns on the Bus," holding listening tours to find common ground with disaffected white conservatives. In the lead-up to the 2016 presidential election, on a stop in Indianapolis, she listened as a white man railed at her about the immigrants and Muslims invading "his" country. His parents worked hard, his grandparents worked hard, and for what? He was going to vote for Trump, because Trump understood him. Sister Simone wanted to tell him that the economic policies that would actually help him were championed by progressives, not Trump. But she stopped herself. She pushed herself to be curious. *You have a story, and I need to hear it,* she thought. She kept listening—and then she heard his pain. She picked up on a refrain that his parents worked hard and wanted a better future for him. "It sounds like you feel ashamed that you did not live up to your parents' expectations," she said. His eyes filled with tears. That was it. The need to belong. To be seen. To be loved. To succeed. To matter. His rage was a symptom of his pain.

"Pain that is not transformed is transferred," says Franciscan priest Richard Rohr. When we leave people alone with their pain, their alienation becomes the precondition for radicalization. But in listening to people's pain, we can help them transform it. If you are like Sister Simone, you might be in a position to listen to disaffected white people in your family or community who are terrified by our nation's demographic transition. You might be able to help them grieve the illusion that America ever belonged only to them. Maybe you can invite them to see that they do not need to fear or hate us. Maybe you can show them spaces where white people and people of color are congregating around common pain to push for change—in health-care, criminal justice, and education. Then again, maybe you can't move them at all. But what you learn can still help someone like me. I want to hold up a vision of an America that has a place for all of us—them, too.

"You can't lead people you don't love," says Van Jones, a lifelong activist and innovator who models for me how to listen to our politi-cal opponents. "We must not become what we are fighting." So I partner with people like Van and Sister Simone who keep me honest in the labor. I now use the words "white supremacy" publicly, be-cause we can't solve a problem we don't have the courage to name. And every time I am tempted to hate, I hear Van's voice: "When it gets hard to love, love harder." I retreat. I rage. Then I return again to labor in love—and try to listen.

❧

How is it that I could hear the pain behind the slurs of self-avowed racists, but I could not yet hear the pain in my own beloved grandfa-ther? I finally began to wonder: What was Papa Ji afraid of losing? I returned home to listen harder, this time with my mother at my side.

"You did not care what Papa Ji would think when you fell in love with Sharat," Papa Ji said. "You did not think about your family or your future generations."

I began to tear up again.

"Don't cry," he said. "I tried to be happy about it, but I cannot change the force of the programming inside me. I cannot agree to this."

My mother stepped in and took her father's hand.

"You and all the poets celebrate love when you hear ghazals and *kahani*s," she said. "You hear the poetry of Heer Ranjha and raise your hands to the sky and say, 'Vah vah vah!'" Heer and Ranjha were the Romeo and Juliet of Punjabi folklore. "But when love actually appears before you," she said, pointing to me, "you reject it. You are against love!"

Papa Ji had tiny droplets of tears in his eyes like golden grain. I noticed the saliva in the corner of his mouth and the way his legs shook back and forth and how his hands trembled in ours. My grandfather, my great sage, had become my opponent. But he was trying hard to listen to me. Sometimes the hardest people to listen to are the ones closest to us. But our closeness can give us resilience so we can listen longer. So, Papa Ji and I kept listening to each other through the long hours, my mother at our side, stepping away to breathe, returning again.

"I do not want to push you away," he said, "but I do not want to be dishonest with you, either. Please keep coming to see me. I am not going to be with you very long."

My grandfather was dying. But our patience in listening to him assumed that there was, even in this dying man, something vibrant and alive and open to change.

"I love you so much, Papa Ji," I said.

"I love you, too," he said. "I am an old man. I want to see you happy. This pains me, and I see that it pains you, too. This pain is not my doing. It is predestined by God. I will celebrate the happiness of my granddaughter on her wedding day."

I could hear the struggle in him—he wanted to disown me, he wanted to bless me.

"Let us stop worrying about the future," he said. "Let us be present now."

I hugged him. The bobby pins in my hair got stuck in his white beard.

"Of course, I get stuck to you," I said.

"Careful," he chuckled. "You will get stuck again and then you cannot go."

"I'm always stuck to you," I said. "You have shaped my life, Papa Ji."

"Thank you, dear, thank you," he said. "And I will always be here to bother you and make you cry, too. I hope you can use the things that you dislike in me, and I can learn how to use the things I dislike in you."

I went home to Sharat in Los Angeles and spent a lot of time by the sea, listening to our conversations replay in my mind. What does it mean to listen to the ones we love when we are in the middle of a fight? I thought of the dance, from myself to another, myself to another. In my hardest conversations, I often need to leave the scene in order to process my rage and grief in safe containers—sometimes for days or months or years—and then return to listen again. I am sometimes tempted never to return again. It seems easier to just cut someone out of my life. But returning *always* takes place anyway, if not in person then in our imagination. Even though I had left Papa Ji's side, I could close my eyes and see his face—glassy watery eyes, gray hair, tiniest trace of saliva, graceful lips, his majesty, his wrinkles, his unbending judgment, his tender heart. Our lives are long and our circles are small. We remain linked to the ones we have loved, if only in our minds. The question is how to be in right relationship with them, even if we may never agree with each other, or even see each other again. Right relationship is knowing that we are interconnected and finding a form of connection that allows us peace. Sometimes right relationship means reentering each other's lives. Sometimes it means staying apart. I knew that Papa Ji and I had not yet found peace. I knew that we still needed to return to each other somehow. I just hoped that we would have time to do it on this earth.

"Think about Papa Ji's life," Sharat said. He pointed me to a thick spiral-bound book on our shelf, Papa Ji's autobiography, *Yaadan da Praga,* Basket of Memories. I once sat with Papa Ji for an entire summer as he dictated his life story in perfect detail. That was many years ago. I opened the book and began to read.

Papa Ji grew up playing under a great banyan tree in the heart of his village. He was born in 1921 in Basupanu in Punjab. At eighteen years old, he joined the British Indian Army and became a mechanic in World War II, serving in Sudan, Ethiopia, Egypt, Libya, Iraq, Iran, and Palestine. Fire rained down from German aircraft at night, but he slept through the air raids, because his father told him that there was no bullet meant for him. When his British superior tried to force him to remove his turban on the front lines, he refused. "God gave me my helmet," he said. When his friend was riddled with German bullets, he took off his turban, wrapped his friend's body with the cloth, and brought him back to the base. After the war, the British left India in 1947 and, upon departing, partitioned the country in two. Papa Ji was caught on the Pakistan side of the new border. He saw trains filled with dead bodies rolling into the station and barely escaped the bloodshed. Mummy Ji, my grandmother, wore white, the color of mourning, until he reappeared on the other side of Punjab. They had children and he worked in Kashmir, Sikkim, Bangalore, and Joshimath, where the music of the River Ganga stirred him to write poetry. In 1984, he hid on rooftops in New Delhi during the anti-Sikh pogroms and watched as rioters threw tires over fleeing Sikh men and set their bodies on fire. That's when my grandparents decided to leave India and join their daughter and son-in-law in America, tend a garden, publish books of poems, and help raise my brother and me.

Papa Ji's life was an epic chronicle of courage in the face of death, and, through it all, his faith shielded him from the hot winds. He had passed down his faith to me. He did not want me to lose it. I wanted to show him that loving Sharat was not making me abandon my faith but rather deepening it. To me, our faith tradition was not a dead boulder we had the burden of carrying, unchanged, a fixed thing to pass on to the next generation, hoping it withstands the erosion of time. Instead I saw our faith tradition more like a river, a current of rituals and songs and stories that flows down to us from the past, influenced by each generation before us, ours to deepen and direct into the future. But I could not force Papa Ji to understand me. I could only be responsible for my effort to understand him. In listening to his life, I was beginning to see that inside his unbending judgment was his attempt to express unending love. He was afraid of losing me. I understood because for as long as I could remember I was afraid of losing him.

When I was a little girl, I would curl up beside Papa Ji and study the ivory curve of his feet.

"Papa Ji, will you die?" I asked one night.

"I have cheated death many times," he said, stroking my forehead with the hand that trembled. "I'm going to live a long time, as long as your father's father. But then I will die."

"I won't be able to bear it," I said.

"You will, my dear," he said.

"Will you send me some sign after you die?" I begged. "It will be our secret experiment."

He paused and agreed. "If you summon me, I will come."

"Promise?" I sat up to look at him.

"Promise," he said.

꧁꧂

A few months later, my mother called to tell me that the Parkinson's was shutting down Papa Ji's body. Sharat and I rushed back to Clovis and into the hospital room. Papa Ji's eyes were bulging out and he was gasping for breath.

"My beautiful Papa Ji!" I ran to his side and set my hands on his belly, like I did as a child when he was convinced I cured him from shingles. We breathed together, and he calmed down, his eyes focused on mine. Sharat and I sat at his bedside for hours each day, taking turns with my parents. Love is not an exchange economy: I was going to choose to love Papa Ji even if he did not know how to love me. I pressed my fingers to his temples and recited the prayer he taught us in childhood. *Tati Vao Na Lagi*. The hot winds cannot touch you.

One night, Papa Ji opened his eyes and looked up at Sharat and me—and smiled. We took his hand.

"Forgive me," he mouthed. "Forgive me, I was a fool. I bless you. I bless both of you."

"Papa Ji, you made me a warrior." I wept. "You made me such a strong warrior that I turned around and fought you! And now you are letting me win."

"Because you are right," he said.

Then he turned to Sharat.

"If you take care of her," he said, "she will take care of you."

Sharat held his hand and looked at him and looked at me, his eyes gentle.

Then Papa Ji asked me to find peace with Roshan. I did not yet know what that meant, but I promised I would. He told me to leave the hospital and return to my work. I refused and he insisted.

"I am not going anywhere," he said. "We are always going to be together."

A few weeks later, my mother called me in the morning while I was getting ready. My parents had brought Papa Ji home from the hospital so that they could take care of him themselves. He had been "traveling" for days, talking to people at his bedside who were long gone. Then suddenly he became lucid. He could no longer speak but he could listen. My mother held the phone to his ear. I recited to Papa Ji the story of Shiva's hair. In a time of great need, the people prayed to the heavens and the deities released a torrent of divine waters. The force of the waters would have shattered the earth. So the deity Shiva, in the form of the Supreme Yogi, caught the waters in the coils of his long matted hair. The River Ganga flowed out of Shiva's hair, nourishing the earth and all the people. "Today, let the divine waters flow through your body, Papa Ji!" I could hear him laugh. I hung up. An hour later, the phone rang again.

Papa Ji had died.

"It's just as you wrote it," my mother said to me. When I had taken down Papa Ji's autobiography, I had asked him his last wish at the time of his death. He said, "That I could give a smile to all the people around me. This is the only one wish I have. I want to go smiling to my master."

"He looked at each of us around his bed," my mother said with a watery voice. "We took turns giving him amrit and he smiled at each of us." He waited until Mummy Ji brought the cloth soaked in sacred water to his lips. He took the cloth into his mouth, swallowed it, sighed, and died. "It was a saint's death," she said.

I sat still for a long time in my apartment and waited for the sign that Papa Ji had promised to send. I knew that it was not rational but it did not matter. He had promised. "If you summon me, I will come." The star lantern on the shelf trembled. But no other sign came. The next day, I went looking for him in the cemetery. I was like a lost child, wandering the woods, the parks, the streets, searching for him, but still there was no sign. Nothing. I was angry. Our last years together were marred by pain, and he had left me without teaching me the secret to his fearlessness.

I went to see Joyce Frazier, a neuromuscular therapist whose treatment room had become a sanctuary. She was a wise woman who knew how to listen deeply.

"Papa Ji was like a great redwood tree," Joyce said to me. "He was ancient and life-giving at the heart of the forest that is your life. The tree provided shade and you didn't know how the forest could be without it. Then one day, the tree fell—there was a thunderous crash, and it threw up dirt and shook the entire forest. Every time you walk through the forest now, you stumble over the fallen tree and bloody your knees, over and over. You do not know how to move through the forest without crashing into it. In time, you will slowly learn to walk around the tree. And then one day, you will decide to sit on its great trunk and notice how moss is growing over it, and flowers now, and it is becoming part of the forest. You will learn to be still and take in the beauty and be in it. Then you will find him."

That night, I had a dream. Papa Ji was there, standing at the bottom of the stairs in our old house. I ran down the stairs and wrapped my arms around him, pressing my face into his brown sweater vest, the one that smelled of sweet musk.

"Papa Ji, how are you here?" I asked.

His spirit had flown to India, but he could see nothing there, only a vast blank void.

"The dead can only see those they love," he said to me. Then I woke up.

I walked to a park, sat on a bench, and looked out at the geese gliding across the shimmering lake.

"Papa Ji, you are here," I repeated. "You have been here all along. The dead can only see those they love. The dead can only see those they love."

I closed my eyes and placed my hands on my lap, palms facing up. I took a deep breath and listened to the rippling water and wind in the trees. Then I felt it: the texture of his hand close over mine, the memory that was the texture, the texture that was the memory.

How do we make peace with beloved ones who become ghosts? The secret is to understand that our relationship with them has not ended even though they are gone. If haunting is possible in death, then healing is possible, too. The dance is endless: The circle of listening goes on even after death when their voice becomes internal to us. The moment I get quiet enough to listen, I can hear my grandfather's voice humming inside me, and I can feel his love, the sweet labor that nourished me through childhood and sustained us even through the years when we could not understand each other, the love that returned us to each other on his deathbed and is returning me to him even now—love that outlasts life.

Institutions in our society need reinventing. Time has come for a new dream. That's what being a revolutionary is.

—*Grace Lee Boggs*

6.
reimagine.

IN MY EARLY LIFE AS AN ACTIVIST, MARCHING IN THE STREETS, BULLHORN to lips, I used the language of resistance. Resistance—to everything from war to white supremacy to the destruction of the earth—was necessary for survival. In the traditional activist playbook, we resist the actions of our opponents with the goal of removing them from power. But the longer I spent listening to the stories of marginalized people, tending to their wounds, the more I heard a deeper longing—for a future where we were all safe and secure in our bodies, free to pursue our dreams, where our social, political, and economic institutions supported not just our survival but our flourishing. We could resist with all our might and never deliver such a future. We needed to do more than *resist*. We needed to *reimagine* the world.

The greatest social reformers in history did not only resist oppressors—they held up a vision of what the world ought to be. Nanak sang it. Muhammad led it. Jesus taught it. Buddha envisioned it. King dreamed it. Dorothy Day labored for it. Mandela lived it. Gandhi died for it. Grace Lee Boggs fought for it for seven decades. They called for us not only to unseat bad actors but to reimagine the *institutions of power* that ordered the world. Take any crisis and notice its antecedents—in the United States, some of the same detention camps that hold migrant children today once held Japanese Americans and before that indigenous people; the criminal justice system controls more black people today than were enslaved in the year 1850; the military-industrial complex that President Eisenhower warned about in the 1950s has run a war on terror for so long that distant war has become a normal feature of American life. Any social harm can be traced to institutions that produce it, authorize it, or otherwise profit from it. To undo the injustice, we have to imagine new institutions—and step in to lead them.

I was slow to arrive at this conclusion. As I began to listen more to my opponents as human beings and understand the self-inflicted wounds of cruelty, I did not just want to hold them accountable; I wanted to change the institutions that allowed them to harm us. I finally took my college professor's advice and applied to law school. My friends Shannon and Jess from the Pocket made the same choice. We thought it would be Justice School, a place to learn how to fight the machine. What followed was an education in what it *really* takes to change institutions of power—institutions like an elite law school, a corrupt police department, a notorious military base, and a supermax prison.

The Law School

Yale Law School sits like the crown jewel of the university, Gothic spires puncturing the sky. Inside there is one grand hallway where nearly all of the life of the law school takes place. The school is small—only about two hundred students in my class. I knew my way to the dining hall, the library, and the lockers. But the rest of the law school was impenetrable to me—a series of mazes and half floors so opaque that they may well have contained shifting staircases. The building is adorned with stained glass and stone sculptures that depict fantastic scenes of law and justice—a frowning judge, a criminal holding a decapitated head, a witness with flowing tears, a talking parrot, a queen.

"It's like Hogwarts!" my friend Zach exclaimed as he tossed me a juggling ball on the New Haven Green. "You're a student of magic!" I liked that idea and decided that I would learn the law as if it were a set of magic spells, incantations that when spoken in the correct order had the power to compel individuals and institutions to do things in the world. It was up to us whether the magic was used for good or ill. I painted the words "Book of Spells" on parchment paper in gold paint and hung it above my bookshelf. When professors and judges in black robes passed me in the great hallway, I imagined them as witches and wizards.

Classes began. I took my seat and opened my casebook highlighted in multiple colors, my questions scribbled in the margins of the page. The professor opened up a class chart and began to call on students: *State the facts of the case. Apply the law to the facts. Deliver the result. Demonstrate why the result would or would not apply in other cases.* And I said nothing. Throughout the class. Every class. I looked down at my notes, confused. My questions about the people in these cases—their lived experience, their social location, the context of their actions—did not seem to matter here. I had nothing to offer. Traditional legal pedagogy was about training students to "think like a lawyer." My questions were outside the scope of legal analysis.

I started dreading class. "Ms. Kaur, what is the applicable statute?" My heart beat in my ears. Other students would come to my rescue. Had I seen *The Paper Chase,* I would have realized that my professors were using a light version of the Socratic method, opining about theory much more than at other law schools, and not *trying* to shame students. No matter, I did that to myself. Clutching books to chest, I looked up at the portraits of famous scholars and alumni on the walls of the law school. Nearly all of them were graying white men. I imagined them coming alive, peering down at me, demanding passwords I did not know. I started to tie my long hair back at the nape of my neck. I stopped wearing earrings. I de-feminized myself without realizing it, as if that would make me think like a lawyer.

One morning, a few months into law school, I went to meet Reva Siegel, my constitutional law professor, a legend in the field for her scholarship in law and social movements. We were supposed to discuss my legal memo on the First Amendment and freedom of speech. I had just gotten the news that Papa Ji had died. I was sad and depressed and did not know why I was here, so far from home, in a place where my voice had no value. Reva said that my shawl was beautiful and I said that I was wearing white because my grandfather had just died and she put down my memo and teared up and said: "I remember your grandfather from your film." I didn't know she had seen my film. "I see you," she said. "I see your grandfather in you. I also see that you are resisting the law."

How did she know?

"I want to tell you that the law will not change who you are," she said. "The law is about who we are as a society, and you came here with passions about how we should be as a society. It would be a tragedy if you let the law destroy your imagination. It is possible for you to learn the language of the law and still retain the rest of yourself. But you must do things in a twofold way while you are here: You must reason as a lawyer so that you are paying attention to what constitutes a legal reason, *and* you must watch what is happening to you as you do this. How is the law intending to change you? What does it include and what does it leave out? What are the other lenses you choose to protect? If you protect the rest of your imagination while you are here, you will leave this place with your sense of self intact. You will use the law as one of many tools. It will make you more powerful. But you have to stop resisting the law first."

I wrapped my shawl tight around my shoulders.

"Don't let the law change how you think," Reva said. "It is your job to change how the law thinks."

I could hear Papa Ji's instruction. "Do not abandon your post."

I nodded.

Knowing I could not do this alone, I thought of my small group—Lauren, Tommy, Tafari, and the thirteen of us who had been grouped together in a cohort. They were the most brilliant people I had met. We had every class together and studied together and shared meals and drinks together, so we weren't intimidated by each other. I called Lauren over to my apartment and confessed to her that every time I opened my casebook, I could hear a voice in my head that said that I was not smart enough or good enough. "Oh my god, me too!" she said. Lauren had served in the Peace Corps in West Africa before coming to law school and carried within her the stories and struggles of people whose voices were absent here. It was a relief to know that we were not alone. "If the law is a language of power, we will become fluent in it," I declared, channeling Reva. "But we will not let the law colonize the other ways of knowing, speaking, listening, and reasoning we cultivated before we came here." Lauren and I started meeting regularly, and our meetings became more important as we became aware of how the law school worked.

Yale Law School does not have class rankings or grades. But in an institution consistently ranked as the top law school in the country, competition is fierce. Students just compete in ways that are harder to see. Most of our class arrived with public interest aspirations. Lauren and I watched as those aspirations fell to the wayside in an effort to attain each new marker of prestige—clinching a position on the journal, landing a summer job at a big law firm, impressing professors enough for a recommendation letter, securing a clerkship with a federal judge. None of these things were wrong in themselves. It's just that many of our classmates pursued them because they were markers of success, not because they advanced a vision of how they wanted to serve the world. There was even a name for it—"prestige-chasing." Law school is not designed to produce revolutionaries who overturn institutions of power but to initiate new generations of elites into how power works.

We upped our game. Lauren and I took a vow together to make the law more loving—to remember the people we came here to serve, find ways to bring them into the room, and let *them* guide our metrics for success. Our meetings turned into rituals. We lit candles, opened journals, and took turns asking each other questions: *What are you grateful for? Why are you here? What changes are you ready to make to stay true to yourself?* We made a tiny space for ourselves in the law school— our own pocket of sisterhood. When we started to suspect that we were not alone in our longing, we began to gather other women in my apartment, where we would all share our struggles. It felt like the only place where we could be vulnerable. I eventually became co-chair of the Women of Color Collective, a law school affinity group. Nearly every day someone was on my couch, working through their tears or fears. Soon my little apartment on Lynwood Place became a meeting space outside the law school, a place to rage and listen and reimagine the law and ourselves in it.

❧

The most powerful institutions in the United States were not built for most of us to be there, let alone hold any kind of power inside them. Law schools were not originally built for women or people of color, certainly not women of color. But that doesn't mean that we don't belong there now or that we cannot change them. Our task is to protect our sense of self-worth when such places make us feel ashamed of who we are or how we think. It begins with finding the people who will listen to you deeply, ask the right questions, "hear you into being," and draw out your imagination. I discovered that meeting regularly in safe spaces outside the walls of the institution is necessary to nurture bravery. At first these gatherings will feel like pockets of resistance, acts of survival. Then you might invite a new person to join you. And then another. And another. Soon that space might grow. Before you know it, you will not be resisting anymore. You will be embodying a different set of norms. From here, you can see the institution with new eyes and find opportunities for intervention. Or revolution.

I did not think that those sacred spaces we held through law school would amount to anything except our own survival. I could not have known that ten years later, the women of Yale Law would wage an all-out revolt, occupying the great hallway in sit-ins, calling for equity and justice. Such a revolution, messy, complicated, and still under way, seemed impossible when I was a student. But isn't that how social change works? A thousand small acts that don't seem to make a difference, until a critical mass bursts into public consciousness. The spaces for solidarity and sisterhood we had created were necessary for future generations to go further, just as Reva and her generation of women had made it possible for us. I did not know any of this in my first year. I was just relieved I had kept my promise: I did not abandon my post.

❧

I immersed myself in the study of Constitutional Law, the subject that Reva taught. I can't say much for my performance in my other first-year classes, but Con Law I mastered. Reva, my only woman professor, ran her seminar more around shared inquiry than interrogation. I don't know how things would have gone without her. All I know is that I found a way into the law. It began with a simple but profound revelation: The founders crafted the U.S. Constitution to consolidate power for white Christian men of an elite class. The rest of us were not counted in "we the people." The law was designed to colonize and control the rest of us, not set us free. And yet the founders had invoked words whose power even they could not constrain—justice, freedom, equality, the guarantee of life, liberty, and the pursuit of happiness. These were magical words that had a power of their own and seized the imagination of the people for whom they were never meant. In every generation, people had risen up in movements to unleash the magic of these words, to bleed for these words and expand the "we" in "we the people" to include more and more of us. Constitutional Law was an archive of these expansions and contractions.

And so, in case after case, I witnessed the fate of our nation's progress hinge on the invocations and interpretations of words in the Constitution—the technicalities of classifications, the particular shape of the linguistic baskets of life, liberty, and property, the procedural and substantive adjustments in the execution of due process. At some point, from somewhere deep under the words on the page, I began to hear the roar of the "revolutionary river" that scholar-activist Vincent Harding describes, a current flowing through centuries of history streaked with the blood of people who gave their lives to movements that secured victories now enshrined in the law. I was beginning to feel differently in my body. The more I read, the more I felt my weight sagging down into the page, heavier and heavier each time, until the text tore and I fell through. I had stopped resisting. I was inside the law now, my feet in the river, words running up and down and sideways, a matrix that ordered the world around me, and I was cracking the spells.

Then I found the basement.

In our second semester of law school, Lauren and I walked down the long pristine hallway, crossed the courtyard, opened a door, and stepped into a basement we did not know existed. It was a different world, frenetic and urgent, coffee cups strewn on tables, students strategizing behind closed doors about their clients—inmates on death row, immigrants in deportation proceedings, detainees at Guantánamo. Yale is one of the few law schools in the country where first-years can apply to clinics. Here students represent real clients in real cases under the supervision of professors. It was as if two schools existed in one—one removed from the world, one enmeshed in the world; one for learning the spells, one for using them. The minute we walked in, we knew that we had found our home. Lauren joined a human rights clinic and I joined an immigration clinic. We had found our Justice School.

Professor Michael Wishnie was the mastermind of the Worker and Immigrant Rights Advocacy Clinic, known as the most demanding clinic at the law school. Mike was a passionate educator and die-hard advocate with legal genius and supreme calm. Under his direction, the clinic won complex civil rights cases and developed new legal strategies that served as templates for the rest of the country. His co-professor was Muneer Ahmad, a Muslim American lawyer and visionary scholar whose work had deeply influenced me even before law school. Mike, Muneer, and a series of clinical fellows made the clinic a training ground for future revolutionaries. My clinic teammates would go on to remake the nation's social justice landscape— Becca Heller built the International Refugee Assistance Project, the organization that fought policies like Muslim bans and won lifesaving protection for refugees; Ady Barkan became the face of Medicare for All after his diagnosis of ALS and spearheaded the organizing force Be a Hero; Chesa Boudin was elected district attorney of San Francisco with an ambitious plan to reform criminal justice. One day *our* portraits would be up on the walls of the law school to inspire future generations.

In our first meeting, Mike introduced the docket of cases. The clinic had a heavy load. Each new student was to join two cases, a litigation case and a nonlitigation project such as legislative or media advocacy for an organization. By the time Mike was done describing all the cases, I was dizzy. "One more thing," he said. A local priest had just reached out to the clinic. His parishioners were coming to him with complaints about the police. The priest was going to hold a meeting at the church. "There's no room for a new case on the docket," Mike said, "but would anyone like to go?" *Police abuse,* I thought. I raised my hand and volunteered.

The Police Department

February 5, 2009, was a cold night. I crunched through the snow and went down into the basement of St. Rose of Lima, a Catholic church a few miles from the law school. Families sat in a circle with children on their laps. I took a seat next to a classmate in the far corner. Father James Manship welcomed us and opened with a prayer in Spanish. Inspired by Catholic social teachings, he focused on the needs of the most vulnerable people in his congregation. He stood next to Sister Mary Ellen Burns, a nun in full habit who had just founded a legal organization to serve local immigrants. Father Jim wrote on the board:

"PODER."

"Quien tiene poder en esta ciudad?" he asked. Who has the power in this city?

People called out, *"La policia!" "Los politicos!"*

Father Jim drew two columns: "the world as it is" and "the world as it ought to be." In the world as it is, yes, the police and politicians have the power. But what about the world as it ought to be?

Silence—until someone in the back said: *"El Dios!"*

And someone in the front whispered: *"La gente."*

Yes, the people have power when they stand together with God in their hearts, Father Jim summarized. He was inviting them to imagine a world in which they had not only dignity but power. One by one, people stood to tell their stories. Some pulled back their sleeves to show scars they had received at the hands of the police.

East Haven, a small New England industrial town, was also home to a growing Latinx population, and the racial resentment was palpable. The local police department already had a troubled history with people of color, most notably the police killing of a young black man, Malik Jones, in 1997. Now East Haven police officers were stopping and detaining Latinx residents without reason, sometimes beating or tasering them. Shopkeepers watched officers waiting to harass customers outside their stores. Families were afraid to walk or drive through parts of town. In story after story, we heard terror in people's voices. When asked whether they would tell their stories in public, they shook their heads. It was far too dangerous.

"But we are not alone," said Father Jim. "We have our lawyers here!"

All eyes flew to the corner of the room to my classmate and me. I swallowed hard. I had only completed one semester of law school—but I knew how to listen to stories. I returned to the clinic with a stack of testimonies to persuade Mike to put East Haven on our docket.

"If you want to take on the case as your nonlitigation project," said Mike, "it's yours."

We were collecting more stories of police abuse when we got the news. Father Jim had been arrested. A Latinx shopkeeper had called the priest when police officers began to harass him in his store. Father Jim arrived and started recording them with a digital camera. The officers ordered him to stop recording, seized the camera, and led him out in handcuffs. The arrest of their priest enraged and emboldened the community. On the steps of the courthouse after Father Jim's court appearance on March 4, community members broke their silence to the press for the first time. I stood proudly by their side.

A few nights later, I was hosting a dance party in my tiny apartment. This was still our first year of law school, and our small group was inseparable. Lauren and I were laughing, Tommy was serving drinks, Tafari was telling a joke. My phone rang.

"Please come!" a woman cried. "The police are arresting people in front of my store."

"Everyone clear out!" I said. My friends moaned and collected their things. I only had to say one word to explain—"Clinic."

"Tafari, let's go!" I said.

"Right there with you, Kaur."

Tafari and I were working on the case together. He had a broad smile, quick wit, and serious passion to stomp out corruption. Raised by a black single mother who was a teacher and community organizer in Denver, his arrival at Yale Law School was as improbable as mine. We drove to the scene. The police were retaliating against the people who had spoken in public, trailing them home, stalking their businesses. I was racked with guilt. We had encouraged them to step forth, but we were the privileged law students who had little to lose. They had everything to lose. I told them that they could back down. But they had seized upon the magic in the words we had offered them: "You have *rights*. The police are violating your *civil rights*. In the world as it ought to be, the police are here to serve and protect you, not terrorize you." Undaunted, they were ready to take on the police department, if we stayed by their side.

We planned our first major press conference to alert the public to the scope of abuse and pattern of retaliation for March 11. The evening before, Marcia, John, Pedro, and Angel prepared their testimonies; Tafari and I worked with them long into the night. In the morning, we sat with them in the empty church and waited as the press set up downstairs. After so much frenetic work, it was our first moment of quiet. Dust motes floated in the sunlight that poured through the stained glass windows. Father Jim stood to speak. I glanced at the clock. The press conference was scheduled to begin. We didn't have time to pray!

"Today, you are going to speak your truth," said Father Jim softly. "We will stand with you."

I turned around and the pews had filled with dozens of people from the community, no longer in the shadows. Everyone rose to their feet, and, as we walked out of the church doors, the people broke into a song—a song in Spanish, a song of longing and liberation that seemed to flow down to us through the centuries like a river, sweeping us up in the current. My heart soared, and my eyes welled up with tears. *Vismaad*. We were no longer leading, we were being carried forth, from that dark night in the basement church into the light of day.

Our people took the podium and faced the cameras. In their stories and tears, they were invoking the right to equal protection under the law guaranteed in the Constitution. The right to interpret the Constitution does not belong to lawyers and judges alone. It belongs to the people. It always has. Our job as their lawyers was to help make their song heard. The Fourth Amendment protects against "unreasonable searches and seizures." The Fourteenth Amendment promises "equal protection under the law." Reva had taught us these spells; Mike was showing us how to cast them. We presented a formal complaint to the Department of Justice calling for a federal investigation:

The East Haven Police Department has engaged in and continues to engage in a pattern or practice of racial profiling that deprives Latinos in East Haven of rights, privileges, or immunities secured or protected by the Constitution (including the

Fourth and Fourteenth Amendment) or the laws of the United States, in violation of 42 U.S.C. § 14141(a).

These words launched a full-throated campaign. My clinic team drafted memos, organized press conferences, crafted complaints, all while listening to the community. I was also listening to our opponents: Through the public statements of police officers, I began to understand the culture of the department. It was not going to be enough to go after individual officers as if they were a few bad apples. They operated inside an institution that condoned and rewarded officers who targeted Latinx people in police stops and then called on immigration officials to deport them. Our campaign persuaded the Department of Justice Civil Rights Division to open an investigation. This was only the second such investigation opened by the Obama administration; the first was of Sheriff Joe Arpaio's department in Maricopa County, Arizona. East Haven was thrust into the national spotlight. The police did not respond well.

"Is he following us?" I asked late one night. Father Jim was driving me home after our meeting at a parishioner's store in East Haven. We turned, the police car followed. We made a U-turn and headed in the other direction. The police car trailed us. We pulled into a parking lot, and the officer waited on the other side. I held my breath. He followed us until we reached the city limits of East Haven, as if chasing us out of town. Soon the legal battle heated up. The police department hired Hugh Keefe, an aggressive trial lawyer and formidable adversary who had long represented police departments in the state. This was going to be an uphill battle.

Tafari and I worked the case through law school—it defined our legal education. In the basement of the clinic and the basement of the church, I was learning what kind of lawyer I was—a movement lawyer. Traditional lawyering is about representing an individual client within an adversarial system and using law as the dominant tool. Movement lawyering is about accompanying communities in broader movements for social change. It requires integrating the law into other strategies—and that means *harnessing the rest of our imagination*. In this case, we pursued public, administrative, legislative, and media advocacy before we ever filed a lawsuit. And we won.

The Justice Department released the results of their investigation in December 2011, almost three years after we launched the case. It found that the East Haven Police Department had engaged in widespread "biased policing, unconstitutional searches and seizures, and the use of excessive force." I testified in a grand jury about the intimidation and retaliation I witnessed. Four white police officers, including the one who tailed me, were arrested on charges of conspiracy, false arrest, excessive force, and obstruction of justice. Two officers pled guilty, and the two others went to trial and were convicted on all counts. All four officers, along with the longtime chief of police, left the department—nearly 10 percent of the entire force. It was now time to reform the department.

In long meetings in the church, clinic students asked community members how *they* would reimagine the police department, then translated those ideas into seven demands delivered to the DOJ. The Justice Department pursued six of the seven demands and orchestrated a consent decree, an agreement that forces police officials and mayors to enact reforms by a deadline. Two years later, a federal report said the town had made "remarkable" progress. A year after that, Attorney General Loretta Lynch called East Haven a model for improving police-community relations, and it has since been used in reforming police departments around the country, from Ferguson to Baltimore.

Meanwhile, clinic students after us and their co-counsel filed a civil rights lawsuit, *Chacon v. East Haven Police Department*. It was a way to pursue the seventh demand: sanctuary policies to separate the police department from Immigration and Customs Enforcement. The suit culminated in a groundbreaking settlement with the Town of East Haven in 2014. The town agreed to pay $450,000 and adopt a new policy to limit the police's involvement in immigration enforcement. It became the strongest sanctuary ordinance in Connecticut. "With this settlement, East Haven has now adopted some of the strictest constraints on immigration enforcement of any city or town in the nation," Mike explained. "This settlement is a testament to the courage and patience of the plaintiffs, who committed themselves to seeking justice not just for themselves, but for the community," said his co-counsel. Years later, when the Trump administration would unleash a deportation force to initiate mass raids across the country, East Haven would not comply, by order of this settlement. The East Haven Police Department is not perfect. But the community had ended the police's reign of terror—and then remade the department. This was more than resistance. This was transformation.

❧

In the years to come, when working on other cases and campaigns, whenever things felt impossible, I would look back on the story of East Haven. From the start, we were part of a diverse coalition that built grassroots power—faith leaders, lawyers, students, small business owners, and community members. The coalition centered the community and tried to follow their lead. In listening to our opponents, we determined that our goal was not just to remove bad actors but to remake an institution. Under the direction of Mike and Muneer, we engaged the right strategies at the right time and sustained advocacy for years with the formidable resources of the law school. But none of this would have been possible had the church basement not been a place for the community to reimagine the world *as it ought to be*.

Every social justice movement in the United States has been infused with the energy of faith leaders who ignite our moral imagination and connect us with our ability to re-create the world around us. We do not need religion to imagine the world we want. But we do need more spaces to imagine and wisdom about how to do it. Prophetic teachers and faith leaders can offer sacred spaces for collective imagining, rituals for resilience, and stories and songs of ancestors that infuse our struggles with purpose. They can lift our gaze beyond immediate victories toward the world we are longing for, as Father Jim and Sister Mary Ellen did for us in that church basement. When we hold fast to a vision of the world as it ought to be, we can better discern which institutions can be reimagined, and which cannot.

I would soon learn that some institutions are so monstrous that they cannot be remade. Instead we have to imagine the world without them.

The Military Base

In my second year of law school, I took a seminar about the U.S. detention centers in Guantánamo Bay, Cuba, taught by Professors Eugene Fidell and Linda Greenhouse. I had spent the summer as a legal intern on the Senate Judiciary Committee on Capitol Hill, writing memos for congressional hearings about the atrocities that had taken place at Guantánamo. Now I was spending hours in the library, going deeper. When Professor Fidell needed a legal observer to go to the base to report on the military commissions on behalf of his organization—the National Institute of Military Justice—I volunteered. I wanted to understand this place before it became a relic of history.

On October 5, 2009, I flew to Guantánamo Bay, Cuba, with a few dozen military personnel, lawyers, and reporters. I clutched a three-hundred-page binder I had assembled for this trip. It was filled with newspaper stories, human rights reports, and law review articles on atrocities that had taken place here: beatings, sleep deprivation, stress positions, force-feedings, waterboarding, and other forms of torture, as well as solitary confinement, suicides, and homicides. The iconic images of prisoners who first arrived here in January 2002 were seared into my mind: brown men in orange jumpsuits, their eyes and ears masked, their hands tied, kneeling in the gravel, caged like animals.

The Bush administration had used Guantánamo to hold prisoners in the war on terror—nearly eight hundred prisoners, all Muslim, most without charge or trial. On the campaign trail, President Obama said, "In the dark halls of Abu Ghraib and the detention cells of Guantánamo, we have compromised our most precious values." On his second day in office, he signed an executive order to close the prison. Nine months later, I thought we would be among the last visitors here.

I stepped off the plane and caught my breath. The Caribbean Sea spread before me, shimmering blue. The air was crisp and clear, and green mountains loomed in the distance, covered in mist. I was a dark smudge against the sunlit coast. I did not expect awe to be my first experience of Guantánamo. Nervously, I rode the ferry across the bay, flanked by military personnel, and was escorted onto the naval base to find . . . *America*. There was a Starbucks with a view of the bay. Palm trees swayed in front of McDonald's. The bowling alley was attached to the Taco Bell, where television screens played reruns of *Friends*. We passed restaurants, tennis courts, state-of-the-art sports fields, indoor gyms, and outdoor movie theaters. The Commissary had everything one would find in a local Walmart. I walked into the specialty gift shop to find T-shirts, baby bibs, shot glasses, cookie jars, and snow globes, all with bright letters painted on the side: GUANTÁNAMO BAY! It was a fantastical cross between small-town America and a Caribbean seaside resort.

"This is the nicest military base I've ever seen," said my military escort. He stopped the car at a road disappearing behind gigantic windmills and pointed ahead. "Just over that hill are the detention centers. That's restricted. It's too bad, because the golf course is down there."

Right, the golf course. Maybe I just needed to squint slightly to see the prison as another feature of everyday life, like the windmills on the hill, the shells on the beach, or the school down the road. Or maybe the plane to Guantánamo transported me into some alternate dimension where the things I thought happened had not happened, at least not for the people here: The world had not roundly condemned torture and indefinite imprisonment at Guantánamo; our new president had not signed an order to close the prison; it was not a symbol of shame; we had not done unspeakable things.

"Are you a family member of one of the detainees?" asked a military officer. I was startled back into awareness of my body. When I said that I was not, he asked, "Well, what country are you from?"

I was repeatedly mistaken for anything but an American legal observer. The workers running the cash registers and sweeping the floors were Filipino, Haitian, and Jamaican migrants, third-country nationals contracted to work on the base for years for a few dollars an hour. In this place, brown and black migrant workers served a multiracial U.S. military that incarcerated Muslims. I could be a migrant, a soldier, or a detainee's sister.

"It's weird being here," I said to another legal observer.

"Oh yeah, I know what you mean," he said. "I was just like you my first time here: There's a Starbucks on Guantánamo?! But on my umpteenth trip, I'm like, where's my latte?"

I was dropped off at "Camp Justice"—a clearing of about a hundred semipermanent khaki military tents designated for lawyers, reporters, and observers of the military commissions. They separated us into far corners of the camp, so that it seemed like I was the only one there. Under the full moon, Camp Justice felt like an otherworldly suburbia, a tent city on gray asphalt bordered by barbed wire and orange barricades at the edge of the bay. I ducked into the tent to find a mattress, small refrigerator, and wooden dresser with a fake orchid in a corner. The growling air-conditioning unit kept the tent frigid. Like a homesick child, I wolfed down the *idli sambar* that Amma, Sharat's mother, had packed for me that morning. But did I ever leave home? Today I had ordered nachos, sat on a beach, passed a McDonald's, and had already been asked, "Where are you from?" I dragged my plastic lawn chair out of the cold tent into the orange glow of a floodlight and wrote in my journal, "I've fallen down the rabbit's hole." I didn't know whether I had landed on the southeastern tip of Cuba, a chipped-off piece of the United States, or a dark anomalous zone willed into the world by sheer imagination.

I opened up my binder. Guantánamo Bay is technically Cuban territory. The United States occupies the land that makes up the forty-five-square-mile base under a colonial-era lease that gives it "complete jurisdiction and control" over the land. Yet the U.S. government has argued that Guantánamo lies outside the jurisdiction of the United States—and therefore beyond the reach of the U.S. Constitution. The government first made this argument in the 1990s when it intercepted thousands of Haitian refugees on the high seas and detained those who tested HIV-positive at Guantánamo. The Clinton administration claimed that the Haitians "had no constitutional rights whatsoever." My clinic professor, Mike Wishnie, had been part of the clinic team that took the administration to federal court when *he* was a student at Yale Law School. Back then, they argued that the Constitution reaches Guantánamo—and won. The government shut down the HIV camp and allowed Haitians to come to the mainland, but then successfully negotiated for the court decision to be vacated—in other words, wiped clean from the books. One moment, the Constitution reached Guantánamo. The next, Guantánamo disappeared once again into a legal black hole.

Fast-forward to 2002—President Bush chose Guantánamo as the destination for terrorism suspects after 9/11 precisely so that the detainees would not have the constitutional right to contest their detention. He declared that detainees in the war on terror were not "prisoners of war" protected under the Geneva Conventions but "unlawful enemy combatants" who had no rights at all. And the American public let it happen. The government relied on fear of "Muslim terrorists" as subhuman monsters, so savage that they were not worthy of the protection of the laws of the civilized world. They were "the worst of the worst," beyond the circle of human beings who had

rights. The truth is that nearly all of these prisoners were not dangerous operatives. Most would be held for years without any evidence
against them.

Once again, civil rights lawyers challenged the government's position that Guantánamo was outside the reach of the U.S. Constitution.
Words like "due process" simply did not fall into the sea. The magic
of those words reached these shores that were controlled by the
United States. Years of legal battle followed. The Supreme Court
found that detainees had the right to challenge their detention in federal courts, but the government blocked their every effort to reach
them. While the courts and Congress and the president wrestled back
and forth on the reach of the Constitution, prisoners waited in cages.
Even three sweeping Supreme Court victories—*Rasul v. Bush* in 2004,
Hamdan v. Rumsfeld in 2006, and *Boumediene v. Bush* in 2008—made no
meaningful difference in the lives of most prisoners: Not one has been
released as a result of a court order. By 2009, there was one change.
Some detainees were able to be heard in the military commissions that
the U.S. government set up on the base. These were not federal courts.
They were military commissions created specifically for prisoners in
the war on terror. It took years of advocacy just to secure the rights of
reporters and nongovernment organizations to witness them. That's
why I was here: to observe one of these hearings and report back to
the world.

On the morning of the hearing, I dressed in a gray suit, trying not
to let my pants touch the dirty wooden floor of my tent. It felt like a
costume. I made my way up the hill that overlooked Camp Justice and
took my seat inside a plain courtroom. A soldier in front of me waited
patiently, clutching a thick spiral book with a bold title on the cover:
Manual for Military Commissions. A few dozen military personnel, lawyers, and spectators chatted casually—until the doors swung open and
four soldiers led in the defendant. The room fell silent and all eyes fell
on Omar Khadr.

The first thing I noticed was Omar's hands, held at shoulder level,
fingers spread delicately in a surprisingly tender posture, barely touch-

ing the soldiers leading him. The softness in his hands did not seem to go with the body that followed. Omar was no longer a boy. He had a fuzzy black beard and his broad shoulders and chest filled out his white uniform. Omar was fifteen years old when U.S. soldiers captured him on the battlefield in Afghanistan. They say he threw a grenade that killed a soldier. Omar was taken to Bagram Prison and then Guantánamo, where it is believed that he was tortured during interrogations, detained in isolation for months at a time, forced into painful stress positions, threatened with rape, confronted with barking dogs, and once used as a "human mop" after he urinated on the floor during an interrogation session. Omar had been imprisoned seven years and had just turned twenty-three. He grew up at Guantánamo. Muneer Ahmad, my clinic professor, had once represented Omar and argued that he had the rights of a child soldier under international treaty, but the U.S. government insisted on continuing to try him as an adult in Guantánamo's military commissions. It was Omar's sixteenth visit to this courtroom.

Omar took his seat at the defense table and asked for a pen. He spent the hearing doodling on a yellow legal pad. "I don't care how old he is," a welfare officer whispered to me, "he has the mindset of a fifteen-year-old."

Omar spoke twice during the hearing. He repeated "Yes, sir" when the judge asked him whether he wanted to change his legal counsel. The judge then spent the majority of the hearing considering whether Omar had the right to protect the privacy of his own legal notes.

As the judge and lawyers went back and forth, I gazed around the room. It looked like a courtroom. It felt like a courtroom. But it lacked the legal precedent to resolve basic legal issues like attorney-client privilege. Without a foundation in centuries of American law, these judges and lawyers turned to other judicial systems in order to figure out how to proceed. But this, too, was arbitrary: They compared commissions to other systems to support one position, then claimed Guantánamo's exceptionalism to support another. The hearing began to feel more like theater than a court proceeding. The absence of legal precedent exposed the illusion. It was like gazing into a dark hole where the law should have been. In the end, the government spent at least $100,000 over the course of four days to hold a twenty-nine-minute hearing devoted almost entirely to a detainee's right to his legal notes, an issue that would not have been an issue at all in federal court—and left it unresolved.

All of this made no difference to Omar, who continued to doodle. "What does 'habeas corpus' mean?" Professor Fidell had asked in class. "Bring me the body!" The right to file a writ of habeas corpus in order to contest your detention meant that the state must produce your body before the law. It must lift you up from the shadows into a courtroom where you are seen and heard by others. I thought of it as the most powerful spell. It was a writ of habeas corpus that was filed in the effort to free my turbaned Sikh grandfather from his detention on Angel Island when he arrived in America a century ago. I would not exist without this spell. Here at Guantánamo, where people were detained not just for months but for years, the Bush administration had insisted that detainees like Omar did not have the right to habeas corpus. But the Supreme Court had ruled that habeas corpus reached this island. Omar had been given the right to speak. His speech was constrained by the made-up rules of the commissions, but still something took place. At the very least, Omar appeared. We saw him, and he saw us. He only said four words in the entire hearing, but it was as if his body said, "I am here," and the words echoed in me and shook me and made me want to shout out over the ocean to the mainland: *Listen.*

After the hearing, I went to O'Kelly's Irish Pub to write notes in my journal. The bar roared behind me as the Yankees scored another run. The pub was loud and crowded, billed as "the newest addition to the Bay's night life." The fake fireplace crackled in the corner, and a mishmash of Irish paraphernalia covered the walls. The bartender wiped glasses clean and served draft beer, scores of bottles glistening behind him. Soldiers and navy officers sat at wooden tables, eating, drinking, watching the game on one of the four plasma screens, or throwing darts at the wall. I could not look in the eyes of any of the men who surrounded me. Omar's face was seared into my mind. Now that I had seen him, nothing felt the same. Any semblance of normalcy around me was a sham.

That's when a soldier plopped down in front of me.

"I see you writing in your book," he said. Which was another way to say, "I see you judging us."

This soldier worked as a guard at the detention centers over the hill.

"Look, the rest of the world doesn't see what I see," he said. "The guards act with professionalism and respect. And the detainees are really intelligent—you have to admire their dedication. They don't play by the rules. They throw bags of feces and urine at us, like, every day."

This soldier, like many here, spoke as if all of Guantánamo's prisoners were guilty.

"We cater to these prisoners," he went on. "We treat them really, really well, as long as they're compliant. And you know what? They get *more freedom* than we do."

He leaned forward. "They make it *easy* for us to hate them."

Rage flushed through my body, my throat closed in, my fists clenched. I wanted to get up and leave. The bar broke out into a roar, a run in the game. But the soldier did not look up. He was looking into his beer. I noticed the sweat on his brow, the way his hands fidgeted. I took a breath. *He has a story. He has a story,* I thought. I forced myself to look into his eyes. Wonder is an act of will.

"Why?" I asked him.

"They get to say anything they want. They get to do anything they want," he said slowly. "We don't." He fidgeted with his purple wristband and took another sip of beer. Soldiers had to wear wristbands to drink when they entered this bar.

Then it happened—I saw a lonely, frail young man. He was a child when 9/11 happened. He signed up for the military to serve his country. He needed to believe that he was fighting for freedom when he watched bombs kill his friends on the battlefield. He needed to believe the people he guarded at Guantánamo were guilty. He resented the world's sympathy for the prisoners and described *himself* as a captive of Guantánamo. *How dare he?* I thought. But all the soldiers here were young—eighteen, nineteen, twenty-two—rotated in batches every year. They were prisoners of a different kind, servants to institutions that trained them to participate in the project of dehumanization. That's how oppression works—it captures generations and assigns each of us roles. On this military base, it had captured *our* generation. *All* of us were young—Omar, this soldier, and me—the prisoner, the guard, the witness. We had not created Guantánamo. We had inherited Guantánamo. In fact, we had inherited *Guantánamos*.

I looked around the bar. O'Kelly's Irish Pub could have been anywhere in the United States. There were pubs and palm trees and Starbucks cafés outside prisons all across America. There must have been an Irish pub somewhere outside the detention center where I had been held in New York. Every prison is located somewhere that feels normal. And yet what takes place behind those doors is not normal. The United States incarcerates more people than any country in the history of the world. In the past thirty years, our prison population increased from around three hundred thousand to more than two million, the majority of the increase attributed to nonviolent drug offenses. The launch of the War on Drugs in 1982 led to a dramatic overhaul in criminal law and sentencing policies, resulting in the rapid mass incarceration of black and brown people, virtually all of them from poor communities. On any given day, one-third of all black men in their twenties are behind bars or on parole. Inside these prisons, violence is routine—murder and rape at the hands of fellow inmates, beatings by guards, inadequate healthcare, and inhumane living conditions. Yet not far from every overcrowded prison, jail, detention center, and migrant camp is just another downtown. We have made a prison society feel normal, and when we glance at the prison doors—whether in Guantánamo Bay, Cuba, or "Guantánamo on the Hudson"—we are tempted to tell ourselves a story that makes it feel normal. We will not be free of Guantánamos until we reimagine a world in which the quarantine of bodies is no longer required to make us believe that we are safe.

I began to understand that magic spells had a limit. Law was a strong tool to reform broken institutions. But these prisons were not broken. They did exactly what they were designed to do. We could not reimagine them—there was no version of them that did not inflict harm. No, we had to dismantle them. We had to imagine America *without* them. We had to imagine a world where *all of us* are free of cages, including the ones who hold the keys to our cells.

I left the bar, returned to Camp Justice, walked down to the beach, and waded into the water, stepping on crushed shells and rocks. I had helped a community stand up to corrupt police officers back in East Haven. But I still had not made peace with the officer who hurt me in "Guantánamo on the Hudson." I closed my eyes and pictured Lieutenant Campo. This time, I did not see a monster. I saw in his hardened face the cost of participating in oppression—the shrunken capacity to love. I felt a softening in my body and the first stirring of compassion for him. I wanted him to be free of Guantánamos, too.

On my last day on the base, I went to the white chapel that stood on a bluff by the sea. At the entrance was a shrine with a woman made of wood, tall and grand, wearing a long blue and gold cloak, holding a baby, with a golden orb around her head. Sailors lost at sea gazed up at her, their eyes wide and hungry, their hands clasped to their chests or clinging to their oars in the storm. They were begging for her help. Her name was Our Lady of Charity—*Nuestra Señora de la Caridad del Cobre*—the Patroness of Cuba and the country's most popular image of the Virgin Mary. Hundreds of years ago, when enslaved Africans were forced to convert to Christianity, they held on to their goddess of love, Oshun, and mapped her onto Mary, hiding their truth in plain sight. She was a benevolent presence above the crying men. But she did not look down at them—her eyes were fixed on the people who entered the chapel. Her eyes were fixed on us—the living. Her eyes were fixed on me.

The Supermax Prison

I returned to law school and couldn't stop thinking about Guantá-namo. I had seen the power of the law, and its limits. Guantánamo was defined by total control, exclusion, and isolation. Social change is only possible when communities are able to mobilize and tell stories that reclaim our imagination. I wanted to help movement lawyers better harness the power of stories in advocacy. I imagined a sort of clinic that trained law students to make films. Sharat came out to Yale, we pitched the idea to Dean Robert Post and Professor Jack Balkin, and with their support we founded the Yale Visual Law Project. Lau-ren and I graduated from law school with our souls intact. She began a child protection fellowship in Haiti on human rights and develop-ment, and I stayed on as a fellow to direct the project. I had found a way to take Reva Siegel's instruction to heart: to try to change the way the law thinks.

We made two films in the first year of the project: *Stigma* told the stories of young black men challenging the police's "stop and frisk" policy in the streets of New York City, and *Alienation* followed Latinx families swept up in immigration raids in Baltimore. Both films played a role in grassroots campaigns for policy change. That's when Profes-sor Hope Metcalf called me into her office. A brilliant and devoted advocate, Hope was known for the compassion she showed to her stu-dents and clients. She represented inmates in a nearby prison and made frequent trips to see them.

"It's like crossing the River Styx," Hope said. "You cross over from bucolic neighborhoods into the prison complex, and you're in a different world. You go down this long hallway and shake your cli-ent's hand, and, in many cases, it's the first time he has touched a human being in years."

Less than an hour from Yale Law School there was a prison that held men in conditions of solitary confinement rivaling the ones at Guantánamo. Solitary confinement has been practiced in U.S. prisons for more than a century. But supermax prisons—*entire* institutions solely designed to hold inmates in isolation—only emerged as a response to Black Power and other movements in the 1970s. Hope described the overwhelming size and concrete mass of these prisons. "It's as if people are buried alive," Hope said. "The supermax is a mass grave with barbed wire." There are as many as eighty thousand people in the United States held in solitary confinement, a third of them in supermax prisons. Today nearly every state has one supermax. Northern Correctional Institution in Connecticut held around four hundred people in solitary, most of them young black and brown men.

Hope knew that we needed more than policy reports to challenge Northern—we needed to make people care. Sharat and I built a team of dedicated students—Eric, Ivy, Jane, Aseem, and Aeryn. "The way we make change is just as important as the change we make!" I declared at our first meeting. No grinding our bones to the ground. The team agreed we would model advocacy that was caring and sustainable. For one year, we investigated the prison together, cameras in hand.

First we talked to inmates and their families. Ros was a mother who routinely made the hour-and-a-half-long drive to visit her son Leighton. He was sent to Northern after he got into a fight during a basketball game at a lower-level prison.

"It's been a blur, like he's always been there," she said, fatigue in her voice. "Visits are half an hour, behind the glass, on a telephone. If we're lucky, it's a phone without static. . . . He'll try to seem like he's okay when we have our visit. He smiles. He'll make jokes with me. But his eyes are, are . . ." she choked up. "They don't reach his eyes, you know."

Ros had reason to worry. Solitary confinement entails twenty-three hours a day in lockdown with one hour of recreation in a larger cage. The cells are the size of a bathroom. The United Nations Special

Rapporteur on torture had determined that spending fifteen days in solitary confinement causes irreparable damage. Yet solitary confinement is not yet considered "cruel and unusual punishment" by U.S. courts. It would be up to the public to invoke the words of the Constitution, exercise our own interpretation, and demand that the courts follow suit.

"You only can take so much," Darnell told us. He was originally sent to prison for dealing drugs. While incarcerated, he was assigned to several facilities, including the state's mental health prison. He was transferred to Northern after disciplinary infractions. "I ended up trying to hang myself. The lieutenant came in and instead of opening up the door and cutting off the noose, because I was unconscious, he maced me. I coughed up blood. I kept coughin' and coughin' and coughin'. They maced me again."

Darnell spent three and a half years in Northern. There are three phases that make up the "Administrative Segregation Program" at the facility. One could complete the program in ten to twelve months. But an inmate in phase three could commit infractions and crash back down to phase one and face another year in the system. Some had been there for years on end. When Darnell was finally released, he was sent directly to the streets.

"That first day I was free, it was like happiness—and confusion," he said. "I had to learn how to be a person again. To this day, I don't feel comfortable around crowds. I still have a problem walking, pronouncing my words, saying words. It's like I had to learn how to talk all over again. I had to be a person again. Because I was an animal for three and a half years."

Commissioner Leo Arnone, the head of the Department of Correction, insisted to us that inmates at Northern were "the worst of the worst." But the majority of inmates we met were nonviolent offenders like Darnell. No one is *sentenced* to Northern. It is a prison for inmates who receive disciplinary tickets in general population. We met a seventeen-year-old, Keishar, who was never convicted of a crime.

While awaiting trial, he was accused of assaulting a correctional offi-cer, given a disciplinary ticket, and sent to Northern. "It was hor-rific," he recalled. "They want you to think of yourself as an animal, as not being human."

We had enough footage to stop there, more than enough. But I was still haunted by the prison guards I met at Guantánamo. I wanted to know what we would find if we listened to our opponents in this story, too. We started to reach out to wardens and former correctional officers who were willing to talk to us. Some of our classmates at the law school were outraged when they found out. *Why should the guards get the same airtime as the prisoners? Why should their stories matter when they are the ones inflicting violence?* My teammates responded that there had been plenty of prison documentaries about inmate stories that didn't change policy. We needed to take the risk. We visited the homes of correctional officers, set up our camera in their living rooms, and lis-tened.

"These officers are the best officers," Mark told us. He was a newly retired correctional officer who had served a decade in Northern. "We're all on the same page. We're all going through the same thing. We're doing it for our families. We're in there doing something no one else wants to do to provide for our families—because we love them."

Love. I was disgusted.

Mark's daughter walked in. He rushed to give her a hug, handed her the car keys, and his smile followed her out the door. "Drive safe!" he called after her. I found my breath and tried to listen harder.

"What is it like to go to work each day?" one of us asked him.

"Like crossing into a war zone," he said. Then he began to describe the high rates of alcoholism, depression, and suicide among the cor-rectional officers.

"Maybe they should have kicked me out of there ten years ago," Mark said as he reflected on the mental toll of working in Northern. "But I stuck it out and stayed. The reason I stayed is because all my other buddies stayed and I'm staying there with them. I got their back and they got my back. I work with some great guys and I'll go into battle with those guys."

"It's that constant stress and pressure of someone in a combat situation," said Wayne, another correctional officer who had just retired. "You know it's coming. When is it going to come and what's going to happen? I've seen staff members, their whole personality change. They may abuse alcohol, or get caught up in a drug situation, their family life changes, they withdraw. I know of several people who committed suicide."

Wayne and Mark were worried about their friend Pete, a fellow correctional officer. Pete's throat was slit by an inmate who used a razor blade affixed to a plastic spork handle.

"How twisted we become because of that job," Pete said. "We sit around and we talk about a guy who was eating his feces and kind of laugh it off. If you did it at a family picnic, your relatives would be picking up the kids and leaving."

Pete's eyes darted from one corner of the room to the other as he spoke. He had been diagnosed with PTSD. He jumped up when he heard loud noises or people running.

"The COs themselves are trapped in this house of mirrors," Hope told us. "All they're seeing is the day-to-day struggle between *us and them*."

"Of course they're animals and they're monsters," Pete said of the inmates. "Otherwise that place wouldn't be there. Even their families have written them off, what families they had."

It was revolting to hear Pete talk like this, but I could no longer see the correctional officers simply as the "bad guys" now that I saw their wounds. The suffering of the prisoner and that of the prison guard, the oppressed and the oppressor, were *not* morally equivalent. But understanding their brokenness expanded my view. What would it take to free *all of us*—victims, oppressors, and witnesses—from institutions that organize violence? We lifted our camera lens to the prison building itself. We tracked down the architect of Northern.

"When we were designing it, there was a desire that their first experience would make an impression," said James Kessler. "The limited environment, the lack of stimulus, it's all about essentially the hope, the belief, that these individuals can change. They put them through this drama. There is nothing soft. It's hard, and they wanted that."

The architect insisted that he never intended for people to lose hope at Northern, that the "choreography" of the prison was designed to compel inmates to complete the program. Instead it brought out the worst of the worst in them, and in the officers. Not to mention it was outrageously expensive. The average cost of incarcerating an inmate at Northern exceeded $100,000 per year, more than twice the cost of housing an inmate in any other facility in Connecticut, or, for that matter, paying tuition at Yale.

Our team spent endless hours in the editing room, distilling hundreds of hours of stories into thirty minutes. We wanted to honor people's stories while making an argument—casting a lawyer's spell with an activist's heart and a filmmaker's magic. Our film *The Worst of the Worst* presented the stories of inmates, correctional officers, wardens, psychiatrists, and officials to show how the supermax prison hurt all who walked through its doors, those behind bars *and* those guarding the cells, their families and communities. The film accompanied a report produced by Hope's clinic and amplified the demands from grassroots community organizers. It made an impression inside Connecticut's halls of power. The Department of Correction began to take steps to reform the prison. Within months of the film's release, Commissioner Arnone began to shut down housing units—two, then six, then eight. The prison population at Northern was reduced from around four hundred to about forty.

I wish the story could end there. A clean victory. A blueprint for reform. If we could do it in Connecticut, then we could help advocates do it in other states, too. If we emptied one supermax at a time, then we could clamp down on the practice of solitary confinement in the United States. We shared the story of Northern as a success story.

But, a few years later, the prison population at Northern quietly began to climb again. The inmates at Northern had been relocated to other prison facilities in the state. Now those same kinds of prisoners were being sent back into solitary. The Department of Correction insisted that it needed Northern. As long as the prison remained in operation, it would continue to be used to sequester inmates from human contact. The change we made did not stand the test of time.

I had focused my attention on Northern and Guantánamo but the "institution" was never any single prison. It was the carceral state. It was not enough to reimagine one prison—we had to reimagine the entire system.

All along, I shared these sorrows and revelations with my friends from the Pocket. Jess was now an immigration attorney, providing direct services to immigrants seeking asylum and relief. Shannon was a psychiatrist, having also gone to medical school, and was working inside the mental health unit of a jail. They, too, had seen our nation's immigration, national security, and criminal justice systems up close. They, too, had reached the same conclusion I had: We needed to support reforms, but we could reform endlessly and still not get the world we wanted. It was time to imagine more boldly and bravely than ever before.

Now the three of us seek out places where people are imagining big—where scholars like Michelle Alexander are calling us to decarcerate America, where Bryan Stevenson seeks abolition of the death penalty, or where Ruth Wilson Gilmore calls for us to abolish prisons altogether and establish new institutions in their place. I am inspired by people creating alternatives to retribution, like restorative justice models that bring communities together to repair harm, rehabilitate offenders, and offer restitution to victims. I start to imagine what might be possible if we poured the resources used to punish people into housing, healthcare, education, art, and job creation. Or if we directed the resources spent on militarized borders and detention centers on border governance, welcoming refugees instead of incarcerating them. Any time my friends and I worry we are dreaming too big, we remind one another that every unjust social institution in history seemed permanent until it was imagined otherwise.

"Slavery, lynching, and segregation are certainly compelling examples of social institutions that, like the prison, were once considered to be as everlasting as the sun," writes activist Angela Davis. "Yet, in the case of all three examples, we can point to movements that assumed the radical stance of announcing the obsolescence of these institutions."

This is *our* moment to declare what is obsolete, what can be reformed, and what must be reimagined. I hold fast to the instruction Reva gave me—to master the world as it is, and labor for what it ought to be. When we create spaces to imagine *together,* like Lauren and I did in law school, or the East Haven parishioners did in their church basement, then we can begin to *feel* the world we want in our bodies. It feels safe and brave and free. It becomes like a memory we carry. We might even find ways for that feeling to expand. We might get chances to create the world we want in the venues of our own lives, here and now.

❧

Sharat and I lived together in New Haven for three years, running the Yale Visual Law Project. We treasured the work but were exhausted all the time. One summer night, he said that he was going to make me dinner. I came home to find our tiny apartment filled with delicious smells. I sat at the kitchen table, and he served us course after course. My "Book of Spells" painting was on the wall behind us. He had put it in a gold frame when I graduated, my real diploma.

"This is a culinary trip through our life together!" he exclaimed. It was a welcome break from talking about prisons.

Each course represented a beautiful memory—roasted garlic and bread from when we fell in love in Chicago, Mexicali chopped salad from a favorite café in Los Angeles, patatas bravas from a romantic restaurant in Boston, late-harvest sauvignon blanc from California wine country, and fresh berry tart with toasted nut crust from Rose Café in Venice Beach. He made everything from scratch. We had been together for six years now. In each course, I tasted our memories.

At the end of dessert, he kneeled down on one knee and asked me to marry him.

"Sure, someday," I said. Until I realized that he was asking for real. Like, right now. This was him proposing. My heart leapt up. Joy flooded through me. My body said *yes,* but my mind said *hold on.* We had weathered so much pain from people who never wanted us married. I also had doubts about the whole institution. I thought of the Punjabi aunties sitting on the *manjee*s in India, relaying story after story of pain. Marriage was a social and legal institution that had cast women as property and cemented traditional gender roles for centuries. Traditional Indian marriages had rituals like dowries and *doli*s, palanquins that literally "transferred" a woman from one family to another. During the wedding ceremony, the bride followed the groom around the fire or around the scripture. I was not going to follow. There was also the small matter that in the course of our scrappy artist-activist lives, Sharat and I had not saved any money for a wedding. I sat him down on the couch and interrogated him for an hour.

"What if we made it ours?" Sharat asked.

He knew how to talk to me. We pulled out paper and markers and began imagining our wedding. If we could make the wedding our own, then we could make marriage ours, too. We asked ourselves: When had we felt most at home in our bodies and at home in the world? What were the elements that made us feel that way? We wrote and dreamed and toasted and planned.

We made our wedding from scratch, out of the United States, far from the city, in the rain forest. It was a week of music and singing and dancing and feasting, weaving together rituals from Sikh and Hindu traditions. During the wedding ceremony, we walked together around the scripture side by side, hand in hand, by the roaring ocean and setting sun. Linda officiated, Zach juggled, Jessica sang, Tafari and Jess emceed, Lauren got me ready, my brother drummed, Sharat's brother Manu toasted, my father beamed, my mother read the *laavan* in Sikh scripture, and Brynn read the poem that married us. Everyone had a role. His parents gave us the words of Sharat's grandfather, the poet Gopalakrishna Adiga: "Let the vessel of my heart float / the river of your smile / dancing to the rhythm of / wave after wave." A little starved hound wandered into the festivities, and we adopted her and named her Shadi, which means "wedding," as if she was our wedding gift from the rain forest. None of our ancestors had chosen their partners or crafted their own ceremony as equals. We were the first generation to do so. In the clearing, we had imagined something new. *We create the beloved community by being in beloved community*. It was New Year's Eve and we danced into the night with fireworks exploding above us. And I felt Papa Ji's blessing.

"The future is an infinite succession of presents, and to live now as we think human beings should live, in defiance of all that is bad around us, is itself a marvelous victory," said historian Howard Zinn.

When we returned, Sharat and I were supposed to go on a honeymoon, but we got consumed by work, which just seemed to get harder. Guantánamo never closed; the inmate population at Northern began to increase. It started to sink in that the labor of institutional change required not months or years, but decades. I knew how to craft big spectacular moments of beloved community—a wedding in the rain forest! a swim with dolphins!—but I did not know how to create respite and communion where it most mattered, in the smaller, humbler moments of daily life. I kept getting sick, again and again. I had come a long way in learning how to love others and even my opponents, but I had not yet learned how to love myself.

part III.

breathe and push
loving ourselves

We have all known the long loneliness and
we have learned that the only solution is love
and that love comes with community.
—*Dorothy Day*

7.
breathe.

THIS TIME, IT HAPPENED AT HOME. MY SKIN BROKE OUT IN A SWEAT, MY legs gave way, and I collapsed on the steps, my back arched. I felt like a mongoose gripped by a boa constrictor, gasping between slow deliberate squeezes. Sharat carried me the rest of the way upstairs, peeled off my clothes, and lowered me into the bath, but my body would not stop writhing. When the contractions came, there was no language in my mind except a voice that said, "Breathe." Sharat held my wrists as I twisted in the water. I leaned over the edge of the bathtub and vomited. He held my back, strong and steady. When the wailing quieted and the water stilled, he laid me on the bed. Our dog, Shadi, came out of hiding and curled up next to me. My back throbbed and the stone in my belly burned, but I fell asleep. Later, when Sharat leaned over me with a cup of herbs, he said that my lips had gone gray. This time it lasted six hours. It would be another twelve hours before I could eat. And another twenty-four hours before I would be able to get out of bed again.

Neither of us called 911, because we knew the pattern and let it run its course. The first episode happened in 2008 while I was volunteering in Barack Obama's campaign headquarters in Austin, Texas. I was rushed to the emergency room, but by the time I arrived, the contractions had quieted and the doctor shrugged, saying it must have been a bad virus. It happened almost every month after that, always at the onset of my period, suddenly, dramatically, without warning. Like labor without the gift. All through law school, my friends Lauren and Tommy were my secret team who knew the drill if Sharat wasn't there. They would bring me clear broth and cover for me when I disappeared for thirty-six to forty-eight hours. Then I would show up in the law school again and walk the great hallway as if everything was fine, as if the contracting and bleeding had never happened, as if my body had not just drowned my mind for two days. Until it happened again the next month. It went on like this for four years.

"Why didn't you tell me?" asked Appa. I had an episode while staying at Sharat's parents' house and they heard me moaning in the bath. Now his father was asking me what was wrong, as a medical doctor with good bedside manner would do. Dr. Tonse Krishna Raju was among the nation's foremost experts on prenatal research, the chief of pregnancy and perinatology at a branch of the National Institutes of Health. I should have told him, but shame kept me silent. It was not my shame alone. I think it was also the ancestral shame of women who for centuries endured a culture where reproductive maladies like mine would cast them out of the house. This ancestral shame ran so deep that it could still live in my body, half a world away. Sharat's family had only showed me love. They were an educated family of letters, my father-in-law an actual scientific expert on conditions like mine. But I did not want them for even a second to regret their son's choice of a partner. So, for four years, I had tried to heal myself—I cut out gluten, dairy, white sugar, and alcohol from my diet; took needles into my skin for acupuncture; drank bitter herbs; and burned moxa on my body at night. But none of it had worked. And now I had to come clean.

"It happens every month, Appa," I said.

He made a call. A specialist at Yale saw me right away and diagnosed the problem: endometriosis. Cells similar to the uterine lining were growing on my ovaries and intestine, bleeding at the onset of my period each month. The intestinal twist from scar tissue caused the abdominal contractions. The condition was correlated with vaginismus. The specialist recommended surgery.

I was lucky. Nearly nine million women and girls in North America suffer from endometriosis, yet it remains underdiagnosed and undertreated, an "invisible" women's disease. On average, women and girls wait eight to eleven years and see five doctors before a confirmed diagnosis. Girls who complain of painful periods are simply not believed. Women of color and low-income women often suffer far longer without access to care. Had I not had a father-in-law who could make a call on my behalf, my condition would have gotten worse, setting me up for organ dysfunction and infertility. The more I learned, the more I blamed a healthcare industry that did not commit enough resources to the health of women and girls. But I did not take time to reflect on why I did not do more to seek out help. I did not think about the shame I still carried under my skin. Or what my decision to suffer silently for four years said about my relationship to my body and how little I prioritized my health. It was hard to see my own suffering as worthy of attention when I was witnessing and working with communities enduring hate, torture, and violence.

At this point, Sharat and I were married and living in New Haven, running the Yale Visual Law Project. I had also become a senior staff member at Auburn Seminary, a two-hundred-year-old progressive seminary in New York City, where I was building an initiative called Groundswell to connect and equip faith leaders working on social justice campaigns. I was inspired by my experience in East Haven, Connecticut, watching church leaders transform a corrupt police department. I wanted Groundswell to give faith groups everywhere access to the same tools to build solidarity and change policy. Groundswell soon became the largest online multifaith organizing community in the country.

I started getting calls to appear on MSNBC as a political commentator and became a regular guest on Melissa Harris-Perry's show. Each day, I commuted between New Haven and my office in Manhattan, working on the train, either creating a Groundswell presentation, arranging a film shoot for my students, or prepping for a television interview. I started sleeping in my NYC office without anyone knowing it. My career was flourishing on the outside, while stress was eating away at me on the inside. The endometriosis episodes got worse each month, but I was too busy to see it. When my diagnosis finally came, I scheduled surgery for August like it was any other event on my calendar.

Then—Sunday, August 5, 2012.

An aerial view of a Sikh gurdwara on the television screen and the words: ACTIVE SHOOTER.

Sharat and I were on our way home from a conference at the White House, where I had spoken on a panel about the now decade-long struggle to combat hate violence against Sikhs. We received frenetic texts, pulled over at a fast-food restaurant somewhere on Highway I-95, and found a television screen. That morning, a white supremacist had entered a Sikh gurdwara in Oak Creek, Wisconsin—and opened fire. Seven people were dead, including the gunman, and many more were injured. It was the most violent hate crime against Sikhs in U.S. history. At that point, it was also the bloodiest attack on any faith community in the United States since the 1963 Birmingham church bombing that had killed four little girls.

The first hours of national media coverage were dismal: Television screens showed images of turbaned men in tears, and the primary response of reporters and audiences was not sympathy but confusion: *Who are these people?* Reporters called us Hindus, Muslims, or foreigners, mispronounced our names, and misrepresented our beliefs. When Sikh advocates finally got through to the right producers at the right television networks, a handful of us were thrust in front of the cameras with a near-impossible task: to explain who Sikhs were in the first place, help people see us not as outsiders but as Americans like them, place this shooting in the broader context of ongoing hate violence since 9/11, invite them to grieve with us, and call them to action, all in two-minute sound bites. As I went from interview to interview, I don't remember feeling much at all except raw in my throat.

"The news is reverberating through every Sikh American household," I said in one interview. "When I saw the television screen, I thought: *That is my gurdwara, those are my aunts and uncles, my brothers and sisters, our children caught in the gunfire, and so . . . right now, every expression of support, every candle lit, every prayer, every story, every message is being deeply felt, not just by the Sikhs in Milwaukee, but across the country.*"

A few days later, Sharat and I went to Oak Creek to grieve with the families of the dead. We were supposed to be there a week but stayed longer. We played multiple roles—reporting on television, print, and radio; coordinating the support of the interfaith partners; counseling the families; and directing our little film team to document the story as it unfolded. We would soon recruit teammates from around the country to join us—Ivy, Aseem, Jonathan, Hilda, Don, and Deep would shuttle in and out of Wisconsin. I had long since canceled my surgery. Days turned into weeks, weeks into months. As time went on, Oak Creek became my second home, the local community my extended family, and what I experienced there changed my life.

I had always called the victims of hate crimes just that—*victims*. We as Sikhs were *invisible* victims, and so I thought that our role as advocates was to call the nation's attention to our suffering—to jump up and down and wave our hands in the air and ask America to see us. In the immediate aftermath of 9/11, Muslim, Arab, and South Asian American (MASA) advocates jumped into action to respond to the onslaught of discriminatory policies by the state and hate crimes in the street. The threats never ceased, so we became masters of crisis management. We built infrastructure for crisis management. We got funded for crisis management. Crisis management protects victims from immediate harm. It does not easily make space for those victims to be seen as survivors who have something to teach the rest of the nation.

That all changed for me in Oak Creek. Sikhs had something to teach America about *how* to respond to the violence of white nationalism, socially, politically, and spiritually. I saw the practices of revolutionary love at work—we wondered, grieved, and fought; we raged, listened, and reimagined the future. All of this was anchored in breath.

☙❧

Breathing is life-giving. In every breath, we take oxygen into our bodies to nourish and sustain us. We inhale the molecules we need; we exhale what we do not need. Breath is constant: Its rhythm moves within us whether or not we are aware of it. Buddhist, Hindu, and many other wisdom traditions have taught conscious breathwork for centuries: When we pay attention to our breath, our minds are called to the present moment. Not the past, not the future. Here and now. Inhale. Exhale. Breathing creates space and time to be present. Present to emotion. Present to sensation. Present to surroundings. Present to one another. Present to ourselves.

Deep breathing, and paying attention to sensations in our bodies as we breathe, increases our resilience. Shallow breathing makes us more vulnerable to stress and illness. Breathing from the diaphragm engages the parasympathetic nervous system and vagus nerve, inducing calm in the body. It changes our blood pressure and heart rate and reduces the risk of inflammatory diseases, including those caused by social trauma and chronic stress. Breathing is perhaps the most universally available wellness tool. Try it now: Take one deep breath. Notice the sensations in your body as you do this. The ability to notice and slow down our breath connects us to a sense of agency: Even in dire circumstances, even when we cannot control anything else, we can consciously take one breath, and then another.

Breathing creates space in our lives to think and see differently, enliven our imagination, awaken to pleasure, move toward freedom, and let joy in. For those of us who live in bodies that are denigrated by society, breathing like this is a *political* act. The world sends a barrage of signals that our bodies—as women, people of color, women of color, queer people, trans people, and disabled people—are not beautiful or strong or worthy of love. Taking the time to breathe—literally and metaphorically—is a way to assert that our bodies are worthy and beloved. Loving our bodies is the first and primal act of loving ourselves.

When I arrived in Oak Creek, I was not taking the time to breathe in my life, but it was in Oak Creek that I learned how to breathe. Most people don't remember the Oak Creek mass shooting, if they even heard of it in the first place. Oak Creek did not receive nearly the same media coverage as other mass shootings. It disappeared from the nation's consciousness almost as soon as it occurred. But I invite you to hear this story. I invite you to grieve with us and, in doing so, to love us. Listening to a story about mass violence is labor. But labor is bearable when we breathe together.

The Story of Oak Creek

Inhale.

Fields stretched on all sides as we made our way from the Milwaukee airport to Oak Creek, a predominantly white suburb with a population of thirty thousand on the southern edge of Milwaukee County. In the late 1990s, local Sikh families established the Sikh Temple of Wisconsin. They were immigrants from India who worked as taxi drivers and gas station attendants and built small businesses to pursue their dreams, as had countless immigrants before them. Their families gathered in rented halls until they could build their own Sikh gurdwara, a brick building set back from the main road on South Howell Avenue. Like all gurdwaras, it was not only a house of worship but also a community center bustling with activity each day—families prayed together and cooked together and argued together and counseled each other, children played in the hallways as the elderly scolded them, couples met and got married, new babies were blessed. The gurdwara was where life happened.

On Sunday morning, August 5, there were about forty people inside the gurdwara preparing for the day's services. By ten A.M., aun-

ties were in the kitchen, cooking *langar,* the communal meal, to feed
the few hundred people who would soon arrive. They were bringing
cha to a boil, stirring enormous steel pots of dal and tossing rotis between their hands, letting the rotis puff up, *gol-gol,* on the stove before
piling them on a tray. In the living quarters at the other end of the
gurdwara, uncles chatted as they tied their turbans. They were granthis
and ragis trained in India who lived and served in the gurdwara for
months or years at a time, leading ceremonies, reciting scriptures, and
singing *kirtan* during the services. In the *diwan* hall, the main prayer
hall, a few had come for quiet meditation. Children played throughout the gurdwara before their Sunday school classes began.

Two children, Amanat Singh and her little brother, Abhay, were
sitting out in front of the gurdwara, giggling and singing, when they
saw a white man pull up in a red pickup truck. The man approached
two granthis who were talking to each other in the parking lot—
Ranjit and Sita Singh, two brothers in their forties. Their wives and
children in India had been separated from them for sixteen years while
they sent money home, waiting to be reunited. Meanwhile, they performed religious services at the gurdwara each day. The brothers prepared to greet the man. He was probably lost and needed directions.
Maybe he would come inside for tea. The children saw a gun and
heard popping sounds. Smoke drifted above Ranjit Ji's turban. Ranjit
Ji staggered toward the gunman, then fell onto the pavement. His
brother Sita Ji fell on top of him, bleeding.

Narinder Kaur witnessed the killings from her parked car. She
managed to drive out of the parking lot, hands shaking, and made the
first 911 call. Amanat and Abhay ran inside the gurdwara and cried,
"Someone killed the Baba Ji!" Everyone began to run. They rushed
into closets, hid behind doors, and ran down to the basement. From
the street, Narinder Auntie called her friend inside the gurdwara, who
answered in a whisper, "Someone save us!" The gunman was now
inside.

Wade Michael Page, armed with a 9 mm semiautomatic handgun,
was stalking the building. He saw a woman behind a large column in

the main foyer and fired, grazing her with a bullet. Amarjit Kaur ran down the hallway into the kitchen, where other women pulled her into the pantry and tended to her wounds with napkins. The pantry was small and dark and hot, sixteen women and children crammed inside, clutching each other as they heard more gunshots.

Page stepped into the *diwan* hall and found Paramjit Kaur, a forty-one-year-old mother of two sons. She served the gurdwara nearly every day of the week. He shot her in front of the Guru Granth Sahib, the sacred scripture. She died where she fell; her blood soaked the carpet. He then proceeded down the hallway toward the kitchen where he had seen Amarjit Auntie disappear.

In the meantime, the aunties in the pantry had smelled something burning. Pammi Kaur and her friend snuck out to turn off the burners on the opposite side of the kitchen. Just then, Pammi Auntie turned to see Page on the other side of the counter that separated the kitchen from the *langar* hall. He was staring at her. He had no expression on his face. He lifted his gun and began firing. Bullets flew and grazed both of them before they dove back into the pantry. Page must have thought that the pantry door led outside. Had he pursued them, all sixteen women and children in the pantry would have been dead.

Page returned down the hallway into the main foyer when he saw an elderly man coming out of the library. Suveg Singh Khattra, an eighty-four-year-old grandfather, had come to live in Oak Creek with his son after retiring from his life as a farmer in Punjab. His son dropped him off at the gurdwara nearly every morning. He spent the day praying and playing hide-and-seek with the children. Page shot him in the head. Page continued down the hallway toward the living quarters on the far side of the building.

Baba Punjab Singh had been tying his turban in one of the bedrooms. He was a renowned Sikh teacher, a man of many words who traveled the world to speak and teach in gurdwaras, splitting his time among Wisconsin, California, New Jersey, and India. His sons and grandchildren loved him as much as the thousands of people who flocked to listen to him. Page forced down the door and shot him in the face. The bullet entered his jaw and permanently damaged his spinal cord. He would survive—but he would never again move or speak.

Page crossed the hallway to the other bedroom, where three more granthis were hiding along with Satwant Singh Kaleka, the president of the gurdwara. They called 911 when they heard gunshots. One of them, Gurmail Singh, hid in the bathroom and heard what happened next. Page entered the room. Prakash Singh was the first to be killed, shot in the head through the eye. He was a thirty-nine-year-old father who had just moved his family from India to serve the gurdwara. His wife and children were hiding in the basement.

Santokh Singh, one of the granthis, faced Page and said, "What is your problem? Why are you doing this?" Page lifted his gun and shot him twice in the stomach. Page pulled the trigger to shoot again but the gun did not fire. He stopped to reload. Clutching his belly, Santokh Uncle pushed through the door and ran down the hallway and outside while Page tried to follow him. He was running and bleeding and breathing "Waheguru, Waheguru." He staggered to a nearby house and collapsed on the front lawn where the neighbor called 911. He would survive.

Meanwhile, Satwant Uncle made a final 911 call. Page then returned to the room and killed him. Police found a butter knife near Satwant Uncle's body. The FBI told his sons Pardeep and Amardeep Kaleka that they believed he had died while trying to fight the gunman.

At 10:28 A.M., Lt. Brian Murphy arrived on the scene. Lieutenant Murphy, a former Marine who had served on the Oak Creek police force for twenty years, was not supposed to work that day. He had traded days off with another officer who was attending his son's ROTC graduation. As he pulled down the driveway, he turned off his lights and sirens. Brian saw the bodies of the brothers in the parking lot, one on top of the other, and called for an ambulance. Sita Ji's eyes were open and fixed. Brian knew they were dead. He saw movement out of the corner of his eye. Page had emerged from the gurdwara.

"Police! Stop!" yelled Brian. Both men raised their guns at the same time and pulled the trigger. Brian missed. Page did not. The bullet hit Brian in the chin, tore through his voice box and larynx, and lodged in his trapezius. Brian dove behind a car for cover as bullets flew around him. There was a lull. Brian crawled out to look for Page but he wasn't there. Page suddenly appeared behind him and opened fire less than fifteen feet away. The next bullet tore off half of Brian's left thumb and knocked the gun from his hand. Page shot him again in the thigh and upper arm. *Better get small,* thought Brian. He flipped over and crawled under the car as more bullets hit the back of his vest.

As he lay under the car, losing blood, the world started to get quiet, heavy, and warm. He started to close his eyes. He was losing consciousness. He was about to give in to the powerful urge to sleep when he thought of his wife and children. He wasn't going to die in this parking lot. He willed himself awake.

There was a lull as Page reloaded his gun. Drawing up the last energy he had, Brian began to crawl across the pavement to his car to retrieve his shotgun. But Page fired again, hitting the back of his arm and leg. At this point, Brian made eye contact. There was nothing in Page's face. Not hate. Not anger. Not emotion. A final round pumped a bullet in the back of Brian's head.

Sirens. Officer Sam Lenda arrived on the scene. Page shot a bullet that shattered the windshield of his police car. Lenda fired back six times. Wounded, Page dropped to the ground, crawled a few feet, and shot himself in the head. It was over.

Exhale.

When the gunshots ceased, everyone hiding in the gurdwara began to stir. Two children who huddled in the basement, Palmeet and Prabhjot, climbed the stairs. Their father had told them to run into the basement to hide and then left to warn others. Now the children were looking for him. They walked past dead bodies and went from room to room until they found their father on the floor of one of the bedrooms. They shook Prakash Singh's body and begged him to wake up. Palmeet touched her father's face around his missing eye. There was blood on her hand. The children hid in the bathroom for another hour until police entered the building and led everyone out. The police asked everyone to put their hands behind their heads as they left the gurdwara. Kulwant Kaur, who had been hiding in the pantry, saw her father-in-law's body in the foyer and started to rush to him, but the police told her to keep her hands up.

Outside in the parking lot, Brian felt his fellow officers lift him up. He could hear stress in their voices. He was their boss. He thought, *Calm it down. Autogenic breathing. Breathe in for four counts, hold for four counts, and out for four counts. It lowers the heart rate, calms the nervous system.* But he couldn't speak to remind them. He had twelve bullets in his body.

As ambulances rushed people to the hospital, the parking lot filled with police cars, FBI agents, media trucks, and family members looking for their loved ones. Kamal and Harpreet Saini, twenty and eighteen, were searching for their mother. Every road was blocked. Kamal fought his way through with a picture of his mother on his phone. "Have you seen her?" he kept asking. The brothers spent all day searching in hospital after hospital. Kamal returned at night to the bowling alley across the street from the gurdwara. Classic Lanes had been transformed into a temporary morgue, interviewing location, and family assistance center. "Do you want to tell him or do you want me to?" an agent asked his father. Everything went dark for a few minutes. Kamal went home to tell his brother, "Mom's not coming home, because she's looking over us from above."

"I've only had one dream about her," Kamal told me. "I told her I was hungry and she made me *saag*." Spinach with butter and spices. "If I could have her back just one day," he said, "I would eat the food she made for me, food from her hands."

I was sitting with Kamal and Harpreet in their mother's bedroom. The shooting had happened three days ago. Both sons were tired and grief-stricken but they knew it was better not to be alone. Thousands of people had shown up on Tuesday night for a vigil for their mother and the others who were killed. They wanted to keep people around them.

"We heard from the medical examiner that she died a painful death," Kamal said. "I know the last thing that probably went through her mind was *'Mere Preet da kee hovega?'* What will become of my Harpreet? She loved him. I know she believes that I'm here for him."

Kamal was the older, independent brother. Harpreet was the shy younger one, the one who never left his mother's side. She was his best friend. "I was bullied through my childhood," Harpreet said quietly, "but I never thought that this would happen to my mother." She had tried to wake them up in the morning to go to gurdwara with her that day, but they turned over and went back to sleep. "If only we had gone with her," they kept saying.

Their father was an alcoholic and had a history of beating their mother. The boys always threw their bodies between them to protect her. They thought he might kill her one day. But she died a different way—at the hands of another man. Now they felt like orphans.

Every weekend, their mother used to make them their favorite food, *gobhi wale pronthay*. The brothers opened the fridge and found the *prontha*s their mother had prepared for them. They sat together and ate her food for the last time, savoring each bite. They would move out of the house a few weeks later.

Suddenly there was a buzz of movement in the rest of the home. Wisconsin's Governor Scott Walker entered the tiny living room of Kamal and Harpreet's house with an entourage of men in black suits.

Inhale.

Governor Walker took a seat and wore a solemn expression as family and neighbors gathered around and the boys described their mother. "Why did he have a gun?" their father moaned. The governor agreed that guns should not be in the hands of deranged people. He then said, "We offer not only our condolences but also our love." He quoted Dr. King: "Darkness cannot drive out darkness. Only light can do that. Hate cannot drive out hate. Only love can do that."

I quietly thought: *King also said that love was not emotional bosh but sustained committed action*. "What will you do to prevent another Oak Creek?" people asked him. He didn't have a good answer. In the days to come, elected leaders like Governor Walker and Representative Paul Ryan and other lawmakers would show up to offer condolences with words like "love" on their lips—but they refused to support gun safety laws, curb hate crimes, or actively combat white nationalism. Their silence would become even more deadly during the Trump era.

Sitting there in that cramped living room, watching the governor nod politely as community members desperately sought his help, knowing that he would do nothing, my fists clenched. I felt the colossal force of rage rise within me. It was not rage against the gunman: It was rage against the lawmakers. I witnessed the rage and let it have me. And then I took the next breath.

Exhale.

On Thursday, August 9—just four days after the shooting—the FBI allowed the community to reenter the gurdwara. The FBI typically cleans crime scenes, but the Sikh community insisted on doing this labor themselves. Media cameras were not allowed inside but family members had asked us to be there to document it.

When we walked into the gurdwara, it was a site of massacre. Blood in the carpets. Bullet holes in the walls. Sacred places are extensions of our bodies. When we step inside them, their familiarity—their smells and colors and sounds—shows up in our bodies as felt sense. It is the feeling of ease and safety and belonging. If we cannot feel at home anywhere else, we can be at home here, even if just for a Sunday morning. When a sacred place is ravaged, it's as if our bodies themselves have been violated. As my eyes darted around to each smudge of blood, I felt dizzy, and nausea overcame me. Here is your home back, full of death.

Prayers sounded softly over the loudspeakers. I watched the same aunties and uncles who had survived the shooting roll up their sleeves and get to work. They ripped out the blood-soaked carpets with their own hands. They painted over the bullet holes in the walls, scrubbed the floors, drilled in new doors, and repaired shattered windows. Over the next few hours, I watched this community literally rebuild itself before my eyes, reciting and breathing "Waheguru, Waheguru" as they worked. They were restoring the gurdwara, and they were restoring themselves. By midday, they were already cooking *langar* and serving food.

"I'm not scared," Pammi Auntie told me. She was the auntie who had rushed out of the pantry to turn off the burners. *"Mainu seva karan to nahi rokya javega."* I will not be stopped from serving.

Inhale.

That night, Thursday night, the Department of Justice organized a town hall meeting. One by one, nearly every Sikh who took the open mic told the panel of officials onstage that the shooting was not an isolated incident but one in a long pattern of hate crimes since 9/11 and long before. Our children are bullied and our people profiled at airports, barred from military service, and subject to racial slurs and hate crimes that are not specifically tracked by the government, they said. Just three days after the shooting, a Sikh cabdriver in Oak Creek reported that a white man asked him to roll down the window, pantomimed shooting a gun, and said, "This isn't over." I was reminded how Rana Sodhi was shown a knife at a stoplight shortly after his brother was killed after 9/11. These were the same stories I had heard repeated for a decade.

"A picture is worth a thousand words," one Sikh uncle said. "Can President Obama please come and take a picture with us to show the country that we are Americans, too?" We were begging for . . . a picture. The officials listened and nodded politely.

The Obama administration implemented a strong and swift response to the Oak Creek shooting. The FBI and Department of Justice investigated the attack as both an act of domestic terrorism and a hate crime. Flags flew at half-mast for us. But our community longed for more. We longed for the deeper spiritual and emotional assurance that we were welcome in a nation that had produced the gunman, the kind of assurance that could have been provided by a presidential visit.

Or at least a photograph. A few weeks earlier, President Obama suspended a day of campaigning and flew to Colorado in the wake of a horrific mass shooting in a movie theater in Aurora. He mourned publicly with the families before they buried their dead. He said that he hugged his daughters closer, imagining them in the theater. In his condolences after Oak Creek, the president referred to Sikhs as members of the "broader American family" as if we were distant relatives. Obama did not come to Oak Creek. In the president's stead, Attorney General Eric Holder attended the memorial. Community members were quietly disappointed. I had conflicted feelings: President Obama should have shown up for us. It was the right thing to do. But it was also difficult to criticize a president who had been maligned since his appearance on the national stage, accused of being a Muslim as if that somehow made him less American. How do we hold leaders accountable when we see them attacked by the same oppressive forces we are seeking to transform? I bit my tongue.

Exhale.

The memorial service was held on Friday, five days after the shooting, in the gym of Oak Creek High School. Sharat and I got there early. There were wooden risers, electronic scoreboards, and conference championship banners on the walls. It could have been any high school gym in America. Sikhs were laying white sheets on the hardwood floor like in a gurdwara. A procession of black hearses arrived. Family members came together and carried a casket inside the gym, chanting "Waheguru, Waheguru," then went back outside to carry in another, then another, and another. They set the caskets down beneath an enormous American flag that hung on the gym wall. When some of the family members had asked my advice about whether the caskets should be open or closed, I said open. The world needed to see.

But I wasn't prepared for the moment they pulled back the white sheets. I looked into the faces of people who looked like my family. Next to each casket stood their sons and daughters. Satpal Kaur Kaleka threw herself over her husband's body and sobbed as other women held her. Kamal and Harpreet stood next to their mother's body, hands clasped, trying to stand tall. The doors opened, and the gym filled with people—Sikhs in turbans and *chunni*s and *ramal*s, then a flood of mostly white people from the local community. Some were dressed for church, others wore Brewers and Packers T-shirts. Police officers in uniform tied on *ramal*s, head coverings worn at Sikh services. I was in awe. Three thousand people had come to mourn with us.

"In the recent past, too many Sikhs have been targeted and victimized simply because of who they are, how they look, and what they believe," said Attorney General Eric Holder. "This is wrong. It is unacceptable. And it will not be tolerated." He echoed President Obama's words: "It is that fundamental belief that I am my brother's keeper, I am my sister's keeper, that makes this country work." He named the shooting an act of domestic terrorism. This was significant. Since 9/11, the Justice Department routinely declined to label white Far-Right extremists "terrorists" even when their crimes met the legal definition of terrorism: "ideologically motivated acts that are harmful to human life and intended to intimidate civilians, influence policy, or change government conduct." It's as though the government reserved that label only for those for whom it wanted to conjure the threat of collective peril: When the perpetrator was Muslim, he was called a terrorist. When he was white, he was called a lone wolf or mentally ill. The label signified whose security was a priority. By calling the Oak Creek massacre an act of terrorism, Holder was making an official statement about the severity of the crime—and the government's commitment to protect us. "We will discuss how to change our laws and hearts in the coming days," he said. Sikhs called out, *"Bole So Nihal,"* and thousands responded, *"Satsriakal!"* May it be so!

Family members took the podium and brought the audience to tears. "I couldn't speak in front of twelve kids in speech class," Kamal whispered to me, "but I just spoke to thousands, and my voice didn't shake. It was my mother's spirit."

It was time to pay our respects to the dead. Everyone lined up. Police officers wept as they approached the open caskets. A priest

walked by each one silently making the sign of the cross. An indigenous leader left a dream catcher. When it was my turn, I touched the
foot of each casket and said, "Waheguru." It was difficult to breathe as
I looked into the lifeless face of each person. On the way back to my
seat, I saw a familiar face—Amardeep Singh Bhalla, the program director of the Sikh Coalition. Amar had been on the ground all week
working alongside other advocates, including Sapreet Kaur, who ran
the Sikh Coalition; Jasjit Singh, who directed the Sikh American
Legal Defense and Education Fund (SALDEF); Deepa Iyer, who led
South Asian Americans Leading Together (SAALT); and Dr. Puni
Kalra, who had brought her team of mental health professionals. Most
of us had worked alongside one another since 9/11. But our bonds
ran deeper than professional ties. We saw one another as sisters and
brothers in the trenches. What was it all for, this decade of advocacy,
if not to prevent a massacre like this? Amar hugged me—more like he
caught me—and, for one long moment, we let ourselves breathe together. "We may not live to see the fruits of our labor in our lifetime,"
Amar said to me, "but we labor anyway." I returned to my seat, and
Sharat saw my tears. We had been professionals all this time, trying to
capture the story on camera, but in that quiet corner of the bleachers,
we wept together and let ourselves become mourners. The bodies of
the dead were cremated after the ceremony. In most cases, ashes were
returned to Punjab and poured in the sacred river Sutlej to merge with
the ancestors.

Inhale.

After the memorial ended on Friday, Republican presidential candidate Mitt Romney—who had referred to "the people who lost their
lives at that sheik temple"—announced that he had chosen a vice presidential running mate, Paul Ryan. Oak Creek was in Ryan's district.
Ryan did not speak at the memorial but he was present, so Romney
waited until the memorial was over before making the announce-
ment. In an instant, I watched the media trucks in Oak Creek pack up
and disappear. I was booked to talk about the shooting on weekend
television shows, as were other advocates, but all of us were bumped

from our slots. We had hoped to move the public beyond Sikhism 101 into a national conversation about hate and white nationalism in America. But that was it. It was over. Our window closed. The shooting did not sustain national attention—not even for a week.

But did we ever have the nation's attention to begin with? CNN was the only network that sent an anchor to report live from Oak Creek. None of the other networks gave the shooting the extensive coverage they had given to the shooting in Aurora a few weeks earlier, or that they would give to the mass shootings to come. It took a massacre for Sikhs to receive the most national attention we had ever gotten in more than a century of history in the United States. Thousands of vigils were held across the nation, hundreds of op-eds published, and it still was not enough. We had not succeeded in helping Americans *as a whole* imagine the gurdwara as a house of worship like their own, or see the people with turbans and headscarves as fellow Americans worthy of their attention, let alone their solidarity. To this day, people nod when I mention Aurora, Newtown, and Charleston, but they draw a blank when I say Oak Creek. As scholar Naunihal Singh reflects, had the shooter been Muslim and the victims white churchgoers, it's hard to imagine that anyone today would not know Oak Creek.

And yet, as Amar said to me, the labor continues. After the media trucks left that day, we stayed on to help tell the story of what happened next.

Exhale.

On Sunday, exactly one week after the shooting, the community reopened the gurdwara. In the morning, hundreds of Sikhs from all over the country, especially the Midwest, arrived at the gurdwara, now a site of pilgrimage. As we pulled in, Kamal and Harpreet showed us where to park. Amardeep Kaleka, whose father was the deceased gurdwara president, introduced the program. I was astonished. Just a week after the shooting, the children of the dead had organized this service in the same place their parents had been killed.

First, the community gathered outside around the Sikh flag—the

Nishan Sahib. We washed the flagpole with water and milk, replaced its gold cloth, and raised the flag again to the buoyant sound of our call-and-response: *"Bole So Nihal!" "Satsriakal!"* Then we entered the main foyer of the gurdwara, now filled with flowers and portraits of the dead. The granthis had just finished the *Akhand Path,* the continuous reading of the Guru Granth Sahib that takes three days, a way we honor the dead. At the doorway to the *diwan* hall, a single bullet hole remained and beneath it the words: WE ARE ONE. 8-5-12. It was an embodiment of the Sikh spirit of *chardi kala,* an act of defiance, a declaration that we were not going to be deterred from rising up.

The service, like all Sikh services, was comprised of *kirtan.* We listened to the poems in our scripture become song and music. The sounds filled my chest and certain lines echoed in me:

> *Meditate and vibrate upon the One,*
> *and you shall cross over the terrifying world-ocean.*

> *Listen, you do not have to go to the house of death.*

> *Meditate on the Name and you shall dwell in the fearless Divine.*

> *The world is just a dream. None of this is yours.*

> *As bubbles in water rise up and disappear again, so is the universe created.*

> *Nothing is permanent.*

> *My strength has been restored and my bonds have been broken,*
> *now I can do everything.*

A granthi rose to deliver the *Ardas,* the final prayer in every Sikh service that invokes the sacrifice and resilience of our ancestors through history and culminates in a prayer for here and now. We rose to our feet. I closed my eyes during the familiar chants. Then came the part that was for this moment, and we prayed for all who had been killed in the shooting. I heard the names of the dead—"Sita Singh, Ranjit Singh, Suveg Singh Khattra, Satwant Singh Kaleka, Prakash Singh, Paramjit Kaur." I heard the names of the wounded—"Lt. Brian Murphy, Baba Punjab Singh, Santokh Singh."

Then I heard his name. "Wade Michael Page."

I looked around. Everyone's eyes were closed, hands folded in prayer. I took a breath and closed my eyes again. Wade Michael Page. Behind the expressionless face that stalked these halls was a pained white man who, too, deserved peace.

The final line of the *Ardas* rang out:

Nanak Nam Chardi Kala Teray Banay Sarbat da Bhalla.
In the name of Divine Oneness, we find ever-rising high spirits.
Within your will, may there be grace for *all* of humanity.

During the service, Kamal and Harpreet sat together in the spot where their mother had bled to death, the spot where the FBI told them they wrapped her body. "When I sit here, I feel at peace," Harpreet whispered to me. "It's like feeling her hug me." For a fleeting moment, these young men wanted to find the white power group that radicalized Page and exact revenge. But that impulse had receded. They were surrounded by *sangat*—community—and breathing as one. They were breathing through guilt and rage and grief and letting breath anchor them. "I don't think much about the gunman anymore," Kamal later declared. "Our community is not about retaliation, just love."

After the prayers ended, speakers took the podium in the gurdwara. I presented bound books that contained four thousand prayers and letters Groundswell had collected from people across the country—so that families could remember in quiet moments that they were still surrounded by support. It would become a practice that we would repeat in the years to come. In the aftermath of every mass shooting in a house of worship—a church in Charleston, a synagogue in Pittsburgh, mosques in New Zealand—we would collect prayers and letters and funds to show that our solidarity lasted long after media trucks left.

"We must live together as brothers and sisters or die apart as fools," said the Reverend Jesse Jackson to the community that day, echoing King. The media was not there to hear his words. "Let your pain fortify your strength. In this place of worship, you were shot down, slaughtered, your worst fears realized, but you turned to each other, your Maker, and you turned to joy and hope. Sikhs, keep living, keep sharing, keep building, keep loving. There is power in your faith."

Inhale.

After the Sunday service, I learned that Baba Punjab Singh, the renowned teacher who had been wounded in the shooting, was being treated at Froedtert Hospital down the hall from Lt. Brian Murphy. His sons Raghuvinder and Jaspreet were in India and got the news over the phone that their father was dead. Their mother, Kulwant Kaur, overheard and went into shock. Another phone call came that night—their father was alive but in critical condition. The sons flew to the United States, rushed to the hospital, and found their father hooked up to a ventilator, his hands and feet swollen. They got to work. They massaged his body until the swelling went down and stayed at his bedside day and night, day and night, to the constant sound of prayers on a small radio. Their father had walked eight miles every morning, so they circled his legs each morning at the same time to keep up his routine. When Baba Punjab Singh opened his eyes for the first time on Tuesday, ten days after the shooting, he moved his lips to try to speak to his sons. But no sound came out. They weren't discouraged. "He has doctors and family but also the power of God, healing power, from within," Raghuvinder told me. His father was his best friend. He had to get better.

Now their mother had arrived from India, and I accompanied her to the hospital to see her husband for the first time. Mata Ji was quiet, draped in a shawl, prayer beads in her hand, "Waheguru" on her lips. We followed her into the hospital room and saw him—a Sikh grandfather cocooned in white sheets, hooked up to monitors, mouth agape, his long gray hair neatly tied in a small bun, skin glowing, eyes closed. Mata Ji set her head down at her husband's feet and wept quietly. She grasped his hand and pressed his forehead and asked him to open his eyes. "Waheguru, Waheguru," she recited with each breath.

"Baba Ji, rise up and tell us one of your great stories!" said Raghuvinder. "The *sangat* is waiting. All are praying for you!" But no response. I took Baba Punjab Singh's hand, warm in mine, and gazed into his face. He looked like my grandfather. He looked like Papa Ji.

Outside the room, Raghuvinder told us, "People didn't really know about Sikhs in this country before, did they? Millions of people know who we are now." I remember hearing the same words from Rana Sodhi more than a decade ago, after Balbir Uncle was killed. I wondered how many more of us had to die before the nation "knew" who we were. We didn't need simply to be known. We needed to be loved.

Exhale.

I was seeing that the Sikh community's response to this massacre had something to offer the nation—how to grieve together, how to breathe through hate and violence together, how to practice love together. I wrote an open letter to President Obama, asking him to come to Oak Creek. CNN ran the letter. "If Trayvon Martin could have been your son," I wrote, "and the kids in the Aurora theater your daughters, then the aunts and uncles shot while praying that Sunday could have been your own, too." A colleague from the White House gave me a call. They were going to send Michelle Obama.

On Thursday, August 23, eighteen days after the shooting, the First Lady arrived at Oak Creek High School to meet the families privately. After she left, I saw something new on their faces—I saw them smile.

"She spent time with each family in turn, asking questions and listening to our pain and hope," said Kamal.

"She told me that my father was a hero," said Amardeep, whose father died fighting the gunman. "That meant a lot to me."

"I'm really glad that the First Lady came," said Harpreet. "I want to go into law enforcement to protect people and fulfill my mother's dream, but I don't want to give up my *pag*." His turban. "The First Lady said that she would work on this for me, and I was shocked. She said that maybe one day I could become Secret Service and protect her!" Harpreet was beaming.

"Look, our parents were just grateful that flags were lowered to half-mast," said Sandeep Khattra, whose grandfather had been killed. "But we grew up in this country, so we wanted more. We wanted to be heard. The First Lady's visit feels like the first step."

In the meeting, the sons and daughters of Oak Creek—Kamal, Harpreet, Amardeep, Sandeep—presented Michelle Obama with a gift: a simple orange wristband with the words "I Pledge Unity. August 5, 2012." She pulled up a chair and said, as they remember it: "We have much work to do as a nation. I'm ready to do my part."

Years later, when I got to spend a few minutes with her, I thanked Michelle Obama for coming to Oak Creek to grieve with us. "Thank you for showing us your love," I said. "It made a difference." The First Lady's visit did not capture the nation's attention as a president's visit would have, but it did give us the energy we needed—not only to grieve, but to fight.

Inhale.

The Sikh community was poised to pursue policy change. In the past decade, we had grown existing community organizations in scope and impact—South Asian Americans Leading Together, the Sikh American Legal Defense and Education Fund, United Sikhs—and we had built new organizations, including the Sikh Coalition. Shortly after 9/11, I had filmed one of the Sikh Coalition's first meetings in an empty office building in Manhattan not far from Ground Zero, where the rubble was still smoking. I watched Amar Bhalla organize a band of young Sikh lawyers to respond to the torrent of calls and emails from Sikhs reporting hate violence in the hours and days following the terrorist attacks. Eleven years later, the Sikh Coalition was the nation's largest Sikh civil rights organization, leading the policy response to Oak Creek. We had never had so many allies before. If we waited too long to act, everyone would disperse. We had to act now. We harnessed all of that energy into a single razor-sharp policy goal: to demand that the government track hate crimes against Sikhs and other minority groups.

"There is no box for me to record the six homicides at the gurdwara down the street as anti-Sikh crimes," said Oak Creek Police Chief John Edwards. He was puzzling over Form 1-699, the Hate Crime Incident Report. "How can we combat a problem we are not even measuring?"

Statistics collected on this form allow law enforcement officials to analyze trends in hate crimes and allocate resources. But, under the FBI's tracking system, there was no category for anti-Sikh hate crimes. They were lumped in with "anti-Muslim" crimes. The same was true for Hindus and Arabs. Sikhs had been asking for years for separate categories. Longtime Sikh advocates Simran Jeet Singh and Prabhjot Singh wrote an op-ed in *The New York Times* that began, "Do American Sikhs count?" They called on the government to track anti-Sikh violence and got national attention. The coalition pushed for a Senate hearing.

On September 19, the Senate Judiciary Committee held a hearing on "hate crimes and the threat of domestic extremism," chaired by Senator Dick Durbin. Just forty-five days after his mother's murder, Harpreet Singh Saini became the first Sikh in U.S. history to testify before Congress.

"I had my first day of college and my mother wasn't there to send me off," Harpreet said. More than four hundred people sat behind Harpreet and in the overflow room. People wept quietly as he spoke.

"I want to protect other people from what happened to my mother," said Harpreet. "I want to combat hate—not just against Sikhs but against all people." He told the senators that he and his brother wanted to be police officers like Lieutenant Murphy so that they could serve and protect others just as he did for our community. Then he made our policy asks.

In the same hearing, former Department of Homeland Security

analyst Daryl Johnson testified that the government had effectively turned a blind eye to right-wing domestic extremism. At DHS, Johnson authored a 2009 report on the alarming rise of white supremacist hate groups after President Obama's election. The department caved in to the political backlash and shut down Johnson's team of five. It left just one analyst to focus on domestic terrorism by non-Muslims in a time of "heightened extremist activity throughout the country." The Southern Poverty Law Center had tracked Page for a decade, but the government did not have a case on him. Could Oak Creek have been prevented if our government had made *our* protection a priority?

"Finally, Senators, I ask that you stand up for us," said Harpreet. "As lawmakers and leaders, you have the power to shape public opinion. Your words carry weight. When others scapegoat or demean people because of who they are, use your power to say that is wrong."

The Oak Creek massacre had taken place during the 2012 election season amid a resurgence of anti-Muslim propaganda. Political candidates were now actively vilifying Muslim Americans in order to win votes, using propaganda created by a mini-industry that had not existed before. The Center for American Progress reported that between 2001 and 2009, seven foundations poured $42.6 million into well-organized think tanks to promote anti-Islam ideologies through blogs, books, and films. As the anti-Islam industry grew, the nation saw a disturbing rise of hate groups, now a thousand strong. The number of hate groups had grown by more than 50 percent since 2000. Muslim American advocates like Wajahat Ali raised the alarm about the Islamophobia industry, but the public paid little attention. We did not know it then, but these were signs of the white nationalist "awakening" that would come to define the Trump era.

After the Senate hearing, we gathered for a press conference in the hall outside. I joined longtime champions Deepa Iyer and Linda Sarsour behind the podium, alongside our black, Christian, Jewish, and queer allies. We called for an end to hate in America with one voice. It was the kind of deep solidarity we would need in the years to come.

That night, Sharat and I took Harpreet and Kamal to see the monuments in Washington, D.C. It was their first time. We went from the Lincoln Memorial to the Martin Luther King, Jr. Memorial. We gazed up at the words etched into the monument of Dr. King: OUT OF THE MOUNTAIN OF DESPAIR, A STONE OF HOPE. Harpreet said, "I feel my mom is still watching over us. That's what made today happen."

In the ten months that followed, the Sikh Coalition and allies led a full-throated campaign to change how the government tracked hate crimes against Sikhs, Hindus, Arabs, and other at-risk communities. Senator Durbin and more than a hundred members of Congress from both parties supported the policy change. Three thousand people of all faiths signed petitions collected by Groundswell. We fought for this single policy change together—and finally won. In 2015, for the first time, the U.S. government began tracking hate crimes against Sikh Americans, along with Arabs, Buddhists, Mormons, Jehovah's Witnesses, and Orthodox Christians.

"It makes me feel we did something for our mom," Harpreet told me, fighting back tears, when the policy victory was announced. "The grief feels the same as it did the day she died. But at least I know that she would be proud."

Exhale.

"I see a lot of victims," Police Chief John Edwards told me. "I am used to seeing people want revenge. Meeting this group of people changed me. All I've seen is compassion and love and support—not only for us but for the entire city. For Wade Michael Page, too. It's changed a lot of people. My officers spend a lot of time at the gurdwara now. They stop in, they go to the services—that's unusual."

Today the gurdwara in Oak Creek is a meeting place not only for Sikhs but for the whole community. That white man sharing a meal in the *langar* hall is Steve Scaffidi, the small-town mayor who was thrust onto the national stage as he managed the crisis. He's now a national voice for gun safety laws. "I'm proud to represent Oak Creek," he said. "Not as a scene of violence, but as a symbol of what one small community can do."

This white man over here sharing a cup of *cha* with a family is

James Santelle, the state's U.S. attorney who assured the community that it would have full access to government resources. He is now fluent in Sikh concepts and history and can even speak a little Punjabi with us.

And if you come on a quiet morning, you may find a certain police officer in the *diwan* hall, sitting quietly, head bowed in prayerful silence. Lt. Brian Murphy survived the shooting rampage but not without a lot of pain. In those first weeks in the hospital, Brian dreaded the moments in the middle of the night when nurses came to suction out his trachea. It felt like drowning. But then he would look up at the thank-you letters pinned on his wall—thousands of letters pouring in from Sikhs across Wisconsin and the United States and around the world—and think, *I got thousands of people behind me, my family and friends and the entire law enforcement community . . . and now the Sikh community, too.* He became a legend to Sikhs worldwide. There are framed pictures of him on the walls of Sikh gurdwaras around America. To the Sikhs in Oak Creek, he is also a friend. When he addressed the gurdwara for the first time, Brian said to the congregation in a hoarse whisper, "My voice has been replaced by yours of *chardi kala*." Ever-rising spirits.

Brian doesn't like to talk about himself. I asked him to help me understand what it is like to take twelve bullets and live. His voice box was permanently damaged, but he could still speak in a whisper. "On a good day it feels like someone holding you by your neck," he confided. "On a bad day it feels like someone squeezing you by the throat. There's no point in any day that I'm released from this pain."

Brian's injuries forced him to retire from the police department. He was racked with survivor's guilt. A few months after the shooting, President Obama honored him and told his story during his State of the Union address in 2013. Brian decided he would use his time on this earth as best he could. He began to train police officers around the country on crisis response. Brian asks police officers to treat every person they meet during a routine stop or in the middle of a crisis as a member of their own family. Once, in a televised CNN town hall meeting, he asked then candidate Trump how he proposed "to protect the constitutional rights of minority groups like Muslims, Sikhs, Hindus, and Jews." The candidate evaded the question.

When Kamal reached out to Brian a year after the shooting, Brian stepped up to become a father figure to him and Harpreet. By that time, the brothers had moved into their own apartment. They had created a makeshift memorial for their mother in their living room. They placed the white shoes she was wearing that day at the foot of her portrait and draped her face with the *chunni* she was wearing that morning. "It still smells like her," Kamal said. Next to the portrait was a piece of carpet from where her body was found. Kamal bought a jewelry box where he put the rings and necklace she was wearing that day. "I come home to her every day," he said. "It's the first thing I see when I walk through the door. I *matha tek* to her, and say 'Hey, mom.'" Kamal often slept on the floor of the living room, at her feet.

Kamal, inspired by Brian, joined the Marines. He still returns home for the anniversary of the shooting every year on August 5. Together the brothers help organize an annual memorial walk and run in the field behind Oak Creek High School in honor of the dead under the theme "Chardi Kala." They string banners, blow up orange and blue balloons, and arrange speakers and music, reclaiming life out of death. No matter where they are, when the clock strikes 10:50 A.M. on August 5, the minute they were told their mother died, Kamal and Harpreet always step away from the fray and spend the moment alone, Kamal's arm over Harpreet's shoulders, taking a deep breath together. They spend the rest of the time with other sons and daughters whose lives were transformed that day, including Pardeep Kaleka.

After his father was killed, Pardeep, a schoolteacher in his thirties, was desperate for answers. Then he saw Arno Michaelis on television. Arno was a former white supremacist who founded the white power skinhead group that radicalized Page. Arno spent seven years in the white power movement as an active organizer, leader, and recruiter. When he renounced his allegiance, he became an eloquent and powerful messenger about life after hate. But Arno was racked with guilt after the Oak Creek shooting and was searching for what to do. When Pardeep reached out, Arno agreed to meet him.

"Why?" Pardeep asked Arno. He wanted to know what drove the gunman to kill his father.

Arno explained how the skinhead group gave him a sense of belonging and filled a void in his life. Until all the people he was trying to hate—a Jewish boss, a gay supervisor, black and brown co-workers—showed him kindness again and again. Hate became too exhausting. Arno described the suffering and loneliness of the young men in the white power movement. He believed that the solution was to meet hate with love, even for them.

It was the beginning of an unlikely friendship. Pardeep and Arno began to call each other brothers. They teamed up with other young Sikhs in Oak Creek, including Mandeep Kaur and Rahul Dubey, and formed Serve 2 Unite, an initiative that works with Milwaukee-area schools and calls for love and action in response to hate. Every year, on August 5, they all return to the gurdwara as a site of pilgrimage, a place to reunite with other families and survivors and allies, their bonds strong, their lives changed.

Inhale.

There was one family, however, for whom time had stood still. As days turned into weeks, weeks into months, months into years, the grandfather and teacher Baba Punjab Singh's condition never changed. He remained in a hospital bed, unable to move or speak, except to blink his eyes. His sons Raghuvinder and Jaspreet remained by his side around the clock. Neither saw their wives or children in India that first year. Jaspreet's wife had given birth to a baby girl, Ekom, and he had yet to hold her. The sons moved their families to the United States so that they could take turns caring for their father.

"It's still August fifth," Raghuvinder told me five years after the shooting. "It has always been August fifth. The pain is evergreen. A year feels like a week. Every day we go to the hospital, and every day we see him in the same condition. Nothing has changed."

There was anguish around Raghuvinder's mouth, and weariness

around his eyes, but he somehow still radiated warmth and kindness. He tied his turban in the same style as his father; I started to see gray in his black beard. We had spent so much time together since the shooting that I called him "Veer Ji," elder brother.

"Every day we live in *chardi kala*," Veer Ji said.

There was the invocation of *chardi kala* again. I grew up with this phrase. *Chardi kala* was woven into Sikh scriptures and our vernacular, commonly translated as "relentless optimism." But what I witnessed in Oak Creek and what I was learning from this family was different from optimism. This was not about the future at all. This was about a state of being in the present moment, as if now is all there is. Now and now and now. It is moving from Moment with a capital M to Moment with a capital M. This is a state of joyfulness inside the struggle—an energy that keeps us in motion, a breathing that keeps us laboring, even inside the pain of labor. Hope is a feeling that waxes and wanes, sometimes brilliant and luminous, sometimes a faint sliver in the sky, sometimes gone completely. No matter how hopeful or hopeless we feel, we can choose to return to the labor anyway. Sometimes we receive the gift of our labor. Sometimes we do not. But it does not matter. Because when we labor in love, labor is not only a means but an end in itself.

I made a pilgrimage with Veer Ji and his family to the Golden Temple in Amritsar, Punjab. It is the most revered gurdwara for Sikhs in India and around the world. The moment we walked in, the noise and dust and chaos disappeared behind us, and we were surrounded by peace on all sides. The Golden Temple shone like a shimmering palace on blue waters. The smell of sweet *prashad* filled the air. I sat next to Veer Ji on the cool marble, prayed for his father, and gazed at the gurdwara. Blood had been spilled here, too, even in these pure waters, as recently as 1984, before and during the pogroms. And yet our ancestors had cleaned the blood with their own hands, made the sanctuary anew, and cleared the way for new life. As we listened to the prayers, baby Ekom played around us, and she giggled as Veer Ji scooped his niece into his arms. Her name means "Oneness"—Guru Nanak's vision that we belong to each other. I took a deep breath. Just then *Tati Vao Na Lagi* began to sound on the loudspeakers, Papa Ji's prayer: The hot winds cannot touch you. Sitting there, with the sound of our ancestors all around us, the shining temple before us, and new life in our arms, I was finally learning how to breathe. *Vismaad*. So that's the secret to living inside of *chardi kala*—ever-rising spirits even in darkness, joy even in struggle—one breath at a time.

Exhale.

These days, each visit to Baba Punjab Singh is the same. I walk into his room and the sound of ever-constant prayers. I help his granddaughter Amrit and Veer Ji wash his hair and make one long braid. Like them, I call him Papa Ji, which means "Father." I rub oil into his skin and massage his legs. I take his hand in mine. His eyes open. His eyes sparkle.

"Papa Ji, do you recognize me?" I ask. He can only blink to communicate—once for no, twice for yes.

He blinks twice.

"Papa Ji, we are all praying for you. Do you feel our prayers and our love?" I ask.

He blinks twice.

Veer Ji asks his father: "Papa Ji, are you in *chardi kala*?"

And his father blinks—twice.

Yes, I am in chardi kala.

If Baba Punjab Singh can live in a state of *chardi kala,* so can I.

The family wishes that no one take photographs of his face, so every time, before I leave, I spend a long time looking into his eyes so that I can take him with me. Baba Punjab Singh represents the state of the Sikh community. We arrived in America more than a century ago with vitality, potential, wisdom, and many words—but hate in the form of white supremacy has tried to kill us. Hate paralyzes our bodies and silences our voices. It finds us in our homes and houses of worship, our schools and streets, and online. Hate strips us of language and denies us recognition. To this day, America cannot pronounce our names or remember our tragedies. Our turbans mark us as terrorists, not seekers of truth and justice. America forgets us, or never knew us to begin with. Yet we go on living; we refuse to die. In fact, we find a way, beyond all odds, to communicate that we are still residing in the Sikh spirit of *chardi kala*. We blink twice. That is our defiance—to practice love even in hopelessness. And to show you. So that you might take our hand, and love us, too.

During those first months in Oak Creek, I barely ate or slept. I was organizing in the trenches alongside other advocates, reporting, filming, writing, and counseling. And I was bleeding. At the end of each day, I discarded pads soaked with blood. I had canceled my surgery for endometriosis and not rescheduled it, hoping to get by on medication. But now instead of bleeding every month, I was bleeding every day—bleeding inside my body and from my body while my community was bleeding. But the community was breathing, too, breathing through rituals and traditions of music and song and meditation, and, in time, I was breathing with them, breathing even as I bled.

I returned home for my surgery three months after the shooting, November 2012. I wrote to friends and family and asked them to envision my surgery as a healing ritual. I received a wave of wishes as Sharat wheeled me into the surgery room and felt an elated joy, rising like buoyant warmth. It surprised me. I marveled at it and rested in it as the anesthesiologist counted down from ten. The surgeon used saline water to wash my intestines, ovaries, and organs. He pumped water into my veins through the IV to hydrate me. My body had been the container for dying, each month my eggs dying, the lesions bleeding. Now my body was being washed clean.

"Your surgery was successful," the doctor told me. "But remember: The endometrial tissue grows back." I had a small window of time if I wanted to have biological children.

A few weeks later, in December 2012, we returned to Oak Creek with a short film Sharat and I had made for the community. We screened it for families in a theater, just for them, before releasing it online. After the film ended, Kamal, Harpreet, and Pardeep stood up to tell their stories, moved the audience, and inspired new connections.

As we flew back home, I thought about what I witnessed in Oak Creek. In the wake of the shooting, many people chose to *wonder* about us and hear our stories and share our pain. The Sikh community knew how to *grieve* together, and we made space for others to join us. In grieving together, we built bonds strong enough to organize together, and our allies followed our lead to *fight* for various social and policy changes. Along the way, we offered one another safe containers for *rage*—rage for the gunman, and rage for lawmakers who did nothing, or not enough. Some of us had the ability to *listen* to people like Arno who helped us understand the gunman's context. This information helped us focus on the change we wanted to make—to hold our institutions responsible for fanning a culture of hate. To start, we chose to *reimagine* how our government prioritizes, tracks, and responds to hate violence. Throughout, we were helping one another *breathe,* taking care of one another in the labor.

Sharat had been breathing with me the whole time, by my side. When the plane touched down in Hartford, Connecticut, the two of us had one task left for the year: to pack our carry-ons and finally go on our honeymoon.

I glanced at my phone as the plane taxied to the gate and saw the breaking news: twenty children and seven adults killed in a mass shooting inside Sandy Hook Elementary School in Newtown, Connecticut. This happened in our own backyard, less than an hour from New Haven. We had traveled from the site of one mass shooting to another. Instead of going home, we drove toward Newtown and saw people in cars sobbing over their steering wheels. A few churches were holding vigils that night, including Newtown Congregational Church, UCC. By the time we arrived, an army of media cameras waited outside. Inside the church, families mourned openly in each other's arms. Sharat and I embraced people we did not know. We were breathing together in this church, just as we had in the gurdwara.

I thought—*This is it*. Newtown will be the tipping point in the movement to end gun violence in America. The massacre of children will wake the nation's conscience.

But it would not be enough. In the years to come, the list of mass shootings would only grow—a queer nightclub in Orlando, a concert in Las Vegas, a high school in Florida, a store in El Paso, among hundreds of others—and Congress would fail to pass any meaningful laws to stop them. Not even background checks. Not even when the majority of the country wanted them. "Thoughts and prayers" would become the refrain of lawmakers who did nothing. Oak Creek would become the first of many houses of worship attacked by white nationalists. The death toll would rise rapidly: two people at a Jewish community center in Kansas City in 2014; nine people in a historically black church in Charleston in 2015; six people in a mosque in Quebec in 2017; eleven people in a synagogue in Pittsburgh in 2018; fifty-one people in mosques in Christchurch, New Zealand, in 2019; one in a synagogue in Poway near San Diego shortly after. I could not have imagined we would see so many Oak Creeks in succession. Back then, we had to link the massacre in Oak Creek to the 16th Street Baptist Church bombing in Birmingham, the last major attack on a faith community, separated by fifty years, just to get people to understand the terror it inflicted. Now such massacres are routine. White nationalists are a globally connected network; each new shooter leaves behind a manifesto or example to inspire another. And behind each of the headlines are stories of the dead and living that are just as complex and deep as those we saw in Oak Creek.

It did not have to be this way.

After Oak Creek in 2012, our nation could have named white nationalist violence a national and global threat and poured resources into fighting to protect our communities. We could have held tech companies accountable for the rapid spread of hate and misinformation on social media platforms. We could have passed strong laws that prohibited racial profiling and created task forces modeled after the National Church Arson Task Force of the 1990s. We could have modeled for the world how to respond to tribal nationalism and initiated local and national dialogues on ending white supremacy. We certainly could have limited the free flow of guns.

As it was, our tiny community had to fight with all our might just to add a box to a federal form. We are not helpless in the wake of this violence. But it will take *all of us* to remake the culture and institutions that authorize hate—and to reimagine a society where no human being is disposable.

In the church in Newtown, grieving those small children, holding Sharat's hand, I felt my face wet with tears in the long night. The choir sang one last hymn to end the service, and we all joined our voices together in the "Hymn of Promise":

> *In the cold and snow of winter, there's a spring that waits to be,*
> *unrevealed until its season, something God alone can see.*

There was so much work to do. I turned to Sharat.

"Do we need to cancel our honeymoon?" I asked.

Sharat had never left my side. His hand was on my back, steadying me as we stared into the abyss in Oak Creek, and before the world went dark in the minutes before my surgery. Our honeymoon had already been postponed by a year. But he didn't answer my question. He just repeated my own words back to me:

"The *way* we make change is just as important as the change we make."

"I said that?"

"This is your test," he said. How much longer was I going to sacrifice my body, and his, for the cause?

❧

There is a pervasive form of contemporary violence to which the idealist most easily succumbs: activism and overwork. . . . To allow oneself to be carried away by a multitude of conflicting concerns, to surrender to too many demands, to commit oneself to too many projects, to want to help everyone in everything, is to succumb to violence. The frenzy of our activism neutralizes our work for peace. It destroys our own inner capacity for peace. It destroys the fruitfulness of our own work, because it kills the root of inner wisdom which makes work fruitful.

—*Thomas Merton*

I had been made to believe that overwork was the only way to make a difference. I had come to measure my sense of worth by how much I produced, how well I responded, and how quickly. I had worked for so long, and so hard, and at such great speeds, that I had become accustomed to breathlessness. I could not remember the last time I had a long night of rest. Or gazed at the night sky. Or danced. I told myself that it was for good reason, that the need was so great, and our work too important. Perhaps you too have felt this way.

This is what I want to tell you: You don't have to make yourself suffer in order to serve. You don't have to grind your bones into the ground. You don't have to cut your life up into pieces and give yourself away until there is nothing left. You belong to a community and a broader movement. Your life has value. We need you alive. We need you to last. You will not last if you are not breathing.

Place a hand on your chest. Take a deep breath. Feel your belly fill up. Hold the inhale for four counts. Feel the suspension. Now exhale for eight counts. Feel your heart beating in your chest. You are alive. You are here. Look around you. What is the most beautiful thing that you can see right now? Look at it for a moment. Notice its color, and shape, the way the light falls on it. Let yourself wonder at it. No matter what is happening out there in the world right now—no matter how dark or violent or cruel—this beautiful thing also exists. The world *right here* is just as real as the world *out there*. Take another deep breath. Notice how it's a little easier. Now—who can share this beautiful thing with you?

"When we see something that beautiful, we call it breathtaking, but we really should call it breath*giving*," my friend Rabbi Sharon Brous says to me. "Because when suffering constricts the heart, awe stretches it back out, making us more compassionate, more loving, more present."

✧✧

Loving ourselves is frontline social justice work. Audre Lorde said: "Caring for myself is not an act of self-indulgence, it is self-preservation, and that is an act of political warfare." And bell hooks wrote, "I have seen that we cannot fully create effective movements for social change if individuals struggling for that change are not also self-actualized or working towards that end." Without loving ourselves, our other efforts to love fail. When asked why we should practice radical care for ourselves, Angela Davis responded: "Longevity." "As we struggle, we are attempting to presage the world to come," she said. "If we don't start practicing collective self-care now, there is no way to imagine, much less reach, a time of freedom." That means finding ways to breathe life *into* the world we want, here and now.

Perhaps it is time to shift the terms from "self-love" to "loving *ourselves*." Loving *ourselves* happens in community. Black feminists in my life show me how. My colleague Lisa Anderson, a black queer theologian, leads retreats and convenings that support the wholeness and wellness of black and brown cis, queer, and trans women. She says, "Movements for social justice will no longer happen on our backs, or over our dead bodies." Activist adrienne maree brown has created a handbook on reclaiming pleasure as essential to the health of our movements in what she calls "pleasure activism." Melissa Harris-

Perry, my friend and big sister, is shifting public discourse from self-care to collective-care. The term "self-care" implies that caring for ourselves is a private, individual act, that we need only to detach ourselves from our web of relations and spend our resources on respite or pampering. But Melissa reminds us that care is labor that we all do for one another, in seen and unseen ways. It should not come with a price tag. It should be available to all of us. Melissa calls for "squad care"—a way to be in relationship with people committed to caring for one another: "Squad care reminds us there is no shame in reaching for each other and insists the imperative rests not with the individual, but with the community. Our job is to have each other's back."

Loving ourselves can begin by breathing together. We carry in our bodies and psyches the trauma of our ancestors but also their resilience. How did *they* breathe together? What were *their* rituals? Singing, chanting, dancing, drumming, shaking, bathing, plunging, burning, walking, writing, resting, eating, sleeping, meditating, expressing gratitude, retreating, bodywork, and being in nature. Notice which practices your body wants. If some practices come from someone else's tradition, seek out people who are sharing such teachings in a culturally respectful way. Now think in rhythms: What can you do every day? Every week? Every month? Every year?

The self-help industry profits from "spiritual bypassing"—the belief that we are changing the world by investing in our own spiritual wellness, even as we continue to participate in the same systems that oppress people. But we can act consciously so that our wellness does not come at the expense of others. If we pay for childcare or housekeeping, we can ensure that domestic workers, often poor black and brown women for whom such respite is not accessible, have fair wages and hours so that they, too, can breathe. If justice work is a matter of choice for us, we can reach out to support those for whom it is not. When the next crisis comes, we can step into the fire to respond, so that others can step back to rest. Perhaps we can cook a meal for a family, volunteer childcare, organize an action, or help another grieve, rage, and breathe. In any given moment, each of us has a role in the labor of revolutionary love.

❧

"What is the life you want for every person on this earth?" my mother asked me.

"Um, let's see, safety, shelter, food, water, healthcare, education, and . . ."

"And time with the people they love," she said. "Go on your honeymoon, please."

I realized what was stopping me: an inflated sense of self-importance. I was acting as though things would fall apart without me, that others could not do the work as well as I could. But, really, I was just terrified that I would no longer have worth if I shifted from *doing* to *being*. I had grown so accustomed to the breathlessness of crises that paying attention to my own breath in my body was the new frightening thing. It was time to find the bravery to surrender my ego and equip others to lead. I made calls and connected advocates in Oak Creek to those in Newtown, and they began to build solidarity directly. Sharat and I then packed for our trip —two months to explore the world and ourselves, breathing together, wondering together, remembering all that was beautiful and good and worth fighting for.

I boarded the plane and held Sharat's hand and took a deep breath as we lifted into the sky—higher and higher and higher—until we turned toward the horizon. In the moment the plane was sideways all we could see was sea and sky, sea and sky.

I think the inability to love is the central problem, because that inability masks a certain terror, and that terror is the terror of being touched. And if you can't be touched, you can't be changed. And if you can't be changed, you can't be alive.

—*James Baldwin*

8.
push.

W HEN I WAS FINALLY READY TO LOVE MYSELF, I HAD TO LEARN HOW to *breathe and push* through my grief, rage, and trauma. On the other side, I found what seemed utterly impossible before: healing, forgiveness, and even reconciliation.

Healing

Sharat and I boarded a plane for our honeymoon with nothing but two carry-ons, a camera, and a sketchbook. We used the money people gave us for our wedding to backpack around the world: Costa Rica, Turkey, Tanzania, New Zealand, and Indonesia. We knew we were lucky: We had the economic means to travel and freedom to take time off from work, privileges out of reach for most people in the marginalized communities I worked with. Every time I felt a surge of guilt, I remembered my mother's instruction: to allow myself the pleasures I wanted for everyone on earth. My gratitude returned me to the present moment. Each place expanded the aperture of what I could *see* and therefore how much I could *breathe* in, and with each breath, I was learning how to love my body and its place among things—the wide wet earth, the sweep of human civilization, the kingdom of animals, the timeline of evolution, and the stars in the universe. I was accessing the force of life within me.

Costa Rica—Breathing the Earth

The rain forest was like a womb—warm, wet, safe, and sustaining. We walked through the cloud forest in Monteverde among trees whose tears created an entire ecosystem. The green trees climbed high into the sky, covered with thick moss and ferns dripping with rain. Orchids and air plants hung on every branch, seeping nutrients from the mist around us. I turned my face up to find the sunlight, eyelashes wet with dew, and spotted a single spiderweb, unspooled in the nook of a great tree, its threads glistening like gold. I drank in every detail.

Some miles away, we waded into the Rio Perdido. The river looked like any other in the rain forest, but the water was hot to the touch. My mother and father were traveling with us for a few days (of course our honeymoon involved my family, too), so we all waded into the thermal river together. I closed my eyes and my mother placed her hand on my belly over my surgery stitches and closed her eyes, and it was as if the river and my mother and the earth were breathing through me.

Turkey—Breathing the Past

We backpacked from Istanbul to Pamukkale to Konya to Cappadocia, and, in each place, we touched remnants of empires from long ago, layers and layers of human civilization stretching back fifteen thousand years. In Ephesus, we walked through the ruins of one of the greatest cities of the Roman Empire. Ephesus had been famous for the worship of Artemis, who absorbed the local goddess before her to become the goddess of fertility. The Temple of Artemis was one of the seven wonders of the ancient world, for thousands of years a place where people prayed for fertility. Now little remained other than stones overgrown with brush and a single column with a stork's nest on top. Sharat and I rested on a rock. I closed my eyes and imagined the thousands of people who had come to this place to pray to the goddess for life to continue in them and through them. I listened to the sounds all around us—birdsong in the trees, cows in the distance, tall grass swaying in the wind—and heard the murmuring song of those prayers whispered long ago. Sharat and I made our own prayer and joined our song to theirs.

Tanzania—Breathing Life

The Serengeti was an ocean—a sea of grass stretching on all sides so that one could think that the entire world was only this. It was like entering a poem. The name "Serengeti" comes from the Maasai name "Siringet," which means "the land of endless space." We camped in endless space for a week. Each morning, we climbed into the rattling jeep and set off down dusty, bumpy roads as our guide followed the map in his mind of the Serengeti floor. Binoculars in hand, we scanned the horizon, plains, and rocks, and once we spotted animals—the thrill! Time stood still as we observed them, Sharat's camera clicking away, my pen running wild on the pages of my sketchbook. Drawing is a contradictory art. In spending so long studying a thing, you seize the thing and disappear into it at the same time. You take and disappear in the taking—until the thing starts to go away. "I love you, elephant"—we would actually say this out loud. "Oh, but we love you, don't go!" I was in awe of them—the elephants on the plain, leopards in the trees, lumbering giraffes, spotted hyenas crossing the road, lionesses crouching on the kopjes, hippos in pools flicking their ears, one bulging eye on us, wildebeest with long, mournful faces, even the grotesque family of vultures, pulling at flesh. *You are a part of me I do not yet know.*

Outside the Serengeti, the Ngorongoro Crater is the most biodiverse place on earth: Once the tallest volcano in the world, the land collapsed millions of years ago and now forms a fertile paradise for thousands of animals. I secretly wanted to imagine the crater as a Garden of Eden where the lion, leopard, cheetah, and hyena ate only plants, and other forces controlled the populations of species. But the wild is brutal. We watched five lions on the golden plain stalk the last in a line of Cape buffalo. They disappeared over the hill so we did not see the kill. The earth is organized by violence—the routine termination of life, the bloody killing of creatures who think and feel and have societies of their own. The earth is also organized by labors of love. I saw it in the gestures between mothers and babies—a mama hippo leads her baby across a swampy lake in the savanna; a baby giraffe, umbilical cord still showing, eats leaves on a bush his mother finds at his exact height; a baby vervet monkey sees food on a higher branch and looks to her parent, waiting for her green light; a baby elephant meets humans in a safari jeep for the first time and looks to his herd to learn that we are in fact safe; a chicken in the corner of an Iraqw hut on the Crater Highlands squawks loudly, feathers flying in the air, to protest Sharat sitting a little too close to her nest of newly laid eggs. In these gestures, there was an impossible love—a wellspring that resided in us, too.

At the Olduvai Gorge, Sharat and I saw a mold of three-million-year-old footsteps in volcanic ash, left by the first humanoids to walk the earth. Our human ancestors migrated from here fifty thousand years ago and spread to every landmass on earth, multiplying our species into billions. Of all the people who have ever been alive on this planet, half are alive today. We, too, are hardwired like the animals to reproduce, to preserve and pass on our genetic code, but there is no one to control our population size or how we manipulate our environment other than us. When I considered all of human history in one breath—our trajectory from warring peoples who killed and enslaved others to nation-states that aim missiles at one another—it seemed like we had made little progress. Perhaps what was truly new and revolutionary on the face of the planet was the notion of universal human dignity, that each person has inherent and equal worth. In every culture, in every part of the world, there have been those who have expanded the idea of "us" beyond family, tribe, and nation to *all* of humanity, insisting that even as we are primed to see the world in terms of "us and them," we are also able to tap the depths of that wellspring of love within us—and choose to love beyond our own kin. At the very tip of the timeline of history, we were the people alive right now who could imagine alternatives to violence and labor for it. This, too, filled me with awe.

New Zealand—Breathing the Universe

We came here to look at the stars. Dark sky reserves are spots on earth where people have agreed to keep light pollution low enough to see the starry night. In the South Island, we entered the largest dark sky reserve in the world—the Aoraki Mackenzie International Dark Sky Reserve. My knees went weak, just like when I was a little girl on the farmland behind our house. My father once introduced me to the concept of the cosmic calendar. "Imagine the entire history of the universe mapped onto months on a calendar, starting with the big bang," he said, filled with excitement. "Then *all* of recorded human history would take place on the last day, December thirty-first, in the final hour, the final minute, and the *final fourteen seconds* of the year!" A blink of an eye. Sharat and I lay on our backs and gazed into the cloudy center of the Milky Way galaxy, as if looking back into time. We watched shooting stars over mountain peaks. *Vismaad*. Ecstatic wonder.

I had forgotten the stars, burning so strong and long that their light reaches us long after they have died. Isn't that what our lives and our activism should look like? Not the supernova, a single outburst under pressure. We must be the long-burning star, bright and steady, contained and sustained, for our energy to reach the next generation long after we die. Oh, and to be part of constellations! Let us see ourselves as part of a larger picture, even if we are like the second star on Orion's Belt, or the seventh of the Seven Sisters. For there is no greater gift than to be part of a movement larger than ourselves. That means that we only need to be responsible for our small patch of sky, our specific area of influence. We need only to shine our particular point of light, long and steady, to become part of stories sewn into the heavens.

Bali, Indonesia—Push

Sharat and I made pilgrimages to Tirta Empul and Pura Besakih and all the great temples of the island, listened to gamelan music, tasted wet grains of rice, tucked flower petals between fingers, and made prayers for fertility; that is, to become vessels for life in *every* sense of the word—biological, intellectual, emotional, and spiritual. And in each place, the prayers gained the force of a river that was like a hot thermal current. The river had been gathering momentum all along, all through our travels, while I was focusing on breathing in the beauty and wonder of the world around me. The river was coursing through me, quietly releasing me from the hold of memories of trauma and shame that had been stitched into my skin since childhood—the cruelty of the boy's mouth in the schoolyard, the night the hand turned my thighs into wooden things, the lieutenant's dark-rimmed glasses as he receded from the body in pain, the shape of the arm that hung limp, the barrel of the gun spinning in sunlight, the bloodstains in the carpets of the prayer hall, the abyss that appeared when looking into caskets of people who looked like my family, the boa constrictor that squeezed the breath out of me, the voice in me that let it because I was not good enough, not strong enough, not beautiful enough, not suffering enough to be saved. No, I was finding a home in my body now, on this earth, in this timeline, as the skies circled around me humming: *You are stardust*. The world was good enough, strong enough, beautiful enough, and worthy enough to be saved, and my body was part of the body of the world. In order to love the world, I had to love myself.

It was time to push.

On our last day in Bali, Sharat appeared with a tray holding a glass of water, a single piece of chocolate he'd cut into the shape of a heart, and a cool wet towel. "Madame, we have ordered the rain for you," he said, because we loved to pretend. "It is arriving shortly. Are you ready for your treatment to begin? It includes a hair crème bath." We opened all the windows of our room and the cool wind rushed around us. He washed my hair and brushed it straight.

"Breathe with me," I said. We spent hours breathing together, his body hovering over mine like the breath of God, and between each breath, he pushed a little closer and I pushed my muscles a little more apart, and I felt the hot river flow from the crown of my head down through my body and said, "I open to you," and we held each other tightly, tears in my eyes. For the first time in my life, there was no searing pain. The thunder boomed through the valley and the clouds opened and the rain poured at a distance until it enveloped us. The world was sky and rain and radiance, release and wholeness, and I saw the future double up and return to me and tell me that I was wondrous and inexhaustible, like the green earth, and that I will be my whole life through.

Healing is the long journey of returning to our bodies. It is a kind of labor that requires breathing and pushing—resting and then going deeper. We must be willing to notice and befriend sensations, including pain and discomfort. "Physical self-awareness is the first step in releasing the tyranny of the past," writes trauma researcher Bessel van der Kolk. Talking about our emotional trauma doesn't necessarily alter our relationship with it. We must be able to *feel* where the trauma lives in our bodies and invite our bodies to orient to the safety of the present moment.

But for survivors of trauma, just noticing our bodies can be terrifying. "Many of us have left our bodies—we're not embodied creatures, we're not living inside our own muscles and cells and sinews. And so we're not in our power, we're not in our energy," says playwright-activist Eve Ensler. In working with women who have survived violence and sexual assault around the world, she has seen that "the more traumatized people are, the less connected they are to their own source of strength, their own source of inspiration, intuition, heart—everything." It was performing in Eve's play *The Vagina Monologues* in college that introduced me to my vagina. Now her work was teaching me that vibrant activism required harnessing the energy and life force of our whole bodies: "It is where we do not live that the dying comes."

I had not been living in my pelvic floor for most of my life. I had told myself a story of damage from assault, vaginismus, and endometriosis, even after pain had passed. But Joyce Frazier helped me change that. She was my neuromuscular therapist who was now a mother figure. "This is a warrior's body!" she declared as she worked on me. In weekly sessions, she taught me how to breathe from my diaphragm and experience a new relationship with my body. Under her care, I pursued varieties of bodywork—acupuncture needles, neuromuscular therapy, somatic trauma therapy, manual pelvic floor therapy, and surgery. I was fortunate and privileged: I had a patient and caring partner, access to resources, and the attention of skilled practitioners. In one somatic therapy session with Tommy Woon, I described the sexual assault when I was a teenager and noticed my thighs clench. I was ashamed and angry that after so many years, my body was still holding the trauma in such a way that it literally shaped my posture and the way I walked. But Tommy told me to say to my thighs, "Thank you for protecting me." I took deep breaths and thanked my muscles for being so vigilant for so long. To my surprise, my legs began to relax and release. The bodily responses that we may be most inclined to reject often occur to protect us and will persist until we properly acknowledge them, feel them, even honor and thank them. I was developing a new relationship to my pelvic floor, not as a site of trauma and pain but a seat of creativity and pleasure. I was learning how to make friends with my body.

What is the place in your body where you are not yet living? Can you put your attention there? It's okay if you can't sense much. Breathe. Sometimes we just need to stay here and breathe and slowly allow awareness to come. Sometimes we are ready to feel more and more of our sensations. Be curious. *You are a part of me I do not yet know.* What is the story you have told about that part of your body? What new story is ready to emerge?

Trauma therapies that use mind-body techniques are available more than before, backed by recent breakthroughs in neuroscience. Somatic trauma therapy, like what I did with Tommy, helps people release traumatic memories by working through sensations. EMDR (eye movement desensitization and reprocessing) helps integrate trauma into the past. Biofeedback lowers the heart rate through slow breathing. Tapping, or emotional freedom technique, calms the sympathetic nervous system and prevents going into fight-or-flight mode. Yoga, historically a system for healing and liberation, trains us to inhabit our bodies through mindful movement. Many of these healing practices originated in indigenous traditions, yet such support is rarely accessible to marginalized people who most need it. It is time to change that. It is time to demand the freedom and opportunity to heal our bodies as a human right. It is time to organize not just around our trauma but around our collective healing.

❧

I returned from our honeymoon feeling rest and joy in my body. I wanted to be able to access that feeling even when the work picked up again. My friend Jessica lived next door to us in New Haven. She was a tenure-track political science professor who was navigating the pressures of academia as an Asian American woman. Yet she knew how to bring joy into her daily life. She spent a little time with me each day and taught me how to bake currant scones, plant a vegetable garden on my balcony, cook her recipe for mapo tofu, bike for pleasure, and dance to blues. Jessica became my closest friend. And whenever the world threw me into darkness, trauma, and despair, she helped me breathe and push through it. Healing did not mean the end to suffering: It meant the freedom to return home, again and again, to our bodies and to one another.

Forgiveness

Grandmother was dying. Sharat and I flew back to California and our farmland, rushed into the old house, and found my mother by Grandmother's side. Grandmother was my father's mother. She put my mother through misery when she was young, but here was my mother, swabbing Grandmother's mouth with a sponge. I had watched my mother work through her grief, rage, and trauma through the years. Now my mother was helping Grandmother die.

"Waheguru, Waheguru," my mother sang softly. I joined her. Grandmother gazed at both of us, moving her lips with ours.

"I love you," she mouthed.

Grandmother died the next morning, on my birthday. My parents did not return her ashes to the sacred rivers of Punjab. Our family had lived in California for a century now. *This* land was as much our ancestral home as that one. So instead my parents went out on a boat off the coast of California with my aunts and uncles—my *chacha*s, *chachi*s, *foofar*, and *bhooa*. They scattered her ashes in the Pacific Ocean, just as they had done for Baba Ji.

"How did you do it?" I asked my mother. "How did you forgive her?"

"Time," she said. "It doesn't happen instantly."

"But *how*?" I asked.

My mother looked at me softly with tears in her eyes. She was as beautiful as ever.

"Forgiveness is for you, not for the person who hurt you," she said. "For you, not them. For *you*."

Somewhere in her healing journey, my mother saw Grandmother in her fullness: a Punjabi farmwoman who worked the fields of California, shovel over her shoulder, boots dripping with mud. Grandmother taught herself how to read, sign checks, and sell peaches at a profit. She created a small empire out of dirt. She bore four children and brought all her siblings and their families from India to America. It was a miracle that she had become the matriarch. She was beloved by everyone, but she was cruel to my mother because her in-laws were cruel to her. She did not have the wisdom to stop the cycle of oppression. My mother did.

"It's easy to love people who love you back," she said. "When somebody gives you pain, how do you love that person? That's the real test of love."

Forgiveness is not forgetting: Forgiveness is freedom from hate.

Two days after nine black people were massacred by a white supremacist in a historic black church in Charleston in June 2015, their family members showed up at his bond hearing, looked into his eyes, and said: "I forgive you." I felt sick to my stomach. This man did not deserve their forgiveness. I worried that saying these words too quickly cut short our right to express our divine rage, publicly and internally. Yet these family members chose to forgive as a declaration of their own autonomy, as if to say no matter what you do to us, we will not allow you to make us hate you. I thought about my own community's choice to pray for the gunman after the mass shooting of Sikhs in Oak Creek, Wisconsin. Forgiveness was not a substitute for justice; it had *energized* us in the fight for justice. It reframed justice not as retribution but as cultural and institutional transformation.

Perhaps our task is to honor all the different ways people relate to forgiveness. Survivors of violence should never be criticized if they choose to forgive. Nor should they be expected to forgive, either. Sometimes the choice to withhold forgiveness is an act of agency, too.

I thought of Roshan. It was my rush to forgiveness that landed me in that empty park and endangered me in the first place. Since his assault with the gun, I had focused on the security of my body. Soon after, Roshan had sent me a letter begging for forgiveness and asked me to release him from his pain. But demanding forgiveness when a survivor is not ready or willing to give it amplifies their original loss of agency. I experienced it as another assertion of his power. I refused, and Roshan left me alone. Now, after watching my mother forgive my grandmother, I felt a new desire to let go of the animosity I was still holding. Forgiveness appeared to me as a gift for *myself* at the end of a long, internal healing process.

I began to forgive him in my heart. I freed myself.

I thought that would be the end of our story. It would have been enough. But sometimes forgiveness opens up the previously unimaginable possibility of reconciliation.

Reconciliation

One day, Roshan called me out of the blue. It had been ten years since the assault with the gun. He was now an engineer and had a fiancée. He called to invite me to his wedding in London, where he was about to move with his new wife. He was reaching out for reconciliation; I recoiled. On his deathbed, Papa Ji had asked me to find peace with Roshan. I knew that survivors did not need to reconcile with their assailants in order to find peace. I had to decide whether this was something I wanted. I told Roshan that I would think about it.

Reconciliation rests on accountability. It requires perpetrators to accept full responsibility for their actions. In truth and reconciliation commissions, the survivor shares the impact of the harm; the offender accepts responsibility, finds a way to repair it, and is reintegrated into the community. Such commissions had been used in more than thirty countries around the world, and, although imperfect, they were powerful alternatives to retribution. I began to imagine what our own truth and reconciliation commission would look like. "Is he aware of the impact of his actions on your life?" Sharat asked.

I called Roshan back and asked if he would be willing to undergo this process with me. "Yes, anything," he said. My mentor Tommy Woon helped me prepare questions about accountability. A few days later, I found a quiet place, took a deep breath, called Roshan, and our first truth and reconciliation session began. Each of my questions began with, "Do you acknowledge that . . . ?" Roshan dutifully acknowledged that he molested me when we were teenagers and that he pulled a gun on me in the park. He was quiet and remorseful. He acknowledged that my trauma caused me panic attacks and nightmares.

"Do you acknowledge that I was scared for years that you were going to find me and kill me?" I asked.

"I didn't know that," he said. He began to sob. This was the moment that a voice in me panicked: "What are you doing to him?" I reminded myself that it was not my job to make him feel better. That was the old way. Tommy had taught me that when a perpetrator reckons with what they have done, they must be allowed to feel intense emotional pain: It is the first step to reconnecting with their empathy and compassion. I waited and let him cry. Then I took a breath and asked:

"Do you acknowledge it?"

"Yes." He wept. He regained his composure. I pushed on.

"Do you acknowledge that I had to work for years with many different practitioners to heal from the trauma of sexual and physical assault?" I asked.

"I didn't know that . . . yes," he said. "I'm so sorry."

"Do you acknowledge that I still let the rest of the family love you and help you, even though it was hard for me?"

"Yes."

"Do you acknowledge that my body still activates when I see you, and that I may not wish to be in your presence, even after we have gone through this process?"

"Yes," he said.

Reconciliation mends what has been torn asunder, but it does not return us to a point before the harm happened. Perpetrators and survivors can just leave each other alone after that. Roshan acknowledged that, even after his apology, I still did not owe him a relationship. I told him that I would come to his wedding if his fiancée knew what he had done. He told her, and Sharat and I made plans to go. I didn't realize how hard the wedding would be for me. My skin crawled, my throat ached. I resented being there. But when I watched Roshan circle the Guru Granth Sahib four times, get married, and start a new chapter in his life, I exhaled—I could feel my grandfather's gratitude even in death.

❧❧

Two years later, the #metoo movement swept the nation, holding powerful men accountable for sexual harassment and abuse in a public reckoning. Millions of women were breaking their silence for the first time. I learned that the #metoo movement began more than a decade ago, the phrase coined by civil rights activist Tarana Burke, who works primarily with poor women and black and brown girls who have survived sexual violence. Burke believed in "empowerment through empathy": Sharing our stories and connecting to other survivors help us heal. She also knew that for women who stand at the intersection of sexism, racism, ableism, poverty, and bigotry, breaking our silence comes at a much higher cost.

I added my voice to the movement, knowing that many Sikh women in my own community did not yet have the resources or support to say the simple words "Me Too." Some of my Sikh sisters reached out to share their stories, and we tended to one another in private safe spaces. The impact of the movement ran deep: We were practicing revolutionary love for one another publicly and privately on a mass scale—*wondering* about one another's stories, *grieving* together, and *fighting* alongside one another.

As time went on, and more abusers were led away in handcuffs, I realized that I had never seen a man who committed sexual or physical assault make a public apology, a sincere and complete public apology. Our society's dominant response to violence was punishment, but I found myself hungering for something else. "Survivors have to be the ones who define what justice looks like," Burke says, "but most survivors aren't punitive and the reason why is because we have such close relations with the people who harm us most of the time." She adds, "Part of our work is teaching people how to dream about another world while actively being safe in this world." I began to wonder: *Could we protect spaces for women to* rage *and heal and find justice, and also for men to claim their own process of accountability, apology, and transformation to earn a pathway back to community?*

I thought back on my exchange with Roshan—how he took full responsibility for his assault and apologized in a way that was satisfactory to me—and I found myself wondering: *How in the world was he able to do that?* I really wanted to know. My desire to know was more powerful than any aversion in me. So, three years after we had our first truth and reconciliation commission, I called him in London and asked him to tell me *his* story of what happened. We chose a day to spend on the phone. I sat in the little garden in our backyard, dialed his number, and opened our second truth and reconciliation commission. This time, I was the one listening.

"What was your sixteen-year-old self thinking the night the assault happened?" I asked.

"I wasn't thinking," he said. "I was confused. I didn't know what I was feeling. I was in a state of unawareness. Not being fully conscious, not being unconscious. It was a dream-like state."

My legs clenched under me. The rest of my body was at ease, but these muscles still felt the residue of the trauma. The body does not forget. I looked up at the garden, the jasmine on the fence, and returned to the safety of the present moment. I took a breath and asked the next question.

"What do you feel now when you look back at that sixteen-year-old?" I asked.

"Anger," he said. "There was something broken inside me that should have been addressed earlier. But it's all me. There's nothing else that I could put this on."

He was taking responsibility for something that he experienced as if in a dream. He wasn't qualifying it or making excuses. I had only heard men say that they did not remember what happened, that they were too drunk or too young or too confused. Roshan was taking full responsibility no matter his intent, no matter how long ago.

I asked him about the times he threatened Sharat.

"Yes," he sighed. "I had anxiety around collective loss. Losing the most sacred parts of our community. Losing our land. Losing our culture. Losing our collective existence. I thought that I was somehow the savior who needed to save future generations. It was naïve."

He talked about intergenerational trauma in Sikh families, going back to the Partition. Still, he managed to express remorse in every sentence. I had never seen a man do this before: identify the forces that drove him to commit violence while taking responsibility for the harm.

"Why did you ask me to meet you in the park that day?" I finally asked.

"I was ashamed and disgusted with what I had done to you," he said. "Everything that was suppressed exploded. For a couple weeks, I didn't sleep much or eat much. I felt this heavy sense of hate. I thought about self-harm. I thought that you wanted to see me punished."

Roshan had believed that people should be punished, not helped, when they commit harm. So, when he faced the harm he had caused, he thought the only solution was to punish himself. In the park that day, I thought he was going to kill me, but he wanted to kill himself in front of me, *for* me. I did not know which was worse.

"After you walked away from me," he said, "I put the gun to my chin and pulled the trigger and nothing happened. I didn't have the right ammunition. They were the wrong bullets."

Both of us got quiet, imagining what might have been.

The healing process for a perpetrator of violence is different than for a survivor. I had to release my trauma and reclaim my power; Roshan had to stand the heat of his internal shame and guilt. His healing was a process of *self-reconciliation,* accepting the darkest parts of himself and integrating them into who he knew himself to be. My healing did not depend on his accountability, nor did his healing depend on my forgiveness. But when he was ready to make a genuine apology, *and* I wanted to hear it, we had found a way into this reconciliation. I thought about Arno Michaelis, the former white supremacist who was now a vocal advocate against hate. His journey was similar to Roshan's. Those who have forsaken wrongdoing can become some of our greatest allies and accomplices in the work of social change.

"Have you found closure?" I asked Roshan.

"Closure is co-dependent on you and your journey," he said. "It's inseparable. I can't have closure when my actions are still causing any harm. Every time I learn something more about the impact of my actions on your life, I feel like I have repeated the harm to you all over again."

Why should a perpetrator be held accountable for what he did years ago? Because the survivor lives with the consequences of those actions for the rest of her life. It runs through her life. Roshan said he was standing by for anything he could do, always.

"To surrender like that is to risk everything," I said.

"Yes," he said.

"How does this process feel to you?" I asked.

"Cathartic," he said, "like a new way of being in the world."

"It's taken a very long time," I said.

We both tried to laugh but only managed to sigh.

We were breathing and pushing through reconciliation, each time creating more space and understanding than we thought possible. The sexual assault had taken place twenty years ago, the physical assault thirteen years ago. It took that damn long to do the work.

❧

I thought about what made Roshan's apology genuine. First, he was willing to wonder about himself, his psyche, family, and conditioning, and to investigate the reasons he committed harm. Second, he was willing to wonder about me and imagine how I felt when he hurt me and in all the suffering that followed. Third, he admitted what he had done. He was specific and detailed. He took full responsibility for the consequences of his actions, regardless of his intention. Finally, he did the work of reparation. Eve Ensler calls these four elements the alchemy of the apology—a process that can be taught, modeled, and practiced. "The mandate is never on the victim to forgive," she says. "But the alchemy of the apology can free us."*

---

* Eve Ensler wrote the apology she had always wanted to hear from her father, who abused her as a little girl. In the process of imagining his apology, years after his death, she freed herself from her father's power over her. Imagination is a powerful tool in our own healing and liberation.

The labor of reconciliation is complicated, unpredictable, and painful. In most truth and reconciliation commissions, a third party leads survivors and offenders through the process. We took a risk by doing it on our own, and we got lucky. Somehow, led by the deepest wisdom within us, Roshan and I pushed together to the other side and transitioned our family into a new place—broken *and* whole, wounded *and* healed, which is, I think, the best shape for a family to be in. Sometimes reconciliation happens in the course of healing; sometimes it does not. What matters is the insistence that our liberation is possible. Pushing *together* through healing, forgiveness, and reconciliation was the labor of revolutionary love.

"Each of us is more than the worst thing we've ever done," says civil rights leader and death penalty abolitionist Bryan Stevenson. "We are all broken by something. We have all hurt someone and have been hurt. We all share the condition of brokenness even if our brokenness is not equivalent." When I was a student, Bryan came to my law school to speak. Now his message echoed in me: In tending our wounds, we show mercy to ourselves and perhaps a corresponding need to show mercy to others. We are released from our attachment to punishment. We evolve our pursuit of justice from retribution—an eye for an eye—to collective liberation.

I began to wonder what such liberation could look like for our society as a whole.

America, too, had committed assaults on people it claimed to care about. America, too, had told itself a story of its own goodness. America, too, had suppressed memories and histories of the traumas it had caused. America, too, could not confront the ways those assaults ran through generational lines, or how oppression took new forms in the present. America, too, did not know how to reconcile the dark parts of its history with the nation it aspired to be. America, too, just wanted us to forget and move on. The prospect of reckoning with truth was too overwhelming, the consequences too unimaginable. But our willful forgetting keeps re-creating the conditions for all that suppressed grief, rage, and shame to erupt in cycles of violence.

What does it mean for us to love ourselves as a people? What does it mean for us to push as a nation?

America needs to reconcile with itself and do the work of apology: To say to indigenous, black, and brown people, we take full ownership for what we did. To say, we owe you *everything*. To say, we see how harm runs through generations. To say, we own this legacy and will not harm you again. To promise the non-repetition of harm would require nothing less than transitioning the nation as a whole. It would mean retiring the old narrative about who we are—a city on a hill—and embracing a new narrative of an America longing to be born, a nation whose promise lies in the future, a nation we can only realize by doing the labor: reckoning with the past, reconciling with ourselves, restructuring our institutions, and letting those who have been most harmed be the ones to lead us through the transition.

❧

Sharat and I moved through the seasons of our life. We decided to return to California after a decade on the East Coast. I wanted to live by the sea that my grandfather crossed to begin our story in America. I wanted to try to start our own family on the land that had been home for generations. Sharat became a director in the film and television industry, and I got a job as a fellow at Stanford Law School that allowed me to work remotely. We found a tiny apartment in Los Angeles on Venice Beach. It felt like a two-chambered peanut, but we loved it. It was like living at the edge of the world, next to a circus of life on the boardwalk, among a community of artists and activists. It was the final years of the Obama era.

I did not know it then but the reconciliation process in my own family would prepare me for what was about to happen next in our nation.

All that you touch
You Change.
All that you Change
Changes you.
The only lasting truth
Is Change.
—*Octavia E. Butler*

9.
transition.

I HELD A POSITIVE PREGNANCY TEST IN MY HAND, STUFFED IT INTO AN EN-velope, and left it for Sharat with a note to meet me at the ocean. I dug my fingers into the sand and gazed at the horizon, laughing and crying at the same time. It didn't have to happen. Between the endo-metriosis and vaginismus, the odds were not in our favor. But we had managed to pluck a zygote from the star nursery, the nebula in Orion's Belt.

"Our next great adventure!" Sharat said when he found me.

We floated in a state of bliss—until the nausea hit the next day. I vomited while Sharat held my hair. Every day after that, I experienced every "normal" symptom pregnant women endure: fatigue, leg cramps, hemorrhoids, sacroiliac joint dysfunction, acid reflux, and surges of prenatal depression. I once threw up on our dog's face. Poor Shadi. But each morning, I managed to walk along the ocean and hum the *shabad*s, and when I saw a little body on the ultrasound for the first time, I said, "Hello, I will love you for the rest of my life."

Labor began at dawn on a December morning. Sharat prepared a bath and lit a candle and squeezed my hands through the contractions, which we called waves. In the ocean, if you make your body rigid as a wave approaches, you get knocked down and beaten up; if you decide to dive beneath the wave, you emerge on the other side with ease. I decided that I would dive under the waves. It worked through early labor. But by nightfall, my labor sped up suddenly, and I wailed dur-ing every contraction. Sharat pressed down on my sacrum with all his might. My mother cleaned the vomit from my hair and made a single strong braid. Mucus and blood appeared on my clothes. I did not know it then but I had already started to transition.

My father drove us to the hospital through the dark night. I was on my hands and knees in the back of the car, wailing. I lifted my face to gaze at the black ocean. White frothy waves rolled in and crashed onto the shore, lit by the moon. *Ocean waves. These are ocean waves,* I kept thinking. But the ocean is vast and dangerous and unflinching. Waves can crush you, waves can kill you. Sometimes there's no way to dive deep enough beneath them. *Breathe,* I heard a voice in me say. When the wave subsided, there was no pain at all, like floating on the sea. I started to cry, feeling sorry for myself. *Save your energy.* I dropped my head against the car window and released my shoulders and face. I focused on rest and luxuriated in the rest. I noticed some still sacred part of me watching all this, alert, attentive, repeating *Breathe*.

By the time we got to the hospital, the waves were not waves. They were tsunamis. "So, on a scale of one to ten, what's your pain level?" asked the receiving nurse. Was she out of her mind? "TEN!" I cried between the contractions. My mom was stroking my forehead. I think Sharat said I love you. But they were distant voices on the shore and I was out at sea, and the only thing I could do was choose to rest between the tsunamis, trusting that they would manage the outside world.

The midwife arrived and said she could see the baby's head, but all I could feel was a ring of fire. My muscles pushed down, but I was resisting and pulled the little body stuck in the ring back into me. There was only one way out and that was to go *through*—I had to push *into* the fire.

The midwife said, "Breathe and push."

I turned to my mother and said, "I can't."

My mother whispered in my ear Papa Ji's prayer, *"Tati Vao Na Lagi."* The hot winds cannot touch you. "You are brave," she said. "You are brave." I didn't believe her. Just then, I saw my grandmother standing behind my mother—and her mother behind her, and her mother behind her, and her mother behind her, a long line of women who had pushed through the fire before me, disappearing into the distant horizon.

You are brave, you are brave.

I saw a woman floating over me, hair flowing, smiling down tenderly. She had my face.

You are brave, you are brave.

I took a breath. I pushed. The fire burned brighter and hotter, and I was screaming, flesh searing, until I pushed all the way through the ring—baby's head. Another push—baby's body.

The fire went out. I heard crying and saw a baby covered in milkiness and blood attached to a long blue spirally cord. They pulled him up onto my chest and my mouth was open and my eyes were wide and my mind was struggling to understand that what I had just survived was somehow connected to this baby. I began to sob and shake and shake and sob. Sharat had tears in his eyes. He cut the umbilical cord. The nurse said that I had to push again to release the placenta. *What?* I pushed one last time. They stitched me up. I had a second-degree perineal tear that required a packet of sutures. That was the fire.

There were no cords or IVs or monitors attached to me, just my own body and bangles and the pendants dangling from my neck. The baby was born as soon as I got to the hospital. I could have been in the woods or in a cave. I was animal and divine.

My father had been behind the curtain, fighting back tears as he heard me wail and the baby cry. He was by my mother's side now, so proud of me. Sharat turned to my parents and announced our son's name: "Kavi Singh Raju." Kavi means "poet" in Sanskrit. Singh binds him to the Sikh tradition of warrior-sages. He was a newborn in our arms, but of course I could see the spirit of his poet-warrior great-grandfathers in him. He lifted his eyes to me, his tiny hands still around my necklaces. He moved on his own down my chest to nurse, slept between my breasts, and wonder melted into me: *You are a part of me that I do not yet know.*

As I held Kavi on my chest, still shaking from the rush of oxytocin flooding my body, my mother was already preparing to feed me spoonfuls of dal and *chol*—feeding her baby as I fed mine. I began to see my mother with new eyes. She had never stopped laboring for me, from my birth to my son's birth. She already knew what I was just beginning to name: *Love is more than a rush of feeling. Love is sweet labor— fierce, bloody, imperfect, and life-giving. A choice we make over and over again.*

I looked up at the clock and announced, "Kavi is five hours old." Then "seven hours old." Then "twelve hours old." I felt the forward pull of time. Time moves like a swift strong current and we can slow it down when we pay attention to it, but there's no stopping it. I felt an exquisite ache knowing that the hours and days of Kavi's life would pull him forward into the future, including a future without us. I realized that the only thing I knew for certain about his life was that it would one day end.

Joy is the gift of love. Grief is the price of love. Anger protects that which is loved. And when we think we have reached our limit, wonder is the act that returns us to love.

❧

The final stage of birthing labor is the most dangerous stage, and the most painful. As the cervix stretches to ten centimeters, contractions are less than a minute apart, and there is barely time to breathe. The medical term is "transition." Transition *feels like dying* but it is the stage that precedes the birth of new life. After my labor, I began to think about transition as a metaphor for the most difficult fiery moments in our lives.* In all our various creative labors—making a living, raising a family, building a nation—there are moments that are so painful, we want to give up. But inside searing pain and encroaching numbness,

---

* Only a subset of women give birth this way, *or* give birth at all. But the ability to create and nurture is a *human* right, not a biological one. I use birthing labor as a metaphor for *any* person in the midst of creative endeavors. If the metaphor of war offers wisdom for how to face injustice and fight the good fight, then perhaps the metaphor of birth can offer all of us wisdom about the courage needed to create something new.

we might also find the depths of our courage, hear our deepest wisdom, and transition to the other side.

During my transition on the birthing table, when the pain was at its worst, there was a voice in me that said, "I can't." But there was also the voice in me whispering, "Breathe," and echoing my mother's words, "You are brave." Who were these voices inside me? Who are the voices of fear and wisdom inside all of us?

I think the voice that said "I can't" has been inside me since childhood, ever since the boy in the schoolyard first held up a mirror to my small, brown, female body and showed me that I had reason to feel afraid. The voice was fully formed by the time I was a teenager. It told me that I was not beautiful enough, smart enough, strong enough, or good enough to do the things I wanted to do. It was the voice that shamed and judged me. In junior high school, I used to pull my long black hair like curtains on either side of me in class so that no one could see my crooked nose or how ugly I was. The voice was just part of my stream of conscious thoughts, but as it got stronger over time, I began to notice its patterns and tone. I named it "the Little Critic" and called it a "he." My inner life became a constant process of tuning out the Little Critic and trying to do the brave thing anyway. The voice grew loud in college when I dated Ram, who amplified my fears in the single refrain: "What will people think?" As the Little Critic grew big and fat from his words, he took the form of a ragged bird who liked to sit on the throne of my mind. He reached great heights during law school. Every time I decided to pursue passion projects instead of prestige, he liked to squawk: "What's wrong with you?" He got the most riled up right before I was about to put my art or voice into the world. "They're going to eat you alive." He made me feel small. His was the presence in me when I turned to my mother at the moment of transition on the birthing table, and said, "I can't."

But there was always another voice in me, too—the power projected into me when my grandfather saw me as a warrior, leading me to knock on the church door, pick up my camera after 9/11, hold on to the megaphone, walk away from the spinning gun, enter prisons and places of violence, find reconciliation, and breathe and push through pain. This was my internal wisdom, growing in presence and clarity through the seasons of my life. I did not know how strong it was in me until I started to notice that every time my friends or students asked me for advice, I sounded like this very wise woman. Tender and truthful and so very wise! In these moments, the Little Critic was always very quiet. He had nothing to say. I began to wonder whether the Wise Woman in me was the one I saw on the birthing table—the one with long flowing hair floating above me, watching me with compassion, the woman who had my face. She had echoed my mother's refrain, "You are brave, you are brave." After Kavi was born, I heard myself speaking like this all the time to him. "Oh, my love," I whispered into his ear. "You are beloved in the world. You are strong and smart and loving and brave."

"Why don't you speak to *yourself* that way?" Sharat asked me.

"Oh!" I said. Sharat was often the one who had to step in when the Little Critic was filling me with doubt or anxiety. Now he was asking for backup.

"We can learn to mother ourselves!" Audre Lorde once declared. So I decided to *practice* listening to the Wise Woman in me. I got a simple blank journal, carried it with me, and wrote in it every day, sometimes three times a day, and simply let her speak. It always began the same way: "Wise Woman here. Wise Woman says . . ." She always began by telling me the state of my body. "Oh, my love, you are tired today. It's okay, I got you." Then she told me what to do next—to rest or work. "Go do this piece of the work and come back and report to me in three hours." She never berated me if I failed. She simply made a new plan and sent me off again. Listening to her voice, literally every few hours, is how I began to *practice* loving myself.

Here's what I discovered about Wise Woman: Her voice is quiet. There is so much noise in my mind—the Little Critic but also the cacophony of noises from the outside world, an endless stream of breaking news and social media and other people's thoughts. I have to get really quiet in order to hear her. How do I know when I am hearing her voice? She is tender and truthful. She is not afraid of anything or anyone. She does not give me all the answers, but she does know what I need to do in this moment—to wonder, grieve, fight, rage, listen, reimagine, breathe, or push. She helps me show up to the labor as my best self.

I believe that deep wisdom resides within each of us. Some call this voice by different sacred names—Spirit, God, Jesus, Allah, Om, Buddha-nature, Waheguru. Others think of this voice as the intuition one hears when in a calm state of mind. My friend Jeremy calls the voice his Inner Professor, his teacher. My teammate Melissa calls hers Best Friend. Whatever name we choose, listening to our deepest wisdom requires disciplined practice. The loudest voices in the world right now are ones running on the energy of fear, criticism, and cruelty. The voices we spend the most time listening to, in the world and inside our own minds, shape the way we see, how we feel, and what we do. When I spend time listening to people who are speaking from *their* deepest wisdom, I can feel understanding, inspiration, and energy nourish the root of my own wisdom. But I must not lose myself at the feet of others. My most vigilant spiritual practice is finding the seconds of solitude to get quiet enough to hear the Wise Woman in *me*.

This practice became urgent and necessary after Kavi was born.

My shoulders were sore, my nipples were raw, and I did not recognize my body. Sharat and I were in a baby cave, sleep-deprived, immersed in love, still learning that love was sweet labor. We labored all hours of the clock—nursing, soothing, bathing, feeding, diaper changing, rocking, sleeping just enough to function, if that. Luckily, we had an intergenerational home—my parents or his parents lived with us for months at a time—so childcare and housekeeping were always divided among the four of us, and the labor was porous enough to let joy in: long cuddles under blankets, strolls along the sea, story time and dance time after sundown. For weeks, the rest of the world was far away—until Deah, Yusor, and Razan were killed.

On February 10, 2015, a gunman entered the home of three Muslim college students in Chapel Hill, North Carolina, and shot them in the head execution-style. Deah Barakat was twenty-three years old; his wife, Yusor Abu-Salha, was twenty-one; and her sister Razan was seventeen. The police maintained that the gunman was motivated by a parking dispute, despite overwhelming evidence of the gunman's hate. The killing generated a wave of grief and rage through our communities, but like many crimes where hate is identified as one of several motives, it would never be officially classified as a hate crime.

I bundled our eight-week-old son in blankets and took him to his first candlelight vigil at the University of Southern California, organized by Muslim and Sikh students. They saw themselves in Deah, Yusor, and Razan. The three of them were exemplary students who cared deeply about public service. Deah and Yusor were training to become dentists; Razan was studying architecture and environmental design. I looked at their radiant smiles in the photos and imagined Kavi their age one day. Dean Varun Soni asked me to speak. "When I was a college student, the murder of Balbir Singh Sodhi was *my* catalyst for action," I said to the students. "Let this moment be yours."

Then I went back to work, writing policy reports about net neutrality for Stanford Law School. Kavi ate his first solids. Took his first steps. Said his first words. But I was spending my off-hours responding to more hate crimes, fanned by candidates running on platforms of hate during the election season. I had called those grieving college students to action, but even I could not have guessed that, as we approached the 2016 election, hate violence would reach a scale and scope that we had not seen since the aftermath of 9/11.

By the end of the year, I was exhausted. On Christmas Eve, Kavi and I carefully put the milk and cookies by the fireplace for Santa Claus. After he went to sleep, I promptly drank the milk and ate the cookies. I wanted Kavi to wake up in the morning and see them gone; I wanted him to believe in a world that was magical. Then we got the

news that another turbaned Sikh grandfather had been beaten in my
hometown of Fresno. Amrik Singh Bal had been walking to work the
morning after Christmas when he heard, "ISIS. Terrorist. Let's get
him." Two men started to beat him. "Please don't kill me," he said,
blocking his face with his lunch bag and water bottle. When he tried
to run, one of them ran over him with a car, breaking his collarbone.
It was one of several high-profile attacks on Sikh fathers and grandfathers that would cause Fresno—where my family had lived for more
than a century—to be described as "a hotspot of anti-Sikh violence."

This time, Sharat found me on the bed under a sheet of tears where
Kavi could not find me. My chest had finally cracked open.

"How will we do it?" I cried. "How will we keep him safe?" I was
reckoning with the fact that our son—a little brown boy with long
hair who might one day wear a turban as part of his faith—was growing up in a nation more dangerous for him than it was for me. I knew
the data on school bullying—that about seven out of ten turbaned
Sikh boys are harassed at school. There would be moments on the
street or in the schoolyard when we would not be able to protect him.
I cried as though my revelation was something new. But I was simply
being inaugurated into the pain that black and brown mothers have
long known on this soil. We cannot protect our children from white
supremacist violence. We can only make them resilient enough to face
it. And insist, until our dying breath, that there be no more bystanders.

"I can't," I said.

"What does Wise Woman say?" Sharat asked.

"Breathe," I said.

"And then?"

"Push."

A few months later, I left Stanford Law to found the Revolutionary Love Project.

❧❧

Election night, November 8, 2016. Sharat and I watched the television in our tiny living room, waiting for the results, as Kavi played at our feet wearing "I Voted" stickers. Finally, this violent election season was coming to an end. Polls began to close, results started to appear, the unthinkable became possible, then inevitable, and I put my hand over my mouth. Panic rose. My face was hot, my breath was shallow. Sharat and I reached for each other's hands.

No, no, no.

It felt like dying. It felt like the death of everything we believed in, the death of equality and freedom, the death of promise and progress, the death of democracy, the death of America, and our place in it.

"Evening Edition!" said Kavi, tugging at my shirt. We looked down at him, our faces blank. Evening Edition was our name for our bedtime routine of stories, dances, and *shabad*s we did together each night to get him to go to sleep.

I turned to Sharat and said, "I can't."

"You said *every* night," Sharat reminded me. "Your rules."

I looked at him. He looked at me.

"Okay," I said.

We turned off CNN, sat on the red cushion, and Kavi handed me *The Little Engine That Could.* I think I can? I wanted to throw the book out the window. I read it anyway.

"Dance time, Mommy!" said Kavi.

That's the last thing I can do right now.

But Sharat turned on the music. I got to my feet and shifted from side to side, looking miserable. Then Kavi leapt into my arms. The music rose.

Baby you're a firework. . . .

I tossed Kavi in the air, and he laughed, and then—I laughed. And we were dancing, Sharat and Kavi and me. We were dancing on election night. I felt energy in my body. *I felt joy.*

Boom, boom, boom. Even brighter than the moon, moon, moon.

Joy returns us to everything that is good and beautiful and worth fighting for. In joy, we see even darkness with new eyes. I was not alone. I was one in millions. I was part of a movement, one in a constellation. I had to shine my light in my specific slice of sky. I could do that.

I did not know then all the crises yet to come: the rise of white nationalists who hailed this presidency as their "great awakening," mass detentions and deportations, Muslim bans, zero-tolerance policies separating migrant children from their parents, attacks on the rights of queer and trans people, assaults on women and women's rights, and new mass shootings and hate violence against Sikhs, Muslims, Hindus, Jews, black people, Latinx people, indigenous people, and immigrants. All I knew was that the future was dark, and that as it got darker and more violent, people would get tired, go numb, and retreat into whatever privilege they might have. I wanted to help people stay in the fire; I wanted to help *myself* stay in the fire. I concluded that revolutionary love was the call of our times—and started building the tools to practice it.

❧❧

One summer night in Los Angeles, Kavi was riding on my father's shoulders, on top of the world, waiting for a boat to ferry them home from a summer concert, when they heard an irate voice. My father tried to intervene, and the woman spun around and yelled at him.

"Go back to the country you came from!"

My parents came home shaken. No one had said anything, just like last time, when my father was walking on the beach with my son, wearing a baby carrier, and a man called him "suicide bomber."

That night, while putting Kavi to sleep, I asked him where he felt sadness in his body. He pointed to his belly. I kissed him and stroked his forehead and sang *"Tati Vao Na Lagi."* He started to fall asleep. My mind wandered. I had just returned from a memorial event in Kansas City, where a young engineer named Srinivas Kuchibhotla was shot and killed by a man who yelled, "Go back to your country!" These were words that preceded violence. Now they were mouthed by the president of the United States. Srinu's widow, Sunayana, told me: "Not one more Srinu. Not one more Sunayana." I could not promise her that. My mind raced with panic; my heart beat in my ears.

Suddenly Kavi put his ear on my mouth.

"Mommy, I don't hear you breathing. You have to breathe to sleep."

"Oh!" I said.

"Breathe and push, Mommy, just *breathe and push*."

All this time, I thought Kavi had no idea about my work in the world. Now here was my son, giving my tools back to me.

Oh my god, I thought. *My son has become my midwife.*

We took long deep breaths together and fell asleep.

෧෨

Is this the darkness of the tomb, or of the womb? I still ask myself this question every day.

Looking back on the events of my life, I was so impatient for change. In the aftermath of 9/11, we organized to quell the hate, but violence on the street was followed by violence by the state. So, we protested the war on terror and organized a strong antiwar movement, but the wars began anyway and brought more destruction. So we built a broad-based movement that elected Barack Obama, and I thought that we had transcended history. But progress during the Obama era was slow and incremental, and meanwhile white nativist forces gained enough power to help deliver the Trump presidency. New executive orders, policies, and assaults rained down on us so hard and so fast that we barely had time to breathe between them. Then, at the onset of a global pandemic, our government failed to take action to stop the spread of COVID-19, leading to mass suffering and death and deepening injustice. If we take a linear view of history, then we are sliding backward.

But if we see the story of America as one long labor, then we have a different view. Progress during birthing labor is cyclical, not linear.

It is a series of expansions and contractions, and each turn through the cycle brings us closer to what is being born. I see this pattern through U.S. history: A generation fought to abolish slavery and free people from bondage, but it was followed by a Jim Crow system. Another generation built a civil rights movement to end segregation and win equal rights, but it was followed by criminal justice, immigration, and national security systems that continue to punish black and brown people. The labor is ongoing, the injustice relentless. But each time people organized, each turn through the cycle opened a little more space for equality and justice. It also created ancestral memory: We carry the memory of movements that came before us. Like the body in labor, we have gained more embodied knowledge about what to do when the crises come. Even when the crises are unprecedented, we can still turn to the wisdom of our ancestors for *how* to labor—to wonder, to grieve, to fight, to rage, to listen, to reimagine, to breathe and to push, and to find the bravery we need for transition. It is our task to innovate and apply these practices in the new reality we find ourselves in.

"Our struggle is also a struggle of memory against forgetting," said bell hooks. She did not just mean remembering our ancestors' trauma but remembering also their deepest wisdom. It is time to seek out the deepest wisdom of those who have been most silenced by the forces of history. When I am in a place that *begins* by recognizing indigenous peoples, *centers* black lives, and *leads* with women of color, I am in a place of deep solidarity. We can model solidarity in all our movement spaces, both in person and virtual. These days, I honor indigenous peoples before I speak, for their memory is the correct starting point for history in the Americas. I seek out ways to center black lives, for black liberation is central to our collective liberation. I follow the lead of women of color who are also queer, disabled, or poor, for they show us how to leave no one behind.

Transition is the most painful and dangerous stage, but it's also where we begin to see what comes into the space we open up. Fresh horrors arrive daily, but our responses are smarter and our solidarity deeper than ever before. In the Trump era, we marched in the streets, protested at airports, and held vigils at the border on a scale we hadn't seen before. Indigenous and Japanese American elders linked arms with Latinx immigrants in front of detention camps in displays of ancestral solidarity. Women ran for public office at every level of government in unprecedented numbers. Disability justice activists modeled how to lead movements in a way that was inclusive and sustainable for all of us. In the quieter venues of our lives, I saw people gathering in classrooms, in houses of worship, and around kitchen tables, caring for one another even when it was hard. Then, at the onset of the COVID-19 pandemic, when it was no longer possible to gather in person, I saw millions of people rise up in new ways—creating virtual gatherings, singing on rooftops, cheering essential workers, organizing mutual aid societies to support the poor, sick, and elderly, filling the vacuum left by government, and reimagining systems that safeguard the most vulnerable among us. I don't know how this will end or how much worse it will get. But in such moments, I see glimpses of a nation waiting to be born, the society we aspire to be—an America that is multiracial, multifaith, multigendered, and multicultural, a nation where power is shared and we strive to protect the wellness and dignity of every person and work to save our earth and our collective future. Each of us has a role in this long labor, no matter who is in the White House. That means when a voice in us says "I can't," our most urgent task is to find the wisdom to stay in the fire.

⚬⚬

As I began to speak out more boldly about revolutionary love during the Trump era, I could hear the voice of the Little Critic inside me getting louder, too. "You're a lawyer! You can't use the word 'love'! No one will take you seriously!" I thought about terminating the Lit-

tle Critic as a birthday gift to myself, but Wise Woman talked me
down. "No," she said. "We need this little guy. He is a part of you. We
just don't need him in charge." So, I began to think about some kind
of ritual. Rituals have the power to usher in transformation that we
are ready for. After two years of practice writing in my Wise Woman
journal each day, I wanted to invite Wise Woman to take her rightful
place on the throne of my mind. No more power struggle. I wanted
her to lead me the rest of my days.

I had started to bring Sikh women together in annual retreats and
forged a sisterhood of Sikh women activists. My bonds with two of
these sisters ran deep: Nirinjan Kaur, a scholar of Sikh studies and
percussionist of Sikh music, and Jasvir Kaur Rababan, a virtuosa of
the *rabab,* a sacred Sikh instrument used by Guru Nanak. I asked if
they would help me find a way to install Wise Woman on the throne.
They said that they wanted to do it, too. It was hard to break away
from the daily work of mothering and activism, but I found twenty-
four hours. We met at a hot spring surrounded by rocks and crafted a
ceremony for ourselves.

Wise Woman Ceremony

Part One: Mapping the Body

We found a quiet spot by the water, sat in a circle, held one another's
hands, and closed our eyes. We hummed for a few minutes, tuning in
to each other, our voices harmonizing into one clear sound.

"If there is a place where the Wise Woman dwells, our deepest
wisdom, where is it in our bodies?" I asked.

I imagined mine in the center of my head, an image of myself
standing in front of an empty gold throne. Jasvir located her Wise
Woman in her heart in the form of a crown. Nirinjan sensed a great
hawk hovering above her. Every person has their own physiological
histories and the location of their deepest wisdom will be specific to
them.

"If there is a place where the Little Critic dwells, where is it?" I asked.

I saw mine perched on top of my head, on the left side, in the form of a ragged bird. Nirinjan saw something similar in herself. Jasvir sensed cobwebs and a big fat spider inside her head.

Now it was time to listen to the Little Critic.

"What do you want to say? What do you have to tell me?" we asked the Little Critic. We wrote down what popped into our minds on paper. Then we spoke the words out loud, taking turns.

"I'm scared."

"You're not good enough."

"You're not smart enough."

"You're not beautiful."

"They don't like you."

"I'm scared."

It sounded like a single chorus of self-judgment and fear. Any of the other Little Critic statements could have been our own. We wiped away tears. Perhaps the Little Critic is our most intimate opponent, the one who is hardest to listen to. But when we wonder even about his voice, we learn something new. I began to wonder: Why was my Little Critic so afraid?

I once had a front-row seat to Sonya Sotomayor's confirmation hearing as Supreme Court justice. I sat behind the senators as a staffer and had their view. Sotomayor was a lone Latinx woman—a wise Latinx woman—looking up at mostly white men in black suits. I watched as Republican senators viciously attacked her. Ten years later, many of those same senators defended Brett Kavanaugh during his confirmation hearing, even when Dr. Christine Ford alleged sexual assault. Her testimony was brave and composed. Still she was dismissed. Men in power do not respond kindly to Wise Women. All this time, the Little Critic was trying to keep me small, because it was the only way to survive. He was trying to protect me. But my Wise Woman knew better. When one Wise Woman leads, she inspires others to join her. When all our Wise Women lead, we not only inspire the world, we remake it.

Part Two: Releasing the Little Critic

I stood at the edge of a pool of icy water. I could not stand cold water, but the only way to set the Little Critic free was to do something shocking. I thought of all the years the Little Critic spent tormenting me, and how I depended on him. I needed to thank him for his years of service and release him from duty. I looked at the cold water plunge and began to whimper. I actually cried. Nirinjan and Jasvir kneeled on either side of me and chanted, "Waheguru, Waheguru."

I plunged into the water and cried out, "Hoooo, hoooo!" I moaned and took deep breaths. I began to speak to the Little Critic: "I see you." *Plunge*. "I honor you." *Plunge*. "I thank you." *Plunge*. "I release you." *Plunge*. "It's okay, I got this. It's okay." I pictured a ragged bird amazed to be acknowledged like this for the first time. I went under the cold water for a long time, my sisters' hands on my shoulders. The Little Critic flapped his wings and flew away. The golden throne room was empty. When I came up, Nirinjan sprinkled water on the crown of my head, and Jasvir followed.

It was their turn. They, too, plunged into the water, wept, and said the words to release their Little Critics. "You did it!" we cried to one another. We formed a circle, hummed, and turned our attention inward. My throne room was empty and ready, the Little Critic far away. Jasvir's head was clear of cobwebs, the spider nowhere to be found. Nirinjan's bird was no longer on his perch, either.

Part Three: Installing Wise Woman on the Throne

"Let's now call our deepest wisdom to the forefront of our consciousness," I said. "Let Wise Woman see through my eyes and speak through my mouth. Let us see one another. Let us speak to one another."

Our Wise Women took turns speaking to one another: "You are a warrior. You are a *sevadar*. You are a lioness. You are a Mai Bhago of our time." It felt like deep witness. We bowed our heads, our three crowns touching. We stood for *Ardas,* the prayer that is part of all Sikh services. Joy filled us: "I feel like I can fill up this whole room!" "I feel like I can mount a horse and go into battle!"

I longed to hold on to this feeling. I had an idea: In Sikh tradition, the wedding ceremony is called the *Anand Karaj,* or Joyful Union. I longed for union with the Wise Woman in me. Could I *marry* her?

We wrapped ourselves in a wedding shawl. Jasvir began to recite the four *laavan* of the *Anand Karaj.* The sound of the poetry reverberated in us as we circled a pool of blue water. The *laavan* describes marriage between the bride and bridegroom as a metaphor for human beings marrying the divine. Each circle represents an ascension into higher states of consciousness and union. We moved as one. As we completed the fourth and final *laav.* I imagined my Wise Woman finally taking her seat on her throne. "I will be faithful to you all my days," I said. We tasted *prashad* by the fire, honey on our palms. "Her reign is sweet!" we said as we laughed.

I went home to Sharat and told him I was married twice.

"Thank god!" he said. Wise Woman made his job so much easier.

Ritual can take many different forms. It does not require being part of a faith or spiritual tradition. It requires an act of imagination and co-creation. For thousands of years, people have innovated within their spiritual traditions to breathe life into them, reviving old rituals with new energy and meaning. We were participating in that great current of history, crafting our ceremony from the cloth of our Sikh tradition. The Wise Woman in me is the way that Waheguru resides in me. Our wedding ceremony was my commitment to honor and listen to the divine within me for the rest of my life.

I wish I could say that I never heard from the Little Critic again. The truth is that the Little Critic still likes to come flapping his wings and sit on his perch and squawk in my ear. The difference is that he's not in charge anymore. He knows that he has no business near the throne, unless Wise Woman scoops him up to soothe him. Wise Woman sits on the throne. Each morning, when I run my head under the shower, I imagine the water clearing the throne room again until it sparkles, and she can take her seat and reign for the day. I try to listen to her, but I am easily distracted. It's hard to get quiet enough to hear her. I am the warrior *and* the deserter. Sometimes I want to call it quits. But I made a vow. So I open my journal each day and let her write to me. I record voice memos of her speaking to me, then listen to them a few minutes later, surprised by what I hear. My sisters and I meet every year in order to renew our vows. Wise Woman has become our internal guide—the one who tells us how to show up to the labor in this moment.

Led by the Wise Woman in me, I knew when it was time to return to the gas station.

❦

As we pulled into the Mesa Star in the desert suburb outside Phoenix, the images rushed back at me: yellow police tape, body facedown, turban knocked to the ground, and the brothers who stood in front of media cameras weeping, declaring the words "love" and "justice." This gas station was the site of Balbir Uncle's murder.

Each year, on September 15, the Sodhi family transformed the gas station into sacred space. They spread white sheets over the asphalt next to the small memorial plaque, set out trays of hot food, and served *cha* to a small gathering of family and neighbors. Drivers continued to pull in and pump gas, looking at us, putting the pieces together. Sometimes they joined us for a minute before driving away. The floodlights came on before the stars came out.

I had made a pilgrimage here many times, but this time, sorrow was heavy in the air. It had been fifteen years since the murder. The violence was endless, the memorials blurred together. Joginder Auntie sat quietly with neighbors, holding a cup of *cha* in her hand. She was still dressed in white, the color of mourning. She caught my gaze and smiled. Husband murdered, brother-in-law murdered, sons' safety threatened daily, and hate crimes at an all-time high, yet here she was, still offering a smile. I introduced her to Kerri Kelly, my friend whose stepfather was killed on 9/11. I had just grieved with Kerri at Ground Zero; now she was here to grieve with us. Joginder Auntie embraced her. It was the first time anyone who lost family on 9/11 had come to mourn her husband. We took our seats together, arm in arm. As the sun set, we listened to *kirtan* and lined up to place our red roses and candles on the cool marble in the spot where he died. When it was my turn, I sat on the marble and whispered to Balbir Uncle, "I have a son now. His name is Kavi. He's going to know your story."

Rana Sodhi sat down next to me. He had spent the past fifteen years telling his brother's story wherever he could, from schools to churches to interfaith vigils.

"Nothing has changed," he said. He looked tired.

I felt a deep longing for relief, and a desire to change the story. I thought of my reconciliation with Roshan and how it had created a new story for both of us. I realized that in all the places I had mourned, the perpetrator was always missing. At Ground Zero in New York, the terrorists who flew the planes into the towers were dead. In Oak Creek, the white supremacist who opened fire on the Sikhs was dead. In my hometown, the young man who beat the Sikh grandfather after Christmas Day was released from custody on bail and then killed himself. They were all dead, and along with them any possibility of redemption. As Rana, Kerri, and I sat at Balbir Uncle's memorial and the darkness gathered around us, I felt an absence I had never felt before. *Who have we not yet tried to love?*

Frank Roque was in an Arizona prison a few miles from the Mesa Star, serving out a life sentence. A few days before his killing spree, Roque had told a waiter at Applebee's: "I'm going to go out and shoot some towel heads," and "We should kill their children, too, because they'll grow up to be like their parents." When the police arrested him after his shooting rampage, he yelled, "I am a patriot!" and "I stand for America!" He told the court that voices told him to "kill the devils." He was sentenced to death, a sentence that was later reduced to life in prison. We had not heard from him since. This man had always been dead to me. But Frank Roque was not dead. He was alive. He was here. I felt the strong urge to conjure him out of the prison, that place of totalizing isolation and erasure, just to hear his voice. I began to *wonder* who he was now and whether he felt remorse.

I turned to Rana. "Would you talk to Frank Roque if you could?" I asked him.

"I would talk to him," he said. He did not hesitate. It was a response born of fifteen years of *grieving*.

That night, before we all went home, a Navajo family who lived near the gas station asked if they could make an offering. They performed a water blessing so that the vows and prayers of love we had made there that night might soak through the roots in the soil beneath our feet and connect to all the other roots in the earth and spread around the globe.

In the morning, Rana and I huddled together around my cell phone and called the prison that held Balbir Uncle's murderer. My teammate Aseem had reached out to the prison to arrange the call. The phone rang. My heart beat in our ears.

"Hello? Is this Frank?"

"Yes, this is." His voice was gruff.

I introduced myself and Rana, and thanked him for taking our call.

"Why did you agree to speak with us?" I asked.

"I've always told the truth about what happened to me," he began. "The events of 9/11 so broke me down as a man that I could not control what happened. I would never have done what happened of my own free will. What happened was a result of mental breakdown. I'm sorry to say it cost his brother's life but it also destroyed mine.

"After three days of solid crying for all the people that died, it turned to anger," he went on. "How could people crash planes full of people into buildings full of people?"

"We were *all* watching the towers fall," I said. "We *all* saw the people jumping from buildings. Balbir Sodhi also did. There are different ways to channel the pain. I know you chose violence."

"I'm sorry for what happened to his brother," he said, "as I'm sorry for what happened to the thousands of innocent people who died on 9/11."

I felt the energy of *rage* in me. All I could hear was a man who refused to take responsibility for murder. Inside me, the Little Critic said: "End the call! What are you doing to Rana?" But the Wise Woman in me held me to my post. I took a *breath* and *pushed*.

"The only life you can take responsibility for is the one *you* took," I said. "We are talking to you about the life that *you* took."

As Frank and I went back and forth, Rana kept *listening*. He heard what I could not hear.

"Frank, I'm hearing you. I'm so thankful for what you say," said Rana. "This is the first time I'm hearing from you that you feel sorry."

A few years ago, Rana had recognized Roque's daughter and wife at Costco while he was buying flowers for the anniversary of his brother's death. "Your dad killed my brother," he told them. Rana invited them to join him at Balbir Uncle's memorial that night for dinner. Frank said that he remembered his daughter telling him the story and was deeply moved that Rana showed compassion to his family. His voice grew soft.

"I want you to know from my heart, I'm sorry for what I did to your brother," Frank said. "One day, when I go to heaven to be judged by God, I will ask to see your brother, and I will hug him, and I will ask him for forgiveness."

"We already forgave you," Rana said, choking back tears. *Forgiveness is not forgetting: Forgiveness is freedom from hate*.

"If I had the power to take you out from prison, I would do it right now," Rana said. "If one day you come out, we can both go to the world and tell the story."

Rana had never wanted him put to death, because it foreclosed the possibility of apology and transformation. Now here he was, *reimagining* our story, recruiting Frank as his brother and *transitioning* us all into someplace new.

"I know I can't give you back what I wish I could, which is your brother," Frank said, "but I hope you find some comfort in knowing that I'm very sorry for what happened to your brother and your whole family and his wife and everyone."

We all agreed to meet again. The call ended. We exhaled and wiped away tears.

"That's just amazing," Rana sighed.

I felt relieved and also sober. Reconciliation is a process, as I had learned from my journey with Roshan. It requires accountability. Frank did not express full responsibility for the murder, nor did he seem to grasp the impact of his brutality. He could not talk about the murder without naming the damage it caused his life. But in hearing Frank's story, I was understanding more deeply the unresolved rage that fuels white supremacist violence, the inner turmoil that results from hateful ideologies. Our meeting was not an end but a beginning, like opening a door.

And so Rana and I agreed to meet Frank again. We were doing it not for him but for ourselves. Our reconciliation with this man will not change the institutions and policies that perpetuate white supremacy. But it will give us information and energy for that broader transformation. Meanwhile, we are reclaiming our sovereignty, not as victims in this story, but as what we have always been, agents of revolutionary love.

❧

Transition is an imperfect metaphor: There is no one point when a new society is born. We always find ourselves in the middle of a cycle. At this moment, you may be seeing around you the earliest stages of a movement taking form. Or you may be seeing the president's pen on a civil rights bill. Often when you bear witness to the first, you will not be in the room for the second. What matters is the choice to show up to the labor in front of you, with the specific gifts you have been given, to play your particular role. When we labor in love, we not only make future victories possible. We also begin to transform the world within us and around us, here and now. In my darkest moments, when I want to give up, I remember the darkness of the womb and turn to the practices of revolutionary love. I remember to measure my success as a person not by what I produce, but by my faithfulness to this labor. I want to last. I want *you* to last. I want to grow old. I want to grow old with you. I believe revolutionary love is our best chance as individuals and societies to stay in the fire long enough to deliver the world longing to be.

༄

Once, when I was still a student, I had a lucid dream while under acupuncture needles on Valerie Courville's treatment table. I was falling through layers of consciousness until I landed with a thud. I saw a boy sitting and dangling his legs, his back to me. I threw my arms around the boy's shoulders. I thought it was Sharat but his shoulders were tiny. I leaned down to see who it was. A little boy in a red jumper smiled at me, and I was overcome with a love so intense that it enveloped both of us. I had never experienced such bright intensity before.

"Who are you?" I asked, but I already knew he was my son. I had always wanted a daughter. Yet here he was.

The boy saw that I was afraid. He transformed into a forty-year-old man before my eyes and smiled at me. I looked into his aged face and felt the same radiant love. He was showing me that it would be okay. He returned to his child self. I savored being with him. I wanted never to leave him. When he began to disappear, every fiber in me cried out: *No!*

"You have to find me," I heard him say. "You have to find me."

And he was gone. My eyes opened. It was unlike any dream I had had. I did not know whether it was my subconscious easing my fear of having a son, or a visit from another realm, or both. I just wanted to return to him.

Seven years later, Kavi came into the world. I stopped thinking about the dream.

One night, when Kavi was three years old, I was busy wrestling him into his pajamas on the bed. Suddenly he stopped his squirming and babbling and looked at me.

"How you found me?" he said.

"Um." I stopped and looked at him. "Well, I had to look for you and then I found you."

"How you found me?" Kavi asked with the same gentle inflection.

"Well, we moved across the country and went all the way to the star nursery," I said.

"How you found me?" he asked again.

"Appa and I found you together," I said.

Only then was he satisfied.

Falling asleep that night, Kavi put his hand on my cheek.

"This is the Mommy I wanted," he said.

I don't know how love works beyond life and death. Some moments strike in me such wonder that I let myself fall into the glassblower's breath. *Vismaad*. All I can do is hold on to the vision of the world longing to be—a world where *every* child feels found, and *every* person is beloved. A world where we can look upon *any* face—even those we might fear—and find recognition. A world where we beckon each other to return to love. This work belongs to all of us. Not just mothers. We all have the ability to participate in this great love story. Imagine the stories we will tell, the institutions we will build, and the lives we will lead when we affirm that every person *is* a person. Imagine the world we will birth when we see no stranger.

Lifetime Practice

After Papa Ji died, I thought that he left me without teaching me the secret to his bravery. Then I realized that his final lesson was the *way* that he died. If I wanted to live and die as bravely as he did, I had to practice. *Practice. Practice. Practice.*

"Think of today as an entire lifetime," Wise Woman says to me before I fall asleep.

"What was the hardest part in this lifetime? Notice where you sense that hardship in your body. Now how did you get through it?" We somehow managed to make it to the end of this day, the end of this lifetime.

"What was the most joyful part of this lifetime?" Every day and every lifetime, no matter how hard, contains moments of joy. "Notice what made it joyful. Sense what joy feels like in your body."

"What are you most grateful for in this lifetime?" Every day and every lifetime offers a new reason for gratitude. "Sense that gratitude in your body."

"Now are you ready to let go of this lifetime? Are you ready to think of the work you have done today and know that it is enough? Are you ready to behold everyone and everything you have ever known and loved, kiss them, and let them go? Are you ready to die a kind of death?"

Each night, I die a kind of death. Each morning, I wake to the gift of a new lifetime. In between, I labor in love. It is enough.

Now you think I won't know you
From the clouds that surround you
But you exalt everything
That cannot contain you—

I'll know you by your joy.
    —*Brynn Saito*

epilogue.
joy.

As I began writing this book, Joyce was dying. She was a mother figure, the wise woman who had helped me heal my body and bring out the Wise Woman in me. I first met Joyce on her treatment table when I moved to New Haven to start law school. She had mothered me for ten years. Now she was dying from multiple myeloma. I called to tell her that my mother and I were coming to help her, as we had promised.

"I'm glad you're coming, darlin'," she said. Her voice was weak. "This is a time to love each other."

"Yes," I said.

"This is a time to consolidate our love."

When my family and I burst through the hospital door, she looked up from her bed and smiled.

"Joyce Auntie, where you going?" three-year-old Kavi asked.

"To heaven," she said sweetly.

"Where that?" Kavi asked.

"Right here," she said. "And very far away."

Kavi gave her a red rose.

"Are you ready for this transition, Joyce?" I asked.

"Oh, not yet, darlin'," she said. "But with every minute, more and more."

I held her hand all night. Her oxygen mask kept slipping, and I kept putting it back over her nose. Her eyes fluttered open when the nurses came in. She swallowed pills with great focus. "You are amazing, Joyce. You are brave," I said. "You are brave." She smiled at me.

When she needed to slow down her breathing, the Wise Woman in me began to guide her inhales and exhales, speaking to her:

There is no time
You are a baby
In your mother's womb
You are a baby
In your mother's arms
You are a little girl
Running free
You are a young woman
Your body so young
You are a woman
Fully matured
You are an artist
You are a healer
You are a friend
You are a daughter
You are a sister
And you are the zygote
Waiting to be born
You are all these things
All at once
There is no time

You are me
And I am you
You are part of me
I am part of you
You are part of everything
You are connected
To everything
You belong to everything

And now it's time
To belong to everything

She hummed "Yes." She was breathing and pushing through pain. I did not know that the labor of dying mirrors the labor of birthing.

When Joyce stopped breathing, it was so imperceptible that my mother and I continued to whisper in her ear. We cried out and took her hands and kissed her forehead and wept on either side of her, our tears soaking the white sheets. We remembered our promise and asked the nurse for a bowl of water, washcloths, and scissors. It is a Sikh tradition for the children to wash and prepare the bodies of their parents after death. Sons do this for their fathers. Daughters do this for their mothers. My mother washed the bodies of my grandmothers, but I was not allowed in because I was still a grandchild. Now it was my turn. I thought it would be difficult, but I followed my mother's lead, hummed the prayers, and learned from her gestures.

I dipped the white washcloths into warm water and dabbed her forehead, her cheeks, her mouth. We thanked each part of her body for serving us. We cut away the hospital gown and dressed her in her royal blue silk *kurta*. Sharat and my father brought piles of flowers. We set purple, pink, and yellow flower petals on all sides of her and placed the red rose Kavi had given her in her hands. Her body was still warm. Adorned with flowers, dressed in royal blue, she looked majestic. At the crematorium, my mother and I recited *Tati Vao Na Lagi*. The hot winds cannot touch you. We pushed the coffin into the furnace and pressed the button. A roar of wind. The flames went up. Her body was burning. My duties as daughter were complete.

The next morning, we woke up to new snow. While eating my mother's soup, I felt tingling in my breasts, and my spoon paused midair. I realized I was pregnant. All those hours I held Joyce's hand, as cells inside her bone marrow were multiplying in order to take her life, cells inside my body were multiplying to make life. I handed

Sharat another note: "Life and death and life again." We called our zygote Little Joy.

I wrote this manuscript while I was pregnant with Little Joy and grieving Joyce. I vomited every hour for the first four months, sick with hyperemesis, and was wheelchair-bound the rest of the time. But I wrote each day as if it was an act of survival, and read each word out loud, as if these stories were all I could give my daughter. I delivered the first draft of the book to my editor and went into labor forty-eight hours later. It happened when I was sitting at my writing desk trying to write a letter to my baby.

"I don't know what to say to Little Joy," I said to Sharat.

"Write what you need to write in order to bring her into the world," Sharat said.

So I wrote my letter and read the last words out loud:

You are beloved
Just as you are.
You are worthy
Of this earth
And its seas and skies
And the gifts it has to offer
Just as you are.
And the earth will receive
All the gifts you give it
As long as the gifts that you give
Are given in joy.
Let joy in every day.
Every day, my love.
Let joy be your lifeblood.

I read the last line, stood up, and immediately went into active labor. She was born four hours later. No image of the ancestors this time. No line of women who had pushed through the fire before me. No Wise Woman floating above me. I had prepared myself to call upon these images, but they did not come to me. I needed them the first time. This time, I needed *her*. I closed my eyes and saw a meadow with flowers. The contraction hit. When it passed, I was in the meadow again, lying on a blanket under the shade of a great tree. She was next to me, looking at me, laughing, cooing, and giggling. I felt joy rushing through me and smiled. The next contraction came and I dropped out of the meadow. I wailed, until I could return to the meadow again and be with her. We picked flowers together. Sat under an umbrella and watched the rain. Now she was fourteen years old with long curly black hair, her head in my arms, looking up at the sky. It was so *joyful* to be with her. This time, I needed the future, not the past. This time, she was my Wise Woman. She came to me, unexpectedly. Not by the ocean. Not in the star nursery. Not in any place chosen by me. But in a wide clear meadow filled with flowers and sunlight and the sound of her cooing. When she landed on my chest, warm and wet, I threw my head back and laughed and wept. She was with me in the meadow and now she was here in my arms.

"Ananda."

In Sanskrit, her name means "joy."

Joy is possible even amid great labors—the labor of dying, the labor of birthing, and the labors between. We cannot force it. But when we create moments to breathe between labor pains, and surrender our senses to the present moment, notice the colors and light and feeling of being alive, here, together, joy comes more easily. It is a felt sense in our bodies. In the face of horrors visited upon our world daily, in the struggle to protect our loved ones, choosing to let in joy is a revolutionary act. Joy returns us to everything good and beautiful and worth fighting for. It gives us energy for the long labor. Letting in joy, therefore, is the tenth practice of revolutionary love, the core practice that sustains all others. *Joy is the gift of love:* It makes the labor an end in itself. I believe laboring in joy is the meaning of life. May we look up at that night sky. May we let joy in. For we will be someone's ancestors one day. If we do this right, they will inherit not our fear but bravery born of joy.

revolutionary love compass.

I HAD CRAFTED THE FRAMEWORK AND PRACTICES OF REVOLUTIONARY LOVE for social justice work out in the world. Then, in the course of writing this book, I noticed that I was starting to use these practices in my home, too. I now envision revolutionary love as a compass, a tool to orient myself in *all* of my labors. As with any tool, I invite you to pick up this compass if it is useful to you.

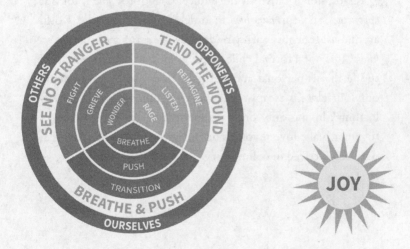

Point the compass toward whomever you want to practice loving— another, an opponent, or yourself. The name of the practice is the outermost ring; the actions for that practice are within. Discern which action you need for the moment. The inner ring of the compass (*wonder, rage, breathe*) contains internal actions, where transformation happens primarily within one's own mind and body. The middle ring (*grieve, listen, push*) contains interpersonal actions, where transformation happens in relationship with other people. The outer ring (*fight, reimagine, transition*) is made up of social actions, where transformation happens within the context of a community. All three levels of transformation—internal, interpersonal, and social—are engaged in the labor of revolutionary love.*

Definitions

• Love is a form of *sweet labor:* fierce, bloody, imperfect, and life-giving—a choice we make over and over again. Love can be taught, modeled, and practiced. It engages all our emotions: Joy is the gift of love. Grief is the price of love. Anger protects that which is loved. And when we think we have reached our limit, wonder is the act that returns us to love.

• "Revolutionary love" is the choice to labor for *others,* for our *opponents,* and for *ourselves* in order to transform the world around us. It begins with wonder: *You are a part of me I do not yet know.* It is not a formal code or prescription but an orientation to life that is personal and political, sustained by joy. Loving only ourselves is escapism; loving only our opponents is self-loathing; loving only others is ineffective. All three practices together make love revolutionary, and revolutionary love can only be practiced in community.

---

*   This compass is a construct. In practice, the actions of love are fluid and fused together. Imagine the inner, middle, and outer rings always moving (i.e., rage is also how we love ourselves, wonder is also how we love our opponents, and so on). I offer the compass as a tool to aid your own inner wisdom, and this configuration of the compass as one starting place.

Loving Others: See No Stranger

> Seeing no stranger begins in wonder. It is to look upon the face of anyone and choose to say: *You are a part of me I do not yet know*. Wonder is the wellspring for love. Who we wonder about determines whose stories we hear and whose joy and pain we share. Those we grieve with, those we sit with and weep with, are ultimately those we organize with and advocate for. When a critical mass of people come together to *wonder* about one another, *grieve* with one another, and *fight* with and for one another, we begin to build the solidarity needed for collective liberation and transformation— a solidarity rooted in love.

See no stranger has become a practice that defines my relationships. At home, I have to wonder about my son and daughter every day in order to figure out what they need. They change so fast that wondering about them gives me information for how to care for them each moment. When they are hurt or angry, holding them close and grieving with them for a moment can help them process their emotions. Often aggression comes from unresolved grief—the need to mourn the loss of not getting what they wanted. Sometimes, I have to fight to protect and provide for them in this tumultuous world. In this way, wondering, grieving, and fighting are daily practices in our home. The day I stop wondering about my husband is the day our marriage starts to die a little, but when I nurture my curiosity, I feel our relationship revive and flourish.

Out in the world, I notice the unconscious biases that arise in me when I look at faces on the street or in the news. To practice seeing each of them as a sister or brother or family member, I say in my mind: *You are a part of me I do not yet know*. Through conscious repetition, I am practicing orienting to the world with wonder and preparing myself for the possibility of connection. (Sometimes I do this with animals and the earth, too!) It opens me up to pay attention to their story. When their story is painful, I make excuses to turn back—"It's too overwhelming" or "It's not my place"—but I hold the compass and remember that all I need to do is be present to their pain and find a way to grieve with them. If I can sit with their pain, I begin to ask: *What do they need?* Listening to more stories, learning about a community's history, or showing up to vigils or marches or memorials gives me information for how to fight for them. I seek out organizations that are already fighting for them and offer my voice or time or money or labor to assist them. When I worry that I'm not enough, I ask myself: *What is* my *sword and shield? How will I fight? What will I risk?* When I get overwhelmed, I ask: *What is* my *role in* this *moment?* I remember that I have only to shine my light in my corner of sky.

Loving Opponents: Tend the Wound

An opponent is any person whose beliefs, words, or actions causes violence, injustice, or harm. The word "enemy" implies permanence, but "opponent" is fluid. We have a range of opponents at any given time, distant and near. Even the people closest to us can become our opponents for a moment. It is daring to put all these people in one big category, but it is useful, for whether our opponents are political or personal, persistent or fleeting, we can practice tending the wound— ours, and if it is safe, theirs. We can *rage* in safe containers to process our pain, *listen* to understand the contexts that enable our opponents to cause harm, and use that information to *reimagine* cultures and institutions that protect dignity for all of us. Tending the wound is not only moral but strategic: It is the labor of remaking the world.

When the person in front of me becomes an opponent, and my impulse is to push them away or shake them, I find ways to *tend the wound*. I practice this a lot with my small children! When they throw epic tantrums, my face flushes and my fists clench. I used to feel ashamed of my anger—was I a bad mother?—until I learned to tend to my own wound first. I remember that rage is not shameful. I find a safe container, a place where I can express my emotions that will cause no harm. Even a closet where I can throw pillows to the floor. I stay there until I am able to wonder about them again. What are their unmet needs? I return to listen and reimagine the conditions driving their behavior. It doesn't work all the time, but it works often enough for it to be my practice. I now use this whenever I get into conflicts with my husband, teammates, or friends: I step away to rage until I can return again to listen and reimagine solutions.

Out in the world, I notice the rage that courses through my body when I face my political opponents. I remember that my rage carries vital information and find safe ways to engage it. It becomes a kind of dance—to release raw rage in a safe container, in order to send divine rage into the world, like focused fury. Sometimes I find a room to shake or cry in for a minute. Other times, in the wake of a hateful policy or hate crime, I gather a group of friends on a video call so that we can rage and grieve together—and recommit to the labor. I now see movement spaces where we can tend to our own wounds as essential justice work. Sometimes I just need to stay there with people, especially when it is my own community in harm's way. But sometimes, when I find enough safety in my body, I am able to listen to my opponents. I remember that I do not need to feel empathy or compassion for my opponents in order to practice loving them. Love is labor that begins in wonder. So, I wonder about them. Beneath the slogans and sound bites, I begin to hear their pain and understand the wounds behind their words. I see their humanity—*I see no stranger*. When listening gets hard, I focus on taking the next breath. Listening does not grant the other side legitimacy. It grants them humanity—and preserves my own. I ask myself: *What is my role in changing the conditions that drive oppression?* I find organizations and leaders who move beyond the language of resistance to visions of the world we want. I focus not only on fighting my opponents but reimagining and remaking institutions and cultures that can free *all of us*.

Loving our opponents is *hard*. If we cannot summon love for all of our opponents in every moment, we have not failed. Revolutionary love is not an all-or-nothing metric. It is an ethic that sometimes feels like an aspiration rather than a reality. But the aspiration to love our opponents is itself revolutionary: It opens up space for us to let *other people* love those opponents when we cannot. Revolutionary love is not about making martyrs of ourselves but rather partaking in the labor that we are ready for at any moment. Tending wounds is the practice of a community, not the sacrifice of an individual.

Loving Ourselves: Breathe and Push

Loving ourselves is a feminist intervention: It is choosing to care for our own bodies and lives as a priority. In all of our various labors—making a life, raising a family, or building a movement—we can care for ourselves by remembering the wisdom of the midwife: breathe and push. We can *breathe* to draw energy and power into our bodies and let joy in. We can *push* through fear and pain to become our best selves, including through healing, forgiveness, and reconciliation. And in the most convulsive moments of our lives, we can summon our deepest wisdom and find the bravery to *transition,* undertaking the fiery and life-giving labor of moving from one reality into another. Laboring in love is how we birth the world to come.

When I turn the compass to myself, I hear the words: *breathe and push*. I never used to give myself a moment of rest. I labored around the clock. But there is a rhythm to breathing and pushing that sustains labor. The midwife does not say "Breathe" once and "Push" the rest of the way! It goes: *Breathe. Push. Breathe. Push. Breathe again.* At home, amid all kinds of labor, I now ask myself: *Do I need to breathe right now?* If yes, I walk outside and look at the sky. I close my eyes and recite a *shabad*. Sometimes I only have time for one long breath before I enter the house or step into the fray. Breathing slows down time for me and increases my resilience: It creates a moment to separate myself from the chaos of consciousness and the fire of the fight and feel my body in its wholeness—until it's time to push again. When I need to push, I remember that going through uncomfortable emotions, sensations, or situations is how change happens.

Out in the world, I seek out spaces where people are coming together to breathe as a community—in music and movement and ritual and healing. I find ways to join communities who are pushing for change together, caring for one another in the process, showing up as one another's midwives, and working to change the conditions that harm us all. We carry in our bodies and psyches the trauma of our ancestors but also their resilience. How did they breathe and push together? What were their rituals? I practice thinking in rhythms: What can I do every day? Every week? Every month? Every year? Sometimes, when the labor gets hard and my emotions are painful and the situation is unbearable, a voice in me says, "I can't." In such times of transition, we need midwives—those who summon our bravery. Sometimes another person. Sometimes our ancestors. Sometimes our own deepest wisdom. I call upon a friend on the phone, or my grandfather in my mind—or the Wise Woman in me who tells me when to breathe, how to push, and where to turn the compass now. I think of each day as a lifetime: I honor how I got through the hardest moments of that lifetime, and offer gratitude for the most joyful moments. At the end of the day, no matter how long, hard, dark or violent, I try to share a song and dance with my children—and let joy in. Joy returns us to everything that is good and beautiful and worth fighting for.

❦

Revolutionary love is practiced in community. Each of us has a role in any given time. We can all be midwives in this time of great transition. The future might still feel dark and unknown, and we might not live to see the world to come, but when we choose to show up with love, our labor becomes an end in itself. We can measure our lives not by what we produce, but by our faithfulness to the labor. Revolutionary love is demanding labor, but it is also creative, transformative, and joyful labor— immeasurably complex and messy, tumultuous and re-velatory, marked by wonder, and *worth it*. Revolutionary love is how we last.

☙❧

The Learning Hub

I invite you to visit the Revolutionary Love Learning Hub—an on-line hub to help you bring revolutionary love into your life. Explore educational guides, training courses, videos, music, artwork, and home practices. Four years in the making, the learning hub brings to life the revolutionary love compass, backed by research and infused with ancestral wisdom. You can use the learning hub to create your own pocket of revolutionary love—in your home, school, organiza-tion, house of worship, or community. My vision is to inspire and equip a critical mass of people to build beloved community where they are.

Visit the Revolutionary Love Learning Hub:

valariekaur.com

Sikh *shabads*.

Sikh *SHABAD*s ARE THE DEVOTIONAL POEMS THAT COMPRISE THE GURU Granth Sahib, the sacred canon of the Sikh faith. *Shabad*s are meant to be recited, sung, or set to music. Several *shabad*s are mentioned in this book. I offer them here in the original Gurmukhi, followed by an English transliteration and my translation.

Mul Mantar—The Root Verse

੧ਓ ਸਤਿ ਨਾਮੁ ਕਰਤਾ ਪੁਰਖੁ ਨਿਰਭਉ ਨਿਰਵੈਰੁ ਅਕਾਲ ਮੂਰਤਿ ਅਜੂਨੀ ਸੈਭੰ ਗੁਰ ਪ੍ਰਸਾਦਿ ॥
ਜਪੁ ॥
ਆਦਿ ਸਚੁ ਜੁਗਾਦਿ ਸਚੁ ॥ ਹੈ ਭੀ ਸਚੁ ਨਾਨਕ ਹੋਸੀ ਭੀ ਸਚੁ ॥

Ik Onkar. Satnam. Karta Purakh. Nirbhau. Nirvair. Akaal Murat. Ajuni. Saibhang. Gurprasad.
Jap.
Aad Sach. Jugaad Sach. Hai Bhi Sach. Nanak Hosi Bhi Sach.

Oneness. True by Name. Source of Creation. Without Fear. Without Enmity. Timeless Form. Beyond Birth. Self-Illuminated. Known by Grace.
Recite.
True at the beginning. True through the ages. True now. Oh Nanak, will be true.

—SRI GURU GRANTH SAHIB, *Japji*, 1:1–4

Jo To Prem Khelan Ka Chaao—If You Want to Play the Game of Love with Me

ਜਉ ਤਉ ਪ੍ਰੇਮ ਖੇਲਣ ਕਾ ਚਾਉ ॥
ਸਿਰੁ ਧਰਿ ਤਲੀ ਗਲੀ ਮੇਰੀ ਆਉ ॥
ਇਤੁ ਮਾਰਗਿ ਪੈਰੁ ਧਰੀਜੈ ॥
ਸਿਰੁ ਦੀਜੈ ਕਾਣਿ ਨ ਕੀਜੈ ॥

Jo to prem khelan ka chaao
Sir dhar tali gali meri aao
It maarag pair dhareejai
Sir deejai kaan na keejai

If you want to play the game of love with me
Step forth with your head on your palm.
When you place your feet on this path,
Give me your head, and care not what anyone says.

—SRI GURU GRANTH SAHIB, *Raag Slok Varan te Vadhik,* 1410

PAGE 5

Tati Vao Na Lagai—The Hot Winds Cannot Touch Me

ਬਿਲਾਵਲੁ ਮਹਲਾ ੫ ॥
ਤਾਤੀ ਵਾਉ ਨ ਲਗਾਈ ਪਾਰਬ੍ਰਹਮ ਸਰਣਾਈ ॥
ਚਉਗਿਰਦ ਹਮਾਰੈ ਰਾਮ ਕਾਰ ਦੁਖੁ ਲਗੈ ਨ ਭਾਈ ॥
ਸਤਿਗੁਰੁ ਪੂਰਾ ਭੇਟਿਆ ਜਿਨਿ ਬਣਤ ਬਣਾਈ ॥
ਰਾਮ ਨਾਮੁ ਅਉਖਧੁ ਦੀਆ ਏਕਾ ਲਿਵ ਲਾਈ ॥ ਰਹਾਉ ॥
ਰਾਖਿ ਲੀਏ ਤਿਨਿ ਰਖਨਹਾਰਿ ਸਭ ਬਿਆਧਿ ਮਿਟਾਈ ॥
ਕਹੁ ਨਾਨਕ ਕਿਰਪਾ ਭਈ ਪ੍ਰਭ ਭਏ ਸਹਾਈ ॥

Bilaval, Mehla Panjva
Tati vao na lagaee parbrahm sharnaee
Chaugird hamare Ram kar dukh lage na bhaee

Satgur poora bhetya jin bant banaee
Ram nam aukhadh diya eka liv laee (Rahao)
Rakh liyay tin rakhan haar sab byadh mitaee
Kaho Nanak kirpa bhaee prabh bhaye sahaee

The hot winds cannot touch me: I am sheltered by the divine
On all four sides, I am surrounded by the divine; sorrow cannot
    consume me.
I have met the true and perfect One who spun all of this.
I am healed in the divine Name; I am merged with the One.
The Keeper has kept me and taken away what ails me.
Nanak says, Grace has fallen upon me, and the divine has come to
    my side.

—SRI GURU GRANTH SAHIB, *Raag Bilaval,* 819:16–819:18
PAGE 8

Vismaad Naad Vismaad Ved (Asa di Var)— Wondrous Is Sound, Wondrous Is Ancient Wisdom (Song of Hope)

ਸਲੋਕ ਮਹਲਾ ੧ ॥
ਵਿਸਮਾਦੁ ਨਾਦ ਵਿਸਮਾਦੁ ਵੇਦ ॥
ਵਿਸਮਾਦੁ ਜੀਅ ਵਿਸਮਾਦੁ ਭੇਦ ॥
ਵਿਸਮਾਦੁ ਰੂਪ ਵਿਸਮਾਦੁ ਰੰਗ ॥
ਵਿਸਮਾਦੁ ਨਾਗੇ ਫਿਰਹਿ ਜੰਤ ॥
ਵਿਸਮਾਦੁ ਪਉਣੁ ਵਿਸਮਾਦੁ ਪਾਣੀ ॥
ਵਿਸਮਾਦੁ ਅਗਨੀ ਖੇਡਹਿ ਵਿਡਾਣੀ ॥
ਵਿਸਮਾਦੁ ਧਰਤੀ ਵਿਸਮਾਦੁ ਖਾਣੀ ॥
ਵਿਸਮਾਦੁ ਸਾਦਿ ਲਗਹਿ ਪਰਾਣੀ ॥
ਵਿਸਮਾਦੁ ਸੰਜੋਗੁ ਵਿਸਮਾਦੁ ਵਿਜੋਗੁ ॥
ਵਿਸਮਾਦੁ ਭੁਖ ਵਿਸਮਾਦੁ ਭੋਗੁ ॥
ਵਿਸਮਾਦੁ ਸਿਫਤਿ ਵਿਸਮਾਦੁ ਸਾਲਾਹ ॥
ਵਿਸਮਾਦੁ ਉਝੜ ਵਿਸਮਾਦੁ ਰਾਹ ॥
ਵਿਸਮਾਦੁ ਨੇੜੈ ਵਿਸਮਾਦੁ ਦੂਰਿ ॥

ਵਿਸਮਾਦੁ ਦੇਖੈ ਹਾਜਰਾ ਹਜੂਰਿ ॥
ਵੇਖਿ ਵਿਡਾਣੁ ਰਹਿਆ ਵਿਸਮਾਦੁ ॥
ਨਾਨਕ ਬੁਝਣਿ ਪੂਰੈ ਭਾਗਿ ॥

Slok Mehla Pehla

vismaad naad vismaad ved

vismaad jee-a vismaad bhed

vismaad roop vismaad rang

vismaad naage fireh jant

vismaad paun vismaad paanee

vismaad agnee kheydeh vidanee

vismaad dhartee vismaad khanee

vismaad saad lageh praanee

vismaad sanjog vismaad vijog

vismaad bhukh vismaad bhog

vismaad sifat vismaad salah

vismaad ujharh vismaad raah

vismaad nerrai vismaad door

vismaad dekhai hajaa hajoor

vekh vidan rahia vismaad

Nanak bujhan poorai bhag

Wondrous is sound, wondrous is ancient wisdom

Wondrous are the creatures, wondrous are their varieties

Wondrous are the forms, wondrous are the colors

Wondrous are the beings who wander around unclothed

Wondrous is the wind, wondrous is the water

Wondrous is the fire, which works wonders

Wondrous is the earth, wondrous the sources of creation

Wondrous are the tastes we seek and seize

Wondrous is union, wondrous is separation

Wondrous is hunger, wondrous is satisfaction

Wondrous is divine praise, wondrous is divine adoration

Wondrous is the wilderness, wondrous is the right path

Wondrous is closeness, wondrous is distance
Wondrous to face the divine, ever-present now
Beholding these wonders, I am wonderstruck
O Nanak, those who understand this are blessed.

—SRI GURU GRANTH SAHIB, *Asa di Var,* 463:18–464:4
PAGE 9

Na Ko Bairi Nahi Begana—I See No Stranger, I See No Enemy

ਕਾਨੜਾ ਮਹਲਾ ੫ ॥
ਬਿਸਰਿ ਗਈ ਸਭ ਤਾਤਿ ਪਰਾਈ ॥
ਜਬ ਤੇ ਸਾਧਸੰਗਤਿ ਮੋਹਿ ਪਾਈ ॥ ਰਹਾਉ ॥
ਨਾ ਕੋ ਬੈਰੀ ਨਹੀ ਬਿਗਾਨਾ ਸਗਲ ਸੰਗਿ ਹਮ ਕਉ ਬਨਿ ਆਈ ॥
ਜੋ ਪ੍ਰਭ ਕੀਨੋ ਸੋ ਭਲ ਮਾਨਿਓ ਏਹ ਸੁਮਤਿ ਸਾਧੂ ਤੇ ਪਾਈ ॥
ਸਭ ਮਹਿ ਰਵਿ ਰਹਿਆ ਪ੍ਰਭੁ ਏਕੈ ਪੇਖਿ ਪੇਖਿ ਨਾਨਕ ਬਿਗਸਾਈ ॥

Kanarra, Mehla Panjva

Bisar gaee sabh taat paraee
Jab te sadhsangat mohe paee (Rahao)
Na ko bairi nahi begana sagal sang hamko ban aaee
Jo parabh keeno so bhal manio eh sumat sadhu te paee
Sabh meh rav rahia parabh ekai pekh pekh Nanak bigsaee

I have forgotten my envy of others
since I found my sacred company.
I see no enemy. I see no stranger. All of us belong to each other.
What the divine does, I accept as good. I have received this wisdom from the holy.
The One pervades all. Gazing upon the One, beholding the One, Nanak blossoms forth in happiness.

—SRI GURU GRANTH SAHIB, *Raag Kanarra,* 1299:13–15
PAGE 9

Anand Karaj (Laavan)—Joyful Union
(The Four Shabads)

ਸੂਹੀ ਮਹਲਾ ੪ ॥

ਹਰਿ ਪਹਿਲੜੀ ਲਾਵ ਪਰਵਿਰਤੀ ਕਰਮ ਦ੍ਰਿੜਾਇਆ ਬਲਿ ਰਾਮ ਜੀਉ ॥
ਬਾਣੀ ਬ੍ਰਹਮਾ ਵੇਦੁ ਧਰਮੁ ਦ੍ਰਿੜਹੁ ਪਾਪ ਤਜਾਇਆ ਬਲਿ ਰਾਮ ਜੀਉ ॥
ਧਰਮੁ ਦ੍ਰਿੜਹੁ ਹਰਿ ਨਾਮੁ ਧਿਆਵਹੁ ਸਿਮ੍ਰਿਤਿ ਨਾਮੁ ਦ੍ਰਿੜਾਇਆ ॥
ਸਤਿਗੁਰੁ ਗੁਰੁ ਪੂਰਾ ਆਰਾਧਹੁ ਸਭਿ ਕਿਲਵਿਖ ਪਾਪ ਗਵਾਇਆ ॥
ਸਹਜ ਅਨੰਦੁ ਹੋਆ ਵਡਭਾਗੀ ਮਨਿ ਹਰਿ ਹਰਿ ਮੀਠਾ ਲਾਇਆ ॥
ਜਨੁ ਕਹੈ ਨਾਨਕੁ ਲਾਵ ਪਹਿਲੀ ਆਰੰਭੁ ਕਾਜੁ ਰਚਾਇਆ ॥੧॥

ਹਰਿ ਦੂਜੜੀ ਲਾਵ ਸਤਿਗੁਰੁ ਪੁਰਖੁ ਮਿਲਾਇਆ ਬਲਿ ਰਾਮ ਜੀਉ ॥
ਨਿਰਭਉ ਭੈ ਮਨੁ ਹੋਇ ਹਉਮੈ ਮੈਲੁ ਗਵਾਇਆ ਬਲਿ ਰਾਮ ਜੀਉ ॥
ਨਿਰਮਲੁ ਭਉ ਪਾਇਆ ਹਰਿ ਗੁਣ ਗਾਇਆ ਹਰਿ ਵੇਖੈ ਰਾਮੁ ਹਦੂਰੇ ॥
ਹਰਿ ਆਤਮ ਰਾਮੁ ਪਸਾਰਿਆ ਸੁਆਮੀ ਸਰਬ ਰਹਿਆ ਭਰਪੂਰੇ ॥
ਅੰਤਰਿ ਬਾਹਰਿ ਹਰਿ ਪ੍ਰਭੁ ਏਕੋ ਮਿਲਿ ਹਰਿ ਜਨ ਮੰਗਲ ਗਾਏ ॥
ਜਨ ਨਾਨਕ ਦੂਜੀ ਲਾਵ ਚਲਾਈ ਅਨਹਦ ਸਬਦ ਵਜਾਏ ॥੨॥

ਹਰਿ ਤੀਜੜੀ ਲਾਵ ਮਨਿ ਚਾਉ ਭਇਆ ਬੈਰਾਗੀਆ ਬਲਿ ਰਾਮ ਜੀਉ ॥
ਸੰਤ ਜਨਾ ਹਰਿ ਮੇਲੁ ਹਰਿ ਪਾਇਆ ਵਡਭਾਗੀਆ ਬਲਿ ਰਾਮ ਜੀਉ ॥
ਨਿਰਮਲੁ ਹਰਿ ਪਾਇਆ ਹਰਿ ਗੁਣ ਗਾਇਆ ਮੁਖਿ ਬੋਲੀ ਹਰਿ ਬਾਣੀ ॥
ਸੰਤ ਜਨਾ ਵਡਭਾਗੀ ਪਾਇਆ ਹਰਿ ਕਥੀਐ ਅਕਥ ਕਹਾਣੀ ॥
ਹਿਰਦੈ ਹਰਿ ਹਰਿ ਹਰਿ ਧੁਨਿ ਉਪਜੀ ਹਰਿ ਜਪੀਐ ਮਸਤਕਿ ਭਾਗੁ ਜੀਉ ॥
ਜਨੁ ਨਾਨਕੁ ਬੋਲੇ ਤੀਜੀ ਲਾਵੈ ਹਰਿ ਉਪਜੈ ਮਨਿ ਬੈਰਾਗੁ ਜੀਉ ॥੩॥

ਹਰਿ ਚਉਥੜੀ ਲਾਵ ਮਨਿ ਸਹਜੁ ਭਇਆ ਹਰਿ ਪਾਇਆ ਬਲਿ ਰਾਮ ਜੀਉ ॥
ਗੁਰਮੁਖਿ ਮਿਲਿਆ ਸੁਭਾਇ ਹਰਿ ਮਨਿ ਤਨਿ ਮੀਠਾ ਲਾਇਆ ਬਲਿ ਰਾਮ ਜੀਉ ॥
ਹਰਿ ਮੀਠਾ ਲਾਇਆ ਮੇਰੇ ਪ੍ਰਭ ਭਾਇਆ ਅਨਦਿਨੁ ਹਰਿ ਲਿਵ ਲਾਈ ॥
ਮਨ ਚਿੰਦਿਆ ਫਲੁ ਪਾਇਆ ਸੁਆਮੀ ਹਰਿ ਨਾਮਿ ਵਜੀ ਵਾਧਾਈ ॥
ਹਰਿ ਪ੍ਰਭਿ ਠਾਕੁਰਿ ਕਾਜੁ ਰਚਾਇਆ ਧਨ ਹਿਰਦੈ ਨਾਮਿ ਵਿਗਾਸੀ ॥
ਜਨੁ ਨਾਨਕੁ ਬੋਲੇ ਚਉਥੀ ਲਾਵੈ ਹਰਿ ਪਾਇਆ ਪ੍ਰਭੁ ਅਵਿਨਾਸੀ ॥੪॥

Suhi, Mehla Chautha

Har pahilarri laav parvirti karam driṛaia bal ram jio
Bani barahma ved dharam drrirho paap tajaia bal ram jio

Dharam drriho har nam dhiavho simrit nam drriraia
Satgur gur pura aradho sabh kilvikh paap gvaia
Sahj anand hoa vadbhagi man har har meetha laia
Jan kahai Nanak laav pehilee arambh kaaj rachaia ||1||

Har dujrri laav satgur purakh milaia bal ram jio
Nirbhao bhai man hoe haumai mail gavaia bal ram jio
Nirmal bho paia har gun gaia har vekhai ram hadure
Har atam ram pasaria suami sarab rahia bharpure
Antar bahar har parabh eko mil har jan mangal gae
Jan Nanak duji laav chalai anhad sabad vajaee ||2||

Har teejrri laav man chao bhaia bairagia bal ram jio
Sant jana har mel har paia vadbhagia bal ram jio
Nirmal har paia har gun gaia mukh boli har bani
Sant jana vadbhagi paia har kathai akath kahani
Hirdai har har har dhun upji har japai mastak bhog jio
Jan Nanak bole teeji laavai har upjai man bairag jio ||3||

Har chautharri laav man sehj bhaia har paia bal ram jio
Gurmukh milia subhae har man tan meetha laia bal ram jio
Har meetha laia mere parabh bhaia andin har liv laee
Man chindia fal paia suami har naam vaji vadhaee
Har parabh thakur kaaj rachaia dhan hirdai naam vigasee
Jan Nanak bole chauthi laavai har paia parabh avinasiee ||4||

In the first circle
we come to everyday life
as two together.
We embrace right action, letting go
of our faults. We seek to remember
the true divine Name. We revere and adore
the true teacher who sees us whole,
our faults dissolved. Simple
spontaneous joy. What luck!

The taste of the divine is sweet.
Nanak the servant says, this is the first circle.
The marriage has begun.

In the second circle the divine reveals
the true Guru, wondrous person.
In fearlessness, our self-clinging
melts away. Awed by the presence,
we sing praise to the One without stain.
Every being, every space,
inside, outside, filled with grace.
The community bursts into songs of joy.
Nanak the servant says, this is the second circle
where the boundless sound resounds.

In the third circle we find
freedom of the mind. Joined in devotion, we sing
with our friends. How fortunate we are!
We discover what's pure. We sing what we are.
We speak the true Word. Such good fortune!
Joined in humble devotion,
we tell the untellable story of the divine.
The Name, the true Name vibrates—
music in the heart, the calling
written on our foreheads.
Nanak the servant says, this is the third circle.
When the mind is free, divinity flows
naturally.

In the fourth circle,
the mind is simple. We meet without effort.
Wherever we look, there is the Guru.
Mind and body are sweet, the divine is sweet,
we're meditating day and night.
All desires are fulfilled,

the Name resounds.
Hearts bloom as bride and groom
merge in the timeless One.
Nanak the servant says, this is the fourth circle.
It is done!

—SRI GURU GRANTH SAHIB, *Raag Suhi,* 773:16–774:12

PAGE 291

acknowledgments.

I AM GRATEFUL TO EVERYONE WHO TRUSTED ME WITH THEIR STORIES AND
taught me about love—the survivors and activists, justice-seekers
and wisdom-bearers, mothers and warriors and elders who are named
in this book. I am especially grateful to Rana Sodhi and the Sodhi
family for our two-decade-long journey together and to Baba Punjab
Singh, the Sikh grandfather who taught me the meaning of *chardi kala*.
He died shortly after this book was finished. May this book honor
him and all who refuse to succumb to despair, who protect that still
sacred place inside them and insist on "blinking twice."

This book had many midwives. My beloved friend Jessica Chen
Weiss was senior midwife, weaving breath into the labor every day
and bringing out the Wise Woman in me. Her husband, Jeremy Wal-
lace, believed in this book even when it existed as an outline on Kavi's
art easel. My first listeners, my book coven—Melissa Canlas, Nirinjan
Kaur Khalsa, Amy Olrick, and longtime brother Deeptej Singh—
created the sanctuary for me to deliver each new chapter with marvelous witness and radiant care. My cousin and sister Sharmila Kaur
Singh was my final listener, sealing this book with her grace. My long
friendship with Brynn Saito, poet of my life, sister on the quest, gave
this book its music.

My brilliant editor, Christopher Jackson, heard this book into
being and made the journey rich and revelatory. I grew as a writer
because of him. I am indebted to Chris and the entire team at One
World, Random House, including Avideh Bashirrad, Nicole Counts,
Cecil Flores, Erica Min, Rachel Rokicki, and Katie Tull for bringing

forth the voices and visions that are helping birth the America to be. My superb literary agent, Margaret Riley King, found the best home for this book.

To my teammates at the Revolutionary Love Project: Your tireless devotion energized me each day. Amy Olrick nurtured the root of this work with tender care. Kalia Lydgate's strategic genius made this book strong. Senior research scholar Melissa Canlas was our intellectual powerhouse whose deep engagement with this material sharpened the framework for revolutionary love and infused it with her own wisdom. Julianna Piazzola was my right-hand woman and research assistant, who labored by my side and produced the endnotes with me. I am indebted to our passionate team of research scholars who crafted memos for each chapter in their areas of expertise: Lisa Freeman in peacebuilding, Scott Henson in history and politics, Matt Henderson in psychology and many other areas, Jem Jebbia in religious studies, and Clayton McClintock in neuroscience. I also had support from Jhumka Gupta in public health and Sarah Munawar in ethics. Historian Erika Lee, Grant Din, and the Angel Island Immigration Station Foundation helped me find records of my family's story in America. My longtime teammates Aseem Mehta and Ivy Wang contributed to the stories in this book. Elizabeth Keller was our master proofreader.

I am grateful to the friends who read early drafts and gave me thoughtful notes, especially Linda Hess, my college mentor and *sutradhar*, who edited every line of this book, just as she did my senior thesis. Eric Parrie, my longtime accomplice, edited the manuscript three times until the words shimmered, just as he has every speech I've given. Bernie White held me to the truth above all. Ani di Franco, with Justin Tranter, turned drafts of this book into gorgeous songs, which I listened to as I finished the book. America Ferrera and Ryan Piers Williams gave me a writing desk and soft landings, and a vibrant community of artists and activists who carried me through the writing of this book. America and Ani, your sisterhood, artistry, and activism inspire me every day.

My Sikh sisters kept me in *chardi kala* on the hardest days: Nirinjan Kaur Khalsa wheeled me to the café to write, Jasvir Kaur Rababan put a *dilruba* in my hands, and Nitasha Sawhney gave me a game plan. To my beloved cousins Andrea, Anika, Ginny, Neena, Neetu, Serena, and Sharmila: Your fierce sisterhood runs through all the stories told in this book—and all the seasons of my life.

Thank you to the thought leaders and practitioners who mentored me in this project: Michelle Alexander for giving this book its name, Eve Ensler for showing me how to distill the truth, Hille Haker for returning me to the birthing metaphor, Melissa Harris-Perry for opening me to complexity, Van Jones for calling forth a love army, Victor Kazanjian for spiritual sustenance, Scotty and Ellen McLennan for guidance and affirmation, Hope Metcalf for urging me to show the ragged edges, Parker Palmer for keeping me faithful to the labor, and Tommy Woon for returning me to my body's wisdom. Our many exchanges pushed me to grow as a thinker. Thank you to bell hooks for first capturing my imagination and setting me on this path with her declaration of love as a public ethic.

I am grateful to the many students, educators, and activists who informed the ideas in this book over the years, and to my speaking agent, Annette Luba-Lucas, for making these public lectures possible. I am indebted to Kathy Anderson, the first person in the literary world who believed that I had a book in me.

Special thanks to all the volunteers who launched the Revolutionary Love Project, especially Meha Chiraya, Tara Dominic, Simran Grewall, Matt Henderson, John-Michael Parker, and longtime teammate Imran Siddiqui. This project would not exist without them or the support of our champions at several institutions: Isaac Luria at the Nathan Cummings Foundation; Van Jones and Kalia Lydgate at Dream Corps; Eve Ensler, Susan Swan, and Kristina Shea at V-Day; and Varun Soni at the University of Southern California.

Thank you to the many South Asian American advocates whose work informs this book, especially Deepa Iyer: You are our moral anchor who gives us vision *and* the tools to show up. I honor the elders who blazed a path for us, in my case Dr. Jaswant Singh Sachdev: You are the wind at my back. To all my Sikh sisters and brothers in the struggle, especially Amardeep Singh Bhalla, Ravi Singh Bhalla, Kamal Kalsi, Gurjot Kaur, Simran Jeet Singh, Sapreet Kaur Saluja, Arjun Sethi, Jaideep Singh, Prabhjot Singh, and the team at the Sikh Coalition: Your seva prefaces the world to come.

To the Auburn Senior Fellows: You are the prophets of revolutionary love today. Your sermons, congregations, and movements shape the nation's moral imagination—and mine. This book was enriched by my long exchanges with Rev. William Barber II of the Poor People's Campaign who leads our nation's moral revival; Rabbi Sharon Brous of IKAR in Los Angeles whose sermons are my north star; Sister Simone Campbell of NETWORK who models grace and longevity; Stosh Cotler of Bend the Arc who leads with an open heart; Rabbi Stephanie Kolin of Union Temple in Brooklyn who organizes with brilliance; Rev. Jacqui Lewis of Middle Church in New York City, who regularly convenes us in a Revolutionary Love Conference; Rev. Michael-Ray Matthews of PICO who teaches us prophetic resistance; Brian McLaren, who mentored me through the book process; Rev. Otis Moss III of Trinity Church in Chicago who helped me live into the name Jubilee; Bishop Gene Robinson who teaches me that courage is fear that has said its prayers; and sensei angel Kyodo Williams, whose Buddhist teachings on radical dharma help us birth a new America. I am also strengthened by Wajahat Ali, Rev. Traci Blackmon, Rev. Jennifer Butler, Bishop Yvette Flunder, Lisa Sharon Harper, Rev. Peter Heltzel, Rabbi Jill Jacobs, and Linda Sarsour. Immense gratitude to Katharine Henderson, John Vaughn, and the team at Auburn Seminary for equipping us as faith leaders—especially Macky Alston, who trained my media voice; Lisa Anderson, who taught me luscious wellness; and Sharon Groves, who showed me my path in the dark.

Thank you to all the friends, teammates, and accomplices who urged these stories out of me over many years: Matthew and Nicole Blute, K.B., Kimi Buser, Tommy Clancy, Jane Cooper, Dylan Courville, Jodi Elliot, Kim Gillingham, Michelle Goldhaber, Jake Goodman, Sabrina Gordon, Tom Halloran, Mehran Herd, Carline and Lars Jorgenson, Deonnie Moodie King, Kerri Kelly, Linda Kay Klein, Sally Kohn, Derek Kroeger, James Kwak, Tafari Lumumba, Marion and Sab Masada, Matthew Matera, Elizabeth Marez, Tracy Wells Miller, Lauren Oleykowski, Helen O'Reilly, Aeryn Palmer, Don Presley, Delaina Price, Isadore Ramirez, Michael Rosenberg, Julie and Mohsen Sadeghi, Shil Sengupta, T. Sher Singh, Michael Skolnik, Abby Shuman, Jonathan Smith, Najeeba Syed, Ray Treadwell, Zach Warren, Pat and Terry Waterman, and Beth Zemsky. Thank you Dot2Dot and Harness for your warm embrace. Special love to the Pocket, Mohammad Abdul-Carim, Mariah Isely, Jessica Jenkins, Shannon Moore-Langston, Irene Lu, and Irene Yeh.

I am grateful to the educators who gave me the tools to tell this story: Muneer Ahmad, Jack Balkin, Emily Bazelon, Diana Eck, Marshall Ganz, Linda Greenhouse, Michael Jackson, Dale Maharidge, Eboo Patel, Rob Reich, Reva Siegel, Barbara van Schewick, and Michael Wishnie. Special affection for Maren Nielsen, my high school English teacher, and Carole Smoot and Rob Darrow, my History Day coaches, for believing I had stories to tell—and showing me how.

Thank you to the caregivers who helped keep our house in order, played with our children, provided treatments, and made it possible for me to write during a difficult pregnancy: Sidia Alfaro, Melvin Badilla, William Barrondo, Jamie Brewster, Valerie Courville, Veronica Gomez, Roxana Rodriguez, Delia and Sydney Soza, and the educators and parents at Evergreen Community School. Thank you to my (actual) midwives, Shadman Habibi and Elizabeth Keit, and my doula, Maite Onochie, who helped me birth our baby as I birthed this book.

My family gave me the blessing to write this book. Sanjeev Brar, my brother and longest companion, nourished me with his endless creativity and encouragement, along with my beautiful sister-in-law Allison Cleveland. I received affection and support from my aunts and uncles—Bhua Ji and Foofar Ji, Chacha Jas and Chachi Ji, Chachi Kul and Chacha Raj, Jagi Auntie, Mama Ji and Mami Auntie, and Masi Auntie. Our cousins cheered us on, especially April, Corinna, Gavin, Harsha, Kiran, Rachana, Sonny, Tom, and Vikas. My brother-in-law and sister-in-law, Manu Raju and Archana Mehta, uplifted us with their friendship and their powerful work in the world. I am grateful to my grandfather Captain Gurdial Singh and Sharat's grandfather, the great poet Gopalakrishna Adiga, for inspiring a family of writers. To the babies in our family—Anika, Avani, Baghail, Connor, Layla, Marshall, Mayuri, Sairaa, Sanaa, Sanjay, Sonya, and Zamina—I cannot wait to put *your* stories in the red binder!

Sharat's parents, Vidya and Tonse Krishna Raju, were our pillars of strength. Amma cared for our babies during long writing days with tireless affection. Appa made our creative lives possible with his steadfast support and boundless appetite for knowledge.

This book would not exist without my parents, Dolly and Judge Brar. They moved us to the rain forest and back, housed us, fed us, cared for us, and raised our children with us, just so that I could write each day. I am grateful for my mother's laughter and wrap-around care, and my father's radiance through this family adventure. My father appears in the background of this book only because his role in my life has been uncomplicated, defined by unending and unconditional support. My father is who we hope our son grows up to be— sincere, passionate, resourceful, just, and committed to the flourishing of the women and girls in his life.

Sharat moved heaven and earth so that I could write this book. Traversed mountains just to find me the letter N missing on a keyboard. Had faith in me in the midnight hour. Made the labor joyful. Loved this book like it was my third child. Because of him, this vibrant life. To baby Ananda, who heard every word while in the womb and again while nursing and giggling in my arms, and Kavi, who celebrated every completed chapter with popcorn and bubble baths and moving chocolate tastings: *Oh, my loves. Let's dance.*

selected reading list.

On Asian American History

Lee, Erika. *The Making of Asian America: A History.* New York: Simon & Schuster, 2015.

Lee, Erika, and Judy Yung. *Angel Island: Immigrant Gateway to America.* New York: Oxford University Press, 2010.

On the Love Ethic

Fromm, Erich. *The Art of Loving.* New York: Harper Perennial, 2006.

hooks, bell. *All About Love: New Visions.* New York: HarperCollins, 2000.

King, Martin Luther, Jr. *Strength to Love.* New York: Harper & Row, 1963.

Tippett, Krista. *Becoming Wise: An Inquiry into the Mystery and Art of Living.* New York: Penguin Press, 2016.

On Race and Justice

Alexander, Michelle. *The New Jim Crow: Mass Incarceration in the Age of Color-blindness.* New York: New Press, 2012.

Davis, Angela Y. *Are Prisons Obsolete?* New York: Seven Stories Press, 2003.

Kendi, Ibram X. *How to Be an Antiracist.* New York: One World, 2019.

Lorde, Audre. *Sister Outsider: Essays and Speeches.* New York: Ten Speed Press, 1984.

Powell, John A. *Racing to Justice: Transforming Our Conceptions of Self and Other to Build an Inclusive Society.* Bloomington: Indiana University Press, 2012.

Sered, Danielle. *Until We Reckon.* New York: New Press, 2019.

Stevenson, Bryan. *Just Mercy: A Story of Justice and Redemption.* New York: Spiegel & Grau, 2014.

On Human Behavior and Healing Trauma

Sapolsky, Robert. *Behave: The Biology of Humans at Our Best and Worst.* New York: Penguin Press, 2017.

van der Kolk, Bessel. *The Body Keeps the Score: Brain, Mind, and Body in the Healing of Trauma*. New York: Viking Penguin, 2014.

On Democracy

Jones, Van. *Beyond the Messy Truth: How We Came Apart, How We Come Together*. New York: Ballantine, 2017.

Kohn, Sally. *The Opposite of Hate: A Field Guide to Repairing Our Humanity*. Chapel Hill: Algonquin, 2018.

Levitsky, Steven, and Daniel Ziblatt. *How Democracies Die*. New York: Crown, 2018.

Palmer, Parker J. *Healing the Heart of Democracy: The Courage to Create a Politics Worthy of the Human Spirit*. Hoboken, N.J.: Wiley, 2011.

On Nonviolent Social Change

Boggs, Grace Lee. *The Next American Revolution: Sustainable Activism for the Twenty-First Century*. Berkeley: University of California Press, 2012.

Chenoweth, Erica, and Maria J. Stephan. *Why Civil Resistance Works: The Strategic Logic of Nonviolent Conflict*. New York: Columbia University Press, 2011.

Freire, Paulo. *Pedagogy of the Oppressed*. New York: Herder & Herder, 1970.

Lederach, John Paul. *The Moral Imagination: The Art and Soul of Building Peace*. New York: Oxford University Press, 2005.

On Hate in America Since 9/11

Iyer, Deepa. *We Too Sing America: South Asian, Arab, Muslim, and Sikh Immigrants Shape Our Multiracial Future*. New York: New Press, 2015.

Malek, Alia. *Patriot Acts: Narratives of Post-9/11 Injustice*. San Francisco: McSweeney's, 2011.

Sethi, Arjun, ed. *American Hate*. New York: New Press, 2018.

Sidhu, Dawinder S., and Neha Singh Gohil. *Civil Rights in Wartime: The Post-9/11 Sikh Experience*. London: Routledge, 2016.

On the Sikh Faith

Mandair, Arvind-Pal Singh. *Sikhism: A Guide for the Perplexed*. New York: Bloomsbury Academic, 2013.

Shackle, Christopher, and Arvind-Pal Singh Mandair. *Teachings of the Gurus*. New York: Routledge, 2005.

Singh, Nikky-Gurinder Kaur. *The First Sikh: The Life and Legacy of Guru Nanak*. New Delhi: Penguin, 2019.

Singh, Nikky-Gurinder Kaur. *Sikhism: An Introduction*. London: I. B. Tauris, 2011.

notes.

introduction.

vii **There are no new ideas** Audre Lorde, "Poetry Is Not a Luxury," in *Sister Outsider: Essays and Speeches* (New York: Ten Speed Press, 1984), 39.

xiii **"What if our America is not dead"** Reframing America as a nation "waiting to be born" was inspired by social reformers throughout history, such as the poet Langston Hughes: "Let America be America again! . . . / America never was America to me, / And yet I swear this oath— / America will be!" Langston Hughes, "Let America Be America Again," in *The Collected Poems of Langston Hughes,* ed. Arnold Rampersand and David Roessel (New York: Vintage, 1994), 189–190.

xiii **In the weeks that followed** Valarie Kaur, "'Breathe! Push!' Watch This Sikh Activist's Powerful Prayer for America," *The Washington Post,* March 6, 2017, https://www.washingtonpost.com/news/acts-of-faith/wp/2017/03/06/breathe-push-watch-this-sikh-activists-powerful-prayer-for-america/. For additional videos of the address, see Valarie Kaur, "Watch Night Speech: Breathe and Push," ValarieKaur.com (blog), January 8, 2017, https://valariekaur.com/2017/01/watch-night-speech-breathe-push.

xiv **At this moment** Brian Levin, "Why White Supremacist Attacks Are on the Rise, Even in Surprising Places," *Time,* March 21, 2019, https://time.com/5555396/white-supremacist-attacks-rise-new-zealand/.

xiv **The United States is also** See Robert P. Jones, *The End of White Christian America* (New York: Simon & Schuster, 2016).

xiv **Or will we continue** See Steven Levitsky and Daniel Ziblatt, *How Democracies Die* (New York: Crown, 2018), 7. "The weakening of our democratic norms is rooted in extreme partisan polarization—one that extends beyond policy differences into an existential conflict over race and culture. America's efforts to achieve racial equality as our society grows increasingly diverse have fueled an insidious reaction and intensifying polarization. And if one thing is clear from studying breakdowns throughout history, it's that extreme polarization can kill democracies."

xv **The same supremacist ideologies** See Naomi Klein, *On Fire: The Burning Case for a Green New Deal* (New York: Simon & Schuster, 2019), 50.

xv **Black feminists like bell hooks** For an exploration of love as a public ethic, see bell hooks, *All About Love: New Visions* (New York: HarperCollins, 2000), 87. "Culturally, all spheres of American life—politics, religion, the workplace, domestic households, intimate relations—should and could have as their foundation a love ethic."

xv **Love is a form** My definition of love is inspired by bell hooks's foundational work on the love ethic. She writes: "Love is an act of will—namely, both an intention and an action. Will also implies choice. We do not have to love. We choose to love." hooks, *All About Love*, 5. The choice to love is "the primary way we end domination and oppression." hooks, *All About Love,* 76. I am also influenced by philosopher Erich Fromm, who writes that "the essence of love is to 'labor' for something and 'to make something grow,' that love and labor are inseparable." Erich Fromm, *The Art of Loving* (New York: Harper Perennial, 2006), 25–26.

xvii **Revolutions do not happen** Krista Tippett, *Becoming Wise: An Inquiry into the Mystery and Art of Living* (New York: Penguin Press, 2016), 135. Tippett explores peacebuilder John Paul Lederach's idea that revolutions happen slowly, over time, as the result of a "new quality of relationship in small, unlikely groups of people." See John Paul Lederach, *The Moral Imagination: The Art and Soul of Building Peace* (New York: Oxford University Press, 2005), chapter 9, "On Mass and Movement: The Theory of the Critical Yeast."

part I: see no stranger: loving others

chapter 1: wonder

5 **If you want to play** Sri Guru Granth Sahib, *Salok,* 1412:2. This *shabad* by Guru Nanak is found in the Guru Granth Sahib, the primary sacred text of the Sikh faith. For the full *shabad,* see the *Sikh shabad*s section in the book.

8 ***Tati Vao Na Lagi*** Sri Guru Granth Sahib, *Raag Bilaaval,* 819:16–18. This *shabad* is attributed to Guru Arjan, the fifth Sikh guru. For the full *shabad,* see the *Sikh shabad*s section in the book.

8 **But Nanak emerged** The story of Guru Nanak's revelation has been told and passed down through *janam-sakhi*s, legendary stories about Nanak's life preserved through oral tradition. When Nanak emerged from the river, his first utterance is said to have been *"Na ko Hindu, Na Musalman,"* which means "No one is a Hindu. No one is a Muslim." For more about Guru Nanak and the beginning of the Sikh faith, see Arvind-Pal Singh Mandair, *Sikhism: A Guide for the Perplexed* (New York: Bloomsbury Academic, 2013), 17–21, 33, 136; Nikky-Gurinder Kaur Singh, The First Sikh: The Life and Legacy of Guru Nanak (New Delhi: Penguin, 2019).

9 **"I see no stranger"** Sri Guru Granth Sahib, *Raag Kanara,* 1299:14. The fifth Sikh teacher, Guru Arjan, captured Guru Nanak's vision in a *shabad* in the Guru Granth Sahib: "Na Ko Bairi Nahi Begana, Sagal Sang Hamko Ban Ayi." My translation: "I see no enemy. I see no stranger. All of us belong to each other." For the full *shabad,* see the *Sikh shabads* section in the book.

9 *Wondrous are the forms* Sri Guru Granth Sahib, *Asa di Var,* 463:18–464:4. This *shabad* is by Guru Nanak. For the full *shabad,* see the *Sikh shabads* section in the book.

11 **We share a common ancestry** Biologists trace the most recent ancestor of all current life on earth to a single-celled bacterium that lived some three billion years ago. Charles Darwin first proposed the theory of common ancestry in *On the Origin of Species* in 1859. For recent science on our common ancestry, see Bill Mesler and James H. Cleaves, "One Primordial Form," in *A Brief History of Creation: Science and the Search for the Origin of Life* (New York: W. W. Norton, 2016), 223–239; Douglas L. Theobald, "A Formal Test of the Theory of Universal Common Ancestry," *Nature* 465, no. 7295 (2010): 219–222.

11 **The air we breathe contains atoms** See Curt Stager, *Your Atomic Self: The Invisible Elements That Connect You to Everything Else in the Universe* (New York: St. Martin's, 2014); Sam Kean, *Caesar's Last Breath: Decoding the Secrets of the Air Around Us* (Boston: Little, Brown, 2017).

11 **Our bodies are composed of** See Karel Schrijver and Iris Schrijver, *Living with the Stars: How the Human Body Is Connected to the Life Cycles of the Earth, the Planets, and the Stars* (Oxford, U.K.: Oxford University Press, 2015).

13 **This *shabad* was my key** For how repetition of a prayer can stimulate the brain's reward system, see Uffe Schjødt et al., "Rewarding Prayers," *Neuroscience Letters* 433, no. 3 (2008): 165–168.

13 **His followers were called Sikhs** Mandair, *Sikhism;* Christopher Shackle and Arvind-Pal Singh Mandair, *Teachings of the Gurus* (New York: Routledge, 2005); Nikky-Gurinder Kaur Singh, *The First Sikh: The Life and Legacy of Guru Nanak* (New Delhi: Penguin, 2019).

13 **Guru Arjan was martyred** Mandair, *Sikhism,* 40–46.

13 **Baba Deep Singh went on** Khushwant Singh, *A History of the Sikhs,* vol. 1, *1469–1839* (New Delhi: Oxford, 1999), 145–146.

14 **In 1699, the tenth Sikh teacher** For the story of Guru Gobind Singh and the formation of the Khalsa, see Mandair, *Sikhism,* 56–61.

14 **"Truth is high, but higher still"** Sri Guru Granth Sahib, *Sri Raag,* 62:11. ਸਚਹੁ ਉਰੈ ਸਭੁ ਕੋ ਉਪਰਿ ਸਚੁ ਆਚਾਰੁ. This *shabad* is by Guru Nanak. The translation is mine.

16 **Our minds are primed** Robert Sapolsky, *Behave: The Biology of Humans at Our Best and Worst* (New York: Penguin Press, 2017), 388–424. In chapter 11, "Us Versus Them," Sapolsky offers an accessible in-depth discus-

sion of the science behind how our minds see the world in terms of "us and them," with summaries of the studies in the following notes.

16 **This happens *before* conscious thought** The adult brain forms "us and them" dichotomies before conscious thought. Just a fifty-millisecond exposure to the face of someone of another race has been shown to activate the amygdala, the part of the brain involved in fear and aggression. We group faces by gender and social status at roughly the same speed. For the neuroscience behind implicit bias, see Tiffany A. Ito and Geoffrey R. Urland, "Race and Gender on the Brain: Electrocortical Measures of Attention to the Race and Gender of Multiply Categorizable Individuals," *Journal of Personality and Social Psychology* 85, no. 4 (2003): 616–626; Tiffany A. Ito and Bruce D. Bartholow, "The Neural Correlates of Race," *Trends in Cognitive Sciences* 13, no. 12 (2009): 524–531, https://doi.org/10.1016/j.tics.2009.10.002.

16 **Our bodies release hormones** Carsten K. W. De Dreu et al., "Oxytocin Promotes Human Ethnocentrism," *Proceedings of the National Academy of Sciences of the United States of America* 108, no. 4 (2001): 1262–1266.

17 **It is easier to feel empathy** See Alessio Avenanti et al., "Racial Bias Reduces Empathic Sensorimotor Resonance with Other-Race Pain," *Current Biology* 20, no. 11 (2010): 1018–1022; Vani A. Mathur et al., "Neural Basis of Extraordinary Empathy and Altruistic Motivation," *NeuroImage* 51, no. 4 (2010): 1468–1475. When people are shown a video of a hand poked by a needle, they have an "isomorphic sensorimotor" response. Their hands tense in empathy. But their empathy response is blunted when the hand belongs to someone of a different race. Similarly, people show more emotional activation when prompted to think about misfortune happening to a person of their own race as opposed to someone of another race.

17 **We think of *us* as complex** Essentialism is the idea that out-groups have an immutable negative "essence." We tend to view "them" as disgusting, homogenous, and interchangeable, with simpler emotions and less sensitivity to pain. See Jacques-Philippe Leyens et al., "The Emotional Side of Prejudice: The Attribution of Secondary Emotions to Ingroups and Outgroups," *Personality and Social Psychology Review* 4, no. 2 (2000): 186–197.

17 **We are much more likely** See Mark Levine et al., "Self-Categorization and Bystander Non-Intervention: Two Experimental Studies," *Journal of Applied Social Psychology* 32, no. 7 (2002): 1452–1463; Mark Levine et al., "Identity and Emergency Intervention: How Social Group Membership and Inclusiveness of Group Boundaries Shape Helping Behavior," *Personality and Social Psychology Bulletin* 31, no. 5 (2005): 443–453. When people are primed to think of a victim of violence as one of "us," it increases the odds of their intervening. They are less likely to intervene when they see a victim as one of "them."

17 **Such stereotypes are in the air** For an in-depth discussion of stereotypes, see John A. Powell, *Racing to Justice: Transforming Our Conceptions of Self and*

Other to Build an Inclusive Society (Bloomington: Indiana University Press, 2012), 21–23. Implicit biases are our attitudes, assumptions, and feelings about one another outside of our conscious awareness and control. You can explore your implicit biases by taking an Implicit Association Test. See Project Implicit, https://implicit.harvard.edu/implicit/education.html.

17 **Even if we are part of** In the 1940s, researchers found that black children preferred to play with white dolls and gave them more positive attributes. Since then, studies in unconscious bias have consistently shown that nearly half of the members of marginalized groups show less favorable attitudes toward their own group than toward higher-status groups. See John T. Jost et al., "Non-conscious Forms of System Justification: Implicit and Behavioral Preferences for Higher Status Groups," *Journal of Experimental Social Psychology* 38, no. 6 (2002): 586–602; John T. Jost et al., "A Decade of System Justification Theory: Accumulated Evidence of Conscious and Unconscious Bolstering of the Status Quo," *Political Psychology* 25, no. 6 (2004): 881–919; Kenneth B. Clark and Mamie P. Clark, "Emotional Factors in Racial Identification and Preference in Negro Children," *Journal of Negro Education* 19, no. 3 (1950): 341–350.

17 **In sixth grade, I discovered** "What is NHD?," National History Day, accessed February 4, 2020, https://www.nhd.org.

18 **I was researching the Partition of India** For more about the Partition of India, see Nisid Hajari, *Midnight's Furies: The Deadly Legacy of India's Partition* (Gloucestershire, U.K.: 2015); Urvashi Butalia, *The Other Side of Silence: Voices from the Partition of India* (Durham, N.C.: Duke University Press, 2000); William Dalrymple, "The Great Divide: The Violent Legacy of Indian Partition," *New Yorker,* June 22, 2015, https://www.newyorker.com/magazine/2015/06/29/the-great-divide-books-dalrymple.

22 **The indigenous population of California** Benjamin Madley, *An American Genocide: The United States and the California Indian Catastrophe, 1846–1873* (New Haven, Conn.: Yale University Press, 2016), 3.

22 **By the time my family arrived** Alfred Louis Kroeber, *Handbook of the Indians of California* (New York: Dover, 1975), 883.

23 **We bowed our heads** For selections from the Guru Granth Sahib, see Shackle and Mandair, *Teachings of the Gurus*.

26 **In brain-imaging studies** Subjects who were prompted to look at the face of a person of a different race long enough to consider what vegetables they liked—in other words, to think about a person as an individual—dampened their automatic fear response. Our prejudices are automatic but not inevitable. We can undo our automatic responses to faces of different races when we choose to wonder about them as people. See Mary E. Wheeler and Susan T. Fiske, "Controlling Racial Prejudice: Social-Cognitive Goals Affect Amygdala and Stereotype Activation," *Psychological Science* 16, no. 1 (2005): 56–63, https://doi.org/10.1111/j.0956-7976.2005.00780.x.

27 **It actually increases the frequency** When white subjects are primed with a command to "avoid prejudice" during a racial interaction, their performance declines more than when they are told to "have a positive intercultural exchange." See Jennifer A. Richeson et al., "An fMRI Investigation of the Impact of Interracial Contact on Executive Function," *Nature Neuroscience* 6, no. 12 (2003): 1323–1328; Jennifer A. Richeson and J. Nicole Shelton, "Negotiating Interracial Interactions: Costs, Consequences, and Possibilities," *Current Directions in Psychological Science* 16, no. 6 (2007): 316–320.

27 **In recent years, breakthroughs in neuroscience** Joseph Altman and Gopal D. Das, "Autoradiographic and Histological Evidence of Postnatal Hippocampal Neurogenesis in Rats," *Journal of Comparative Neurology* 124, no. 3 (1965): 319–335; Michael S. Kaplan, "Environment Complexity Stimulates Visual Cortex Neurogenesis: Death of a Dogma and a Research Career," *Trends in Neurosciences* 24, no. 10 (2001): 617–620; Guo-Li Ming and Hongjun Song, "Adult Neurogenesis in the Mammalian Central Nervous System," *Annual Review of Neuroscience* 28 (2005): 223–250; Wei Deng et al., "New Neurons and New Memories: How Does Adult Hippocampal Neurogenesis Affect Learning and Memory?," *Nature Reviews Neuroscience* 11, no. 5 (2010): 339–350.

27 **Experience can lead to structural changes** Amelia Mutso et al., "Abnormalities in Hippocampal Functioning with Persistent Pain," *Journal of Neuroscience* 32, no. 17 (2012): 5747–5756; Eleanor A. Maguire et al., "Navigation-Related Structural Change in the Hippocampi of Taxi Drivers," *Proceedings of the National Academy of Sciences of the United States of America* 97, no. 8 (2000): 4398–4403; Katharine Woollett and Eleanor A. Maguire, "Acquiring 'the Knowledge' of London's Layout Drives Structural Brain Changes," *Current Biology* 21, no. 24 (2011): 2109–2114; Peter S. Eriksson et al., "Neurogenesis in the Adult Human Hippocampus," *Nature Medicine* 4, no. 11 (1998): 1313–1317.

28 **I could not have known** For more on Brian McLaren, see "About Brian McLaren," https://brianmclaren.net/about-brian. For more on Parker Palmer, see "Parker J. Palmer," Center for Courage & Renewal, http://www.couragerenewal.org/parker.

chapter 2: grieve

31 **Those who love us never** Alice Walker, foreword to *Barracoon: The Story of the Last "Black Cargo,"* by Zora Neale Hurston (New York: HarperCollins, 2018), xi.

33 **Hannah Arendt calls this** See Hannah Arendt, *The Human Condition* (Chicago: University of Chicago Press, 1958); Hannah Arendt, *Between Past and Future* (New York: Viking Press, 1961); Hannah Arendt, *On Violence* (New York: Harcourt, Brace & World, 1970).

34 **I dreamed of becoming a professor** For an example of a historical account from the "underside" of history, see Howard Zinn, *A People's History of the United States* (New York: Harper & Row, 1980).

34 **In my sophomore year** Trevor Sutton, "Living History Project Shares Voices from the Past," *Stanford Daily,* April 23, 2001, https://archives .stanforddaily.com/2001/04/23?page=1#issue.

34 **I wrote a proposal** For an example of oral histories of the 1947 Partition of India, see Urvashi Butalia, *The Other Side of Silence: Voices from the Partition of India* (Durham, N.C.: Duke University Press, 2000).

35 **The violence was instant** To learn more about hate violence after 9/11, see Alia Malek, *Patriot Acts: Narratives of Post-9/11 Injustice* (San Francisco: McSweeney's, 2011); Dale Maharidge, *Homeland* (New York: Seven Stories Press, 2004); Dawinder S. Sidhu and Neha Singh Gohil, *Civil Rights in Wartime: The Post-9/11 Sikh Experience* (London: Routledge, 2016); Deepa Iyer, *We Too Sing America: South Asian, Arab, Muslim, and Sikh Immigrants Shape Our Multiracial Future* (New York: New Press, 2015).

35 **On city streets across the nation** Community groups reported more than two thousand hate incidents in the aftermath of 9/11. See Human Rights Watch, "United States: 'We Are Not the Enemy'; Hate Crimes Against Arabs, Muslims, and Those Perceived to Be Arab or Muslim After September 11" (report, vol. 14, no. 6 [G], November 2002), 11–14, https://www .hrw.org/reports/2002/usahate/usa1102.pdf.

36 **He was the first of nineteen** Those killed in the aftermath of 9/11 include Balbir Singh Sodhi, Waqar Hassan, Adel Karas, Saed Mujtahid, Jayantilal Patel, Surjit Singh Samra, Abdo Ali Ahmed, Abdullah Mohammed Nimer, Vasudev Patel, Kimberly Lowe, Ali Almansoop, Jawed Wassel, Ali W. Ali, Ramez Younan, Amar Singh Sachdeva, and Sukhpal Singh Sodhi. See Muneer I. Ahmad, "A Rage Shared by Law," *California Law Review* 92, no. 5 (2004): 1259–1330, https://www.jstor.org/stable/3481418; *Divided We Fall: Americans in the Aftermath,* directed by Sharat Raju, written by Valarie Kaur (Los Angeles: New Moon Productions, 2008), https://valariekaur .com/film/divided-we-fall.

36 **I pulled down Harry Potter** J. K. Rowling, *Harry Potter and the Sorcerer's Stone* (New York: Scholastic, 1998).

36–37 **I thought back** For more about the human rights atrocities in India during and after the 1984 pogroms, see Jaskaran Kaur, *Twenty Years of Impunity: The November 1984 Pogroms of Sikhs in India,* 2nd ed. (Portland, Ore.: Ensaaf, 2006), https://ensaaf.org/wp-content/uploads/2018/08/20years -2nd.pdf.

37 **Documentation determined which atrocities** The philosopher Judith Butler writes: "If a life is not grievable, it is not quite a life, it does not qualify as a life and is not worth a note. It is already the unburied, if not the unburiable." Judith Butler, *Precarious Life: The Powers of Mourning and Violence* (London: Verso, 2004), 34.

38 **As far as we know** Maharidge, *Homeland,* 85–86.

39 **From then on** "The Heroes," *Newsweek,* September 26, 2001, https://www
.newsweek.com/heroes-152329.

39 **No correction was issued** Jaideep Singh, "Confronting Racial Violence:
Sikh Americans Have Been Targeted for Harassment and Attack More Than
Any Group Since 9/11," *Colorlines* 6, no. 1 (2003): 23.

39 **The image of turbaned** For an examination of stereotypes of Muslims and
Arabs in entertainment media before 9/11, see Jack G. Shaheen, *Reel Bad
Arabs: How Hollywood Vilifies a People* (Northampton, Mass.: Olive Branch
Press, 2001).

40 **Police caught his assailants** Daniel Massey, "'Ignorant' Teens Beat Sikh in
Richmond Hill," QNS, September 26, 2001, https://qns.com/story/2001/
09/26/ignorant-teens-beat-sikh-in-richmond-hill.

40 **He would be the first of many** Elderly Sikh men who have been attacked
since 9/11 include Surinder Singh and Gurmej Atwal (Lee Romney, "Attack
on Sikh Men Triggers Outcry in Elk Grove, Calif., and Beyond," *Los Angeles
Times,* April 11, 2011, https://www.latimes.com/local/la-xpm-2011-apr
-11-la-me-0411-sikhs-20110411-story.html); Amrik Singh Bal (Angélica
Salceda, "Fresno in Mourning: Two of Our Sikh Neighbors Attacked in One
Week," ACLU Northern California, January 11, 2016, https://www.aclunc
.org/blog/fresno-mourning-two-our-sikh-neighbors-attacked-one-week);
and Sahib Singh Natt ("Caught on Camera: Men Beat, Spit on Elderly Sikh
Man at Manteca Park," CBS Sacramento, August 7, 2018, https://sacramento
.cbslocal.com/2018/08/07/sikh-man-attacked-manteca).

40 **On the morning of September 30** Moni Basu, "Sikhs Under Attack,"
CNN, updated September 14, 2016, https://www.cnn.com/2016/09/14/
us/sikh-hate-crimes-list/index.html.

41 **We sat in the prayer hall** Bella Bru, "Sikh Temple Vandalized in West Sacramento," Free Republic, September 13, 2001, http://www.freerepublic
.com/focus/f-news/522619/posts.

41 **When I came home** *Fresno Bee,* "Hate Graffiti on Fresno Gurdwara,"
March 15, 2004, Harvard University Pluralism Project Archive, https://
hwpi.harvard.edu/pluralismarchive/news/hate-graffiti-fresno-gurdwara.

42 **But the FBI would report** Federal Bureau of Investigation, "Hate Crime
Statistics, 2001," Hate Crimes in 2001—Uniform Crime Reporting, https://
ucr.fbi.gov/hate-crime/2001/hatecrime01.pdf.

42 **When crimes were recorded** See Ahmad, "A Rage Shared by Law."

42 **The most consistent and immediate targets** Laurie Goodstein and Tamar
Lewin, "A Nation Challenged: Violence and Harassment; Victims of Mistaken Identity, Sikhs Pay a Price for Turbans," *The New York Times,* September 19, 2001, https://www.nytimes.com/2001/09/19/us/nation-challenged
-violence-harassment-victims-mistaken-identity-sikhs-pay-price.html
?register=email&auth=register-email.

43 **The journey is often painful** For a clinical study of the importance of grief work and the damage caused by grief suppression, see Erich Lindemann, "Symptomatology and Management of Acute Grief," *American Journal of Psychiatry* 101, no. 2 (1944): 141–148.

44 **Some forms of grief** Brandon Hamber, "Does the Truth Heal?," in *Burying the Past: Making Peace and Doing Justice After Civil Conflict,* ed. Nigel Biggar (Washington, D.C.: Georgetown University Press, 2003), 158. "Psychological restoration and healing can only occur through providing space for survivors of violence to be heard and for every detail of the traumatic event to be reexperienced in a safe environment."

44 **A story of violence** Elizabeth Rosner, *Survivor Café: The Legacy of Trauma and the Labyrinth of Memory* (Berkeley, Calif.: Counterpoint, 2017), 32.

45 **They had witnessed surges** Human Rights Watch, "United States: 'We Are Not the Enemy,'" 11–14.

45 **Social psychologists speak** In terror management theory, threats to mortality cause us to draw closer to those who validate our beliefs and express aversion toward those who are perceived to threaten our beliefs. See Jeff Greenberg et al., "Evidence for Terror Management Theory II: The Effects of Mortality Salience on Reactions to Those Who Threaten or Bolster the Cultural Worldview," *Journal of Personality and Social Psychology* 58, no. 2 (1990): 308–318, https://doi.org/10.1037/0022-3514.58.2.308. For an analysis of the 9/11 attacks through the lens of terror management theory, see: Tom Pyszczynski et al., *In the Wake of 9/11: The Psychology of Terror* (Washington, D.C.: American Psychological Association, 2002).

45 **Many of our grandparents** See Nisid Hajari, *Midnight's Furies: The Deadly Legacy of India's Partition* (Stroud, U.K.: Amberley, 2015); Butalia, *The Other Side of Silence;* William Dalrymple, "The Great Divide: The Violent Legacy of Indian Partition," *New Yorker,* June 22, 2015, https://www.newyorker.com/magazine/2015/06/29/the-great-divide-books-dalrymple.

45 **Some of our parents** See Kaur, *Twenty Years of Impunity.*

45 **Today we know that trauma** See David Matz et al., "Interrupting Intergenerational Trauma: Children of Holocaust Survivors and the Third Reich," *Journal of Phenomenological Psychology* 46, no. 2 (2015): 185–205; Donna K. Nagata et al., "Processing Cultural Trauma: Intergenerational Effects of the Japanese American Incarceration," *Journal of Social Issues* 71, no. 2 (2015): 356–370, https://doi.org/10.1111/josi.12115.

47 **White supremacy had always** Jeannine Hill Fletcher, *The Sin of White Supremacy: Christianity, Racism, and Religious Diversity in America* (New York: Orbis, 2017).

48 **America did not find our lives** See Butler, *Precarious Life,* 32–34. Butler asks whose lives are "grievable" as a way to explore whose count as human.

52 **That morning, he had boasted** "Sodhi Murder Trial Begins," Rediff

.com, September 4, 2003, https://www.rediff.com/us/2003/sep/03sodhi .htm.

52 **After the shooting rampage** Mike Anton, "Collateral Damage in the War on Terrorism," *Los Angeles Times,* September 22, 2001, https://www.latimes .com/archives/la-xpm-2001-sep-22-mn-48573-story.html.

52 **A few days later** Inspired by his Islamic faith, Rais Bhuiyan launched a campaign to fight for a stay of execution for Mark Stroman, the man who shot him and blinded him in one eye and murdered two others in hate crimes after 9/11. Anand Giridharadas captured this story in his book *The True American: Murder and Mercy in Texas* (New York: W. W. Norton, 2015), which is now being made into a film.

53 **Sikhs don't hide** Valarie Kaur and Simran Jeet Singh, "Underneath the Turban: Why Sikhs Do Not Hide," *HuffPost,* updated October 13, 2012, https:// www.huffpost.com/entry/sikhs-turbans_b_1770366?utm_hp_ref=religion &ncid=edlinkusaolp00000008.

57 **I thought of the indigenous peoples** See Benjamin Madley, *An American Genocide: The United States and the California Indian Catastrophe, 1846–1873* (New Haven, Conn.: Yale University Press, 2016); David E. Stannard, *American Holocaust: The Conquest of the New World* (1993; repr., New York: Oxford University Press, 2018); Roxanne Dunbar-Ortiz, *An Indigenous People's History of the United States* (Boston: Beacon Press, 2014).

57 **America does not know how** Legal scholar Reva Siegel calls the process by which white privilege is maintained "preservation through transformation": The rules and rhetoric change, but the systems of racial and social control remain. See Reva B. Siegel, "'The Rule of Love': Wife Beating as Prerogative and Privacy," *Yale Law Journal* 105, no. 8 (1996): 2117–2207; Reva B. Siegel, "Why Equal Protection No Longer Protects," *Stanford Law Review* 49, no. 5 (1997): 1111–1148, https://www-jstor-org.libproxy1.usc.edu/ stable/1229249.

57 **Slavery transmuted into segregation** See Michelle Alexander, *The New Jim Crow: Mass Incarceration in the Age of Colorblindness* (New York: New Press, 2012); *13th,* directed by Ava DuVernay (California: Forward Movement/ Kandoo Films/Netflix, 2016), streaming on Netflix.

57 **I thought of my own community** See Arjun Sethi, ed., *American Hate* (New York: New Press, 2018); Deepa Iyer, *We Too Sing America: South Asian, Arab, Muslim, and Sikh Immigrants Shape Our Multiracial Future* (New York: New Press, 2015); Erika Lee, *The Making of Asian America: A History* (New York: Simon & Schuster, 2015); Juan Gonzalez, *Harvest of Empire: A History of Latinos in America,* rev. ed. (New York: Penguin, 2011).

59 **"We sang our grief"** Joy Harjo, "No," in *Conflict Resolution for Holy Beings: Poems* (New York: W. W. Norton, 2015).

59 **The mind can comprehend** Paul Slovic, "'If I Look at the Mass I Will

Never Act': Psychic Numbing and Genocide," *Judgment and Decision Making* 2, no. 2 (2007): 79–95, http://journal.sjdm.org/7303a/jdm7303a.htm.

59 **"If I look at the mass"** Ibid., 79.

61 **Her stepfather, Lt. Joseph Gerard Leavey** "About [Joseph Leavey]," Lt. Joseph G. Leavey Foundation, accessed March 3, 2020, http://ltjosephgleavey foundation.com/about/; Kevin Flynn and Jim Dwyer, "Fire Department Tape Reveals No Awareness of Imminent Doom," *The New York Times,* November 9, 2002, https://www.nytimes.com/2002/11/09/nyregion/fire -department-tape-reveals-no-awareness-of-imminent-doom.html.

61 **She apologized for some** See Sharon Otterman, "Visitors Fault Sept. 11 Museum's Portrayal of Islam," *The New York Times,* June 1, 2014, https:// www.nytimes.com/2014/06/02/nyregion/sept-11-museum.html.

62 **On the very night of the attacks** President George W. Bush, "Presidential Address," September 11, 2001, C-Span video, 04:47, https://www.c-span .org/video/?165970-1/presidential-address.

62 **In the name of the dead** John Haltiwanger, "America's 'War on Terror' Has Cost the US Nearly $6 Trillion and Killed Roughly Half a Million People, and There's No End in Sight," *Business Insider,* November 14, 2018, https:// www.businessinsider.com/the-war-on-terror-has-cost-the-us-nearly-6 -trillion-2018-11; "Body Count: Casualty Figures After 10 Years in the 'War on Terror'" (report, *International Physicians for the Prevention of Nuclear War, Physicians for Social Responsibility, and Physicians for Global Survival,* March 2015), 15, http://www.ippnw.de/commonFiles/pdfs/Frieden/Body_Count _first_international_edition_2015_final.pdf.

chapter 3: fight

65 **Power without love** Martin Luther King, Jr., "'Where Do We Go from Here?,' Address Delivered at the Eleventh Annual SCLC Convention" (per popular recollection, Atlanta, August 16, 1967), transcript at Stanford University Martin Luther King, Jr. Research and Education Institute, Stanford University, https://kinginstitute.stanford.edu/king-papers/documents/where -do-we-go-here-address-delivered-eleventh-annual-sclc-convention.

67 **My family's story** Kehar Singh's story is similar to that of many Punjabi Sikh migrants who arrived at Angel Island in the early twentieth century. See Erika Lee and Judy Yung, *Angel Island: Immigrant Gateway to America* (New York: Oxford University Press, 2010), chap. 4, "Obstacles This Way, Blockades That Way." For a short documentary that tells the story of Kehar Singh, see *Becoming American,* directed by Sharat Raju, written by Valarie Kaur (Los Angeles: New Moon Productions, 2008), https://valariekaur .com/film.

68 **My grandfather was released** The records of my grandfather's detention and release are in the Angel Island archives. You can find ancestral stories at

the U.S. Immigration Station Museum, Angel Island, California. See also Angel Island Immigration Station Foundation, https://www.aiisf.org.

68 **He was a simple farmer** For a chronicle of early South Asian American history, including the Stockton Sikh Temple, the Gadar Party, and Bhagat Singh Thind, see Suzanne McMahon, *Echoes of Freedom: South Asian Pioneers in California, 1899–1965: An Exhibition in the Bernice Layne Brown Gallery in the Doe Library, University of California, Berkeley, July 1–September 30, 2001* (Berkeley, Calif.: Chinese Popular Culture Project, 2001), also available at https://guides.lib.berkeley.edu/echoes-of-freedom.

69 **Just his dead body** Mike Anton and John Glionna, "Second Brother Dies for Dream," *Los Angeles Times,* August 7, 2002, https://www.latimes.com/archives/la-xpm-2002-aug-07-me-again7-story.html.

70 **In fact, everyone seemed to talk** Legal scholar Muneer Ahmad describes how hate crimes were regarded in the same way as "crimes of passion" in the aftermath of 9/11. Muneer I. Ahmad, "A Rage Shared by Law," *California Law Review* 92, no. 5 (2004): 1259–1330, https://www.jstor.org/stable/3481418.

70 **Outright violence was the tip** See Alia Malek, *Patriot Acts: Narratives of Post-9/11 Injustice* (San Francisco: McSweeney's, 2011); Dale Maharidge, *Homeland* (New York: Seven Stories Press, 2004); Deepa Iyer, *We Too Sing America: South Asian, Arab, Muslim, and Sikh Immigrants Shape Our Multiracial Future* (New York: New Press, 2015).

72 **I discovered it was a work** Eve Ensler, *The Vagina Monologues* (New York: Villard, 1998).

72 **It was based on interviews** Eve Ensler, "Crooked Braid," in *The Vagina Monologues,* 20th anniv. ed. (New York: Ballantine, 2018). When I look back on my college experience, I wish there had been an indigenous woman in our cast to interpret and perform this monologue rather than me. The most necessary voices in telling the stories of indigenous women are indigenous women themselves.

74 **Top members of the Bush administration** See Corbett B. Daly, "Ex-Bush Aide: Iraq War Planning Began After 9/11," CNN, May 6, 2004, http://www.cnn.com/2004/US/03/20/clarke.cbs/index.html; Ron Suskind, *The Price of Loyalty: George W. Bush, the White House, and the Education of Paul O'Neill* (New York: Simon & Schuster, 2004).

74 **A year and a half after 9/11** See John Walcott, "Troubling Questions over Justification for War in Iraq," Knight Ridder Newspapers, May 30, 2003, https://www.mcclatchydc.com/news/special-reports/iraq-intelligence/article24438124.html; Jonathan S. Landay, "Lack of Hard Evidence of Iraqi Weapons Worries Top U.S. Officials," Knight Ridder Newspapers, September 6, 2002, https://www.mcclatchydc.com/news/special-reports/iraq-intelligence/article24433348.html; Warren P. Stroebel, "Data Didn't Back Bush Claims on Iraqi Weapons, Officials Say," Knight Ridder Newspapers,

June 6, 2003, https://www.mcclatchydc.com/news/special-reports/iraq
-intelligence/article24438178.html.

74 **The public was fed** For the statements of lawmakers opposing the war in
Iraq, see Representative Bernie Sanders, "Rep. Bernard 'Bernie' Sanders Op-
poses the Iraq War," October 9, 2002, C-Span video, 05:59, clip created
October 29, 2014, https://www.c-span.org/video/?c4512996/rep-bernard
-bernie-sanders-opposes-iraq-war; Senator Lincoln Chafee, "Sen. Lincoln
Chafee (R-RI) on Iraq War Resolution," October 9, 2002, C-Span video,
04:29, clip created June 3, 2015, https://www.c-span.org/video/?c4539966/
sen-lincoln-chafee-iraq-war-resolution; Senator Robert C. Byrd, "User Clip:
Byrd's Anti-Iraq War Speech February 12, 2003," C-Span video, 49:41,
https://www.c-span.org/video/?c4550037/user-clip-byrds-anti-iraq-war
-speech-february-12-2003.

74 **This man was an actor** The event at Stanford's Memorial Church took
place on February 19, 2003. Actor Aldo Billingslea, an assistant professor in
the Department of Theatre and Dance at Santa Clara University, performed
a dramatic reading of "Beyond Vietnam," a speech that Dr. King delivered in
New York City on April 4, 1967. Billingslea replaced the word "Vietnam"
with "Iraq." The speech was edited by Clayborne Carson, professor of history and director of the Martin Luther King, Jr. Papers Project.

74 **It was time to end the wars** Martin Luther King, Jr., "Beyond Vietnam—A
Time to Break the Silence" (speech, New York, April 4, 1967), Martin Luther King, Jr. Research and Education Institute, Stanford University, https://
kinginstitute.stanford.edu/king-papers/documents/beyond-vietnam.

75 **She had seen the scholar–activist** Edward Said was a Palestinian American
scholar, advocate, and literary critic whose seminal work, *Orientalism,* is considered among the most influential scholarly books of the twentieth century.
See Edward Said, *Orientalism* (New York: Random House, 1978).

75 **She would become an acclaimed poet** See Brynn Saito, *The Palace of Contemplating Departure* (Pasadena, Calif.: Red Hen Press, 2013); Brynn Saito,
Power Made Us Swoon (Pasadena, Calif.: Red Hen Press, 2016). To learn more
about Brynn Saito, see https://brynnsaito.com.

75 **When they were our age** For Brynn Saito's work retelling her grandparents' stories, see Dear—: A Living Archive of Letters & Chapbook Com-
piled by Brynn Saito, website, accessed January 29, 2020, https://www
.youaremissing.com; Yonsei Memory Project, accessed January 29, 2020,
https://www.yonseimemoryproject.com.

75 **They were among 120,000 Japanese Americans** See Densho: The Japanese American Legacy Project, accessed January 29, 2020, http://densho
.org; Lawson Fusao Inada et al., eds., *Only What We Could Carry: The Japanese
American Internment Experience* (Berkeley, Calif.: Heyday, 2014).

76 **They showed up for each other** Japanese Americans stood in solidarity
with Muslim, Sikh, Arab, and South Asian Americans in the aftermath of

9/11 and continue to stand up for marginalized communities today. See Bridget Said, "The Memory Keepers: Japanese American Internment Survivors and Descendants Speak Out," *Vogue,* March 6, 2019, https://www.vogue.com/projects/13549104/japanese-incarceration-women-descendants-california; Brynn Saito and Nikiko Masumoto, "Their Grandmothers Were Interned in WWII. Now Two Fresnans React to Migrant Centers," *Fresno Bee,* July 2, 2019, https://www.fresnobee.com/opinion/readers-opinion/article232194357.html; Lina Hoshino, *Caught in Between: What to Call Home in Times of War,* DVD (San Francisco: IEEHA, 2004); Nikkei Progressives and Nikkei Resisters, "Japanese Americans Condemn Trump Executive Order Detaining Families," *Nichi Bei,* July 5, 2018, https://www.nichibei.org/2018/07/japanese-americans-condemn-trump-executive-order-detaining-families.

76 **Brynn and I decided** Brynn Saito co-founded the Yonsei Memory Project, which uses art and dialogue to connect the World War II incarceration of the Japanese American community with current civil liberties struggles. To learn more about the project, see https://www.yonseimemoryproject.com.

76 **When we feel helpless** See Steven Maier and Martin A. Seligman, "Learned Helplessness: Theory and Evidence," *Journal of Experimental Psychology: General* 105, no. 1 (1976): 3.

76 **The Brazilian educator Paulo Freire** Working with laborers in Brazil, Freire observed that those who came to understand their condition as a result of structures of inequality cultivated "critical consciousness," a sense of agency that led to action. See Paulo Freire, *Pedagogy of the Oppressed* (New York: Herder & Herder, 1970).

77 **College students across the country** Vauhini Vara, "Students Skip Class, Rally for Peace," *Stanford Daily,* March 6, 2003, https://archives.stanforddaily.com/2003/03/06?page=1&section=MODSMD_ARTICLE5#article. The strike at Stanford University was the first major student strike on campus since the Vietnam War.

78 **Flash the turban** Stress makes it easier to learn a fear association and to consolidate it into long-term memory. Stress also makes it harder to unlearn a fear association. See Benedict J. Kolber et al., "Central Amygdala Glucocorticoid Receptor Action Promotes Fear-Associated CRH Activation and Conditioning," *Proceedings of the National Academy of Sciences of the United States of America* 105, no. 33 (2008): 12004–12009, https://doi.org/10.1073/pnas.0803216105; Elizabeth A. Phelps et al., "Extinction Learning in Humans: Role of the Amygdala and vmPFC," *Neuron* 43, no. 6 (2004): 897–905, https://doi.org/10.1016/j.neuron.2004.08.042; Robert Sapolsky, *Behave: The Biology of Humans at Our Best and Worst* (New York: Penguin Press, 2017), 167; Sabrina M. Rodrigues et al., "The Influence of Stress Hormones on Fear Circuitry," *Annual Review of Neuroscience* 32 (2009): 289–313, https://doi.org/10.1146/annurev.neuro.051508.135620.

80 **The image of the brown turbaned** See Deepa Iyer, *We Too Sing America: South Asian, Arab, Muslim, and Sikh Immigrants Shape Our Multiracial Future* (New York: New Press, 2015), chap. 2, "Journeys in a Racial State."

80 **After his release** American Civil Liberties Union, "Civil Liberties After 9/11: The ACLU Defends Freedom" (report, n.d.), 2, accessed January 29, 2020, https://www.aclu.org/sites/default/files/field_document/911_report .pdf.

80 **Under the Alien Absconder Initiative** Kevin Lapp, "Pressing Public Necessity: The Unconstitutionality of the Absconder Apprehension Initiative," *N.Y.U. Review of Law & Social Change* 29, no. 3 (2004): 573–575, https:// papers.ssrn.com/sol3/papers.cfm?abstract_id=1911210.

80 **Then, under the National Security** American-Arab Anti-Discrimination Committee, "End the Shame of NSEERS," https://www.adc.org/legal/end -the-shame-of-nseers. "84,000 Arabs and Muslims registered voluntarily and subsequently 14,000 of them were deported for voluntarily complying with the program. Yet, none, not one, of these registrants has been charged with terrorism."

80 **Meanwhile, the administration began** Bonnie Kristian, "FBI Admits Patriot Act Powers Didn't Help Solve Any Big Terror Cases," *The Week,* May 22, 2015, https://theweek.com/speedreads/556626/fbi-admits-patriot -act-powers-didnt-help-solve-big-terror-cases.

81 **Profiling by the government** Ahmad, "A Rage Shared by Law," 1267. "Within days after the terrorist attacks, racial profiling emerged as the government's primary weapon of choice in the newly declared war on terrorism. Whereas 80% of Americans opposed racial profiling prior to September 11, after the attacks almost the same percentage favored profiling of those assumed to be Arab or Muslim."

81 **This is why hate crimes** "Hate Crime Data: The Value in Expanding Our Sources," USAFacts, August 3, 2019, https://usafacts.org/reports/facts-in -focus/hate-crimes-ucr-ncvs; Kuang Keng Kuek Ser, "Data: Hate Crimes Against Muslims Increased After 9/11," *The World,* PRI, September 12, 2016, https://www.pri.org/stories/2016-09-12/data-hate-crimes-against -muslims-increased-after-911.

81 **State violence fueled public hatred** Ahmad, "A Rage Shared by Law," 1277. "Indeed, physical violence against Arabs, Muslims, and South Asians, and racial profiling of these same communities are best understood as different facets of the same social, political, and cultural phenomena. Each is constitutive of the other: we might view physical hate violence as the end product of racial profiling's flawed logic, just as racial profiling may be viewed as a form of violence—whether psychic or physical—flowing from bias."

81 **The government incarcerated** Brynn Saito's father and elders in her community still carry with them badges and images of "Japanese Hunting Licenses" or "Jap Hunting Licenses" that circulated during that era.

81 **But the administration insisted** Muneer I. Ahmad, "Resisting Guantá-namo: Rights at the Brink of Dehumanization," *Northwestern University Law Review* 103, no. 4 (2009): 1683–1763, https://digitalcommons.law.yale.edu/fss_papers/5255. "Notably, the 'enemy combatant' construct was a legal in-vention of the Bush Administration, distinct from the presumptive 'prisoner of war' status to which the prisoners otherwise would have been entitled, the intended effect of which was to remove the prisoners from the ambit of both the Geneva Conventions and the U.S. courts. In this way, in the eyes of the law, the prisoners were made invisible. Hidden on a remote and mysterious island, which was made inaccessible to lawyers and human rights advocates for nearly two years, the prisoners were nearly erased" (p. 1705–1706).

82 **As the war drums grew louder** Social reformers have long argued that neu-trality is also a position. In his acceptance speech for the Nobel Peace Prize in 1986, Holocaust survivor Eli Wiesel said, "We must take sides. Neutrality helps the oppressor, never the victim." "Elie Wiesel—Acceptance Speech" (Oslo, December 10, 1986), The Nobel Prize, https://www.nobelprize.org/prizes/peace/1986/wiesel/26054-elie-wiesel-acceptance-speech-1986. Archbishop Desmond Tutu, theologian and antiapartheid activist, said, "If you are neutral in situations of injustice, you have chosen the side of the oppressor." Desmond Tutu, interview by Gary Younge, "The Secrets of a Peacemaker," *Guardian* (U.S. edition), May 22, 2009, https://www.theguardian.com/books/2009/may/23/interview-desmond-tutu. More re-cently, Rabbi Sharon Brous said, "Our history has taught us: Either you work to dismantle oppressive systems, or your inaction becomes the mortar that sustains them." Rabbi Sharon Brous, "Building a New America" (ser-mon, Los Angeles, September 10, 2018), IKAR, https://ikar-la.org/sermons/building-a-new-america.

82 **Some even displayed bumper stickers** See Bilal Quereshi, "After Shoot-ing, Sikhs Assess Their Place in America," The Two-Way (blog), NPR, Au-gust 6, 2012, https://www.npr.org/sections/thetwo-way/2012/08/06/158234401/after-shooting-sikhs-assess-their-place-in-america.

82 **This reminded me of** See Jane Hong, "Asian American Response to Incar-ceration," Densho Encyclopedia, https://encyclopedia.densho.org/Asian_American_response_to_incarceration.

83 **"We've been protesting this war"** Shahid Buttar is now a seasoned civil rights lawyer, activist, and organizer and has run for Congress. For more about Buttar, see https://www.shahidbuttar.com.

83 **Direct Action to Stop the War** "Direct Action to Stop the War (DASW) Site," Skyeome Blog, January 8, 2003, http://skyeome.net/wordpress/?p=68; "Direct Action to Stop the War," Internet Archive Way Back Machine, accessed January 28, 2002, http://web.archive.org/web/20030512100748/http://www.actagainstwar.org.

83 **They were inspired by King** The practice of civil disobedience as part of

movements for social change has a century-long history in the United States. See Lewis Perry, *Civil Disobedience: An American Tradition* (New Haven, Conn.: Yale University Press, 2013). Campaigns of nonviolent resistance throughout the twentieth century were seen to be "twice as effective as their violent counterparts in achieving stated goals." See Erica Chenoweth and Maria J. Stephan, *Why Civil Resistance Works: The Strategic Logic of Nonviolent Conflict* (New York: Columbia University Press, 2011), 7. For a current resource, see International Center on Nonviolent Conflict, https://www.nonviolent-conflict.org.

83 **We were trained as legal observers** The National Lawyers Guild is "the nation's oldest and largest progressive bar association" in the United States and works to protect the rights of protesters through their Mass Defense and Legal Observer programs. See "About," National Lawyers Guild, https://www.nlg.org/about.

84 **A few minutes later** President George W. Bush, "Presidential Address on War with Iraq," March 19, 2003, C-Span video, 04:03, https://www.c-span.org/video/?175603-1/president-bush-addresses-war-iraq.

87 **This was something powerful** Anthony Ha and Eric Eldon, "Students and Faculty Protest War in the City, on Campus," *Stanford Daily*, March 21, 2003, https://archives.stanforddaily.com/2003/03/21?page=1&section=MODSMD_ARTICLE1#article. An estimated fifty people were arrested at the protest at the intersection of Third and Market Street in San Francisco, and at least thirty were Stanford students.

89 **I would study police departments'** Police brutality against black people has had a long history, from the era of Jim Crow, when Southern police and the KKK terrorized black communities, to the civil rights movement, during which police used attack dogs and fire hoses on protesters, to the present day, when killings by police have ignited the movement known as Black Lives Matter. See Howard Rahtz, *Race, Riots and the Police* (Boulder, Colo.: Lynne Rienner, 2016); Keeanga-Yamahtta Taylor, *From #BlackLivesMatter to Black Liberation* (Chicago: Haymarket, 2016).

89 **I would learn about histories** Each year, the majority of unarmed victims of police killings are people of color. Black people in particular are more likely to be killed by police, more likely to be unarmed when killed, and less likely to be threatening someone when killed. The names of black people killed by police officers routinely appear in the headlines. In recent years, those have included Eric Garner, Michael Brown, Tamir Rice, Freddie Gray, Alton Sterling, Philando Castile, Sandra Bland, Charles Kinsey, and Botham Jean. Lesser known are the names of trans black women, such as Mya Hall, Kayla Moore, and Duanna Johnson. For more about police violence, see Black Lives Matter, https://blacklivesmatter.com; Mapping Police Violence, https://mappingpoliceviolence.org; Say Her Name campaign, African American Policy Forum, https://aapf.org/shn-campaign.

89 **I watched as America's police** See Arthur Rizer and Joseph Hartman, "How the War on Terror Has Militarized the Police," *Atlantic,* November 9, 2011, https://www.theatlantic.com/national/archive/2011/11/how-the-war-on-terror-has-militarized-the-police/248047; Timothy Roufa, "The History and Purpose of SWAT Teams," The Balance Careers, updated November 6, 2019, https://www.thebalancecareers.com/the-history-and-purpose-of-swat-teams-974567. Since 9/11, police departments across the United States have acquired military weapons, technology, and training in SWAT tactics. In major cities, a police officer today appears less like a "peace officer"—one who is committed to keeping the peace—and more like a "soldier." Rizer and Hartman state, "When police officers are dressed like soldiers, armed like soldiers, and trained like soldiers, it's not surprising that they are beginning to act like soldiers. And remember: a soldier's main objective is to kill the enemy."

89 **Newspapers reported that twenty-two hundred** Associated Press, "Supporters of Iraq War Hold San Francisco Rally," *Daily Press* (Newport News, Virginia), March 23, 2003, https://www.dailypress.com/bal-te.iraq29mar29-story.html; Michael Powell, "Around Globe, Protest Marches; in N.Y., 200,000 Take to Streets," *The Washington Post,* March 22, 2003, A19.

90 **So our season of organizing began** Eric Eldon, "Students Protest Lockheed," *Stanford Daily,* April 23, 2003, https://archives.stanforddaily.com/2003/04/23?page=1&section=MODSMD_ARTICLE3#article; Will Oremus, "Students Protest Bush's War Spending," *Stanford Daily,* May 5, 2003, https://archives.stanforddaily.com/2003/05/05?page=1&section=MODSMD_ARTICLE2#article.

90 **The legend goes** This story is one of many legends passed down in oral tradition about Holi. For more such legends about Radha and Krishna, see: *Gītagovinda of Jayadeva: Love Song of the Dark Lord*, Barbara Stone Miller, ed. and trans. (New Delhi: Motilal Banarsidass, 1977), 124–125.

91 **Even as we watched** Murtaza Hussain, "It's Time for America to Reckon with the Staggering Death Toll of the Post-9/11 Wars," *The Intercept,* November 19, 2018, https://theintercept.com/2018/11/19/civilian-casualties-us-war-on-terror.

91 **A multimillion-dollar industry emerged** See Wajahat Ali et al., "Fear, Inc.: The Roots of the Islamophobia Network in America," Center for American Progress, August 26, 2011, https://www.americanprogress.org/issues/religion/reports/2011/08/26/10165/fear-inc.

91 **Today Americans are seven times** Charles Kurzman and David Schanzer, "The Growing Right-Wing Terror Threat," *The New York Times,* June 16, 2015, https://www.nytimes.com/2015/06/16/opinion/the-other-terror-threat.html. Right-wing extremists averaged 337 attacks per year in the decade following 9/11, causing 254 fatalities. In contrast, there have been 20

terrorism-related plots carried out by American Muslims in 13-plus years, accounting for 50 fatalities.

91 **And Muslim and Sikh Americans** Christopher Ingraham, "Anti-Muslim Hate Crimes Are Still Five Times More Common Today Than Before 9/11," *The Washington Post,* February 11, 2015, https://www.washingtonpost.com/ news/wonk/wp/2015/02/11/anti-muslim-hate-crimes-are-still-five-times -more-common-today-than-before-911.

93 **The Sikh gurus professed equality** For more about feminism and early Sikh history, see Nikky-Gurinder Kaur Singh, *The Birth of the Khalsa: A Feminist Re-memory of Sikh Identity* (Albany, N.Y.: SUNY Press, 2005); Valarie Kaur, "10 Sikh Women You Should Know and Why You Should Know Them," *HuffPost,* March 22, 2012, updated May 22, 2012, https://www .huffpost.com/entry/10-sikh-women-you-should-know_b_1353700.

93 **This village woman Mai Bhago** For one telling of Mai Bhago's story, see Nidar Singh Nihang and Parmjit Singh, *In the Master's Presence: The Sikhs of Hazoor Sahib* (London: Kashi House, 2008). Mai Bhago and her forty soldiers forced the Mughal soldiers to retreat at the Battle of Muktsar in Khidrana. She is credited for protecting the Sikh community and preserving the Sikh faith.

94 **Today we call the forty warriors** The section of the Ardas that honors the forty soldiers or "Chali Mukte" reads: "Panj Piare, Char Sahibzade, Chali Mukte, those living with religious commitment / Those who have connected spiritually, shared freely, fought injustice, and forgiven human shortcomings / Recollecting the actions of those beloved and truthful ones / O Khalsa Ji! Say—Waheguru!" For a full English translation of the *Ardas,* see Gurmat Literacy Project, "Ardas Translation," Surat Initiative, accessed January 29, 2020, https://www.suratinitiative.org/gurmat-literacy-project-1.

95 **"There is no such thing"** Audre Lorde, "Learning from the 60s," in *Sister Outsider: Essays and Speeches* (New York: Ten Speed Press, 1984), 134–144. About a decade before the scholar Kimberlé Crenshaw coined "intersectionality" to describe the oppression experienced by black women, Lorde identified the "multidimensional threats to survival" and the need for solidarity in a speech in honor of the life of Malcolm X.

96 **"Intersectionality," a term coined** Kimberlé Crenshaw, "Demarginalizing the Intersection of Race and Sex: A Black Feminist Critique of Antidiscrimination Doctrine, Feminist Theory and Antiracist Politics," *University of Chicago Legal Forum* 1, no. 8 (1989): 139–167, https://chicagounbound .uchicago.edu/cgi/viewcontent.cgi?referer=&httpsredir=1&article=1052& context=uclf. Intersectionality is often misunderstood as a kind of counting of identities—for example, I am a woman and able-bodied and South Asian American. But intersectionality is an analysis rather than an identity. It is a way of understanding how complex social inequalities are related. Women of color have employed this analytic tool as far back as Sojourner Truth's

"Ain't I a Woman" speech in 1851, when she expressed how racism and sexism intersected in her body.

96 **Sikh women in America** For a compilation of Sikh American women's stories, see Meeta Kaur, *Her Name Is Kaur: Sikh American Women Write About Love, Courage, and Faith* (Berkeley, Calif.: She Writes Press, 2014).

96 **Perhaps a better word is "accomplices"** "Accomplices Not Allies: Abolishing the Ally Industrial Complex," Indigenous Action Media, May 4, 2014, http://www.indigenousaction.org/accomplices-not-allies-abolishing-the-ally-industrial-complex.

97 **But warrior metaphors show** Activists in indigenous communities are reclaiming their warrior traditions in nonviolent ways. In their nonviolent protest against the Dakota Access Pipeline (DAPL), Native American water protectors drew upon their ancestors' resistance to colonization. One elder reflected that in the 1970s, some members of the American Indian Movement (AIM) were armed because they did not know the force they might encounter from government officials. But during protests at the Standing Rock reservation, water protectors ensured that there were no weapons in their camp and pointed to the tools of social media, where they could amplify their message and find protection through solidarity. "Our words are our arrows now," one said. "Our laptops are our shields." See *Rise,* season 1, episode 2, "Red Power: Standing Rock, Part II," written and directed by Michelle Latimer, originally aired January 27, 2017, on Viceland.

97 **Nonviolent movements around the globe** See Chenoweth and Stephan, *Why Civil Resistance Works.* Between 1900 and 2006, campaigns of nonviolent resistance were more than twice as effective as their violent counterparts in achieving their stated goals.

97 **"Only when all other methods fail"** "Chu kar az hameh heelate dar guzasht, Halal ast burdan bi-shamsher dast." Dasam Granth, Zafarnama, 1417:22.

98 **Begin where you are** South Asian American activist Deepa Iyer offers a robust framework for each of us to use to discern our role in the labor for social justice. Roles include frontline responders, healers, storytellers and artists, bridge builders, disrupters, caregivers, visionaries, and builders. Identifying our particular role in any given moment helps us get off the "seesaw of outrage and numbness." For guiding questions, see Deepa Iyer, "My Role in a Social Change Ecosystem: A Mid-Year Check-In," *Medium,* May 13, 2019. https://medium.com/@dviyer/my-role-in-a-social-change-ecosystem-a-mid-year-check-in-1d852589cdb1.

part II. tend the wound: loving opponents

chapter 4: rage

101 **My fear of anger taught** Audre Lorde, "The Uses of Anger: Women Responding to Racism" (speech, Storrs, Conn., June 1981), BlackPast.org, https://www.blackpast.org/african-american-history/speeches-african -american-history/1981-audre-lorde-uses-anger-women-responding -racism.

106 **I had absorbed** For a deep exploration of research on rage and gender starting in childhood, see Soraya Chemaly, *Rage Becomes Her: The Power of Women's Anger* (New York: Atria, 2018).

106 **The opposite of love** Elie Wiesel famously said in a 1986 interview that the opposite of love is indifference. This idea is also found in psychologist Wilhelm Stekel's 1921 writings. See Elie Wiesel, interview by Alvin P. Sanoff, *US News & World Report,* October 27, 1986; Wilhelm Stekel, *The Beloved Ego: Foundations of the New Study of the Psyche* (New York: Moffat Yard, 1921), 16.

107 **It was the opening night** For more on the early days of the Spinning Wheel Festival, see Nicola Mooney, "Charkha Spins in Toronto," SikhChic .com, accessed February 5, 2020, http://sikhchic.com/article-detail.php?id= 1&cat=2.

107 **My senior honors thesis** My thesis, "Targeting the Turban: Sikh Americans and the Aversion Spiral After September 11," received the Golden Medal for Excellence in the Humanities from Stanford University in 2003. "14 Students Honored with Golden Medals, 29 with Firestones," *Stanford Report,* June 18, 2003, https://news.stanford.edu/news/2003/ june18/goldenfirestone-618.html.

107 **Sharat Raju was fresh out** For Sharat Raju's filmography, including his first film, *American Made,* see www.sharatraju.com.

107 *American Made* **told the story** *American Made,* written and directed by Sharat Raju (Los Angeles: Atomic 5/AFI Executive, 2003), https://sharatraju .onfabrik.com/portfolio/american-made-1.

107 **The film would go on** *Independent Lens,* season 7, episode 23, "American Made," written and directed by Sharat Raju, originally aired May 9, 2006, on PBS, https://www.pbs.org/independentlens/americanmade/film.html.

108 **We talked every day** *Divided We Fall: Americans in the Aftermath,* directed by Sharat Raju, written by Valarie Kaur (Los Angeles: New Moon Productions, 2008), https://valariekaur.com/film/divided-we-fall.

108 *Last night the moon came* Rumi, "The New Rule," in *The Essential Rumi,* trans. Coleman Barks (New York: HarperOne, 1995).

111 **Vaginismus is the involuntary tightening** See "Vaginismus," International Society for the Study of Vulvovaginal Disease, accessed January 30, 2020, https://www.issvd.org/vaginismus; *Tightly Wound,* written and di-

rected by Shelby Hadden (Austin: Hadden, 2018), https://www.tightly
woundfilm.com.

111 **It is estimated that one** Very little is understood about vaginismus, which
has made it difficult to find accurate statistics for how many women suffer
from it. However, more research is emerging and the results emphasize the
need for additional studies. Peter T. Pacik and Simon Geletta, "Vaginismus
Treatment: Clinical Trials Follow Up 241 Patients," *Sexual Medicine* 5,
no. 7 (2017): e114–e123, https://www.sciencedirect.com/science/article/
pii/S2050116117300181.

111 **One possible cause for vaginismus** Elke D. Reissing et al., "Etiological
Correlates of Vaginismus: Sexual and Physical Abuse, Sexual Knowledge,
Sexual Self-Schema, and Relationship Adjustment," *Journal of Sex & Marital
Therapy* 29, no. 1 (2003): 47–59, https://doi.org/10.1080/713847095.

113 **One in three women** Sharon G. Smith et al., "National Intimate Partner
and Sexual Violence Survey: 2015 Data Brief," Centers for Disease Control
and Prevention, last reviewed June 19, 2019, https://www.cdc.gov/
violenceprevention/datasources/nisvs/2015NISVSdatabrief.html; "Violence
Against Women," World Health Organization, November 29, 2017, https://
www.who.int/news-room/fact-sheets/detail/violence-against-women.

113 **The solution is more solidarity** V-Day is a global activist movement to
end violence against women and girls. Its One Billion Rising campaign is
the biggest mass action to end violence against all women in human history.
See V-Day website, accessed January 29, 2020, https://www.vday.org/
homepage.html; One Billion Rising website, accessed January 29, 2020,
https://www.onebillionrising.org.

114 **On Sunday, Brynn and I joined** Christine Hauser, "Marchers Denounce
Bush as They Pass G.O.P. Convention Hall," *The New York Times,* August 29, 2004, https://www.nytimes.com/2004/08/29/politics/campaign/
marchers-denounce-bush-as-they-pass-gop-convention-hall.html; Robert D.
McFadden, "The Republicans: The Convention in New York—the March;
Vast Anti-Bush Rally Greets Republicans in New York," *The New York
Times,* August 30, 2004, https://www.nytimes.com/2004/08/30/us/
republicans-convention-new-york-march-vast-anti-bush-rally-greets
-republicans.html.

115 **The warehouse would soon detain** Amy Goodman and Juan Gonzalez,
"Guantanamo on the Hudson: Detained RNC Protesters Describe Prison
Conditions," Democracy Now! video, 31:03, September 2, 2004, https://
www.democracynow.org/2004/9/2/guantanamo_on_the_hudson
_detained_rn; Sarah Ferguson, "Guantanamo on the Hudson," *Village Voice,*
August 24, 2004, https://www.villagevoice.com/2004/08/24/guantanamo
-on-the-hudson.

116 *Ik Onkar. Satnam* Christopher Shackle and Arvind-Pal Singh Mandair,
Teachings of the Gurus (New York: Routledge, 2005), 3–4. The *mul mantar,* the

root verse, opens the Guru Granth Sahib. It is considered the foundation of the Sikh faith. For the English translation, see the *Sikh shabads* section in the book.

116 *Aad Sach. Jugaad Sach* Ibid. This comes at the end of the *mul mantar.*

117 **Nearly eighteen hundred people** Ed Pilkington, "New York Agrees $18m Settlement with 2004 Republican Convention Protesters," *Guardian* (U.S. edition), January 15, 2014, https://www.theguardian.com/world/2014/jan/15/new-york-agrees-settlement-2004-republican-convention; Michael Slackman and Diane Cardwell, "Tactics by Police Mute the Protesters, and Their Messages," *The New York Times,* September 2, 2004, https://www.nytimes.com/2004/09/02/politics/campaign/tactics-by-police-mute-the-protesters-and-their-messages.html.

117 **It appeared that the city** See Joseph Goldstein, "Operation Overlord II: NYPD Planned RNC Arrests," *The New York Sun,* January 31, 2007, https://www.nysun.com/new-york/operation-overlord-ii-nypd-planned-rnc-arrests/47754; New York Civil Liberties Union, "Rights and Wrongs at the RNC: A Special Report About Police and Protest at the Republican National Convention" (2005), 6, https://www.nyclu.org/sites/default/files/publications/nyclu_pub_rights_wrongs_rnc.pdf.

117 **Some fifty detainees were beginning** Sara Kugler, "Judge Orders Protesters' Release," *Lawrence (Kansas) Journal-World,* September 3, 2004, https://www2.ljworld.com/news/2004/sep/03/judge_orders_protesters/.

119 **I started taking classes** To learn more about the work of scholars Diana Eck, Hille Haker, and Michael Jackson, see Diana L. Eck, *Encountering God: A Spiritual Journey from Bozeman to Banaras* (Boston: Beacon Press, 2003); Hille Haker, "The Fragility of the Moral Self," *Harvard Theological Review* 97, no. 4 (2004): 359–381; Michael Jackson, *The Politics of Storytelling: Violence, Transgression, and Intersubjectivity* (Chicago: University of Chicago Press, 2002).

119 **I was captivated** Hannah Arendt, *Eichmann in Jerusalem: A Report on the Banality of Evil* (New York: Viking Press, 1963).

119 *Pain / penetrates me Sappho: A New Translation,* trans. Mary Barnard (Berkeley: University of California Press, 1958), frag. 61.

120 **One night, I attended** There are many approaches to loving-kindness meditation. The particular workshop I attended did not work for me. I have since experienced the benefits of this meditation when led by practitioners sensitive to trauma and healing in the body. For a more sophisticated introduction to loving-kindness meditation, see Sharon Salzberg, *Loving-Kindness: The Revolutionary Art of Happiness* (Boulder, Colo.: Shambhala Classics, 1995).

121 **Abu Ghraib was a watershed** See Dr. Maha Hilal, "Abu Ghraib: The Legacy of Torture in the War on Terror," Al Jazeera, October 1, 2017, https://www.aljazeera.com/indepth/opinion/abu-ghraib-legacy-torture-war-terror-170928154012053.html.

121 **I was assigned the role** Huda Alazawi was one of the few women held in solitary at Abu Ghraib. She told her story for the first time to the *Guardian*. Luke Harding, "After Abu Ghraib," *Guardian* (U.S. edition), September 20, 2004, https://www.theguardian.com/world/2004/sep/20/usa.iraq.

122 **Sergeant Joseph Darby** For more on the soldiers involved in the Abu Ghraib scandal, see Errol Morris, *Standard Operating Procedure,* DVD (Los Angeles: Participant Media, 2008).

123 **I thought of Arendt's analysis** Hannah Arendt's idea of the banality of evil has been supported by social psychology experiments. Stanley Milgram's famous experiments measured the willingness of people to obey directions to inflict pain on others. Participants were instructed by an authority figure to administer shocks of increasing voltage on people who made mistakes recalling words. Despite conflicts with personal conscience, the majority of participants administered shocks at levels that would have been fatal had they been real. See Stanley Milgram, *Obedience to Authority: An Experimental View* (New York: HarperCollins, 1974).

123 **The play ran** Ken Gewertz, "Abu Ghraib Onstage: Multimedia Theatrical Piece Tries to Make Sense of Prison Abuse," *Harvard Gazette,* May 5, 2005, https://news.harvard.edu/gazette/story/2005/05/abu-ghraib-onstage.

123 **It was attacked by the Right** Talk show host Rush Limbaugh criticized the play: "Here you have these dunces . . . at Harvard now doing a play on the travesties of Abu Ghraib, and you know this is going to get back to the people in Baghdad, the insurgents and this sort of thing. It's just typical. These people hate the country, folks. I'm telling you: There's an anti-American bias in the American left." I published an open letter in response. See Valarie Kaur, "Rush Limbaugh's Tortured Logic," *Salon,* May 28, 2005, https://www.salon.com/2005/05/28/harvard_abu_ghraib_play.

126 **I thought of all the women** For a national survey on reasons why women of color are reluctant to call police officers, see American Civil Liberties Union, "Responses from the Field: Sexual Assault, Domestic Violence, and Policing" (report, October 2015), https://www.aclu.org/report/sexual-assault-domestic-violence-and-policing.

127 **He operated on the premise** For more about healing trauma in the body, see Bessel van der Kolk, *The Body Keeps the Score: Brain, Mind, and Body in the Healing of Trauma* (New York: Viking, 2014).

127 **When we face a threat** Ibid., 80–85; Stephen W. Porges, "The Polyvagal Theory: Phylogenetic Substrates of a Social Nervous System," *International Journal of Psychophysiology* 42, no. 2 (2001): 123–146.

127 **Tommy believed that** In my case, "exposure therapy," reliving the trauma over and over again, and cognitive behavior therapy, known as talk therapy, provided relief but was not effective in resolving the problem. For more about somatic experiencing trauma therapy, see Peter Levine, *Waking the Tiger: Healing Trauma* (Berkeley, Calif.: North Atlantic Books, 1997).

130 **Neurobiologists call oxytocin** Oliver J. Bosch and Inga D. Neumann, "Both Oxytocin and Vasopressin Are Mediators of Maternal Care and Aggression in Rodents: From Central Release to Sites of Action," *Hormones and Behavior* 61, no. 3 (2012): 293–303, https://doi.org/10.1016/j.yhbeh.2011.11.002.

130 **Rage is a healthy** Van der Kolk, *The Body Keeps the Score,* 3, 43–46, 63, 136.

131 **"We learned when we were"** bell hooks, *Killing Rage: Ending Racism* (New York: Henry Holt, 1995), 13.

131 **We now have the data** Van der Kolk, *The Body Keeps the Score,* 136, 142. "Rage that has nowhere to go is redirected against the self, in the form of depression, self-hatred, and self-destructive actions" (p. 136).

131 **It results in high rates** Carol Magai et al., "Anger Experience and Anger Inhibition in Sub-Populations of African American and European American Older Adults and Relation to Circulatory Disease," *Journal of Health Psychology* 84, no. 4 (2003): 413–432.

131 **It amplifies our perception** Phillip J. Quartana and John W. Burns, "Painful Consequences of Anger Suppression," *Emotion* 7, no. 2 (2007): 400–414, https://doi.org/10.1037/1528-3542.7.2.400.

131 **For men, rage is often** Lisa A. Martin et al., "The Experience of Symptoms of Depression in Men vs Women: Analysis of the National Comorbidity Survey Replication," *JAMA Psychiatry* 70, no. 10 (2013): 1100–1106, https://doi.org/10.1001/jamapsychiatry.2013.1985; Agneta Fischer and Catherine Evers, "The Social Costs and Benefits of Anger as a Function of Gender and Relationship Context," *Sex Roles* 65, no. 1 (2011): 23–34, https://doi.org/10.1007/s11199-011-9956-x; Ann M. Kring and Albert H. Gordon, "Sex Differences in Emotion: Expression, Experience, and Physiology," *Journal of Personality and Social Psychology* 74, no. 3 (1998): 686–703, https://doi.org/10.1037/0022-3514.74.3.686.

131 **Mass shooters are typically men** Hilary Brueck and Shana Lebowitz, "The Men Behind the US's Deadliest Mass Shootings Have Domestic Violence— Not Mental Illness—in Common," Business Insider, August 5, 2019, https://www.businessinsider.com/deadliest-mass-shootings-almost-all-have-domestic-violence-connection-2017-11?fbclid=IwAR2cltRAix UTtoRgpCZLvt7_VmJ8eUMmvol07zyflPDlr8na79Gdz-mwR7k; Yasmine Issa, "'A Profoundly Masculine Act': Mass Shootings, Violence Against Women, and the Amendment That Could Forge a Path Forward," *California Law Review* 107, no. 2 (2019): 673–706.

131 **For women and girls** Ephrem Fernandez and Dennis C. Turk, "The Scope and Significance of Anger in the Experience of Chronic Pain," *Pain* 61, no. 2 (1995): 165–175, https://doi.org/10.1016/0304-3959(95)00192-U; Kevin T. Larkin and Claudia Zayfert, "Anger Expression and Essential Hypertension," *Journal of Psychosomatic Research* 56, no. 1 (2004): 113–118; Chemaly, *Rage Becomes Her,* 49–64.

131 **Safe containers take many forms** For containment theory in psychoanalysis—the idea that people need safe containers to process emotions—see Wilfred R. Bion, *Learning from Experience* (London: Karnac, 1962); Donald W. Winnicott, *The Maturational Processes and the Facilitating Environment: Studies in the Theory of Emotional Development* (New York: International Universities Press, 1965).

132 **Academics in other parts** See Patton E. Burchett, *A Genealogy of Devotion: Bhakti, Tantra, Yoga and Sufism in North India* (New York: Columbia University Press, 2019).

132 **In Kolkata, Deonnie took me** Deonnie Moodie is now a professor of religious studies and has published the first comprehensive study of the Kalighat Temple. See Deonnie Moodie, *The Making of a Modern Temple and a Hindu City: Kālīghāṭ and Kolkata* (New York: Oxford University Press, 2018). Moodie's book is the first comprehensive examination of Kalighat, the most famous temple for the Goddess Kali.

133 **I thought about Kali's origin story** See Devī Māhātmya, *Mahasaraswati,* 7:5–6; Thomas B. Coburn, *Encountering the Goddess: A Translation of the Devī Māhātmya and a Study of Its Interpretation* (Albany, N.Y.: SUNY Press, 1991), 61; David Kinsley, *Hindu Goddesses: Visions of the Divine Feminine in the Hindu Religious Tradition* (Delhi: Motilal Banaras, 1998), 116–122.

133 **It is the fearsome wrath** Alice Getty, *The Gods of Northern Buddhism: Their History and Iconography* (New York: Dover, 1988), 125–126.

133 **Or the fury of Jesus** Mark 11:11–19 (New Revised Standard Version).

133 **I see it in the indigenous** Jennifer Hassan and Emily Tamkin, "The Power of the Haka: New Zealanders Pay Traditional Tribute to Mosque Attack Victims," *The Washington Post,* March 18, 2019, https://www.washingtonpost.com/world/2019/03/18/power-haka-new-zealanders-pay-traditional-tribute-mosque-attack-victims.

134 **But civility is too often** See Robin DiAngelo, *White Fragility* (Boston: Beacon Press, 2015). "It is white people's responsibility to be less fragile; people of color don't need to twist themselves into knots trying to navigate us as painlessly as possible" (152).

134 **Rather than taming** Judith Butler, "Explanation and Exoneration, or What We Can Hear," *Grey Room,* no. 7 (April 1, 2002): 57–67.

134 **"Anger is loaded with information"** Lorde, "The Uses of Anger."

135 **I had started learning Kathak** Pandit Chitresh Das Ji and his disciple Gretchen Hayden were my teachers. For more about Kathak dance in America and their story, see Sarah Morelli, *A Guru's Journey: Pandit Chitresh Das and Indian Classical Dance in Diaspora,* Music in American Life (Champaign: University of Illinois Press, 2019). You can find their Kathak schools at http://www.chhandika.org, https://kathak.org, https://theleelainstitute.org.

chapter 5: listen.

137 **How do we hold people accountable** Melvin McLeod, "'There's No Place to Go but Up': bell hooks and Maya Angelou in Conversation," *Lion's Roar,* January 1, 1998, https://www.lionsroar.com/theres-no-place-to-go-but-up.

139 **"I shall permit no man"** Booker T. Washington, *Up from Slavery: An Auto-biography* (New York: Doubleday, Page, 1907), 165.

140 **"Hate does that"** Toni Morrison, *Love* (New York: Knopf, 2003), 34.

140 **Sharat and I were still** *Divided We Fall: Americans in the Aftermath,* directed by Sharat Raju, written by Valarie Kaur (Los Angeles: New Moon Productions, 2008), https://valariekaur.com/film/divided-we-fall.

141 **But every time I buried** Filmmaker Prashant Bhargava once told Sharat Raju, "If you run after your project, people will chase you." For more about Bhargava, see Sam Roberts, "Prashant Bhargava, Filmmaker of 'Patang (The Kite),' Dies at 42," *The New York Times,* May 18, 2015, https://www.nytimes.com/2015/05/19/arts/prashant-bhargava-filmmaker-of-patang-the-kite-dies-at-42.html.

141 **Our friends began to volunteer** The team who worked on *Divided We Fall* included Matthew Blute (cinematographer), Don Presley (first assistant camera), Tracy Wells Miller (director of communications), Jessica Jenkins (director of research), Charles Dulin (titles and graphics), and Richard Hilary (graphic design), For a complete list of people who worked on the film, see the film credits starting at 1:31:58, *Divided We Fall,* https://valariekaur.com/film/divided-we-fall.

141 **I began blogging stories** For the first blog post, see Valarie Kaur, "How the Film Began," ValarieKaur.com (blog), July 12, 2005, https://valariekaur.com/2005/07/how-the-film-began. For more on the film, see "Divided We Fall," ValarieKaur.com (blog), https://valariekaur.com/film/divided-we-fall.

141 **We premiered the film** Nick Martin, "Documentary Tells Story of Sikh Slain After 9/11," *East Valley Tribune* (Tempe, AZ), September 15, 2006, https://www.eastvalleytribune.com/news/documentary-tells-story-of-sikh-slain-after/article_dcf81c32-5978-5166-8204-db89196e24d5.html; Valarie Kaur, "A World Premiere," ValarieKaur.com (blog), September 8, 2016, https://valariekaur.com/2006/09/a-world-premiere.

141 **With the family's blessings** Awards for *Divided We Fall* include Best Documentary, New Jersey Independent South Asian Cine Fest 2007; Audience Choice Best Documentary, Indian Film Festival of Los Angeles 2007; Best International Documentary, Reelworld Film Festival (Toronto) 2007; and Opening Night Film, Seattle Human Rights Film Festival 2007. For a full list of awards the film received, see *Divided We Fall,* https://valariekaur.com/film/divided-we-fall.

142 **We were on the road** For more about the tour, see Valarie Kaur and Sharat Raju, "Divided We Fall Year-in-Review," December 2007, http://archive

.constantcontact.com/fs076/1101865578764/archive/1101867243209
.html.

142 **That was the singular power** Film critic Roger Ebert called cinema "the most powerful empathy machine in all the arts." "Roger Ebert's Walk of Fame Remarks," Roger Ebert's Journal, June 24, 2005, https://www.rogerebert.com/rogers-journal/eberts-walk-of-fame-remarks. For more on cinema and empathy, see Linda Holmes, "'A Machine That Generates Empathy': Roger Ebert Gets His Own Documentary," NPR, July 3, 2014, https://www.npr.org/2014/07/03/328230231/a-machine-that-generates-empathy-roger-ebert-gets-his-own-documentary; Jessica Marshall, "Gripping Yarns," *New Scientist* 279, no. 2799 (2011): 45–47; Loris Vezzali et al., "The Greatest Magic of Harry Potter: Reducing Prejudice," *Journal of Applied Social Psychology* 45, no. 2 (2015): 105–121.

142 **The film was forcing people** See Mary E. Wheeler and Susan T. Fiske, "Controlling Racial Prejudice: Social-Cognitive Goals Affect Amygdala and Stereotype Activation," *Psychological Science* 16, no. 1 (2005): 56–63, https://doi.org/10.1111/j.0956-7976.2005.00780.x.

143 **Empathy is cognitive *and* emotional** Hidehiko Takahashi et al., "When Your Gain Is My Pain and Your Pain Is My Gain: Neural Correlates of Envy and Schadenfreude," *Science* 323, no. 5916 (2009): 937–939, https://doi.org/10.1126/science.1165604; Robert Sapolsky, *Behave: The Biology of Humans at Our Best and Worst* (New York: Penguin Press, 2017), 522, 533–535. Empathy for "them" requires cognitive work in order to override automatic fear or disgust responses. As Sapolsky puts it, empathizing with the pain of someone we dislike "is a dramatic cognitive challenge rather than something remotely automatic" (p. 534).

144 **As Hannah Arendt says** Hannah Arendt, *Lectures on Kant's Political Philosophy* (Chicago: University of Chicago Press, 1982), 43.

144 **But witnessing suffering does not** Namwali Serpell, "The Banality of Empathy," *New York Review of Books,* March 2, 2019, https://www.nybooks.com/daily/2019/03/02/the-banality-of-empathy/.

148 **True understanding is not possible** For more on how to cultivate an approach to deep listening, see William Isaacs, *Dialogue: The Art of Thinking Together* (New York: Currency, 1999), 37–48.

148 **White supremacy is a system** See Carol Anderson, *White Rage: The Unspoken Truth of Our Racial Divide* (New York: Bloomsbury, 2017).

149 **Obama joined all our disparate** Barack Obama, "More Perfect Union" (speech, Philadelphia, March 18, 2008), YouTube video, 37:10, posted by NowThis News, February 11, 2019, https://www.youtube.com/watch?v=iA3O2VguXks.

149 **And yet Obama's personhood** See Barack Obama, *Dreams from My Father* (New York: Times Books, 1995).

149 **The campaign used** "What Is Public Narrative and How Can We Use It?," Working Narratives, accessed August 19, 2019, https://workingnarratives .org/article/public-narrative.

150 **After the election** Micah L. Sifry, "Obama's Lost Army," *New Republic,* February 9, 2017, https://newrepublic.com/article/140245/obamas-lost -army-inside-fall-grassroots-machine.

151 **In the meantime** Bryan T. Gervais and Irwin L. Morris, *Reactionary Republicanism: How the Tea Party Paved the Way for Trump's Victory* (New York: Oxford University Press, 2018).

151 **My friend Professor Melissa Harris-Perry** Melissa Harris-Perry, "How Barack Obama Is Like Martin Luther King, Jr.," *Nation,* January 18, 2010, http://www.thenation.com/article/how-barack-obama-martin-luther-king -jr. "Barack Obama is not the leader of a progressive social movement; he is the president. As president he is both more powerful than Dr. King and more structurally constrained."

153 **"The Quran also says"** Qur'an 5:32–34 (Oxford World's Classics). "We decreed to the Children of Israel that if anyone kills a person—unless in retribution for murder or spreading corruption in the land—it is as if he kills all mankind, while if any saves a life it is as if he saves the lives of all mankind."

154 **"Sikhs and Muslims have been"** Arwa Mahdawi, "The 712-Page Google Doc That Proves Muslims Do Condemn Terrorism," *Guardian* (U.S. edition), March 26, 2017, https://www.theguardian.com/world/shortcuts/ 2017/mar/26/muslims-condemn-terrorism-stats.

155 **"Look, I'm not a bigot"** For an excellent resource on how to counter racism, see Ibram X. Kendi, *How to Be an Antiracist* (New York: One World, 2019), 9. "When racist ideas resound, denials that those ideas are racist typically follow. When racist policies resound, denials that those policies are racist also follow. Denial is the heartbeat of racism, beating across ideologies, races, and nations. . . . But there is no neutrality in the racism struggle. . . . One either believes problems are rooted in groups of people, as a racist, or confronts racial inequities, as an antiracist."

156 **It turns out** Taking the perspective of "them" is a dramatic cognitive challenge. See Sapolsky, *Behave,* 531–535.

156 **An invisible wall forms** American sociologist Arlie Russell Hochschild describes her attempt to listen to Trump voters as "scaling the empathy wall." Through hundreds of hours of conversations, she finds what she defines as "deep stories," narrative frameworks that shape the embodied experience of the people she interviews. Arlie Russell Hochschild, *Strangers in Their Own Land: Anger and Mourning on the American Right* (New York: New Press, 2016), 5.

156 **Our goal is to understand them** Krista Ratcliffe, *Rhetorical Listening* (Carbondale: Southern Illinois University Press, 2005), 22, 25–33, 57. Ratcliffe

suggests that we train to become "apprentices of listening rather than masters of discourse" (p. 25). Rhetorical listening includes promoting an understanding of self and other, proceeding within an accountability logic, locating identifications across commonalities *and* differences, and analyzing claims as well as the cultural logics within which those claims function. By focusing on claims and cultural logics, listeners may still disagree with each other's claims, but they may better appreciate that the other person is not simply wrong but rather functioning from within a different logic.

156 **In understanding the cultural forces** For how change agents use a strategic "heartwired" approach to understand their opponents, see Robert Pérez and Amy Simon, "Heartwired: Human Behavior, Strategic Opinion Research and the Audacious Pursuit of Social Change" (strategy guide, Heartwired, 2017), https://heartwiredforchange.com/download-heartwired. "Some have identified gateways to persuasion that previously had been closed to them. Others have pinpointed the barriers to persuasion that were rooted in their audience's values, beliefs, emotions, identities and lived experiences, which created resistance to change. Their research helped to plot the interim changes needed to lay the groundwork necessary for even greater change down the line" (p. 10).

157 **Neuroscientists call it "cognitive load"** See Sapolsky, *Behave,* 534–535. The cognitive load of repeatedly taking the perspective of another whose view is challenging exhausts the part of the brain involved in overriding a habitual behavior (such as clinging to our own beliefs and pain). When our own resources are depleted, it becomes more challenging to draw close to others who are not like us.

158 **I didn't listen as well** Isaacs, *Dialogue,* 37–38. When listening to an opponent, we are only partially listening and spending the rest of our attention on preparing a defense of our own position. We superimpose our own assumptions on what we have heard. The combination of what we actually heard and our assumptions and inferences becomes our reality.

159 **My friend Sister Simone Campbell** "NETWORK's Nuns on the Bus," NETWORK, accessed August 19, 2019, https://networklobby.org/nunsonthebus.

159 **"Pain that is not transformed"** Fr. Richard Rohr, "Transforming Pain," Center for Action and Contemplation (website), October 17, 2018, https://cac.org/transforming-pain-2018-10-17. For more see Fr. Richard Rohr, *A Lever and a Place to Stand: The Contemplative Stance, the Active Prayer* (New York: Paulist Press, 2011).

160 **"You can't lead people"** Van Jones, *Beyond the Messy Truth: How We Came Apart, How We Come Together* (New York: Ballantine, 2017), 192.

160 **"We must not become"** Ibid., 28.

161 **Heer and Ranjha were** Waris Shah, *The Love of Hir and Ranjha,* trans. Sant Singh Sekon (Ludihana, India: Old Boys' Association Punjab Agricultural

College, 1977), http://apnaorg.com/books/english/heer-sekhon/book.php?fldr=book.

163 **Instead I saw our faith tradition** Diana L. Eck, *Encountering God: A Spiritual Journey from Bozeman to Banaras* (Boston: Beacon Press, 2003), 2. "All of us contribute to the river of our traditions. We do not know how we will change the river or be changed as we experience its currents."

165 **In a time of great need** Diana L. Eck, *India: A Sacred Geography* (New York: Harmony), 136–140.

chapter 6: reimagine

169 **Institutions in our society need** *POV,* season 27, episode 2, "American Revolutionary: The Evolution of Grace Lee Boggs," directed by Grace Lee (New York: Cherry Sky Pictures, 2013), originally aired June 30, 2014, on PBS, https://www.amdoc.org/watch/americanrevolutionary.

171 **In the traditional activist playbook** See Saul Alinsky, *Rules for Radicals: A Pragmatic Primer for Realistic Radicals* (New York: Vintage, 1989).

171 **Dorothy Day labored for it** See Dorothy Day, *The Long Loneliness* (New York: Harper & Brothers, 1952); Dorothy Day, *Loaves and Fishes* (1963; repr., New York: Orbis, 1997).

171 **Grace Lee Boggs fought** See Grace Lee Boggs, *Living for Change: An Autobiography* (Minneapolis: University of Minnesota Press, 1998); Grace Lee Boggs with Scott Kurashige, *The Next American Revolution: Sustainable Activism for the Twenty-first Century* (Berkeley: University of California Press, 2012); Robert D. McFadden, "Grace Lee Boggs, at 100; Rights Activist for 7 decades," *Boston Globe,* October 7, 2015, https://www.bostonglobe.com/metro/obituaries/2015/10/07/grace-lee-boggs-detroit-activist-dies/8ldI7FPXUBNDDf7EygPz5O/story.html.

171 **in the United States** Ben Fenwick, "'Stop Repeating History': Plan to Keep Migrant Children at Former Internment Camp Draws Outrage," *The New York Times,* June 22, 2019, https://www.nytimes.com/2019/06/22/us/fort-sill-protests-japanese-internment.html.

171 **the criminal justice system** Michelle Alexander, *The New Jim Crow: Mass Incarceration in the Age of Colorblindness* (New York: New Press, 2012), 180.

171 **the military–industrial complex** Dwight Eisenhower, "President Dwight Eisenhower Farewell Address," January 17, 1961, C-Span video, 16:08, https://www.c-span.org/video/?15026-1/president-dwight-eisenhower-farewell-address; "How the US Learned to Stop Worrying and Love the Forever War," *Nation,* September 11, 2019, https://www.thenation.com/article/archive/afghanistan-forever-war.

172 **The building is adorned** "Architecture," Yale Law School, accessed January 29, 2020, https://law.yale.edu/about-yale-law-school/glance/architecture.

173 **Had I seen** *The Paper Chase,* directed by James Bridges (Twentieth Century Fox, 1973).

173 **I de-feminized myself** For insight into the challenges for women in law schools historically, see Lani Guinier et al., *Becoming Gentlemen* (Boston: Beacon Press, 1997).

173 **One morning, a few months** "Reva Siegel," Yale Law School, accessed January 31, 2020, https://law.yale.edu/reva-siegel.

175 **But in an institution** Jeff Schmitt, "Yale Law School Holds Top Spot in U.S. News Ranking," *Tipping the Scales,* March 12, 2019, https://tippingthescales.com/2019/03/yale-law-holds-top-spot-in-u-s-news-ranking.

176 **I eventually became co-chair** "Women of Color Collective," Yale Law School, accessed January 31, 2020, https://law.yale.edu/student-life/student-journals-organizations/student-organizations/women-color-collective.

176 **I could not have known** Jacob Stern and David Yaffe-Bellamy, "Yale Law School's Reckoning over Brett Kavanaugh," *Atlantic,* September 25, 2018, https://www.theatlantic.com/politics/archive/2018/09/protests-grow-yale-law-school-over-brett-kavanaugh/571225.

177 **In every generation** See Nikole Hannah-Jones, "Our Democracy's Founding Ideals Were False When They Were Written. Black Americans Have Fought to Make Them True," *The New York Times Magazine,* August 14, 2019, https://www.nytimes.com/interactive/2019/08/14/magazine/black-history-american-democracy.html.

177 **Constitutional Law was an archive** Jack M. Balkin and Reva B. Siegel, eds., *The Constitution in 2020* (New York: Oxford University Press, 2009); Paul Brest et al., eds., *Processes of Constitutional Decisionmaking: Cases and Materials,* 7th ed. (Philadelphia: Wolters Kluwer, 2018).

177 **At some point, from somewhere** Vincent Harding, *There Is a River: The Black Struggle for Freedom in America* (New York: Harcourt Brace, 1981), xviii–xix.

178 **Yale is one of the few** "Clinical and Experiential Learning," Yale Law School, accessed January 31, 2020, https://law.yale.edu/studying-law-yale/clinical-and-experiential-learning.

178 **Professor Michael Wishnie** "Michael J. Wishnie," Yale Law School, accessed January 31, 2020, https://law.yale.edu/michael-j-wishnie.

178 **Under his direction** "Worker and Immigrant Rights Advocacy Clinic," Yale Law School, accessed August 22, 2019, https://law.yale.edu/wirac. For a video about the clinic, see https://law.yale.edu/yls-today/yale-law-school-videos/spotlight-worker-immigrant-rights-advocacy-clinic-wirac. For more on clinic victories under the Trump administration, see "Challenging the Refugee and Travel Ban," YLS Today, February 1, 2017, https://law.yale.edu/yls-today/news/challenging-refugee-and-travel-ban; "WIRAC Heads

to Supreme Court in Suit Defending DACA," YLS Today, November 12, 2019, https://law.yale.edu/yls-today/news/wirac-heads-supreme-court-suit -defending-daca; "WIRAC Mobilizes to Reunite Families," YLS Today, July 23, 2018, https://law.yale.edu/yls-today/news/wirac-mobilizes-reunite -families; "WIRAC Reaches Major Settlement on Behalf of Asylum-Seeking Family," YLS Today, June 25, 2019, https://law.yale.edu/yls-today/ news/wirac-reaches-major-settlement-behalf-asylum-seeking-family.

178 **His co-professor was Muneer Ahmad** "Muneer I. Ahmad," Yale Law School, accessed January 31, 2020, https://law.yale.edu/muneer-i-ahmad.

179 **Becca Heller built** For information on the International Refugee Assistance Program, see https://refugeerights.org. For how Heller took on the Muslim ban under the Trump administration, see Miriam Jordan, "A Travel Ban's Foe: A Young Firebrand and Her Pro Bono Brigade," *The New York Times,* May 7, 2017, https://www.nytimes.com/2017/05/07/us/travel-ban-lawyer .html.

179 **Ady Barkan became the face** "What Is a Hero?," Be a Hero, accessed August 22, 2019, https://beaherofund.com.

179 **Chesa Boudin was elected** Derek Hawkins, "Progressive Lawyer Wins San Francisco District Attorney Race, Continuing National Reform Trend," *The Washington Post,* November 9, 2019, https://www.washingtonpost.com/ nation/2019/11/10/progressive-lawyer-wins-san-francisco-district -attorney-race-continuing-national-reform-trend.

179 **One day *our* portraits** Heather Gerken, the first woman dean of Yale Law School, made diversity and inclusion in admissions and faculty a core priority and put the portraits of diverse living alumni on the walls of the school. See Heather Gerken, "Diversity and Inclusion: Message from the Dean," Yale Law School, fall 2019, https://law.yale.edu/student-life/diversity -inclusion. "And our walls boast not just portraits of illustrious alumni from our past, but photographs of the extraordinarily diverse and accomplished alumni from our present."

179 **Father James Manship** For more on Father James Manship, see Mary O'Leary, "The Rev. James Manship of St. Rose of Lima in New Haven Reassigned to Meriden Parish," *New Haven Register,* May 14, 2017, https:// www.nhregister.com/connecticut/article/The-Rev-James-Manship-of-St -Rose-of-Lima-in-New-11313803.php.

179 **He stood next to Sister** For more on Sister Mary Ellen Burns, see "Our Team," Apostle Immigrant Services, accessed January 31, 2020, https:// www.apostleimmigrantservices.org/test-page.

180 **The local police department** James Walker, "Top 50: Malik Jones; an Unwanted Legacy," *New Haven Register,* updated September 9, 2018, https:// www.nhregister.com/news/article/Top-50-Malik-Jones-an-unwanted -legacy-13214977.php.

181 **Father Jim had been arrested** Thomas MacMillan, "Cross-Border Cops Arrest Father Jim," *New Haven Independent,* March 3, 2009, https://www .newhavenindependent.org/index.php/archives/entry/cross-border_cops _arrest_father_jim.

181 **On the steps of the courthouse** Thomas MacMillan, "City Priest Pleads Not Guilty," *New Haven Independent,* March 4, 2009, http://www .newhavenindependent.org/archives/2009/03/new_haven_pries_1.php.

182 **Our people took the podium** Thomas MacMillan, "Priest's Video Contradicts Police Report," *New Haven Independent,* March 12, 2009, https://www .newhavenindependent.org/index.php/archives/entry/priests_video _contradicts_police_report.

182 **We presented a formal complaint** The Jerome N. Frank Legal Services Organization, Yale Law School, to Shanetta Y. Cutlar and Mark Kappelhoff, U.S. Department of Justice, March 26, 2009, http://graphics8.nytimes.com/ packages/pdf/nyregion/20100423HAVEN_pdfs/Complaint_letter_to _DOJ.pdf.

183 **These words launched** Thomas MacMillan, "Report: East Haven Police Target Latinos," *New Haven Independent,* April 23, 2010, https://www .newhavenindependent.org/index.php/archives/entry/report_tickets_show _east_haven_targets_latinos.

183 **They operated inside** Seth Freed Wessler, "How East Haven, Conn., Became Synonymous with Racial Profiling," Colorlines, February 2, 2012, https://www.colorlines.com/articles/how-east-haven-conn-became -synonymous-racial-profiling.

183 **This was only the second** See "U.S. Department of Justice Civil Rights Division Accomplishments, 2009–2012," U.S. Department of Justice, updated November 20, 2015, https://www.justice.gov/crt/us-department -justice-civil-rights-division-accomplishments-2009-2012.

183 **Movement lawyering is about** Betty Hung, "Movement Lawyering as Rebellious Lawyering: Advocating with Humility, Love and Courage," *Clinical Law Review* 23, no. 2 (2017): 663–669, https://www.law.nyu.edu/sites/ default/files/upload_documents/Betty%20Hung%20--%20Movement %20Lawyering.pdf. Hung defines movement lawyering as follows: "Lawyering that supports and advances social movements, defined as the building and exercise of collective power, led by the most directly impacted, to achieve systemic institutional and cultural change" (p. 664). She identifies three essential threads: "i) to be grounded in a place of humility that recognizes lawyering as but one of multiple strategies necessary to advance a social movement; ii) to act from a place of love that affirms the intersectional humanity of the whole person and entire communities in order to build movements together; and iii) to practice courage and be willing to relinquish our privileges in order to act and stand up for justice" (p. 664).

184 **The Justice Department released** Peter Applebome, "Police Gang Tyrannized Latinos, Indictment Says," *The New York Times,* January 24, 2012, https://www.nytimes.com/2012/01/25/nyregion/connecticut-police -officers-accused-of-mistreating-latinos.html. For the full report from the U.S. Department of Justice, see Assistant Attorney General Thomas E. Perez to Mayor Joseph Maturo, Jr., December 19, 2011, https://www.justice.gov/ sites/default/files/crt/legacy/2011/12/19/easthaven_findletter_12-19-11 .pdf. Note: A number of Department of Justice reports on police departments in this era included findings of unconstitutional searches and seizures and excessive force. East Haven was one of the few where the Department of Justice also found pervasive racial discrimination.

184 **All four officers** There were fifty-four police officers on the force at the time.

184 **The Justice Department pursued** U.S. Department of Justice, "Justice Department Enters into Settlement Agreement to Reform the East Haven, Conn., Police Department," press release 12-1396, November 20, 2012, https://www.justice.gov/opa/pr/justice-department-enters-settlement -agreement-reform-east-haven-conn-police-department.

184 **A year after that** David Moran, "U.S. Attorney General Lynch Praises East Haven Police," *Hartford Courant,* July 21, 2015, https://www.courant.com/ news/connecticut/hc-east-haven-attorney-general-loretta-lynch-visit-0722 -20150721-story.html; Paula Reid, "Can a Connecticut City Be a Model for Reforming the Ferguson Police Force?," CBS News, April 2, 2015, https:// www.cbsnews.com/news/can-east-haven-ct-be-a-model-for-reforming-the -ferguson-police-force.

184 **Meanwhile, clinic students after us** Chacon v. East Haven Police Department, 3:10-cv-01692-AWT (D. Conn., 2014), https://www.clearinghouse .net/detail.php?id=13807.

184 **The suit culminated in** Associated Press, "East Haven Settles Suit on Civil Rights," *The New York Times,* June 9, 2014, https://www.nytimes.com/ 2014/06/10/nyregion/east-haven-settles-suit-on-civil-rights.html.

185 **"With this settlement, East Haven"** "Civil Rights Plaintiffs Settle with East Haven, Secure Groundbreaking Immigration Policy," Yale Law School, June 9, 2014, https://law.yale.edu/yls-today/news/civil-rights-plaintiffs -settle-east-haven-secure-groundbreaking-immigration-policy.

185 **"This settlement is a testament"** Ibid.

185 **Years later, when** Davis Dunavin, "Obama-Era Agreement Puts East Haven at Odds with Trump's Deportation Agenda," WSHU Public Radio, March 22, 2017, https://www.wshu.org/post/obama-era-agreement-puts -east-haven-odds-trump-s-deportation-agenda#stream/0.

185 **Prophetic teachers and faith leaders** Today, for example, Auburn Seminary convenes faith leaders pursuing social justice work as part of its Auburn

Senior Fellows, including Muslim American author-activist Wajahat Ali; Rev. William Barber II of the Poor People's Campaign; Rev. Traci Blackmon of the United Church of Christ; Rabbi Sharon Brous of IKAR in Los Angeles; Rev. Jennifer Butler of Faith in Public Life; Sister Simone Campbell of NETWORK; Rev. Dr. Noel Castellanos of the Christian Community Development Association; Stosh Cotler of Bend the Arc; Bishop Yvette Flunder of the Fellowship of Affirming Ministries; Lisa Sharon Harper of Sojourners; Rev. Dr. Peter Heltzel of the Micah Institute; Rabbi Jill Jacobs of T'ruah; Rabbi Stephanie Kolin of Central Synagogue in New York City; Rev. Jacqui Lewis of Middle Church in New York City; Rev. Michael-Ray Matthews of PICO; author-educator Brian McLaren; Rev. Otis Moss III of Trinity Church in Chicago; Bishop Gene Robinson, who is the first gay bishop in Christendom;, Linda Sarsour of MPower; Imam Dawud Walid of the Council on American-Islamic Relations in Michigan; Rev. Dr. Raphael Warnock of Ebenezer Baptist Church in Atlanta; and sensei angel Kyodo Williams, who teaches radical dharma. For more about their work, see "Senior Fellows," Auburn Seminary, https://auburnseminary.org/senior-fellows.

186 **National Institute of Military Justice** See "About Us," National Institute of Military Justice, accessed December 5, 2019, https://nimj.org/about-us.

186 **It was filled with newspaper stories** "A Brief History of Guantanamo Post 9-11," Witness to Guantanamo, accessed September 9, 2019, http://witnesstoguantanamo.com/story-of-gtmo; Clive Stafford Smith, *The Eight O'Clock Ferry to the Windward Side* (New York: Nation Books, 2010); Matt Apuzzo et al., "How U.S. Torture Left a Legacy of Damaged Minds," *The New York Times,* October 8, 2018, https://www.nytimes.com/2016/10/09/world/cia-torture-guantanamo-bay.html; Mohamedou Ould Slahi and Larry Siems, *Guantanamo Diary* (Boston: Little, Brown, 2015); Neil A. Lewis, "Red Cross Finds Detainee Abuse in Guantánamo," *The New York Times,* November 30, 2004, https://www.nytimes.com/2004/11/30/politics/red-cross-finds-detainee-abuse-in-guantanamo.html; "Report on Torture and Cruel, Inhuman, and Degrading Treatment of Prisoners at Guantánamo Bay, Cuba," Center for Constitutional Rights, July 2006, https://ccrjustice.org/sites/default/files/assets/files/Report_ReportOnTorture.pdf; "Solitary Confinement at Guantanamo Bay," Center for Constitutional Rights, accessed September 9, 2019, https://ccrjustice.org/home/get-involved/tools-resources/fact-sheets-and-faqs/solitary-confinement-guantanamo-bay#.

187 **The Bush administration had used** "Guantánamo by the Numbers," Center for Constitutional Rights, November 14, 2015, https://ccrjustice.org/home/get-involved/tools-resources/fact-sheets-and-faqs/guant-namo-numbers; "Guantánamo Timeline," Center for Constitutional Rights, January 2018, https://ccrjustice.org/sites/default/files/attach/2018/01/GuantanamoTimeline_Jan2018.pdf; Katharine Q. Seelye, "A Nation Chal-

lenged: The Detention Camp; U.S. to Hold Taliban Detainees in 'the Least Worst Place,'" *The New York Times,* December 28, 2001, https://www .nytimes.com/2001/12/28/us/nation-challenged-detention-camp-us-hold -taliban-detainees-least-worst-place.html.

187 **On the campaign trail** Barack Obama, "The War We Need to Win" (speech, Woodrow Wilson International Center for Scholars, Washington, D.C., August 1, 2007), transcript and audio available at American Rhetoric, https:// www.americanrhetoric.com/speeches/barackobamawilsoncenter.htm.

188 **I was dropped off** For a video of Camp Justice narrated by *Miami Herald* reporter Carol Rosenberg, see José A. Iglesias, "Touring Camp Justice," *Miami Herald,* March 30, 2018, https://www.miamiherald.com/news/nation -world/world/americas/guantanamo/article205877479.html.

189 **The United States occupies** "Agreement Between the United States and Cuba for the Lease of Lands for Coaling and Naval stations; February 23, 1903," art. III, Lillian Goldman Law Library, Yale Law School, accessed August 27, 2019, https://avalon.law.yale.edu/20th_century/dip_cuba002.asp.

189 **My clinic professor, Mike Wishnie** For the story of how law professor Harold Koh and his team of law students, including Michael Wishnie, fought for the rights of Haitian refugees at Guantánamo, see Brandt Goldstein, *Storming the Court: How a Band of Law Students Fought the President—and Won* (New York: Scribner, 2006).

189 **He declared that detainees** Karen J. Greenberg et al., eds., *The Enemy Combatant Papers: American Justice, the Courts, and the War on Terror* (Cambridge, U.K.: Cambridge University Press, 2014).

189 **They were the "worst of the worst"** Scott Horton, "The Worst of the Worst?," Browsings (blog), *Harper's,* October 2, 2009, https://harpers.org/ blog/2009/10/the-worst-of-the-worst.

190 **The truth is that nearly** Ibid.

190 **Even three sweeping** Boumediene v. Bush, 553 U.S. 723 (2008), https:// www.oyez.org/cases/2007/06-1195; Hamdan v. Rumsfeld, 548 U.S. 55 (2006), https://www.oyez.org/cases/2005/05-184; Rasul v. Bush, 542 U.S. 466 (2004), https://www.oyez.org/cases/2003/03-334.

190 **Not one has been released** David Cole, "'With All Deliberate Speed': Rasul v. Bush Ten Years Later," *New Yorker,* July 1, 2014, https://www .newyorker.com/news/news-desk/with-all-deliberate-speed-rasul-v-bush -ten-year-later.

190 **They were military commissions** Jaclyn Belczyk, "House Passes Amendments to Military Commissions Act," Jurist, October 9, 2009, https://www .jurist.org/news/2009/10/house-passes-amendments-to-military.

191 **Omar was fifteen years old** For Omar Khadr's story, see Michelle Shepard, *Guantanamo's Child: The Untold Story of Omar Khadr* (Hoboken, N.J.: Wiley, 2008).

191 **Muneer Ahmad, my clinic professor** For Muneer Ahmad's insights on representing a detainee at Guantánamo, see Muneer I. Ahmad, "Resisting Guantánamo: Rights at the Brink of Dehumanization," *Northwestern University Law Review* 103, no. 4 (2009): 1683–1763, https://digitalcommons.law .yale.edu/fss_papers/5255.

192 **In the end, the government** For my full report from Guantánamo, see "Valarie Kaur," in *NIMJ Reports from Guantánamo,* vol. 2 (N.p.: National Institute of Military Justice and American University Washington College of Law, 2010), 14–19, https://nimj.org/wp-content/uploads/topics/ guantanamo%20observer%20documents/National%20Institute%20of %20Miltiary%20Justice%2C%20Reports%20from%20Guantanamo%2C %20Vol%202%20%282010%29.pdf.

194 **In the past thirty years** Alexander, *The New Jim Crow,* 6–8.

194 **The launch of** Ibid., 49–96.

194 **On any given day** Dorothy E. Roberts, "The Social and Moral Costs of Mass Incarceration in African American Communities," *Stanford Law Review* 56, no. 5 (2004): 1272, https://scholarship.law.upenn.edu/faculty _scholarship/583.

194 **Inside these prisons** P. R. Lockhart, "America Is Finally Being Exposed to the Devastating Reality of Prison Violence," Vox, April 5, 2019, https:// www.vox.com/policy-and-politics/2019/4/5/18297326/prison-violence -ohio-alabama-justice-department-lawsuit.

195 **Her name was** Emilio Cueto, "The Surprising History of Cuba's Patron Saint," as told to John F. Ross, *Smithsonian Journeys Quarterly: Cuba,* October 27, 2016, https://www.smithsonianmag.com/travel/surprising-history -cuba-patron-saint-cachita-virgin-mary-our-lady-charity-cultural-travel -180960606.

196 **Yale Visual Law Project** "About Visual Law Project," Yale Law School, accessed August 26, 2019, https://law.yale.edu/isp/initiatives/about-visual -law-project.

196 **We made two films** *Alienation,* written, directed, and produced by Megan Corrarino, Nate Freeman, Sharanya Kannikannan, Valarie Kaur, and Sharat Raju (New Haven, Conn.: Yale Visual Law Project, 2011), https://vimeo .com/26903037; *Stigma: Stop and Frisk in New York City,* written, directed, and produced by Stephanie Keene, Valarie Kaur, Ally Lamb, Rebecca Wexler, and Spencer Wolff (New Haven, Conn.: Yale Visual Law Project, 2011), https://vimeo.com/25382610.

196 **That's when Professor Hope Metcalf** "Hope R. Metcalf," Yale Law School, accessed January 31, 2020, https://law.yale.edu/hope-r-metcalf.

197 **But supermax prisons** For the history behind supermax prisons, see Marie Gottschalk, *The Prison and the Gallows: The Politics of Mass Incarceration in America* (New York: Cambridge University Press, 2006).

197 **Northern Correctional Institution** "Northern Correctional Institution," Connecticut State Department of Correction, accessed January 31, 2020, https://portal.ct.gov/DOC/Facility/Northern-CI.

197 **Ros was a mother** Ros's son Leighton Johnson has since been released from Northern Correctional Institution. He is now a vocal leader in the local movement to end solitary confinement in Connecticut. See "Stop Solitary: Connecticut," Stop Solitary CT campaign, accessed January 31, 2020, https://www.stopsolitaryct.org.

197–198 **The United Nations Special Rapporteur** United Nations General Assembly, "Interim Report of the Special Rapporteur of the Human Rights Council on Torture and Other Cruel, Inhuman or Degrading Treatment or Punishment" (August 5, 2011), 8, http://solitaryconfinement.org/uploads/SpecRapTortureAug2011.pdf.

198 **Yet solitary confinement is not** Stephanie Wykstra, "The Case Against Solitary Confinement," Vox, April 17, 2019, https://www.vox.com/future-perfect/2019/4/17/18305109/solitary-confinement-prison-criminal-justice-reform.

199 **I wanted to know** Peacemaker John Paul Lederach teaches that "the moral imagination requires the capacity to imagine ourselves in a web of relationships that include our enemies." John Paul Lederach, *The Moral Imagination: The Art and Soul of Building Peace* (New York: Oxford University Press, 2005), 34.

201 **The average cost of incarcerating** Christopher Reinhart, "Cost of Incarceration and Cost of a Career Criminal" (report 2008-R-0099, Connecticut General Assembly, Office of Legislative Research, February 13, 2008), https://www.cga.ct.gov/2008/rpt/2008-R-0099.htm.

201 **Our film *The Worst of the Worst*** *The Worst of the Worst: Portrait of a Supermax Prison,* written and directed by Valarie Kaur and Sharat Raju (New Haven, Conn.: Yale Visual Law Project, 2012), https://vimeo.com/54826024. For a discussion of this film, see Valarie Kaur, "On MSNBC: Inside America's Prisons," ValarieKaur.com (blog), December 5, 2012, https://valariekaur.com/2012/12/prisons.

201 **The film accompanied a report** In 2019, Hope Metcalf and her clinic submitted a formal letter to the United Nations Special Rapporteur showing that the use of solitary confinement in Connecticut constituted torture. See "Clinic Asks U.N. Special Rapporteur to Declare CT Department of Correction 'Tortures,'" Yale Law School, May 14, 2019, https://law.yale.edu/yls-today/news/clinic-asks-un-special-rapporteur-declare-ct-department-correction-tortures.

202 **The Department of Correction insisted** "Northern will never close or merge with another facility. We need Northern." Deputy Commissioner James Dzurenda, quoted in "Restructuring Northern CI," *P.R.I.D.E. at Work,* newsletter of the Connecticut Department of Correction, June 14,

2012–July 31, 2012, https://portal.ct.gov/-/media/DOC/Pdf/Pride/PRIDE20120731pdf.pdf?la=en.

202 **Now the three of us seek** Alexander, *The New Jim Crow;* Bryan Stevenson, *Just Mercy: A Story of Justice and Redemption* (New York: Spiegel & Grau, 2014); Ruthie Wilson Gilmore, *Golden Gulag: Prisons, Surplus, Crisis, and Opposition in Globalizing California* (Berkeley: University of California Press, 2007).

202 **I am inspired by people** See Danielle Sered, *Until We Reckon* (New York: New Press, 2019); *The Redemption Project with Van Jones,* premiered April 28, 2019, on CNN, https://www.cnn.com/shows/redemption-project-van-jones. For the first alternative-to-incarceration and victim-service program in the United States, see Common Justice, https://www.commonjustice.org.

202 **Or if we directed the resources** For a coalition pursuing humane border policy, see "Southern Border Communities Coalition," SBCC, accessed February 5, 2020, https://www.southernborder.org/about.

203 **"Slavery, lynching, and segregation"** Angela Y. Davis, *Are Prisons Obsolete?* (New York: Seven Stories Press, 2003), 24.

205 **"The future is an infinite"** Howard Zinn, *A Power Governments Cannot Suppress* (San Francisco: City Lights, 2007), 270.

part III: breathe and push: loving ourselves

chapter 7: breathe

209 **We have all known** Dorothy Day, "The Final Word is Love," *Catholic Worker,* May 1980, https://www.catholicworker.org/dorothyday/articles/867.html.

212 **Cells similar to the uterine** "Endometriosis," National Institute of Child Health and Human Development, last reviewed February 21, 2020, https://www.nichd.nih.gov/health/topics/endometriosis.

212 **Nearly nine million women** "Endometriosis Awareness: Why Our Voices Matter," Center for Endometriosis Care, updated April 20, 2018, http://centerforendo.com/endometriosis-awareness-why-our-voices-matter.

213 **On average, women and girls** Zoe Pugsley and Karen Ballard, "Management of Endometriosis in General Practice: The Pathway to Diagnosis," *British Journal of General Practice* 57, no. 39 (2007): 470–476, https://www.ncbi.nlm.nih.gov/pmc/articles/PMC2078174/#b1.

213 **Groundswell** Groundswell website, accessed December 5, 2019, https://action.groundswell-mvmt.org.

213 **I started getting calls** "Melissa Harris-Perry Tag," ValarieKaur.com (blog), accessed August 30, 2019, https://valariekaur.com/tag/melissa-harris-perry.

214 **It was the most violent hate crime** Susan Sonaldson James, "Wisconsin Shootings: Sikhs Faced Discrimination Since 9/11," ABCNews, August 6, 2012, https://abcnews.go.com/Health/wisconsin-shooting-hate-crimes-sikhs-rise-911/story?id=16939326.

214 **At that point** "Who Are Sikh Americans?," SALDEF, accessed March 4, 2020, https://saldef.org/who-are-sikh-americans/#.WjWYu1Q-fq0.

214 **Reporters called us Hindus** See Manjeet Birk et al., "De-Islamizing Sikhaphobia: Deconstructing Structural Racism in Wisconsin Gurdwara Shooting 10/12," *Education, Citizenship and Social Justice* 10, no. 2 (2015): 97–106, https://doi.org/10.1177%2F1746197915583936.

214 **When Sikh advocates finally** See "Sikh Community Activist Simran Jeet Singh: After Wisconsin Attack, I Refuse to Live in Fear," DemocracyNow! video, August 7, 2012, at 35:41 of 50:37, https://www.democracynow.org/2012/8/7/sikh_community_activist_simran_jeet_singh; "Understanding the Sikh Community," CNN, August 6, 2012, video, 05:20, https://www.cnn.com/videos/bestoftv/2012/08/06/exp-point-narinder-singh.cnn.

214 **"The news is reverberating"** Valarie Kaur, interview by Alina Cho, *CNN Newsroom,* August 7, 2012, video, 05:52, posted by Auburn Seminary, https://vimeo.com/47090061.

215 **We built infrastructure** See Deepa Iyer, "A Perfect Storm in the Making for 17 Years: A Reflection and Call to Action," Medium, September 10, 2018, https://medium.com/@dviyer/a-perfect-storm-in-the-making-for-17-years-a-reflection-and-call-to-action-711425228a70.

216 **Breathing from the diaphragm** Roderik J. S. Gerritsen and Guido P. H. Band, "Breath of Life: The Respiratory Vagal Stimulation of Contemplative Activity," *Frontiers in Human Neuroscience* 12, no. 397 (2018): 1–25, https://www.ncbi.nlm.nih.gov/pmc/articles/PMC6189422.

216 **It changes our blood pressure** For the impact of diaphragmatic breathing on the body, see Marc A. Russo et al., "The Physiological Effects of Slow Breathing in the Healthy Human," *Breathe* 13 (2017): 298–309, https://breathe.ersjournals.com/content/13/4/298. For the impact of mindfulness on the body, see Susan L. Smalley and Diana Winston, *Fully Present: The Science, Art, and Practice of Mindfulness* (New York: Hachette, 2010).

217 **In the late 1990s** "Welcome to Sikh Temple of Wisconsin," Sikh Temple of Wisconsin, accessed February 1, 2020, http://sikhtempleofwisconsin.com.

223 **"Darkness cannot drive out"** Martin Luther King, Jr., *Strength to Love* (New York: Harper & Row, 1963), 47.

224 *King also said that love* "I'm not talking about emotional bosh when I talk about love, I'm talking about a strong, demanding love." Martin Luther King, Jr., "'Where Do We Go from Here?," Address Delivered at the Eleventh Annual SCLC Convention" (per popular recollection, Atlanta, 1967), Martin Luther King, Jr. Research and Education Institute, Stanford

University, https://kinginstitute.stanford.edu/king-papers/documents/where
-do-we-go-here-address-delivered-eleventh-annual-sclc-convention. In another speech the same year, he said, "When I speak of love I am not speaking
of some sentimental and weak response. I am not speaking of that force
which is just emotional bosh. I am speaking of that force which all of the
great religions have seen as the supreme unifying principle of life." Martin
Luther King, Jr., "Beyond Vietnam—A Time to Break the Silence" (speech,
New York, April 4, 1967), Martin Luther King, Jr. Research and Education
Institute, Stanford University, https://kinginstitute.stanford.edu/king-papers/
documents/beyond-vietnam.

224 **In the days to come** See Valarie Kaur, "Sikh-Led Prayer and GOP Convic-
tions," CNN, updated August 29, 2012, https://www.cnn.com/2012/08/
29/opinion/kaur-sikh-leads-prayer-rnc/index.html.

225 **One by one, nearly every Sikh** A.C. Thompson, "Sikhs in America: A
History of Hate," *ProPublica,* August 4, 2017, https://www.propublica.org/
article/sikhs-in-america-hate-crime-victims-and-bias.

225 **The FBI and Department of Justice** Eric Holder, "Healing Communities
and Remembering the Victims of Oak Creek," August 2, 2013, U.S. Department of Justice Archives, https://www.justice.gov/archives/opa/blog/
healing-communities-and-remembering-victims-oak-creek.

226 **A few weeks earlier** David Nakamura, "After Aurora Shootings, Obama
Again Takes On Role as Healer in Chief in Colorado," *The Washington Post,*
July 22, 2012, https://www.washingtonpost.com/politics/after-aurora
-shootings-obama-again-takes-on-role-as-healer-in-chief-in-colorado/
2012/07/22/gJQAdEO92W_story.html.

226 **He said that he hugged** Barack Obama, "Weekly Address: Remembering
the Victims of the Aurora, Colorado Shooting," White House, Office of the
Press Secretary, July 21, 2012, https://obamawhitehouse.archives.gov/the
-press-office/2012/07/21/weekly-address-remembering-victims-aurora
-colorado-shooting.

226 **In his condolences** Barack Obama, "Statement on the Shootings in
Oak Creek, Wisconsin," August 5, 2012 (Government Printing Office,
DCPD201200619), https://www.govinfo.gov/content/pkg/DCPD-201200619/
pdf/DCPD-201200619.pdf.

227 **"In the recent past"** Eric Holder, "Attorney General Eric Holder Speaks at
the Oak Creek Memorial Service" (Oak Creek, Wis., August 10, 2012), U.S.
Department of Justice, https://www.justice.gov/opa/speech/attorney
-general-eric-holder-speaks-oak-creek-memorial-service.

227 **Since 9/11, the Justice Department** Elisha Fieldstadt and Ken Dilanian,
"White Nationalism—Fueled Violence Is on the Rise, but FBI Is Slow to Call
It Domestic Terrorism," NBC News, August 5, 2019, https://www.nbcnews
.com/news/us-news/white-nationalism-fueled-violence-rise-fbi-slow-call
-it-domestic-n1039206; Trevor Aaronson, "Terrorism's Double Standard:

Violent Far Right Extremists Are Rarely Prosecuted as Terrorists," The Intercept, March 23, 2019, https://theintercept.com/2019/03/23/domestic-terrorism-fbi-prosecutions.

227 **"We will discuss how to"** Holder, "Attorney General Eric Holder Speaks at the Oak Creek Memorial Service."

228 **Amar had been on the ground** For more about the Sikh American advocacy groups on the ground after the Oak Creek tragedy, see Sikh Coalition website, accessed February 1, 2020, https://www.sikhcoalition.org; Sikh American Legal Defense and Education Fund (SALDEF) website, accessed February 1, 2020, https://saldef.org; South Asian Americans Leading Together (SAALT) website, accessed February 1, 2020, https://saalt.org; Tori DeAngelis, "Healing and Growth After Mass Murder," *American Psychological Association Monitor on Psychology* 47, no. 9 (2016): 22, https://www.apa.org/monitor/2016/10/mass-murder.

228 **After the memorial ended** Philip Rucker, "Romney Confuses 'Sikh' with 'Sheik,'" *The Washington Post,* August 7, 2012, https://www.washingtonpost.com/politics/romney-confuses-sikh-with-sheik/2012/08/07/10beaba6-e0fc-11e1-a19c-fcfa365396c8_story.html.

229 **None of the other networks** Mona Chalabi, "Terror Attacks by Muslims Receive 357% More Press Attention, Study Finds," *Guardian* (U.S. edition), July 20, 2018, https://www.theguardian.com/us-news/2018/jul/20/muslim-terror-attacks-press-coverage-study.

229 **As scholar Naunihal Singh reflects** Naunihal Singh, "An American Tragedy," *New Yorker,* August 13, 2012, https://www.newyorker.com/news/news-desk/an-american-tragedy.

230 *Meditate and vibrate upon* Sri Guru Granth Sahib, *Salok Mahalla,* 1427:3, 1427:12, 1428:5, 1428:13, 1427:16, 1429:4, 1429:7. These lines are fragments from various *shabad*s sung during the service at the gurdwara.

230 **A granthi rose to deliver** For an English translation of the *Ardas,* see Gurmat Literacy Project, "Ardas Translation," Surat Initiative, accessed January 29, 2020, https://www.suratinitiative.org/gurmat-literacy-project-1. For my reflections on the *Ardas* and its significance after the Oak Creek mass shooting, see my April 25, 2014, speech at the first-ever event to commemorate the Sikh faith held at the Pentagon, in "Ardas: The Echoes of a People," Kaur Life, August 25, 2014, https://kaurlife.org/2014/08/25/ardas-echoes-people.

231 **Wade Michael Page** See Marilyn Elias, "Sikh Temple Killer Wade Michael Page Radicalized in Army," *Intelligence Report,* November 11, 2012, https://www.splcenter.org/fighting-hate/intelligence-report/2012/sikh-temple-killer-wade-michael-page-radicalized-army.

231 *Nanak Nam Chardi Kala* The translation is mine. See Gurmat Literacy Project, "Ardas Translation."

231 **I presented bound books** "Groundswell Delivers Messages to Oak Creek Gurdwara & Sikh Community," video, 03:17, posted by Auburn Seminary, August 17, 2012, https://vimeo.com/47723529.

231 **In the aftermath** See "Stand in Solidarity with the Families of Charleston Church Shooting," Groundswell, accessed February 2, 2020, https://action .groundswell-mvmt.org/petitions/send-prayers-to-familes-of-charleston -church-shooting; "In Solidarity with the Tree of Life Synagogue, We Pray and We Pledge!," Groundswell, accessed February 2, 2002, https://action .groundswell-mvmt.org/petitions/in-solidarity-with-the-tree-of-life -synagogue-we-pray-and-we-pledge; "Send Love & Solidarity to the Muslim Families of New Zealand: Pledge to Fight White Nationalism," Groundswell, accessed February 2, 2020, https://action.groundswell-mvmt.org/ petitions/send-a-message-of-love-solidarity-to-the-muslim-families-of -christchurch.

233 **I wrote an open letter** Valarie Kaur, "President Obama, Come to Oak Creek," CNN, updated August 17, 2012, https://www.cnn.com/2012/08/ 17/opinion/kaur-obama-sikh-temple/index.html.

233 **On Thursday, August 23** Valarie Kaur, "Opinion: First Lady Sets an Example After Wisconsin Shooting," CNN, updated August 24, 2012, https:// www.cnn.com/2012/08/24/us/opinion-first-lady-sets-an-example-after -wisconsin-shooting/index.html.

234 **In the past decade** See South Asian Americans Leading Together (SAALT) website, accessed February 1, 2020, https://saalt.org; Sikh American Legal Defense and Education Fund (SALDEF) website, accessed February 1, 2020, https://saldef.org; United Sikhs website, accessed February 1, 2020, https:// unitedsikhs.org.

234 **I watched Amar Bhalla** For our short film on some of the Sikh Coalition's cases, see *Rising Up Against Hate,* directed by Sharat Raju, written by Valarie Kaur (Los Angeles: New Moon Productions, 2008), https://valariekaur .com/film.

234 **Eleven years later** "About Us," Sikh Coalition, accessed September 2, 2019, https://www.sikhcoalition.org.

235 **We harnessed all of that energy** "Hate Crime Tracking and Prevention," Sikh Coalition (website), accessed March 4, 2020, https://www.sikhcoalition .org/our-work/preventing-hate-and-discrimination/hate-crime-tracking -and-prevention.

235 **"There is no box for me"** John Edwards, interview by Valarie Kaur, "Oak Creek Police Chief John Edwards," video, 02:34, posted by Sharat Raju, 2013, https://vimeo.com/50335607.

235 **But, under the FBI's tracking** U.S. Department of Justice, Federal Bureau of Investigation, *Uniform Crime Reporting Handbook* (2004), 122, https://ucr .fbi.gov/additional-ucr-publications/ucr_handbook.pdf.

235 **Sikhs had been asking** "SALDEF December Advocate: Assailants in Sacramento Hate Crime Apprehended," SALDEF, December 16, 2010, https://saldef.org/saldef-december-advocateassailants-in-sacramento-hate-crime-apprehended.

235 **Longtime Sikh advocates** Simran Jeet Singh and Prabhjot Singh, "How Hate Gets Counted," op-ed, *The New York Times,* August 24, 2012, https://www.nytimes.com/2012/08/24/opinion/do-american-sikhs-count.html.

235 **On September 19** U.S. Senate, Judiciary Committee, *Hate Crimes and the Threat of Domestic Extremism: Hearing Before the Subcommittee on the Constitution, Civil Rights and Human Rights,* 112th Cong., September 19, 2012, https://www.judiciary.senate.gov/meetings/time-change__hate-crimes-and-the-threat-of-domestic-extremism.

235 **Just forty-five days after** Valarie Kaur, "After Sikh Temple Shooting, a Historic Hearing," Melissa Harris-Perry (blog), MSNBC, September 21, 2012, http://www.msnbc.com/melissa-harris-perry/after-sikh-temple-shooting-historic-h.

235 **"I had my first day of college"** Harpreet Singh Saini, testimony, in U.S. Senate, Judiciary Committee, *Hate Crimes and the Threat of Domestic Extremism,* at 01:15:48, https://www.judiciary.senate.gov/meetings/time-change__hate-crimes-and-the-threat-of-domestic-extremism. Full transcript available at https://www.judiciary.senate.gov/imo/media/doc/9-19-12SainiTestimony.pdf.

235 **In the same hearing** Daryl Johnson, testimony, in *Hate Crimes and the Threat of Domestic Extremism,* at 01:05:11, https://www.judiciary.senate.gov/meetings/time-change__hate-crimes-and-the-threat-of-domestic-extremism. Full transcript available at https://www.judiciary.senate.gov/imo/media/doc/9-19-12JohnsonTestimony.pdf.

236 **At DHS, Johnson authored** Janet Reitman, "U.S. Law Enforcement Failed to See the Threat of White Nationalism. Now They Don't Know How to Stop It," *The New York Times Magazine,* November 3, 2018, https://www.nytimes.com/2018/11/03/magazine/FBI-charlottesville-white-nationalism-far-right.html.

236 **It left just one analyst** Daryl Johnson, interviewed by Hedi Beirich, *Intelligence Report,* June 17, 2011, https://www.splcenter.org/fighting-hate/intelligence-report/2011/inside-dhs-former-top-analyst-says-agency-bowed-political-pressure.

236 **The Southern Poverty Law Center** "Southern Poverty Law Center Has Tracked Sikh Temple Shooter for More Than a Decade," *Here and Now,* PRI, August 6, 2012, https://www.pri.org/stories/2012-08-06/southern-poverty-law-center-has-tracked-sikh-temple-shooter-more-decade.

236 **"Finally, Senators, I ask"** Saini, testimony.

236 **The Oak Creek massacre** Dalia Fahmy, "The Rise of the Alt-Right: Un-

derstanding the Sociocultural Effects of Mainstreaming Anti-Muslim Sentiment," in *The Islamic Tradition and the Human Rights Discourse*, ed. H.A. Hellyer (report, The Atlantic Council, September 15, 2018), https://www.atlanticcouncil.org/wp-content/uploads/2018/09/12_Rise_of_Alt_Right_-_Fahmy_-_Islam_and_Human_Rights_Report.pdf; John Feffer, "The Right Wing's Election-Year Islamophobia," *Nation*, March 29, 2012, https://www.thenation.com/article/archive/right-wings-election-year-islamophobia.

236 **The Center for American Progress** Wajahat Ali et al., "Fear, Inc.: The Roots of the Islamophobia Network in America," Center for American Progress, August 26, 2011, https://www.americanprogress.org/issues/religion/reports/2011/08/26/10165/fear-inc.

236 **As the anti-Islam industry grew** Mark Potok, "The Year in Hate and Extremism," *Intelligence Report*, March 4, 2013, https://www.splcenter.org/fighting-hate/intelligence-report/2013/year-hate-and-extremism.

236 **The number of hate groups** "Hate Group Numbers Up by 54% Since 2000," Southern Poverty Law Center, February 26, 2009, https://www.splcenter.org/news/2009/02/26/hate-group-numbers-54-2000.

236 **Muslim American advocates** Ali et al., "Fear, Inc."

236 **We did not know it then** Alan Rappeport and Noah Weiland, "White Nationalists Celebrate 'an Awakening' After Donald Trump's Victory," *The New York Times*, November 19, 2016, https://www.nytimes.com/2016/11/20/us/politics/white-nationalists-celebrate-an-awakening-after-donald-trumps-victory.html.

236 **After the Senate hearing** For statements of diverse community groups who supported the hearing, see SAALT, "Diverse Community Organizations Applaud Senate Hearing on Hate Violence Next Week," press release, February 6, 2013, https://saalt.org/diverse-community-organization-applaud-senate-hearing-on-hate-violence-next-week.

237 **In the ten months that followed** "FBI Hate Crime Tracking Campaign," Sikh Coalition, accessed January 31, 2020, https://www.sikhcoalition.org/our-work/legal-and-policy/fbi-hate-crime-tracking-campaign.

237 **Senator Durbin and more than** "Victory! 10 Months After Oak Creek, FBI Group Votes to Track Sikh Hate Crimes," Sikh Coalition, June 5, 2013, https://www.sikhcoalition.org/blog/2013/victory-10-months-after-oak-creek-fbi-group-votes-to-track-sikh-hate-crimes.

237 **Three thousand people of all faiths** "To: Attorney General Eric Holder; Tell the FBI: Track Hate Crimes Against Sikh Americans," Groundswell, accessed January 31, 2020, https://action.groundswell-mvmt.org/petitions/tell-the-fbi-track-hate-crimes-against-sikh-americans-1.

237 **In 2015, for the first time** Valarie Kaur, "One Year After Oak Creek, Why the FBI Tracking Hate Crimes Is a Victory," Melissa Harris-Perry (blog),

MSNBC, August 5, 2013, http://www.msnbc.com/melissa-harris-perry/one-year-after-oak-creek-why-the-fbi.

237 **That white man sharing a meal** For Oak Creek Mayor Steve Scafiddi's first-person story of the mass shooting and its aftermath, see Stephen A. Scaffidi, *Six Minutes in August: A Story of Tragedy, Healing and Community* (Milwaukee, WI: Marketpoint Media, 2015).

238 **President Obama honored him** Barack Obama, "Remarks by the President in the State of the Union Address," White House, Office of the Press Secretary, February 12, 2013, https://obamawhitehouse.archives.gov/the-press-office/2013/02/12/remarks-president-state-union-address.

238 **Once, in a televised** "Full Rush Transcript: Donald Trump, CNN Milwaukee Republican Presidential Town Hall," Anderson Cooper, moderator, CNN, March 29, 2016, http://cnnpressroom.blogs.cnn.com/2016/03/29/full-rush-transcript-donald-trump-cnn-milwaukee-republican-presidential-town-hall.

239 **Together the brothers** "Chardi Kala 6k," Serve 2 Unite, accessed January 31, 2020, http://www.chardhikala6kwi.org. For my essay on the first anniversary of the Oak Creek shooting, see Valarie Kaur, "A Year Later, Sikhs Keep Up Fight Against Gun Violence," CNN, updated August 8, 2013, https://edition.cnn.com/2013/08/07/opinion/kaur-oak-creek-anniversary/index.html.

239 **Arno was a former white supremacist** See Arno Michaelis, *My Life After Hate* (Milwaukee, WI: Life After Hate, 2010); Arno Michaelis, "I Learned the Hard Way How to Stop Hate," CNN, updated August 15, 2017, https://www.cnn.com/2017/08/15/opinions/ex-white-power-compassion-answer-michaelis-opinion/index.html.

240 **They teamed up with** To read Pardeep Kaleka and Arno Michaelis's story in their own words, see Arno Michaelis and Pardeep Kaleka, *The Gift of Our Wounds: A Sikh and a Former White Supremacist Find Forgiveness After Hate* (New York: St. Martin's, 2018). For more about their organization, Serve 2 Unite, see https://www.giftofourwounds.com/serve2unite.

241 **He tied his turban** For an image of Raghuvinder Singh, see his portrait in Amit Amin and Naroop Jhoti, *Turbans and Tales: Portraits of Contemporary Sikh Identity* (London: Unbound, 2019), 179.

243 **A few weeks later** For our short film about Oak Creek, see *Oak Creek: In Memoriam,* produced by Valarie Kaur and Sharat Raju (Los Angeles: New Moon Productions, 2008), https://vimeo.com/52729831.

244 **I glanced at my phone** James Barron, "Nation Reels After Gunman Massacres 20 Children at School in Connecticut," *The New York Times,* December 14, 2012, https://www.nytimes.com/2012/12/15/nyregion/shooting-reported-at-connecticut-elementary-school.html.

244 **We had traveled from** Valarie Kaur, "Journey from Oak Creek to New-

town," ValarieKaur.com (blog; originally for *The Washington Post*), December 16, 2012, https://valariekaur.com/2012/12/journey-from-oak-creek-to-newtown.

245 **In the years to come** Chris Wilson, "37 Years of Mass Shootings in the U.S. in One Chart," *Time,* updated August 7, 2019, https://time.com/4965022/deadliest-mass-shooting-us-history.

245 **Not even when the majority** Lydia Saad, "Americans Widely Support Tighter Regulations on Gun Sales," Gallup, October 17, 2017, https://news.gallup.com/poll/220637/americans-widely-support-tighter-regulations-gun-sales.aspx.

245 **"Thoughts and prayers"** See David Leonhardt et al., "Thoughts and Prayers and N.R.A. Funding," *The New York Times,* October 4, 2017, https://www.nytimes.com/interactive/2017/10/04/opinion/thoughts-prayers-nra-funding-senators.html; James Fallows, "The Empty Rituals of an American Massacre," *Atlantic,* February 15, 2018, https://www.theatlantic.com/politics/archive/2018/02/deeply-saddened/553478; Tribune Wire Reports, "Thoughts and Prayers: Politics of Grief and Gun Control After Latest Shooting," *Chicago Tribune,* December 3, 2015, https://www.chicagotribune.com/opinion/commentary/ct-thoughts-prayers-politics-gun-control-shooting-20151203-story.html.

245 **The death toll would rise rapidly** Emma G. Fitzsimmons, "Man Kills 3 at Jewish Centers in Kansas City Suburb," *The New York Times,* April 13, 2014, https://www.nytimes.com/2014/04/14/us/3-killed-in-shootings-at-jewish-center-and-retirement-home-in-kansas.html; Jason Horowitz et al., "Nine Killed in Shooting at Black Church in Charleston," *The New York Times,* June 17, 2015, https://www.nytimes.com/2015/06/18/us/church-attacked-in-charleston-south-carolina.html; Ian Austen and Craig S. Smith, "Quebec Mosque Shooting Kills at Least 6, and 2 Suspects Are Arrested," *The New York Times,* January 29, 2017, https://www.nytimes.com/2017/01/29/world/americas/quebec-city-mosque-shooting-canada.html; Campbell Robertson et al., "11 Killed in Synagogue Massacre; Suspect Charged with 29 Counts," *The New York Times,* October 27, 2018, https://www.nytimes.com/2018/10/27/us/active-shooter-pittsburgh-synagogue-shooting.html; Charlotte Graham-McLay, "Death Toll in New Zealand Mosque Shootings Rises to 51," *The New York Times,* May 2, 2019, https://www.nytimes.com/2019/05/02/world/asia/new-zealand-attack-death-toll.html; Jennifer Medina et al., "One Dead in Synagogue Shooting Near San Diego; Officials Call It Hate Crime," *The New York Times,* April 27, 2019, https://www.nytimes.com/2019/04/27/us/poway-synagogue-shooting.html.

245 **Now such massacres are routine** Brian Levin, "Why White Supremacist Attacks Are on the Rise, Even in Surprising Places," *Time,* March 21, 2019, https://time.com/5555396/white-supremacist-attacks-rise-new-zealand; Lois Beckett and Jason Wilson, "'White Power Ideology': Why El Paso Is

Part of a Growing Global Threat," *Guardian* (U.S. edition), August 5, 2019, https://www.theguardian.com/us-news/2019/aug/04/el-paso-shooting -white-nationalist-supremacy-violence-christchurch.

245 **White nationalists are a globally connected** For connections between recent terrorist attacks around the world, see Weiyi Cai and Simone Landon, "Attacks by White Extremists Are Growing. So Are Their Connections," *The New York Times,* April 3, 2019, https://www.nytimes.com/interactive/2019/04/03/world/white-extremist-terrorism-christchurch.html.

245 **We could have passed strong** For the policy recommendations of community organizations, see "Written Statement of Deepa Iyer, Executive Director South Asian Americans Leading Together (SAALT)," submitted to U.S. Senate, Judiciary Committee, *Hate Crimes and the Threat of Domestic Extremism,* https://saalt.org/wp-content/uploads/2012/09/SAALT-Statement -of-the-Record.pdf. For more about proposed racial profiling legislation, see "End Racial and Religious Profiling Act," Human Rights Campaign, last updated October 1, 2019, https://www.hrc.org/resources/end-racial -religious-profiling-act.

245–246 **We could have modeled** See Valarie Kaur, "America After the Sikh Temple Shooting," ValarieKaur.com (blog; originally for Common Ground News Service), August 15, 2012, http://valariekaur.com/2012/08/common -ground-news-service-america-after-the-sikh-temple-shooting.

246 **In the cold and snow** Natalie Sleeth, "In the Bulb There Is a Flower (Hymn of Promise)" (Hope Publishing, Carol Stream, Ill., 1986), https://www .hopepublishing.com/find-hymns-hw/hw3983.aspx.

246 **There is a pervasive form** Thomas Merton, *Conjectures of a Guilty Bystander* (New York: Doubleday Religion, 1965), 85. Merton attributes this insight to Douglas Steere, American Quaker author and philosopher.

248 **"When we see something that beautiful"** For Rabbi Sharon Brous's sermon connecting wonder to love and justice, see Rabbi Sharon Brous, "I Need You to Breathe" (sermon, Los Angeles, September 29, 2017), IKAR, https://ikar-la.org/sermons/i-need-you-to-breathe.

248 **"Caring for myself"** Audre Lorde, epilogue to *A Burst of Light and Other Essays* (Ithaca, N.Y.: Firebrand, 1988), 130.

248 **"I have seen"** bell hooks, "Preface to the New Edition: Reflections of Light," in *Sisters of the Yam: Black Women and Self-Recovery* (New York: Routledge, 2015), xi.

248 **Without loving ourselves** bell hooks, *All About Love: New Visions* (New York: HarperCollins, 2000), chap. 4, "Commitment: Let Love Be Love in Me."

248 **When asked why** Angela Davis, "Radical Self Care: Angela Davis," Afropunk video, 04:27, December 7, 2018, https://afropunk.com/2018/12/radical-self-care-angela-davis.

248 **My colleague, Lisa Anderson** Lisa Anderson, "Loving Black Women Hard and Well Can Change the World," Auburn Seminary, accessed September 4, 2019, https://auburnseminary.org/voices/loving-black-women-hard-and -well-can-change-the-world. For information about the fellowships, re- treats, and convenings led by Anderson at Auburn Seminary, see "Sojourner Truth Leadership Circle," https://auburnseminary.org/stlc.

248 **Activist adrienne maree brown** adrienne maree brown, *Pleasure Activism: The Politics of Feeling Good* (Chico, Calif.: AK Press, 2019).

249 **Melissa calls for "squad care"** Melissa Harris-Perry, "How #SquadCare Saved My Life, *Elle,* July 24, 2017, https://www.elle.com/culture/career -politics/news/a46797/squad-care-melissa-harris-perry. For more essays on squad care, see https://www.elle.com/squadcare.

249 **The self-help industry profits** For spiritual bypassing generally, see John Welwood, "Principles of Inner Work: Psychological and Spiritual," *Journal of Transpersonal Psychology* 16, no. 1 (1984): 63–73, https://pdfs.semanticscholar .org/88da/58231b94f12676397195167f4064c5178eee.pdf?_ga=2 .264308680.658861266.1583539420-260789484.1583539420.

250 **I had grown so accustomed** For how a generation of Muslim, Sikh, Arab, and South Asian American advocates are now reckoning with vicarious trauma since 9/11, see Deepa Iyer, "Reckoning with Trauma 16 Years After," *Medium,* September 10, 2017, https://medium.com/@dviyer/https -medium-com-dviyer-reckoning-with-trauma-16-years-after-sept11 -98e063b6197e.

chapter 8: push

251 **I think the inability to love is the central problem** James Baldwin, inter- view in *Advocate*, excerpted in *Utne Reader* (July/August 2002), 100.

257 **Dark sky reserves** "International Dark Sky Reserves," International Dark- Sky Association, accessed September 5, 2019, https://www.darksky.org/our -work/conservation/idsp/reserves.

257 **My father once introduced** Scientist Carl Sagan popularized the cosmic calendar in his book *The Dragons of Eden* (New York: Random House, 1977) and his television series *Cosmos: A Personal Voyage* premiered September 28, 1980, on PBS.

259 **"Physical self-awareness is"** Bessel van der Kolk, *The Body Keeps the Score: Brain, Mind, and Body in the Healing of Trauma* (New York: Viking, 2014), 103.

259 **"Many of us have left"** Eve Ensler, "In the Body of the World," *Library Talks* (podcast), New York Public Library, May 7, 2014, http://new yorkpubliclibrary.libsyn.com/eve-ensler-in-the-body-of-the-world.

259 **In working with women** Ibid.

259 **Now her work was** Eve Ensler, *In the Body of the World: A Memoir of Cancer and Connection* (New York: Metropolitan, 2013), 146.

260 **Somatic trauma therapy** See Peter Levine, *Waking the Tiger: Healing Trauma* (Berkeley, Calif.: North Atlantic Books, 1997); "What Is Somatic Experiencing?," Somatic Experiencing Trauma Institute, accessed September 4, 2019, https://traumahealing.org/about-us.

260–261 **EMDR (eye movement desensitization and reprocessing)** "What is EMDR?," EMDR Institute, accessed September 4, 2019, https://www .emdr.com/what-is-emdr.

261 **Biofeedback lowers the heart rate** Inna Khazan, Biofeedback and Mindfulness in Everyday Life: Practical Solutions for Improving Your Health and Performance (New York: W. W. Norton, 2019).

261 **Tapping, or emotional freedom technique** Peta Stapleton, *The Science Behind Tapping: A Proven Stress Management Technique for the Mind and Body* (Carlsbad, Calif.: Hay House, 2019); "The Ultimate Tapping Guide," Dr. Peta Stapleton, accessed February 3, 2020, https://petastapleton.com/ resources/the-ultimate-tapping-guide.

261 **Yoga, historically a system** Marlysa B. Sullivan et al., "Yoga Therapy and Polyvagal Theory: The Convergence of Traditional Wisdom and Contemporary Neuroscience for Self-Regulation and Resilience," *Frontiers in Human Neuroscience* 12 (2018), https://doi.org/10.3389/fnhum.2018.00067.

263 **Forgiveness is not forgetting** For an exploration of forgiveness, see Helen Whitney, *Forgiveness: A Time to Love and a Time to Hate* (Campbell, CA.: Fast-Pencil Premiere, 2011).

263 **Two days after** Oliver Laughland et al., "'I Forgive You': Charleston Church Victims' Families Confront Suspect," *Guardian* (U.S. edition), June 19, 2015, https://www.theguardian.com/world/2015/jun/19/i-forgive-you -charleston-church-victims-families-confront-suspect.

264 **In truth and reconciliation commissions** "Challenging the Conventional: Can Truth Commissions Strengthen the Peace Process?" (symposium report, International Center for Transitional Justice and Kofi Anan Foundation, 2014), 1, https://www.ictj.org/sites/default/files/ICTJ_TruthCommPeace _English_2016.pdf; G.G.J. Knoops, "Truth and Reconciliation Commission Models and International Tribunals: A Comparison" (symposium report, "The Right to Self-Determination in International Law," organized by Unrepresented Nations and Peoples Organization [UNPO], Khmers Kampuchea-Krom Federation [KKF], and Hawai'i Institute for Human Rights [HIHR], The Hague, September 29, 2006–October 1, 2006, 1–2), http:// www.unpo.org/downloads/ProfKnoops.pdf; "Truth Commissions," fact sheet, International Center for Transitional Justice, 2008, accessed September 9, 2019, https://www.ictj.org/sites/default/files/ICTJ-Global-Truth -Commissions-2008-English.pdf.

264 **Such commissions had been used** Ibid.

266 **Two years later** For more about the #metoo movement, see https://

metoomvmt.org. For more about the legal defense fund founded in solidarity with vulnerable women in the movement, see Time's Up, https://timesupnow.org.

266 **I learned that** Nikki Ogunnaike, "Tarana Burke Started the #MeToo Movement 10 Years Ago," *Elle,* October 19, 2017, https://www.elle.com/culture/a13046829/tarana-burke-me-too-movement-10-years-ago; Tarana Burke, "The Inception," me too, accessed September 5, 2019, https://metoomvmt.org/the-inception.

266 **Burke believed in** Daisy Murray, "'Empowerment Through Empathy'— We Spoke to Tarana Burke, the Woman Who Really Started the 'Me Too' Movement," *Elle* (U.K. edition), October 23, 2017, https://www.elle.com/uk/life-and-culture/culture/news/a39429/empowerment-through-empathy-tarana-burke-me-too.

266 **I added my voice** Valarie Kaur (@ValarieKaur), "#Metoo. But it took years of sisterhood and healing for me to say these words out loud . . . ," Instagram, October 16, 2017, https://www.instagram.com/p/BaUbJMMHJg1.

266 **"Survivors have to be the ones"** Tarana Burke and Mariame Kaba, "Tarana Burke and Mariame Kaba Talk Movements, Survivorship, Radical Community Healing to Open AMC2018," Allied Media Projects, July 27, 2018, https://alliedmedia.org/news/2018/07/27/tarana-burke-and-mariame-kaba-talk-movements-survivorship-radical-community-healing.

268 **I thought about Arno Michaelis** See Arno Michaelis and Pardeep Kaleka, *The Gift of Our Wounds: A Sikh and a Former White Supremacist Find Forgiveness After Hate* (New York: St. Martin's, 2018).

269 **Eve Ensler calls these** Eve Ensler, "The Alchemy of the Apology" (keynote address, Bioneers Conference, San Rafael, Calif., October 2019), Bioneers, https://bioneers.org/eve-ensler-alchemy-apology-zstf1911. For Eve Ensler's imagined apology from her father, who abused her when she was a child, see Eve Ensler, *The Apology* (New York: Bloomsbury, 2019).

270 **In most truth and reconciliation commissions** "Truth Commissions."

270 **"Each of us is more than"** Bryan Stevenson, *Just Mercy: A Story of Justice and Redemption* (New York: Spiegel & Grau, 2014), 17–18.

270 **"We are all broken by something"** Ibid., 289.

chapter 9: transition

273 **All that you touch** Octavia E. Butler, *Parable of the Sower* (1993; repr., New York: Grand Central, 2019), 3.

278 **The medical term is "transition"** "Stages of Labor: Early Labor, Active Labor & Transition Stage," American Pregnancy Association, accessed September 7, 2019, https://americanpregnancy.org/labor-and-birth/first-stage-of-labor.

280 **"We can learn to mother"** Audre Lorde, "Eye to Eye," in *Sister Outsider: Essays and Speeches* (New York: Ten Speed Press, 1984), 173. I use the word "mothering" to describe the capacity to care that resides in every human being. "Mothering, radically defined, is the glad gifting of one's talents, ideas, intellect, and creativity to the universe without recompense." Alexis Pauline Gumbs et al., eds., *Revolutionary Mothering: Love on the Front Lines* (Oakland: OM Press, 2016), xv.

282 **On February 10, 2015** Jonathan M. Katz and Richard Pérez-Peña, "In Chapel Hill Shooting of 3 Muslims, a Question of Motive," *The New York Times,* February 11, 2015, https://www.nytimes.com/2015/02/12/us/muslim -student-shootings-north-carolina.html.

282 **The police maintained that the gunman** Margaret Talbot, "The Story of a Hate Crime," *New Yorker,* June 15, 2015, https://www.newyorker.com/ magazine/2015/06/22/the-story-of-a-hate-crime.

282 **The killing generated** Joseph Neff and Shaila Dewan, "He Killed Three Muslim Students. but Did He Commit a Hate Crime?," *The New York Times,* June 12, 2019, https://www.nytimes.com/2019/06/12/us/hate -crime-muslim-students.html.

282 **Deah and Yusor were** Their families started the Our Three Winners Foundation to honor Deah Barakat, Yusor Abu-Salha, and Razan Abu-Salha. See "Our Story," Our Three Winners Foundation, accessed September 7, 2019, https://ourthreewinners.org/who-we-are.

282 **I had called those grieving** See Daryl Johnson, "Report: Rise in Hate Violence Tied to 2016 Election," Southern Poverty Law Center, March 1, 2018, https://www.splcenter.org/hatewatch/2018/03/01/report-rise-hate -violence-tied-2016-presidential-election; Eric Lichtblau, "Hate Crimes Against American Muslims Most Since Post-9/11 Era," *The New York Times,* September 17, 2016, https://www.nytimes.com/2016/09/18/us/politics/ hate-crimes-american-muslims-rise.html.

283 **Amrik Singh Bal had been walking** Derek Hawkins, "'ISIS. Terrorist. Let's Get Him': Sikh Man's Attacker Found Guilty of Hate Crime," *The Washington Post,* October 27, 2016, https://www.washingtonpost.com/ news/morning-mix/wp/2016/10/27/isis-terrorist-lets-get-him-sikh-mans -attacker-found-guilty-of-hate-crime.

283 **It was one of several** Zak Cheney-Rice, "How Fresno, California, Became a Hotspot for Anti-Sikh Violence in America," Mic, January 20, 2016, https://www.mic.com/articles/132552/how-fresno-california-became-a -hotspot-for-anti-sikh-violence-in-america.

283 **I knew the data on school** Sikh Coalition, "'Go Home Terrorist': A Report on Bullying Against Sikh American School Children" (report, March 11, 2014), www.sikhcoalition.org/documents/pdf/go-home-terrorist.pdf.

283 **A few months later** The Revolutionary Love Project produces stories,

tools, curricula, and mass mobilizations for social justice rooted in the ethic of love. For more about the Revolutionary Love Project, see https://revolutionaryloveproject.com.

285 **I did not know then** Alan Rappeport and Noah Weiland, "White Nationalists Celebrate 'an Awakening' After Donald Trump's Victory," *The New York Times,* November 19, 2016, https://www.nytimes.com/2016/11/20/us/politics/white-nationalists-celebrate-an-awakening-after-donald-trumps-victory.html.

285 **I had just returned** See Anand Giridharadas, "A Murder in Trump's America," *Atlantic,* February 28, 2017, https://www.theatlantic.com/politics/archive/2017/02/srinivas-kuchibhotla-alok-madasani/518160.

286 **Srinu's widow, Sunayana, told me** Sunayana Dumula, Srinivas Kuchibhotla's widow, has since emerged as a powerful advocate for immigrant communities, launching the organization Forever Welcome in Srinivas's memory. See https://www.facebook.com/ForeverWelcome1.

287 **"Our struggle is also"** bell hooks, *Talking Back: Thinking Feminist, Thinking Black* (Boston: South End Press, 1977), 4.

288 **Fresh horrors arrive daily** For platforms of present-day social justice movements that are committed to deep solidarity, see "What We Believe," Black Lives Matter, accessed August 27, 2019, https://blacklivesmatter.com/about/what-we-believe/; "Women's Agenda," Women's March, accessed August 27, 2019, https://womensmarch.com/agenda; "Our Demands," Poor People's Campaign, accessed August 7, 2019, https://www.poorpeoplescampaign.org/demands.

288 **In the Trump era, we marched** See Erica Chenoweth and Jeremy Pressman, "One Year After the Women's March on Washington, People Are Still Protesting En Masse. A Lot. We've Counted," *The Washington Post,* January 21, 2018, https://www.washingtonpost.com/news/monkey-cage/wp/2018/01/21/one-year-after-the-womens-march-on-washington-people-are-still-protesting-en-masse-a-lot-weve-counted.

288 **Indigenous and Japanese American elders** Ben Fenwick, "'Stop Repeating History': Plan to Keep Migrant Children at Former Internment Camp Draws Outrage," *The New York Times,* June 22, 2019, https://www.nytimes.com/2019/06/22/us/fort-sill-protests-japanese-internment.html.

288 **Women ran** Colleen Shalby, "A Record Number of Women Are Running for Office. This Election Cycle, They Didn't Wait for an Invite," *Los Angeles Times,* October 10, 2018, https://www.latimes.com/politics/la-na-pol-women-office-20181010-story.html.

288 **Disability justice activists** Leah Lakshmi Piepzna-Samarasinha, *Care Work: Dreaming Disability Justice Work* (Vancouver, British Columbia, Canada: Arsenal Pulp Press, 2018); Sins Invalid, *Skin, Tooth, and Bone: The Basis of Movement Is Our People*, 2nd ed., https://www.sinsinvalid.org/disability-justice-primer.

289 **I had started to bring** See Lakhpreet Kaur, "Sikh Women Gather at Mai Bhago Retreat," Kaur Life, March 22, 2017, https://kaurlife.org/2017/03/22/sikh-women-gather-first-mai-bhago-retreat.

290 **Sotomayor was a lone** See Lauren Collins, "Number Nine," *The New Yorker,* January 11, 2010, https://www.newyorker.com/magazine/2010/01/11/number-nine.

290 **Ten years later** Paul Kane, "Silent No More, Senate's Angry Republican Men Roar to Kavanaugh's Defense," *The Washington Post,* September 27, 2018, https://www.washingtonpost.com/powerpost/silent-no-more-senates-angry-republican-men-roar-to-kavanaughs-defense/2018/09/27/29430a4e-c27f-11e8-b338-a3289f6cb742_story.html.

292 **In Sikh tradition** Sri Guru Granth Sahib, *Raag Suhi,* 773:16–774:12. For the full *laavan,* see the *Sikh shabads* section in the book.

294 **In my hometown** Rory Appleton, "Teen Charged with Hate Crime on Fresno Sikh Man Commits Suicide," *Fresno Bee,* April 22, 2016, https://www.fresnobee.com/news/local/crime/article73458157.html.

294 **A few days before** "Sodhi Murder Trial Begins," Rediff.com, September 4, 2003, https://www.rediff.com/us/2003/sep/03sodhi.htm; Simran Jeet Singh, "A Unique Perspective on Hate-Crimes: The Story of a Convicted Killer," Huff-Post, updated September 19, 2012, https://www.huffpost.com/entry/a-unique-perspective-on-hate-crimes-the-story-of-a-convicted-killer_b_1685020.

294 **When the police** Mike Anton, "Collateral Damage in the War on Terrorism," *The Los Angeles Times,* September 22, 2001, https://www.latimes.com/archives/la-xpm-2001-sep-22-mn-48573-story.html.

294 **He told the court** Julian Borger, "September 11 Revenge Killer to Die for Shooting Sikh," *Guardian* (U.S. edition), October 10, 2003, https://www.theguardian.com/world/2003/oct/11/usa.julianborger.

295 **In the morning** For a video of the complete conversation between Rana Sodhi and Frank Roque and an essay and radio interview, see Valarie Kaur, "His Brother Was Murdered for Wearing a Turban After 9/11. 15 Years Later, He Spoke to the Killer," *The World,* PRI, September 23, 2016, https://www.pri.org/stories/2016-09-23/his-brother-was-murdered-wearing-turban-after-911-last-week-he-spoke-killer.

298 **I remember to measure** My friend Parker Palmer—Quaker writer, educator, and elder—taught me to measure my success not necessarily by effectiveness but by faithfulness to my values. For more, see Parker J. Palmer, *Healing the Heart of Democracy: The Courage to Create a Politics Worthy of the Human Spirit* (Hoboken, N.J.: Wiley, 2011), 192–193.

epilogue: joy

301 **Now you think** Brynn Saito, "Deep in the Cloud-Filled Valley," in *The Palace of Contemplating Departure* (Pasadena, Calif.: Red Hen Press, 2013), 84.

VALARIE KAUR is a civil rights activist, lawyer, filmmaker, innovator, and founder of the Revolutionary Love Project. She has won national acclaim for her work in social justice on issues ranging from hate crimes to digital freedom. Her speeches have reached millions worldwide and inspired a movement to reclaim love as a force for justice. A daughter of Sikh farmers in California, she earned degrees from Stanford University, Harvard Divinity School, and Yale Law School and holds an honorary doctorate from the California Institute of Integral Studies. She lives in a multigenerational home in Los Angeles with her husband, son, and daughter.

valariekaur.com
Facebook.com/valarie.kaur.page
Twitter: @valariekaur
Instagram: @valariekaur